FORM 990: EXPLORING THE FORM'S COMPLEX SCHEDULES

BY EVE ROSE BORENSTEIN, J.D. AND
JANE M. SEARING, CPA, M.S. TAXATION,
TAX SHAREHOLDER - CLARK NUBER P.S.

Notice to Readers

Form 990: Exploring the Form's Complex Schedules is intended solely for use in continuing professional education and not as a reference. It does not represent an official position of the Association of International Certified Professional Accountants, and it is distributed with the understanding that the author and publisher are not rendering legal, accounting, or other professional services in the publication. This course is intended to be an overview of the topics discussed within, and the author has made every attempt to verify the completeness and accuracy of the information herein. However, neither the author nor publisher can guarantee the applicability of the information found herein. If legal advice or other expert assistance is required, the services of a competent professional should be sought.

**You can qualify to earn free CPE through our pilot testing program.
If interested, please visit aicpa.org at http://apps.aicpa.org/secure/CPESurvey.aspx.**

Course code: **733921**
F990A GS-0417-0A
Revised: **May 2017**

V090356_052318

TABLE OF CONTENTS

Recent Developments

Users of this course material are encouraged to visit the AICPA website at www.aicpa.org/CPESupplements to access supplemental learning material reflecting recent developments that may be applicable to this course. The AICPA anticipates that supplemental materials will be made available on a quarterly basis. Also available on this site are links to the various "Standards Trackers" on the AICPA's Financial Reporting Center which include recent standard-setting activity in the areas of accounting and financial reporting, audit and attest, and compilation, review and preparation.

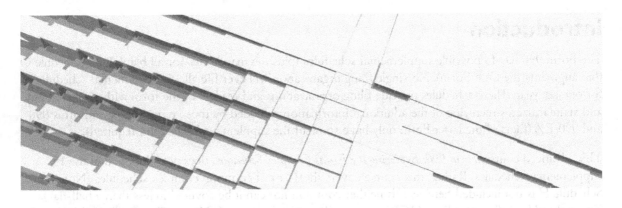

Chapter 1

INTRODUCTION TO SCHEDULES—THE PURPOSE AND FUNCTION OF THE 990's 15 SUPPLEMENTAL SCHEDULES

LEARNING OBJECTIVES

After completing this chapter, you should be able to do the following:

- Recognize the uniformity of reporting that comes with utilizing supplemental schedules.
- Recognize when supplemental schedules are required (or not required) to be completed by filers of Form 990-EZ.
- Identify the significance of the 10 reporting areas covered in the Schedules presented in this course.

Introduction

The Form 990 has 15 possible supplemental schedules (plus the mandatory-for-all blank lines Schedule O that augments the Core Form). No single filing organization will ever file all 15 supplemental schedules for one tax year. These schedules provide filing organizations and readers of the form with comparability and standardized structuring of the additional information provided by those reporting upon Forms 990 and 990-EZ (filers of the latter Form only have some of the supplemental schedules required).

This advanced course, *Form 990: Exploring the Form's Complex Schedules*, does not address all of the 15 supplemental schedules. Rather, this course covers the 10 most common complex schedules (Note: Schedule H is not included here, as it is neither common nor can it be covered in less than a half-day). The authors' basic/intermediate AICPA course, *Form 990: Mastering Its Unique Characteristics*, addresses the entirety of the 990's common schedules,[1] but does not drill down into this course's 10.

---

[1] That course addresses, again, from a basic/ intermediate perspective:
   Schedule A: Qualification by 501(c)(3) Organizations as Non-Private Foundation (Overview of A-I, A-II, and A-III)
   Schedule B: Reporting of Contributors
   Schedule D: Supplemental Financial Statements
   Schedule F: (Overview)
   Schedule G-I: Professional Fundraisers
   Schedule G's Parts II and III (Overview)
   Schedule I: Grantmaking—Domestic
   Schedules J and L: (Overview chapters on each)
   Schedule M: (Overview)

The 16 Schedules of the Form 990 (using Mnemonics)

- **Schedule A—Public Charity Status and Public Support** (required of all 501(c)(3) filers) (A stands for "we ARE NOT a private foundation")
- **Schedule B—Schedule of Contributors** (B stands for "BENEFACTORS providing grants or contributions")
- **Schedule C—Political Campaign and Lobbying Activities** (C stands for "CONNECTIONS to public policy world")
- **Schedule D—Supplemental Financial Statements** (D stands for "Financial DETAILS")
- **Schedule E—Schools** (E stands for "EDUCATIONAL institutions")
- **Schedule F—Statement of Activities Outside the United States** (F stands for "FOREIGN activities")
- **Schedule G—Supplemental Information Regarding Fundraising or Gaming Activities** (G stands for "GAMING and GALAs"—the schedule also includes reporting on professional fundraisers)
- **Schedule H—Hospitals** (H stands for HOSPITALS)
- **Schedule I—Grants and Other Assistance to Organizations, Governments and Individuals in the United States** (I stands for "IMPARTING money to others by domestic grantmaking")
- **Schedule J—Compensation Information** (J stands for "JUDGING compensation practices")
- **Schedule K—Supplemental Information on Tax-Exempt Bonds** (K stands for "KRAZY money")
- **Schedule L—Transactions with Interested Persons** (L stands for "LIGHT" as this schedule is about casting sunlight on such transactions[2])
- **Schedule M—Noncash Contributions** (M stands for "non-MONETARY" donations)
- **Schedule N—Liquidation, Termination, Dissolution, or Significant Disposition of Assets** (N stands for "NOT the same as before")
- **Schedule O—Supplemental Information** (O stands for "OTHER things filer is required to, or wants to, state" or Overflow)
- **Schedule R—Related Organizations and Unrelated Partnerships** (R for "RELATED organizations [and unrelated partnerships]")

---

[2] "Sunlight is the best disinfectant," a well-known quote from U.S. Supreme Court Justice Louis Brandeis.

SCHEDULES THAT APPLY TO FORM 990-EZ FILERS (AND THEIR REACH)

Schedule A—Public Charity Status and Public Support	All filers exempt under 501(c)(3)
Schedule B—Schedule of Contributors	All 501(c) filers with one or more contributors who made gifts ≥ $5k * 501(c)(7), (8), or (10) filers who received any contributions to be used exclusively for the purposes enumerated in 170(c)(4)[3]
Schedule C—Political Campaign and Lobbying Activities, Part I-A & -B not I-C	501(c)(3) filers with direct or indirect political activity
Schedule C—Political Campaign and Lobbying Activities, Part II-A only	501(c)(3) filer which has a 501(h) election in effect for the filing year
Schedule C—Political Campaign and Lobbying Activities, Part II-B only	501(c)(3) filer which has no 501(h) election in effect for the filing year
Schedule C—Political Campaign and Lobbying Activities, Part III	501(c)(4), (5), or (6) filer that received membership dues, assessments or similar amounts (for example, are subject to, unless exempted, Section 6033 notice and reporting requirements (and, potentially, a proxy tax))
Schedule E—Schools	Primary basis of non-private foundation status for the filing year is that under Section 170(b)(1)(A)(ii) (for example, as a school) and thus need report adherence to non-discrimination policies and publication notices
Schedule G—Supplemental Info. Regarding Fundraising or Gaming Activities, Part II	Filer has gross receipts (including gift portion) from fundraising events or fundraising sales > $15,000
Schedule G—Supplemental Info. Regarding Fundraising or Gaming Activities, Part III	Gross income from gaming activities exceeds $15,000
Schedule L—Transactions with Interested Persons, Part I	501(c)(3), (4) or (29) filer required to report an excess benefit transaction with a disqualified person (as defined in Section 4958) due to same either occurring in tax year or discovered as having occurred in prior year but not been previously reported (no dollar threshold)

---

[3] That IRC section provides that donations by an individual to a domestic fraternal beneficiary society or a domestic fraternal society operating under the lodge system are deductible as charitable contributions. The Schedule B inquiry is of organizations who may *believe* they can offer such deductibility.

Schedule L—Transactions with Interested Persons, Part II	Filer had loan between it and an interested person outstanding on the last day of the tax year (no dollar threshold)
Schedule N—Liquidation, Termination, Dissolution, or Significant Disposition of Assets, Part I	Organization fully liquidated, terminated, dissolved or merged into a successor organization during the tax year and ceased operation
Schedule N—Liquidation, Termination, Dissolution, or Significant Disposition of Assets, Part II	Organization sold, exchanged, disposed or transferred >25% of its beginning net assets (other than excepted transactions).
Schedule O—Supplemental Information	All filers—supplements info on 990-EZ pages

KNOWLEDGE CHECK

1. Facts: Filing organization completes Form 990-EZ. The organization is exempt under IRC Section 501(c)(3) and qualifies as a school under 170(b)(1)(A)(ii). The organization would also qualify as a public charity under 509(a)(3). It has several major contributors who made contributions over $5,000. The school's annual gala raises $30,000 annually. The organization has made an election under 501(h) for making lobbying expenditures. What schedules will the organization attach to Form 990-EZ?

    a. Schedule A, B, and E

    b. Schedule A, B, C, E, G and O

    c. Schedule A, C, E, and O

    d. The organization cannot file Schedule 990-EZ because it has made the 501(h) election.

FOCUS OF THIS COURSE

This course looks closely at and takes a deeper dive into the instructions, examples, and fact patterns filing organizations encounter while completing the most common Schedules required of Forms 990 and 990-EZ. It is the case that even the most seasoned professionals will encounter facts which can present ambiguous filing positions. When this occurs, it is important to do the following:

1. Carefully review the Form 990 and schedule instructions
2. Thoroughly explore and understand any relevant glossary definitions
3. Remember the primary goals of the Form 990 redesign:
    a. Compliance
    b. Transparency
    c. Accountability

The key goal in preparation is to ensure that reporting by the filing organization meets the definitions. If reporting position contemplated is not contrary to any written instructions, always ask whether it is in line with the spirit of the reporting goals of the Form 990. That is, does it provide readers with information that would lead them to draw logical conclusions about the filing organization?

SCHEDULES COVERED IN THIS COURSE

Chapter 2: Deep Dive into Schedule R, the First Required Schedule (When Applicable) of the Form 990. This is the starting point of any properly prepared Form 990. It is not a Schedule Required of Form 990-EZ filers. Without first identifying all related organizations, preparers will be forced to go back and make additional inquiries if related organizations are later identified.

Chapter 3: Deep Dive into Schedule A – How a Public Charity is NOT a Private Foundation. All organizations exempt under 501(c)(3) must complete Schedule A to demonstrate why they are not a private foundation. In 1969, Congress bifurcated charitable organizations between private foundations and all other charitable organizations (public charities). Private foundations are subject to more restrictive operating rules and usually an excise tax on net investment income. Private foundations file Form 990-PF. All other charitable organizations file Form 990, 990-EZ, of the 990-N electronic postcard. For filers of the 990 or 990-EZ, Schedule A is required. There are five substantive parts to Schedule A and Part VI is for providing supplemental information.

Chapter 4: Other Revenue Disclosures Important to Fundraising (Schedules G-II and M). This chapter provides a deeper dive into both the Core Form's Part VIII, Line 8, and its tie to Part VIII, Line 1c, as well as Line 1g, and how those lines are further explored with Schedule G—Fundraising Activities, Galas; and Schedule M—Noncash Contributions. Organizations today engage with more creative and entrepreneurial fundraising opportunities and need be careful to both properly account for and report on all of these activities and their results.

Chapter 5: Public Policy, Political Activity, and Lobbying Disclosures on Schedule C. Form 990 is utilized by organizations exempt under 501(a) and 527, and Schedule C provides transparency into permissible and impermissible intervention into public policy, lobbying and political activities of all filers of the Form 990 and 990-EZ.

Chapter 6: The Interested Persons of Schedule L and the Impact of This Schedule on Filing Organizations. Schedule L has two primary purposes. The first is to report impermissible excess benefit transactions under Section 4958 with disqualified persons for which a Form 4720 must be filed and a penalty must be paid and corrective action taken. The second purpose is sunlight. Parts II through IV provide information on transactions between the reporting organization and individuals the IRS has designated through definitions the Service has promulgated. There is no basis for these transactions being good or bad. The judgment is in the eye of the reader.

Chapter 7: Foreign Activities (Grantmaking and Beyond). Filing organizations often mistakenly believe Schedule F is just the foreign equivalent of Schedule I. Schedule F encompasses all foreign activities of the reporting organization, including direct foreign activities, investments, and fundraising, besides direct and indirect grantmaking activities to entities and individuals.

Chapter 8: Fully Disclosing Compensation on Schedule J—The Rest of the Core Form Part VII Story. Schedule J is not required of all filing organizations and it is never required for Form 990-EZ. The Core Form Part VII compensation includes compensation paid by the filing organization and may include compensation from related and unrelated organizations. However, there are exceptions to what must be reported by the filing organization on Part VII for benefit and compensation from related organizations which does not apply for reporting once Schedule J is triggered. The deep dive into Schedule J will highlight and solidify understanding of these concepts.

Chapter 9: Tax Exempt Bonds and Schedule K. Post-issuance compliance has long been an area of concern for the IRS with tax exempt bonds. This schedule is designed to elicit responses raising awareness of compliance, including use of bond proceeds, private business use, arbitrage practices, and procedures for corrective actions, when required.

Chapter 10: The Final Chapter: Schedule N— Exempt Entity Is No More, Is In Wind-Up, or Has Experienced Asset Contraction/ Expansion. When organizations enter into a plan of liquidation, dissolution, termination or have a significant disposition of assets that does not meet one of the exceptions, Schedule N is required. This schedule triggers a front page disclosure on Form 990 and so is a significant disclosure. It generally signifies a going concern disclosure, and if that is not what the organization intends to communicate, care should be taken to communicate otherwise to readers of the Form 990 or 990-EZ.

KNOWLEDGE CHECK

2. When a filing organization is unsure of the correct filing position to take based upon the facts presented, which is NOT a suggested action for arriving at a reasonable position?

    a. Thoroughly explore and understand any relevant glossary definitions.
    b. Remember the three principles of the Form 990 redesign: transparency, accountability and compliance; and check to see if the disclosure fits within these principles.
    c. Call the IRS helpline for assistance.
    d. Carefully review the Form 990 and specific Schedules' instructions.

3. Which realm is NOT the subject of additionally mandated reporting through Form 990's supplemental schedules?

    a. How public charity status is maintained or qualified for by 501(c)(3) filers.
    b. Inside dealings with those managing the filer.
    c. Program operations' enhancements that advance the filer's exempt purposes.
    d. Revenue capture from contributors.

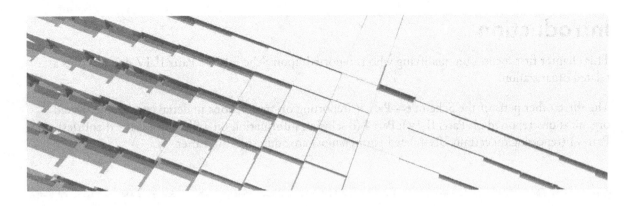

Chapter 2

DEEP DIVE INTO SCHEDULE R, THE FIRST REQUIRED SCHEDULE (WHEN APPLICABLE) OF THE FORM 990

LEARNING OBJECTIVES

After completing this chapter, you should be able to do the following:

- Identify the principles by which control vests when determining parent-subsidiary or brother-sister status between the filer and another not-for-profit (nonstock) entity.
- Identify how control vests, directly and indirectly, over an entity that is a stock corporation.
- Recognize both the characteristics of a disregarded entity and how it reports annually to the IRS.
- Identify how to report required information for a filer's direct and indirect related organizations.

Introduction

This chapter first focuses on qualifying who is reported upon Schedule R's Parts II-IV due to status as a related organization.

The three other parts of the Schedule—Part V (reporting on transactions undertaken with the related organizations reported on Parts II-IV); Part I (disclosing information on a filer's disregarded entities); and Part VI (reporting on certain UN-related partnerships) are addressed thereafter.

WHAT IS A RELATED ORGANIZATION?

Per the Form 990 instructions, a related organization is an organization that stands in any of eight relationships to a filing organization (filer). There are six primary relationships by which a related organization exists [Note: These materials only address related organizations of 501(c)(9) entities by footnote here[1]]:

1. **Parent**—A not-for-profit organization (NFP) or stock corporation that directly or indirectly controls the filer.
2. **Subsidiary**—An NFP or stock corporation that is directly or indirectly controlled by the filer.
3. **Brother/ sister**—An NFP or stock corporation controlled directly or indirectly by the same person or persons that control(s) the filer.

   [For the preceding three categories, it is imperative that one understand the definition of control by which parent/ subsidiary or brother/ sister status vests; the glossary definition of control is reprinted on the following page.]

4. **Supporting/ supported**—Two directions here, as follows:
   a. supporting organization of the filer [for example, an organization that is rostered by the IRS or claims to be classified at any time during the tax year as a supporting organization (within the meaning of 509(a)(3)) of the filer]; or
   b. an entity that is a supported organization of the filer for periods in the year in which the filer itself is a supporting organization under 509(a)(3)
5. *A controlled* **partnership**, or a **limited liability company (LLC)**—Same is defined as the filer being in either of two postures as follow, with respect to the partnership/ LLC:
   a. Filer is one of three or fewer managing partners/ members or in the case of a limited partnership, one of three or fewer general partners; or
   b. Filer has a > 50 percent profits or capital interest in the partnership or LLC.
6. *A controlled* **trust**—Same is defined as the filer having had a > 50 percent beneficial interest in the trust, determined by the filer's actuarial interest in the trust, at any time in the tax year.

---

[1] The two related organization categories that exist with respect to 501(c)(9)s (Voluntary Employees' Beneficiary Associations or VEBAs) are: such filers' sponsoring organization(s) and contributing employer(s). These two categories appear as the last two conditions of the glossary term related organization (reprinted on the next page). Other than these mentions, no other specific address of VEBA's related organizations are made in this course.

IMPORTANT NOTE: Although Schedule R also is used to report the fact of, and certain information related to, a filer's disregarded entities (in Part I of the Schedule), a disregarded entity is NOT a related organization. A disregarded entity exists when an entity (1) is a limited liability company (LLC) with a single-member (that is, sole owner); and (2) has not elected to be treated as a stand-alone taxpayer. If a filer is the sole owner of a disregarded entity, that LLC's activities, revenues, expenses, and net assets are included with those of the filer upon the filer's 990. Disregarded entity is a glossary term and is the subject of the Form 990 instruction's appendix F.

Proper identification of a filer's related organizations and disregarded entities is essential as it affects not only completion of Schedule R, but also

- the Core Form's Part VI (Governance),
- Part VII (Compensation) and Schedule J,
- Part VIII (Revenue),
- Part X (Balance Sheet) and
- Schedules D.

The complete glossary-term definition of related organization (from which the preceding address of six primary versus two VEBA categories is culled) is reprinted here:

An organization, including a nonprofit organization, a stock corporation, a partnership or limited liability company, a trust, and a **governmental unit** or other government entity, that stands in one or more of the following relationships to the filing organization at any time during the **tax year**.
- Parent: an organization that **controls** the filing organization.
- Subsidiary: an organization **controlled** by the filing organization.
- Brother/Sister: an organization **controlled** by the same person or persons that control the filing organization. However, if the filing organization is a trust that has a bank or financial institution trustee that is also the trustee of another trust, the other trust is not a Brother/Sister related organization of the filing organization on the ground of common control by the bank or financial institution trustee.
- Supporting/Supported: an organization that claims to be at any time during the **tax year**, or that is classified by the IRS at any time during the tax year, as (i) a **supporting organization** of the filing organization within the meaning of section 509(a)(3), if the filing organization is a **supported organization** within the meaning of section 509(f)(3); (ii) or a supported organization, if the filing organization is a supporting organization.

> • Sponsoring Organization of a VEBA: an organization that establishes or maintains a section 501(c)(9) voluntary employees' beneficiary association (VEBA) during the tax year. A sponsoring organization of a VEBA also includes an employee organization, association, committee, joint board of trustees, or other similar group of representatives of the parties which establish or maintain a VEBA. Although a VEBA must report a sponsoring organization as a related organization, a sponsoring organization should not report a VEBA as a related organization, unless the VEBA is related to the sponsoring organization in some other capacity described in this definition.
> • Contributing Employer of a VEBA: an employer that makes a contribution or contributions to the VEBA during the tax year. Although a VEBA must report a contributing employer as a related organization, a contributing employer should not report a VEBA as a related organization, unless the VEBA is related to the contributing employer in some other capacity described in this definition.

Note that the first three bullet points refer to another glossary-term's definition, Control, which differs depending on the entity status of the party for whom control is being evaluated. These materials now move to explore when another entity falls within the conditions of control.

Related organization status reaches a filer's parent, subsidiary, or sibling (brother/sister). Such conditions are in play when the other entity, respectively

- has control of the filer;
- is controlled by the filer; or
- is under common control of the same group of persons who control the filer

Control is a glossary-definition term. Its text (discussion of which begins in next section) states that status as a related organization may be found through either direct control or indirect control. What constitutes control depends on the form of entity of the party that is controlled—for example, whether it is a corporation and, if so, organized as a for-profit versus a not-for-profit corporation, or whether it is a trust or a partnership. Control is defined differently for those four types of entities (not-for-profits, stock corporations, partnerships/ limited liability companies, and trusts). Preparers need be fluent with each of the four separate standards, each of which we will now explore.

MEASURING CONTROL OF A NONPROFIT CORPORATION (OR ORGANIZATION WITHOUT OWNERS/ PERSON WITH BENEFICIAL INTERESTS)

The glossary definition sets out the following:

> Control of a not-for-profit organization (or other organization without owners or persons having beneficial interests, whether the organization is taxable or tax-exempt):
>
> One or more persons (whether individuals or organizations) control a not-for-profit organization if they have the power to remove and replace (or to appoint or elect, if such power includes a continuing power to appoint or elect periodically or in the event of vacancies) a majority of the not-for-profit organization's directors or trustees, or a majority of members who elect a majority of the not-for-profit organization's directors or trustees. Such power can be exercised directly by a (parent) organization through one or more of the (parent) organization's officers, directors, trustees, or agents, acting in their capacity as officers, directors, trustees, or agents of the (parent) organization. Also, a (parent) organization controls a (subsidiary) not-for-profit organization if a majority of the subsidiary's directors or trustees are trustees, directors, officers, employees, or agents of the parent.

This definition needs to be parsed sentence-by-sentence:

- The first two sentences discuss who has the right to vote in or appoint (directly or indirectly) a majority of the board of the NFP organization whose relationship to another is being tested (the filer or the third party potential related organization). Here the inquiry is whether
  - a majority of seats on the board are subject to the appointment powers of, or are elected by, the entity who is being tested for status as the filer's related organization; or
  - a majority of seats on the filer's board are subject to the appointment powers of, or are elected by, the entity who is being tested for status as the filer's related organization.
- Of extreme importance is that the third sentence of the definition sets out an alternative condition of control. It mandates a look at who is in the seats of the board of the relevant NFP (such as the filer or any third party potential related organization). Here the inquiry is how the majority of those seated on the NFP's board is composed: the filer's:
  - trustees
  - directors
  - officers
  - employees
  - agents

Note: The precedent for the listed individuals' presence leading to control comes from the income tax regulations' address of control under Section 512(b)(13). Regulations Section 1.512(b)-1(l)(4)(b) sets out that these parties' presence indicates control, regardless of how they are there:

Nonstock organization. In the case of a nonstock organization, the term control means that at least 80** percent of the directors or trustees of such organization are either **representatives of** <u>OR</u> directly or indirectly controlled by an exempt organization. **A trustee or director is a representative of an exempt organization if he is a trustee, director, agent, or employee of such exempt organization.** A trustee or director is controlled by an exempt organization if such organization has the power to remove such trustee or director and designate a new trustee or director.

> ****NOTE:** The 80 percent measure was lowered to greater than 50 percent when Congress amended Section 512(b)(13) in 1997; this regulation has yet to be updated for that change.

The result from such language, that an NPO may be a related organization through de facto control, has generated complaints. AICPA's Technical Resource Panel on Exempt Organizations (EO-TRP), noting the desire of some to interpret control with respect to nonprofit (or nonstock) corporations contrary to IRS intent (and in contradiction to the income tax regulation that it is derived from, as noted previously), said the following in its June 2014 comments to the IRS on the 990 instructions:

> In the case of multiple, affiliated nonstock organizations with nearly identical board members, taxpayers are arguing that notwithstanding overlapping composition of boards of trustees, the trustees of X Charity, acting in that capacity, have no authority to remove, replace, or appoint a majority of the governing bodies of the other affiliates. The board of trustees of each affiliate, acting in its own independent capacity, periodically appoints its own new trustees.

> We believe the last sentence of the definition of control applies as written (and note its parallel expression and result in Regulations Section 1.512(b)-1(l)(4)(b) …) and that it imposes related organization status between the two organizations regardless of whether parent-subsidiary status was intended, as in these cases, a brother/sister relationship exists.

Conclusion:

PARENT/SUBSIDIARY status is measured (in the case in which a not-for-profit organization is controlled and with respect to it being a subsidiary or brother/sister of other entities who are now related organizations of it):

FIRST by looking at who appoints those seated on the board of the NFP and (assuming no majority is then in place by which control is found), then SECOND by looking at *who is sitting* in each seat on the NFP's board. All of that is undertaken to the end of determining whether there is an entity that EITHER is appointing/electing (directly or indirectly) a majority of the individuals on the board of the relevant NFP ... OR SECOND is deemed to be in *de facto* control over the NFP given the presence in majority position on the NPFP's board of individuals beholden/connected to another entity through being on that other entity's board, or by serving it as an officer, employee, or agent. [BROTHER/SISTER status is measured by noting whether a collective group is in the FIRST OR SECOND position while at the same time having control over other entities for whom sibling relationship through common control then exists.]

PRACTICE GUIDE

To determine whether a filer (who is itself a not-for-profit organization) is controlled by another organization (and has a parent), or controls another not-for-profit (and has a subsidiary), or is with another not-for-profit both under common control (and has a sibling), the tasks are as follows:

1. With respect to the filer (a nonstock corporation) having a parent entity,
    a. determine whether serving on the filer's board are board members (such as trustees or directors), officers, employees, or agents of another entity in such number they constitute a majority of those seated on the filer's board at any point in time in the tax year; and
    b. determine whether another party held the right to elect/ appoint—directly or indirectly—at any point in time in the tax year some or all of those serving on the filer's board and whether the number of such seats at that time constituted a majority of all seats.

    IF SO TO *a* or *b*: That entity is a parent of the filer.

2. With respect to the filer having a subsidiary not-for-profit organization,
    a. determine whether the filer's board members (such as trustees or directors), officers, employees or agents make up a majority of those seated on the board of that not-for-profit (at any point in time in the filer's tax year); and
    b. determine whether the filer or its members held at any time in the tax year the right to elect/ appoint—directly or indirectly (the latter being the case if the filer's trustees, directors, officers, or agents, acting in their capacity as trustees, directors, officers or agents of the filer organization)—those serving on the board of that not-for-profit in such number that such seats constituted a majority of all seats on the (subsidiary's) board.

    IF SO TO *a* or *b*: That not-for-profit organization is a subsidiary of the filer.

3. With respect to the filer, itself a not-for-profit organization, having a sibling organization
   a. determine, in the presence of a parent entity (related organization), whether that parent had other subsidiaries within the Schedule R definitions; and
   b. determine whether there are multiple parties whose interests together (for example: considering those parties' interests aggregated within a unified entity) yield both that unified entity being a parent entity of the filer and the parent of other subsidiaries by virtue of the control standards for:
      i. NFPs
      ii. stock corporations
      iii. partnerships/ LLCs

   IF SO TO *a* or *b*, or in combination of *a* and *b*: The identified other subsidiaries found are siblings of the filer.

And finally, as with all other conditions of control (that is, regardless of the form of entity of the party being tested for related organization status), control may exist indirectly. Schedule R's instructions provide an example of indirect control of an NFP that emphasizes de facto board-overlap as creating related organization status:

> Organizations A, B, C, and D are not-for-profit organizations. Organization A appoints the board of Organization B, which appoints the board of Organization C. A majority of the board members of Organization D are also board members of Organization A. Under these circumstances, Organizations B and D are directly controlled by Organization A, and Organization C is indirectly controlled by Organization A. Therefore, Organizations B, C, and D are subsidiaries of Organization A; Organization C is also a subsidiary of Organization B; and Organizations B and C have a brother or sister relationship with Organization D.

- In this example, A and D (both NFPs) are related organizations on a de facto basis because the seats of D's board are comprised, in majority, by those who are connected to A because they are A's board members (they also could have been A's officers, employees, or specific agents). With majority control imputed due to holding a majority presence, D [is] directly controlled by...A.
- The example additionally brings in two other NFPs, B and C. With respect to them, we are told that A appoints the board of B and B appoints the board of C. As a result, A has direct control of B (as A is B's parent) and A has indirect control of C (because B is C's parent).
- Given what we have already noted (A has direct control of D, and B and C are under A's direct and indirect control), the example holds that B and C are each also brothers or sisters of D.

IMPORTANT NOTE RELATED TO THOSE IN GROUP RULINGS: None of the preceding constructs reach filers whose sole connection is derived from status as common subordinates in a group ruling OR by being the central in a group ruling in relationship to one or more subordinates or vice versa.

As to *indirect control*, beginning in 2015 the instructions provide more clarity via a new example 8 detailed below:

Example 8. F is a 501(c)(3) public charity that appoints the governing body of G, another 501(c)(3) public charity. G is supported by H, a Type III supporting organization, but G does not control H. G and H are thus related organizations because of the supporting/supported relationship. Absent other facts, F and H are not related organizations.

And finally, Schedule R speaks to common control (that is, brother or sister connection) with two examples:

Examples of Control by Multiple Persons

Example 1. Organizations A and B each appoint one-third of the board members of Organizations C and D, and are not otherwise related to Organizations C and D. Although neither Organization A nor Organization B is a parent of Organization C or Organization D, Organizations C and D are controlled by the same persons, and therefore are brother/sister related organizations with respect to each other.

Example 2. Organization E has 1,000 individual members who elect its board members. The membership of Organization E is also the membership of Organization F, and elects the board members of Organization F. Organizations E and F are brother/sister related organizations with respect to each other.

KNOWLEDGE CHECK

1. In evaluating control over a not-for-profit corporation, which statement sets out factor(s) not taken into account?

   a. Rights of parties to appoint or elect those who will serve on the governing body with voting rights (hereafter, board members) on an ongoing basis.

   b. The filing organization board members' affiliations as officers, board members, employees, or agents of other entities.

   c. Whether board members have family relationships with board members of another organization.

   d. Whether parties who have rights to appoint or elect board members of one entity also have rights to appoint or elect board members of other entities on an ongoing basis.

2. Which condition that applies to a not-for-profit corporation would not result (absent other factors) in its having related organization status to a filer?

    a. It was created by the filer.

    b. It is a supported organization of the filer within the meaning of IRC Section 509(a)(3).

    c. Its three-member board of directors at one time during the filer's year included the filer's human resources director and CFO.

    d. Its by-laws mandate that the filer's CEO appoints two of the three members of its board of directors.

MEASURING CONTROL OF A STOCK CORPORATION (FOR EXAMPLE, FOR-PROFIT CORPORATIONS AND SIMILAR ENTITIES)

The glossary definition sets out the definition as follows:

> **Control of a stock corporation**
> One or more persons (whether individuals or organizations) control a stock corporation if they own more than 50% of the stock (by voting power or value) of the corporation.

Stock. That is the sole matter at issue per this straightforward definition: ascertaining whether any for-profit is more than 50 percent owned by a filer (who would be in direct control), or by parties who control the filer (in which case, the filer would be in a brother-sister relationship with the for-profit).

As with all conditions of control, same can exist indirectly:

> **Indirect control.** Control can be indirect. For example, if the filing organization controls Entity A, which controls (under the definition of control in these instructions) Entity B, the filing organization will be treated as controlling Entity B. To determine indirect control through constructive ownership of a corporation, rules under Section 318 apply.

The mandate here is to evaluate indirect control in line with Section 318, which mandates multiplication of a parent's percentage (of stock), when same is 50 percent or greater, against the subsidiary's percentage (of stock), garnering an apportioned pro rata stock position. Once one party has 50 percent or more stock of another, drop-down stock ownership is imputed by multiplying the interest of the first party with that of the party it controls:

> Were NFP X to own 60 percent of the stock of Y, and Y were to own 90 percent of the stock of Z, X is considered to indirectly own 54 percent (60 percent × 90 percent) of Z's stock. On these facts, X and Y would be directly related organizations (because X's stock ownership position in Y is greater than 50 percent) and X and Z would be indirectly related organizations (because X is considered to have a 54 percent stock ownership position in Z).

S Corporations are addressed in Section 318 with a slightly different rule.

The instructions for Schedule R provide multiple examples of indirect control of stock corporations illustrating the Section 318 rules:

Example 5. T, an exempt organization described in Section 501(c)(3), owns 40 percent of the stock of U, a taxable C corporation. T and U each own 40 percent of the stock of V, another taxable C corporation. Under these facts, T and U are not related organizations as parent or subsidiary because T does not own more than 50 percent of U's stock. Under Section 318(a)(2)(C), none of U's holdings are attributed to T by virtue of T's ownership of U stock, because T owns less than 50 percent of U stock. Thus T and V are not related organizations as parent or subsidiary.

Example 6. Same facts as in Example 5, except U is an S corporation. Under Section 318(a)(5)(E), T constructively owns 16 percent of V–U (40 percent of U's 40 percent ownership of V), giving T a total ownership interest of 54 percent in V, and making T and V related organizations as parent or subsidiary.

Example 7. Same facts as in Example 5, except that T owns 50 percent of U's stock. T and U are not related organizations as parent or subsidiary because T does not own more than 50 percent of U's stock. Under Section 318(a)(2)(C), U's holdings are attributed to T by virtue of T's 50 percent ownership of U's stock. Thus, T constructively owns 20 percent of V through U (50 percent of U's 40 percent ownership of V), giving T a total ownership interest of 60 percent in V, and making T and V related organizations as parent or subsidiary.

MEASURING CONTROL OF A PARTNERSHIP (INCLUDING LLC'S TAXED AS PARTNERSHIPS)

The glossary definition sets out the pertinent definition as follows:

Control of a partnership or limited liability company
One or more persons control a partnership if they own more than 50% of the profits or capital interests in the partnership (including a limited liability company treated as a partnership or disregarded entity for federal tax purposes, regardless of the designation under state law of the ownership interests as stock, membership interests, or otherwise). A person also controls a partnership if the person is a managing partner or managing member of a partnership or limited liability company which has three or fewer managing partners or managing members (regardless of which partner or member has the most actual control), or if the person is a general partner in a limited partnership which has three or fewer general partners (regardless of which partner has the most actual control). For this purpose, a "managing partner" is a partner designated as such under the partnership agreement, or regularly engaged in the management of the partnership even though not so designated.

Much is captured within that definition's paragraph (the outset of this chapter noted the multiplicity of status possibilities here). There are three scenarios in which a partnership or limited liability company (LLC) is a related organization of a filer:

1. The partnership or LLC is one in which the filer has greater than 50 percent profits or capital interest (directly or indirectly).
2. The partnership or LLC has three or fewer managing partners or members and the filer is a managing partner or member.
3. The partnership is a limited partnership with three or fewer general partners and the filer is a general partner.

Reprising the prior-noted instruction concerning indirect control, the text expands, in the case of partnerships and limited liability companies, to provide more specific information, as highlighted via the following italicized sentences:

> **Indirect control.** Control can be indirect. For example, if the filing organization controls Entity A, which in turn controls (under the definition of control in these instructions) Entity B, the filing organization will be treated as controlling Entity B. To determine indirect control through constructive ownership of a corporation, rules under Section 318 apply. *Similar principles apply for purposes of determining constructive ownership of another entity (a partnership or trust). If an entity (X) controls an entity as a partnership by being one of three or fewer partners or members* [**Authors' note:** *Here the term partners or members is used in reference to a managing partner or, in the case of a limited partnership, a general partner, and for LLCs, a managing member], then an organization that controls X also controls the partnership.*

As to how those similar principles apply to testing a partnership for related organization status, the Schedule R instructions provide three examples:

> **Example 1.** B, an exempt organization, wholly owns (by voting power) C, a taxable corporation. C holds a 51 percent profits interest in D, a partnership. Under the principles of Section 318, B is deemed to own 51 percent of D (100 percent of C's 51 percent interest in D). Thus, B controls both C and D, which are therefore both related organizations with respect to B.
>
> **Example 2.** X, an exempt organization, owns 80 percent (by value) of Y, a taxable corporation. Y holds a 60 percent profits interest as a limited partner of Z, a limited partnership. Under the principles of Section 318, X is deemed to own 48 percent of Z (80 percent of Y's 60 percent interest in Z). Thus, X controls Y. X does not control Z through X's ownership in Y. Y is a related organization with respect to X, and (absent other facts), Z is not.
>
> **Example 3.** Same facts as in Example 2, except that Y is also one of three general partners of Z. Because Y controls Z through means other than ownership percentage, and X controls Y, in these circumstances, Z is a related organization with respect to X. The other general partners of Z (if organizations) are not related organizations to X, absent other facts.

Measuring Control of a Trust

The glossary definition sets out:

> <u>Control of a trust with beneficial interests</u>
> One or more persons control a trust if they own more than 50% of the beneficial interests in the trust. A person's beneficial interest in a trust shall be determined in proportion to that person's actuarial interest in the trust as of the end of the tax year.

Note this definition looks solely at a party's actuarial interest in the trust, not at who is a trustee or controls the trustee(s). (Only with this type of entity does the Schedule R glossary definition of control diverge from the Section 512(b)(13) definition of control, a point that matters solely for reporting in Part V, Line 2.)

If a beneficiary has no determinable interest in the trust, no related organization exists as the control threshold is negated. This is explicitly noted in the instructions:

> In some situations a named beneficiary may have no determinable interest in the trust. For instance, if Trust A allows the trustee to distribute income and principal in the trustee's sole discretion for 10 years to the then-living issue of X, with the remainder (if any) to Charity B, then Charity B has no interest in the trust that can be determined before the 10-year period is ended, and therefore does not control the trust for purposes of Form 990 and Schedule R.

Again, as with the other forms of entity and their conditions of control, control may exist indirectly (however, control by trustees who are banks or financial institutions is ignored to determine parties in common control). On both points, the instructions provide the following information:

Indirect control. Control can be indirect. For example, if the filing organization controls Entity A, which in turn controls (under the definition of control in these instructions) Entity B, the filing organization will be treated as controlling Entity B. To determine indirect control through constructive ownership of a corporation, rules under Section 318 apply. Similar principles apply for purposes of determining constructive ownership of another entity (a partnership or trust).

Bank trustee exception. If the filing organization is a trust that has a bank or financial institution trustee that is also the trustee of another trust, the filing organization is not required to report the other trust as a brother or sister related organization on the ground of common control by the bank or financial institution trustee.

RELATED ORGANIZATION STATUS BY IDENTITY (RATHER THAN THROUGH CONTROL)

Three other ways are described in the glossary definition of related organization by which (aside from parent, subsidiary, or brother-sister status) such status may vest:

> - Supporting/Supported: an organization that claims to be at any time during the **tax year**, or that is classified by the IRS at any time during the tax year, as (i) a **supporting organization** of the filing organization within the meaning of section 509(a)(3), if the filing organization is a **supported organization** within the meaning of section 509(f)(3); (ii) or a supported organization, if the filing organization is a supporting organization.
> - Sponsoring Organization of a VEBA: an organization that establishes or maintains a section 501(c)(9) voluntary employees' beneficiary association (VEBA) during the tax year. A sponsoring organization of a VEBA also includes an employee organization, association, committee, joint board of trustees, or other similar group of representatives of the parties which establish or maintain a VEBA. Although a VEBA must report a sponsoring organization as a related organization, a sponsoring organization should not report a VEBA as a related organization, unless the VEBA is related to the sponsoring organization in some other capacity described in this definition.
> - Contributing Employer of a VEBA: an employer that makes a contribution or contributions to the VEBA during the tax year. Although a VEBA must report a contributing employer as a related organization, a contributing employer should not report a VEBA as a related organization, unless the VEBA is related to the contributing employer in some other capacity described in this definition.

Circumstances applicable to VEBAs are not addressed in these materials other than to note that filers who are exempt as VEBAs (for example, are organizations exempt under Section 501(c)(9)) must report as related organizations their sponsoring organizations and their contributing employers. The 2013 instructions clarified that the reverse is not required (that is, that sponsoring organizations and contributing employers of VEBAS are not to report the VEBA as a related organization unless there is another basis by which related organization status would vest; for example, were the sponsor or contributing employer to have majority seats on the VEBA's board, and control).

On the definitions of supporting organization (a tax classification) and supported organization (a status that derives from another holding the specified tax classification unique to supporting organizations), the glossary definitions are reprinted:

> **Supported organization:** A public charity described in Section 509(a)(1) or 509(a)(2) supported by a **supporting organization** described in Section 509(a)(3).

Supporting organization: A public charity claiming status on Form 990 or otherwise under Section 509(a)(3). A supporting organization is organized and operated exclusively to support one or more **supported organizations**. A supporting organization that is operated, supervised, or controlled by one or more supported organizations is a Type I supporting organization. The relationship of a Type I supporting organization with its supported organization(s) is comparable to that of a parent-subsidiary relationship. A supporting organization supervised or controlled in connection with one or more supported organizations is a Type II supporting organization. A Type II supporting organization is controlled or managed by the same persons that control or manage its supported organization(s). A supporting organization that is operated in connection with one or more supported organizations is a Type III supporting organization. A Type III supporting organization is further considered either functionally integrated with its supported organization(s) or not functionally integrated with its supported organization(s) (Type III other). Finally, a supporting organization cannot be controlled directly or indirectly by one or more **disqualified persons** (as defined in Section 4946), other than foundation managers and other than one or more public charities described in Sections 509(a)(1) or (2).

The tax classification referred to in the definition of supporting organization, set out in Section 509(a)(3), is the basis by which 501(c)(3) entities may claim status as not being a private foundation (and are public charities). Section 509(a)(3) classification is afforded to 501(c)(3) entities organized not only for 501(c)(3) purposes (and with appropriate limitations), but whose organizing document states they are organized to support one or more named organizations,[2] who must be 501(c)(3) public charities or a 501(c)(4), (c)(5), or (c)(6) entity who (if its revenue streams were tested under the public support test used in 501(c)(3) contexts under Section 509(a)(2)) would meet such standards. Supporting organizations are afforded non-private foundation classification even if they would not be publicly supported under the two public support tests[3] because their operations are limited to assisting those who are inherently publicly accountable, and who are presumed to be interested in seeing they operate properly.

SUMMARIZING SUPPORTING OR SUPPORTED RELATED ORGANIZATIONS

The three scenarios in which filers must be prepared to identify related organizations due to the status they hold not related to finding presence of control are:

1. Filers in a supporting organization or supported organization pair under Section 509(a)(3) due to Section 509(a)(3) supporting organization status informing the basis of their non-private foundation classification report the entity or entities on the other side, their supported organization(s) (who need be entities themselves described in Sections 501(c)(3), 501(c)(4), 501(c)(5), or 501(c)(6)).
2. Filers in a supporting organization or supported organization pair under Section 509(a)(3) who are the supported organization(s) of a Section 501(c)(3) entity holding Section 509(a)(3) supporting

---

[2] Originally for this classification, it was not a requirement that one specify one's supported organizations so long as they were named by class (of beneficiary). As a result, longstanding entities may not meet this requirement. Although that is permitted to them under grandfathering rules, it is not permitted to other 509(a)(3) entities, who cannot qualify without designating their supported organizations in their organizing document.

[3] The first of the public support tests is expressed in Sections 509(a)(1) and 170(b)(1)(A)(vi), and is evidenced by completion of Schedule A's Part II. The second of the public support tests is expressed in Section 509(a)(2) and is evidenced by completion of Schedule A's Part III.

organization status as the basis of its non-private foundation classification-qualification report the entity on the other side, the supporting organization, who will be an entity described in Section 501(c)(3).

KNOWLEDGE CHECK

3. Which does not hold status as a related organization?

   a. A filer's supporting organization (that is, an entity holding status under Section 509(a)(3) and reporting to the IRS that the filer is one of its supported organizations).

   b. A limited partnership in which the filer has a 35 percent capital or profits interest (and the filer is not a general partner).

   c. A supported organization of a filer who holds Section 509(a)(3) status and whose mission is to provide support to the supported organization.

   d. A wholly-owned subsidiary of the filer that is a stock corporation in which the filer is the sole shareholder.

Completion of Schedule R Parts Vis-a-Vis Identifying Disregarded Entities and Related Organizations

Once a filer has identified one or more disregarded entities or related organizations, Schedule R-I through R-IV must be completed. The (Core Form) Part IV at Lines 33 and 34 has the trigger questions that denote the need for such completion:

		Yes	No
33	Did the organization own 100% of an entity disregarded as separate from the organization under Regulations sections 301.7701-2 and 301.7701-3? *If "Yes," complete Schedule R, Part I* **33**		✓
34	Was the organization related to any tax-exempt or taxable entity? *If "Yes," complete Schedule R, Part II, III, or IV, and Part V, line 1* **34**	✓	

SCHEDULE R, PARTS I–IV COMPLETION

Each of these parts reports detailed information on each entity being disclosed (related organizations and disregarded entities), but each part requires different data, geared to each part's type of group.

Part I

This part provides details in Columns (a) through (e) that should be easy to procure such as the disregarded entity's identity (name, address, EIN), domicile in which organized, primary activity, income for the year, and total assets at year-end.

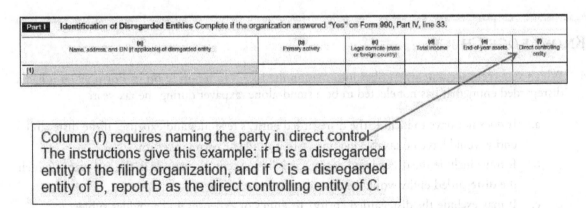

> Column (f) requires naming the party in direct control. The instructions give this example: if B is a disregarded entity of the filing organization, and if C is a disregarded entity of B, report B as the direct controlling entity of C.

Note the impact of the Column (f) instruction were a filer to have a disregarded entity (as shown, B) that itself was the sole member of another limited liability company (again as shown, C) both entities' financial (and program) activities are reported with the filer on the Core Form.

As to the Column (a) header, IRS protocol has changed last several years. IRS is adamant (see newer version of Form W-9) that disregarded entities, regardless of having their own EIN *which as noted in the following tip* IS REQUIRED FOR PAYROLL TAX REPORTING PURPOSES but only for such purposes, are to use the EIN of their sole member.

> **TIP** A disregarded entity generally must use the EIN of its sole member. An exception applies to employment taxes: for wages paid to **employees** of a disregarded entity, the disregarded entity must file separate employment tax returns and use its own EIN on such returns. See Regulations sections 301.6109-1(h) and 301.7701-2(c)(2)(iv).

501(c)(3) organizations have long wanted to have their disregarded entity LLCs able to directly receive charitable contributions. Such result was embraced by IRS Notice 2012-52, effective for charitable contributions made on or after July 31, 2012 (and also, for reliance, for taxable years for which the period of limitation on refund has not expired). It sets out that the IRS will treat a contribution to a disregarded SMLLC created or organized in or under the law of the United States, a United States possession, a state, or the District of Columbia, and is wholly owned and controlled by a U.S. charity, as a charitable contribution to a branch or division of the U.S. charity. It also notes that donee acknowledgment should be provided by the qualified charity that is the sole-member of the LLC.

KNOWLEDGE CHECK

4. Which statement accurately describes information the filer is to report upon its Form 990 if it had a disregarded entity that has not elected to be a stand-alone taxpayer during the tax year?

    a. It does not have to include the disregarded entity's revenues and expenses if the disregarded entity would have no taxable income were it to file its own tax return.

    b. It must include the disregarded entity's activities except for periods in the tax year in which the disregarded entity would be described as tax-exempt.

    c. It may exclude the disregarded entity's revenues or expenses and activities subject to unrelated business income tax if it requires the disregarded entity to file its own tax return solely for those activities and income.

    d. A disregarded entity of the filer must be listed on Part I of Schedule R and all of its activities, revenue, expenses, and net assets reported on the Core Form 990 and schedules as if earned directly by the filer.

Part II

This part's details are specific to the idiosyncratic nature of tax-exempt status (besides providing the same mundane information—name, address, EIN, domicile in which organized, and primary activity information—asked of throughout Parts I-IV). Note: Despite the part's header, governmental entities are reportable upon this part.

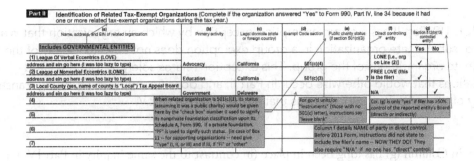

Note: Preceding sample is for a filer, FREE LOVE, with three related organizations reportable here:

- NFP that goes by the acronym LONE [related due to LONE's Board composition—FREE LOVE's employees sat in 3 of LONE's Board 5 seats at one point in tax year]
- NFP that goes by the acronym LOVE [related as it is owned by LONE, which is LOVE's sole voting member and seats LOVE's Board]
- a governmental entity [related because at one time in year, two of FREE LOVE's board members were also serving as two of the three Tax Board Commissioners]

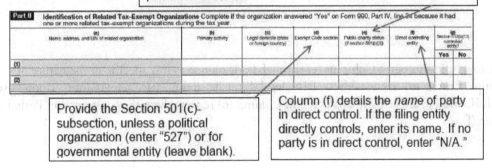

Column (e) instruction not only requires, for a non-private foundation 501(c)(3) related organization, using the Part I, Schedule A line number that corresponds to that entity's public charity status but, notes two points further:

1. for 509(a)(3) supporting organizations, the Type must also be inputted using the Roman numeral, and for Type Ill's, requires denoting functionally integrated or other; and
2. related foreign organizations not recognized as a 501(c)(3) public charity by the IRS but for which the filing organization has made a good faith determination that the entity is the equivalent of a public charity are to be reported BUT if no such determination has been made, Column (e) is to be left blank.

The inquiry in Column (g) has long been in place (in contrast to the same inquiry in Part IV, reporting in particular on stock corporations, which was only added as of the 2012 Form). Its significance comes from the fact that having a tax-exempt entity who is itself a related organization (referred to in the remaining pages of this chapter as RO) does not correlate to that RO being under > 50 percent board control of the filer (which is the condition by which 512(b)(13) controlled entity status vests). The requirement of Column (g) made of the filer is to affirm, if applicable, that such condition is in place.

Should a filer have > 50 percent control (directly or indirectly) over its RO, 512(b)(13) controlled entity status exists. Section 512(b)(13) taints out of unrelated business income tax (UBIT)-modification payments by a controlled entity of rents (from real property), annuities, interest, or royalties. (This topic is returned to in these materials' address of Schedule R Part V, Line 2.)

Part III

The data sought in this part's Columns (e) through (k) is unique as it is specific to the nature of partnerships. Entries for name, address, EIN, legal domicile, and primary activity information (also found in Parts I, II, and IV) are self-explanatory, and Column (d) repeats the task represented in Parts I and II at Column (f).

Column (e) provides info potentially reflecting UBIT-susceptible income coming to the filer from the partnership (note column (f) reports the filer's "share" for the year).

Issue for tax authorities is possible effect the disproportion effects toward reducing the tax liability of *taxable* partners.

Part III	Identification of Related Organizations Taxable as a Partnership Complete if the organization answered "Yes" on Form 990, Part IV, line 34 because it had one or more related organizations treated as a partnership during the tax year.										
	(a) Name, address, and EIN of related organization	(b) Primary activity	(c) Legal domicile (state or foreign country)	(d) Direct controlling entity	(e) Predominant income (related, unrelated, excluded from tax under sections 512-514)	(f) Share of total income	(g) Share of end-of-year assets	(h) Disproportionate allocations?		(i) Code V – UBI amount in box 20 of Schedule K-1 (Form 1065)	(j) General or managing partner?		(k) Percentage ownership
								Yes	No		Yes	No	
(1)													
(2)													

Column (d) details the *name* of the party in direct control. If the filing entity directly controls, enter its name. If no party is in direct control, enter "N/A."

Column (i) reports the UBIT-susceptible income reported by the related organization as the filer's share.

The c3s (and potentially c4s) are limited in extent to which they can conduct activities outside their exempt purposes *with partners who are not exempt.* Issue here relates both to potential lack of exemption qualification (on private benefit or even inurement grounds). Also, there are potential UBIT implications if filer is not in control of the partnership.

Note: If the related organization being reported is NOT one in which the filer is a partner or member (if the filer was the parent of the RO as a managing partner or member or general partner or the filer was in a brother/ sister relationship with the partnership), only Columns (a) through (c) are to be completed AND the all other columns should be denoted as N/ A.

Completion of Column (e):

Column (e) Predominant income. Classify the predominant type of partnership income as:
- Related;
- Unrelated; or
- Excluded from tax under section 512, 513, or 514.

In other words, enter which of the three types listed above is more prevalent than the others.

For classification purposes, use the definitions of columns (B), (C), and (D) set forth in the instructions to the Statement of Revenue in Form 990, Part VIII.

Completion of Column (g)*

Column (g) Share of end-of-year assets. Enter the dollar amount of the filing organization's distributive share of the related partnership's end-of-year total assets, in accordance with the organization's capital interest as specified by the partnership or LLC agreement, for the related partnership's **tax year** ending with or within the filing organization's tax year. Use Schedule K-1 (Form 1065) for the partnership's year ending with or within the organization's tax year to determine this amount by adding the organization's ending capital account to the organization's share of the partnership's liabilities at year end reported on the Schedule K-1.

* Note: For Column (g), the Schedule K-1 is to be used, not what is on filer's books and records.

Two more Part III completion tips:

(1) If the K-1 (Form 1065) is not available at the time Form 990 is completed, the instructions state preparers may provide a reasonable estimate of the required information (K-l's are referenced in the instructions for Columns (f), (g), and (i)); and

(2) The instructions provide (as a tip) that Column (i)'s reporting of Box 20/ Code V unrelated business taxable income amounts are not controlling of the filer's actual UBIT liability (they note that if the organization believes the amount on the K-1 is incorrect, it should consult with the partnership.)

Part IV

This part of the Schedule R does double-duty, reporting *both* upon related organizations organized *as corporations* (but not not-for-profit, nonstock corporations—so *not* tax-exempt 501(c)-entities) and those organized *as trusts*. As with the preceding parts of Schedule R, this part's Columns (a) through (c) input name/ address/ EIN, domicile in which organized, and primary activity. Column (d) of this part mirrors the same asks we saw in all three preceding parts of the Schedule. Column (e) requires denoting the type of corporation or status as a trust. Columns (f) through (h) are self-explanatory.

There is a reason for emphasizing that Column (i) was only added by the 2012 Form—for the first four years of the Redesigned Form 990, the IRS had assumed filers knew that they had a 512(b)(13) controlled entity with a corporation in which the filer had a greater than 50 percent stock position (visible in Column (h)), triggering greater reporting of transactions between said related organization and the filer in Part V of this Schedule. However, the IRS realized that many filers were not aware of what makes an entity a 512(b)(13) controlled entity (and that Part V additional reporting on same was not occurring), so it added this column to specifically highlight the topic.

Illustrative Part IV input:

Schedule R (Form 990) 2012

Note: Preceding sample is for the same filer noted earlier, FREE LOVE, who not only had related organizations reportable on Part II, but also has three corporations or trusts who are related organizations:

- A 85 percent-owned C corp, Widget-Rama
- Two charitable remainder trusts in which its actuarial interest (given the age of the life-income beneficiaries, the youngest of which is 93) is > 50 percent

Columns (a) through (d) represent the same inquiries seen earlier in Parts I-III (with one change for split-interest trusts – same is addressed on next page); Column (e) is self-explanatory, and Column (h) only needs more explanation with respect to trusts. Instructions on the remaining columns, (f) and (g), and the pertinent portion of (h) follow:

Column (f). Share of total income. For a **related organization** that is a C corporation, enter the dollar amount of the organization's share of the C corporation's total income. To calculate this share, multiply the total income of the C corporation (as reported on its Form 1120, U.S. Corporation Income Tax Return) by the following fraction: the value of the filing organization's shares of all classes of stock in the C corporation, divided by the value of all outstanding shares of all classes of stock in the C corporation. The total income is for the related organization's **tax year** ending with or within the filing organization's tax year.

For a related organization that is an S corporation, enter the filing organization's allocable share of the S corporation's total income. Use the amount on Schedule K-1 (Form 1120S) for the S corporation's tax year ending with or within the filing organization's tax year (Part III, lines 1 through 10 of Schedule K-1 (Form 1120-S)).

For a related organization that is a trust, enter the total income and gains reported on Part III, lines 1 through 8 of Schedule K-1 (Form 1041) issued to the filing organization for the trust's tax year ending with or within the filing organization's tax year.

 A section 501(c)(3) organization that is an S corporation shareholder must treat all allocations of income from the S corporation as **unrelated business income**, *including gain on the disposition of stock.*

Column (g). Share of end-of-year assets. Enter the dollar amount of the filing organization's allocable share of the **related organization's** total assets as of the end of the related organization's **tax year** ending with or within the filing organization's tax year. For related C and S corporations, this amount is determined by multiplying the corporation's end-of-year total assets by the fraction described in column (f). For related trusts, this amount corresponds to the filing organization's percentage ownership in the trust.

In the case of a trust, the last sentence of the preceding Column (g) instruction is augmented by the following Column (h) instruction:

For a related organization taxable as a trust, enter the filing organization's percentage of beneficial interest. In each case, enter the percentage interest as of the end of the related organization's tax year ending with or within the filing organization's tax year.

- Also affecting split interest trusts is a provision allowing confidentiality on a trust's identity: the names, addresses, and employer (taxpayer) ID numbers of a RO split-interest trust does not have to be entered. Instead, these trusts are to be reported at Part IV only by type (charitable remainder trusts, charitable lead trusts, pooled income funds). Column (a) reports the type of trust(s), and, if applicable, the number of such types of trusts. Thereafter, Columns (b)–(d) and (i) are to be completed, all others are left blank. See reprint of instruction:

> **Split-interest trusts.** If the related organization is a split-interest trust described in section 4947(a)(2), the organization may enter in column (a) the term "Charitable remainder trust," "Charitable lead trust," or "Pooled income fund," as appropriate, instead of the trust's name, EIN, or address. If the organization was related to more than one of a certain type of related split-interest trust during the tax year, it should enter the number of that type of trust in parentheses after the name. For instance, if the organization had two related charitable remainder trusts and three related charitable lead trusts, it should enter "Charitable remainder trusts (2)" on one line of column (a) and "Charitable lead trusts (3)" on another line in column (a). The organization may leave columns (e), (f), (g), and (h) blank for these lines. Use Part VII if the organization needs space to provide additional information for columns (b), (c), (d), or (i).

Column (i): The purpose of this column, identifying ROs as 512(b)(13) controlled entities, relates to further reporting on transactions with those in such status in Part V. What defines such status depends on the form of the RO's entity, as same vests if either:

- the related organization is under > 50 percent stock control of the filer with corporations with stock -OR-
- the related organization is under > 50 percent filer-over-trustees control of the filer with the related organization being a trust

IMPORTANT NOTE: except for trusts, the Form 990 definition of control as the term relates to finding related organization status employs the same definition as that found in Section 512(b)(13). With trusts, however, status as a RO exists when a filer has a >50 percent *beneficial interest* in the trust whereas status as a 512(b)(13) controlled entity of the filer turns on whether the filer has majority control of the Trust's governors (that is, the same standard by which RO *and* 512(b)(13) control is deemed with respect to not-for-profit or nonstock entities. As to 512(b)(13) controlled entity characterization of a trust, Regulations Section 1.512(b)-1(l)(4)(b), reprinted earlier in this chapter, requires evaluation of whether a majority of the Trust's trustees are board members, employees, or agents of the filer.

KNOWLEDGE CHECK

5. What information is NOT required to be disclosed on Schedule R, Part III for entities taxable as a partnership?

    a. Name of the partnership.
    b. Predominant income source.
    c. Total amount of income that is unrelated or excluded from tax under Sections 512-514.
    d. Share of total income.

6. What information is required to be disclosed on Schedule R, Part IV for charitable remainder trusts?

    a. Name of the trust.
    b. Address.
    c. Taxpayer ID number.
    d. Share of end-of-year assets.

7. What information is NOT required to be disclosed on Schedule R, Part IV for stock corporations?

    a. Name of the corporation.
    b. Legal domicile.
    c. Dollar value of end-of-year assets.
    d. Status as 512(b)(13) controlled entity.

SCHEDULE R'S PART V

This part reports on transfers with the filer's related organizations (such as those disclosed in the Schedule's Parts II—IV). There are only two lines:

Line 1 is completed by all filers and requires checking boxes to denote, by type, the fact that one or more transactions have occurred with the filer's related organizations (for example, the ROs disclosed upon Parts II–IV of this Schedule.

Line 2 completion is only required in two specified circumstances: (1) if the filer is a 501(c)(3) entity and has one or more tax-exempt ROs who are exempt under a NON-(c)(3) Section (for example, exempt under Sections 501(c)(4) or 501(c)(6)); or (2) if the filer has a RO who is a 512(b)(13) controlled entity.

Line 1:

Part V	Transactions With Related Organizations Complete if the organization answered "Yes" on Form 990, Part IV, line 34, 35b, or 36.		
		Yes	No
	Note. Complete line 1 if any entity is listed in Parts II, III, or IV of this schedule.		
1	During the tax year, did the organization engage in any of the following transactions with one or more related organizations listed in Parts II–IV?		
a	Receipt of (i) interest, (ii) annuities, (iii) royalties, or (iv) rent from a controlled entity	1a	
b	Gift, grant, or capital contribution to related organization(s)	1b	
c	Gift, grant, or capital contribution from related organization(s)	1c	
d	Loans or loan guarantees to or for related organization(s)	1d	
e	Loans or loan guarantees by related organization(s)	1e	
f	Dividends from related organization(s)	1f	
g	Sale of assets to related organization(s)	1g	
h	Purchase of assets from related organization(s)	1h	
i	Exchange of assets with related organization(s)	1i	
j	Lease of facilities, equipment, or other assets to related organization(s)	1j	
k	Lease of facilities, equipment, or other assets from related organization(s)	1k	
l	Performance of services or membership or fundraising solicitations for related organization(s)	1l	
m	Performance of services or membership or fundraising solicitations by related organization(s)	1m	
n	Sharing of facilities, equipment, mailing lists, or other assets with related organization(s)	1n	
o	Sharing of paid employees with related organization(s)	1o	
p	Reimbursement paid to related organization(s) for expenses	1p	
q	Reimbursement paid by related organization(s) for expenses	1q	
r	Other transfer of cash or property to related organization(s)	1r	
s	Other transfer of cash or property from related organization(s)	1s	

Line 1's sub-lines represent types of transactions – the instructions define none of the sub-lines but make two pronouncements:

- A single transaction may be described by an reported in more than one line; and
- A transfer, for Part V, Lines 1r and 1s, includes any covenance of funds or property not described in Lines 1a through 1q, whether or not for consideration, such as a merger with a related organization.

Aside from those pronouncements, the most difficult line is Line 1a as it returns to the need to have made an accurate determination of whether any related organization reported in Parts II-IV is controlled by the filer and is within the definition of a 512(b)(13) controlled entity. To the extent one or more related organizations fit such characterization, a "Yes" at Line 1a reflects that the four categories of investment income (interest, annuities, royalties, or rents from real property) obtained from such a controlled entity will be subject to the cited Section's taint into UBIT-taxation.

Although Lines 1a-1s are relatively self-explanatory, Line 2 is not.

The following illustration returns to the prior-noted filer FREE LOVE, and its related organization, LOVE:

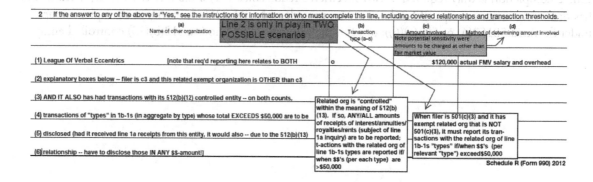

Line 2's application is rather nuanced. It requires reporting <u>details</u> of transactions only in the case (and then a bit disparately) of the filer **EITHER:**

having a 512(b)(13) controlled entity (the filer is a Controlling Organization)	OR	being exempt under Section 501(c)(3) and the RO in question is exempt under 527 or 501(c) BUT NOT under 501(c)(3)
↙		↘
Controlling Organization (in which case reporting is made ONLY with respect to certain transactions with the filer's 512(b)(13)-controlled entity, as follows): The filing organization must report on this line any of the following transactions that it engaged in with a controlled entity of the filing organization, as defined in Section 512(b)(13), during the tax year. <ul><li>All transactions described in Line 1a, which includes all receipts or accruals of interest, annuities, royalties, or rent from a controlled entity under Section 512(b)(13), regardless of amount.</li><li>Any other type of transaction described in Lines 1b through 1s with controlled entities, if the amounts involved during the tax year between the filing organization and a particular controlled entity exceed $50,000 for that transaction.</li></ul>		501(c)(3) and is related to a non-(c)(3) exempt (in which case reporting is made ONLY with respect to certain transactions with that related organization, as follows per the instructions): 501(c)(3) organizations must also report on Line 2 transactions described in Part V, Lines 1b through 1s that they engaged in with related tax-exempt organizations not described in Section 501(c)(3) (including 527 political organizations), if the amounts involved during the tax year between the filing organization and a particular related tax-exempt organization exceed $50,000.

What purpose does Line 2 serve?

Section 512(b)(13) is a UBIT loophole closer. By design it reaches payments made by subsidiaries when same are more-than-50 percent controlled by an exempt parent entity. In light of that section's requirements, Section 6033(h) requires controlling organizations to report certain controlled entity transactions, including loans, fund transfers, and receipt of interest, annuities, royalties, or rents from the controlled entity, on their Forms 990. Because receipts or accruals of interest, annuities, royalties, or rent from these controlled entities are subject to special tax treatment under Section 512(b)(13), they must be reported regardless of amount.

And finally, there is a less-than-helpful instruction regarding Part V's Column (c), and the augmentation of its last sentence with the requirements imposed by Column (d):

Column (c) Amount involved. The amount involved in a transaction is the **fair market value** of the services, cash, and other assets provided by the filing organization during its **tax year**, or the fair market value received by the filing organization, whichever is higher, regardless of whether the transaction was entered into by the parties in a prior year. Any reasonable method for determining such amount is acceptable.

Column (d) Method of determining amount involved. Describe the method used to determine the value of the services, cash, and other assets reported in column (c).

<u>Part VI.</u> Unlike the preceding parts of the Schedule R, this part does NOT report on Related Organizations. Rather, this part reports on *unrelated organizations that are taxable as partnerships*.

Part VI	Unrelated Organizations Taxable as a Partnership (Complete if the organization answered "Yes" to Form 990, Part IV, line 37.)										
Provide the following information for each entity taxed as a partnership through which the organization conducted more than five percent of its activities (measured by total assets or gross revenue) that was not a related organization. See instructions regarding exclusion for certain investment partnerships.											
(a) Name, address, and EIN of entity	(b) Primary activity	(c) Legal domicile (state or foreign country)	(d) Predominant income (related, unrelated, excluded from tax under section 512-514)	(e) Are all partners section 501(c)(3) organizations?		(f) Share of total income	(g) Share of end-of-year assets	(h) Disproportionate allocations?		(i) Code V—UBI amount in box 20 of Schedule K-1 (Form 1065)	(j) General or managing partner?	(k) Percentage ownership
				Yes	No			Yes	No		Yes	No	

WHY IS THIS SOUGHT? The IRS' frequently asked questions stated the case for this part as follows:

Some exempt organizations participate in joint ventures and other arrangements in which the organization does not have a controlling interest that satisfies the Form 990 definition of *related organization*. These arrangements might lead to activities that result in unrelated business income tax, private benefit, inurement, and other exempt status issues, especially when the organization does not control the venture or arrangement. Accordingly, Part VI of Schedule R was designed to collect information regarding participation in partnerships which are not controlled by the organization but through which the organization conducts significant activities. **For this purpose, the organization must report information regarding unrelated partnerships through which it conducts activities constituting at least 5 percent of its total activities, measured by gross revenue or total assets, whichever is greater.** Certain passive investment activities are excepted. **(Authors' emphasis added via bold and highlight.)**

In this part, provide information on any **unrelated organization** (an organization that is not a related organization with respect to the filing organization) that meets all of the following conditions.

1. The unrelated organization is treated as a partnership for federal tax purposes (S corporations are excluded).

2. The filing organization was a partner or member of the unrelated partnership at any time during the filing organization's **tax year**.

3. The filing organization conducted more than 5% of its activities, figured as the greater of its **total assets** at the end of its tax year or its gross revenue for its tax year, through the unrelated partnership.

In determining the percentage of the filing organization's activities as measured by its total assets, use the amount reported on Form 990, Part X, line 16, as the denominator, and the filing organization's ending capital account balance for the partnership tax year ending with or within the filing organization's tax year as the numerator (the amount reported on Schedule K-1 can be used). In determining the percentage of the filing organization's activities as measured by its gross revenue, use the amount reported on Form 990, Part VIII, line 12, as the denominator, and the filing organization's proportionate share of the partnership's gross revenue for the partnership tax year ending with or within the filing organization's tax year as the numerator.

As to the extent and reach of the passive investment activities exception, the instructions provide:

Disregard unrelated partnerships that meet both of the following conditions.

1. 95% or more of the filing organization's total revenue from the partnership for the partnership's tax year ending with or within the organization's tax year is described in sections 512(b)(1)–(3) and (5), such as interest, dividends, royalties, rents, and capital gains (including unrelated debt-financed income).

2. The primary purpose of the filing organization's investment in the partnership is the production of income or appreciation of property and not the conduct of a section 501(c)(3) charitable activity such as program-related investing.

2. The primary purpose of the filing organization's investment in the partnership is the production of income or appreciation of property and not the conduct of a section 501(c)(3) charitable activity such as program-related investing.

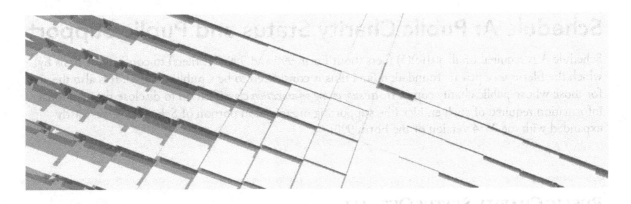

Chapter 3

Deep Dive into Schedule A—How a Public Charity is NOT a Private Foundation

LEARNING OBJECTIVES

After completing this chapter, you should be able to do the following:

- Identify how to properly report the basis of the filer's tax year non-private foundation classification qualification for the tax year being reported upon.
- Identify the different bases by which non-private foundation classification is obtained and how to properly report these upon Schedule A's Part I.
- Recognize the key differences between the two public support tests.
- Identify the completion requirements for the additional parts of Schedule A that need be completed by the filing organizations who report public charity classification under either of the two public support tests.

Schedule A: Public Charity Status and Public Support

Schedule A is required of all 501(c)(3) filers (both Form 990 and 990-EZ filers) to confirm the basis by which the filer *is not* a private foundation (and thus is considered to be a public charity). It is also the site for those whose public charity comes from *supporting organization* classification to disclose the additional information required of such entities (the supporting organization portion of Schedule A was vastly expanded with the 2014 version of the Form 990).

PUBLIC CHARITY STATUS OVERALL

The Internal Revenue Code[1] has, since 1969, provided that all 501(c)(3) organizations are automatically classified as private foundations, unless they meet one of the bases for exception from such classification. The exceptions, that is, the underlying standards by which an organization is classified as a non-private foundation, are set out in IRC 509(a)(1), (2), and (3)[2] (a 501(c)(3) falling within their definitions is commonly known as a public charity or a public charity that is a supporting organization). It is thus important to understand what statuses are covered by Section 509(a)(1)–(3).

However, before exploring how a 501(c)(3) organization is not a private foundation, it is helpful to note what private foundation status brings with it: an excise tax scheme. The scheme is applied via six IRC Sections (4940-4945) within Chapter 42 of the IRC. Those sections are designed to compel private foundations to act appropriately, specifically to:

- Do two things: (1) make qualifying distributions tied to minimum investment return on a timely basis (Section 4942); and (2) pay a tax on their net investment income (Section 4940)

and

- Not do four things: (1) make taxable expenditures (Section 4945); (2) engage in self-dealing with their disqualified persons (Section 4941); (3) maintain excess business holdings (Section 4943), and (4) make jeopardizing investments (Section 4944)

Self-Reporting the Right Classification upon Schedule A, Part I

On each year's annual information return, 501(c)(3) organizations self-identify the basis of their current (current being in effect during the tax year being reported upon) non-private foundation classification. How the IRS rostered such status off of the filer's initial exemption application determination or thereafter does not determine what category a filer is to report for any particular tax year. Instead, taxpayers have fluidity and identify their basis of non-private foundation classification on an each year basis. This is mandated by the Regulations that tie to the Form 990's 2008 redesign (regulations first issued on a temporary basis in September 2008, and then finalized in September 2011).

---

[1] The "IRC" or "Section" All citations are to the Internal Revenue Code of 1986.
[2] IRC Section 509(a)(4) sets out a category of non-private foundations that has become anachronistic (applying to less than 50 entities) and is thus NOT addressed in these materials.

> PRACTICE TIP: It is imperative that preparers understand that they are *not* required to follow the category of classification reflected upon the filer's 501(c)(3) determination letter or current Exempt Organization Business Master File posting (EOBMF).

The Schedule A instructions make this explicit, stating the following in Part I, Reason for Public Charity Status (Lines 1–12):

> Check only one of the boxes on Lines 1 through 12 to indicate the reason the organization is a public charity for the tax year. The reason can be the same as stated in the organization's tax-exempt determination letter from the IRS (exemption letter) or subsequent IRS determination letter, or it can be different.
>
> If an organization believes there is more than one reason why it is a public charity, it should check only one box but can explain the other reasons it qualifies for public charity status in Part VI.
>
> The IRS does not update its records on an organization's public charity status based on a change the organization makes on Schedule A (Form 990 or 990-EZ). Thus, an organization that checks a public charity status different from the reason stated in its exemption letter or subsequent determination letter, although not required, may submit a request to the IRS Exempt Organizations Determinations Office for a determination letter confirming that it qualifies for the new public charity status if the organization wants the IRS records to reflect the new public charity status.

IRS Exempt Organization Business Master File (EOBMF) and Its Recording of Public Charity Classification (That Is, Determinations)

The open to the public excerpt of the IRS' Business Master File for currently-recognized exempt organizations provides information pertaining to the rostering the IRS has for those organizations. Called the Exempt Organizations Business Master File (EOBMF), the IRS has been committed since 2012 to publish the excerpt on a monthly-updated basis (which can most readily be culled, for those looking for confirmation of 501(c)(3) status but not specific non-private foundation basis, by using the IRS' Select Check[3] tool). Each month's issuance reflects the then-most-current information the IRS has recorded with respect to an entity's exempt status including, in the case of 501 (c)(3) organizations, the basis by which the IRS last determined the entity to qualify as a non-private foundation. As noted, such public charity rostering is not definitive, and filers are to complete the Form 990 based on self-assertion of relevant (to the reported upon year) qualification.

Funders of 501(c)(3) entities typically seek confirmation of current 501(c)(3) exemption, and in many cases, public charity or private foundation classification. The latter information is found in the EOBMF and is most readily accessed charity check services such as GuideStar[4] and Foundation Source who access that file's monthly updates. However, the IRS rostering of non-private foundation status reflects a

---

[3] Select Check's master page is located at www.irs.gov/ Charities-&-Non-Profits/ Exempt-Organizations-Select-Check

[4] www.guidestar.org and www.foundationsource.org

moment in time (the taxpayer's initial exemption determination or later reclassification request). Funders are allowed to rely upon such third party services, even though the category of non-private foundation status may have changed.

In light of the increased access by funder to EOBMF data, some exempt organizations [especially those who had been supporting organizations under 509(a)(3) but now can qualify under one of the two public support tests] may want to re-roster their non-private foundation classification status with the IRS in order to have their 990 reporting match the EOBMF. As already emphasized, such re-rostering is not mandated by law or rule. Nonetheless, filers who wish to update their non-private foundation classification on the IRS' EOBMF may make a rulings request to the IRS' Cincinnati Determinations Offices. Form 8940, Request for Miscellaneous Determination may be used to assist organizations with making such requests (although it is not required). The instructions to that form are helpful in spelling out what need be provided in support of non-private foundation reclassification, especially under either of the two public support tests. A user fee (currently $400) must accompany such requests.

IDENTITY CATEGORIES ESTABLISHING PUBLIC CHARITY STATUS

The sections establishing how entities are NOT private foundations first reach those 501(c)(3) organizations who are inherently accountable to public scrutiny by virtue of who they are, from an identity-standpoint:

509(a)(1) includes five identity categories via cross-reference to another Section 170(b)(1)(A):

1. Churches
2. Schools
3. Hospitals and medical research organizations operated with hospitals
4. Governmental units
5. Agricultural research organizations operated in conjunction with a land-grant college or agricultural university (Added in 2016)

> Note: Although 509(a)(1) also includes a category that requires *revenue testing* to test for public support, that status is not identity-based and thus its subject is held for later discussion.

509(a)(3) also sets out an identity category: Supporting organizations—such entities are 501(c)(3)'s whose purpose is to support other 501(c)(3) organizations (or even 501(c)(4), (c)(5) or (c)(6) entities) but only if the supported organization(s) would themselves fit description as non-private foundations under 509(a)(1) or 509(a)(2).

509(a)(4) sets out the last identity category: Groups who test for public safety.[5]

---

[5] The only discussion of this category occurs in footnote 2, where its rarity is noted.

The noted list of identity categories is visible in seven of Schedule A, Part I's box choices as follows:

1. *Churches* (filers claiming such status as primary check Schedule A's Part I, Box 1) (the term also reaches convention of churches and associations of churches):

> 1 ☐ A church, convention of churches, or association of churches described in **section 170(b)(1)(A)(i).**

Filers who hold such status by law meet a filing exception and are not required to file the exempt organization annual return (Form 990 or 990-EZ) or notice (Form 990-N).

2. *Schools* (filers claiming such status as primary check Schedule A's Part I, Box 2):

> 2 ☐ A school described in **section 170(b)(1)(A)(ii).** (Attach Schedule E.)

3. *Hospitals* (including cooperative hospital service organizations) and *medical research organizations* (MRO) operated in conjunction with a hospital (filers claiming such status as primary check Schedule A's Part I, Box 3 or 4, respectively):

> 3 ☐ A hospital or a cooperative hospital service organization described in **section 170(b)(1)(A)(iii).**
> 4 ☐ A medical research organization operated in conjunction with a hospital described in **section 170(b)(1)(A)(iii).** Enter the hospital's name, city, and state: _____

4. *Federal, state, or local government or governmental units* (filers claiming such status as primary check Schedule A's Part I, Box 6):

> 6 ☐ A federal, state, or local government or governmental unit described in **section 170(b)(1)(A)(v).**

5. An agricultural research organization operated in conjunction with a land-grant college or university or a non-land-grant college of agriculture. Similar to organizations claiming MRO status, they must specifically identify the college or university by name and location.

> 9 ☐ An agricultural research organization described in **section 170(b)(1)(A)(ix)** operated in conjunction with a land-grant college or university or a non-land-grant college of agriculture (see instructions). Enter the name, city, and state of the college or university: _____

6. *Organizations organized and operated exclusively to test for public safety* (filers claiming such status as primary check Schedule A's Part I, Box 11:

> 11 ☐ An organization organized and operated exclusively to test for public safety. See **section 509(a)(4).**

7. *Supporting organizations* (filers claiming such status as primary check Schedule A's Part I, Box 12)

KNOWLEDGE CHECK

1. Which phrase can be applied to accurately complete the following sentence: 501(c)(3) organizations who are classified as public charities must _____

   a. pay the excise taxes private foundations are subject to until such time as the IRS has audited their Form 990 filing.
   b. attach a completed Schedule A to each year's Form 990 or 990-EZ.
   c. submit to the IRS a reclassification ruling request whenever their primary basis of non-private foundation classification has changed from the prior filed Form 990 Schedule A.
   d. attach a copy of the ruling letter from the IRS which established them as a non-private foundation to their Form 990 each year.

2. Which organizations would have public charity classification on an identity basis?

   1. A charity whose main function is to advocate to have the needs of teen mothers met
   2. A homeless shelter that is a stand-alone agency operated by the county
   3. A hospital licensed by the state
   4. An organization whose mission is to advance the public's knowledge of various religions' values and teachings
   5. An association of churches linked to a specific denomination

   a. All
   b. 2 through 5
   c. 3 and 5
   d. 2, 3, and 5

3. For a 501(c)(3) filer that has been classified by the IRS as a non-private foundation which statement is correct?

   a. The filer *must* report on Schedule A's Part I by checking all of the boxes by which it qualified (in the tax year reported upon) as a non-private foundation.
   b. The filer *must* report on Schedule A's Part I by checking the box consistent with the status that the IRS originally granted as its qualified exempt status.
   c. The filer *must* report on Schedule A's Part I by checking the box that reflects its current most appropriate primary basis of classification for non-private foundation status and it is not required to communicate with the IRS in advance to gain approval for such status prior to submitting the return. It is not required to but it may provide an explanation on Schedule A's blank lines Part VI.
   d. The filer *must* check its current primary basis of classification AND report at Schedule A's blank lines Part VI that such classification is not the same as that rostered by the IRS. At its option it may note there its intent or lack thereof to seek a ruling from the IRS' determinations unit to seek confirmation of the basis it is meeting and expects to meet in the future.

MORE IS REQUIRED OF SUPPORTING ORGANIZATIONS THAN "CHECK THE BOX"—PREPARATION POINTS FOR PART I, LINE 12

Filers who check Box 12 will confront multiple lines following that box. Lines 12a-g, shown in the following text box, demonstrate that filers asserting such status have multiple reporting requirements, due to Congressional enactments initially effected via the Pension Protection Act of 2006. These were not incorporated into practice (or the 990) prior to regulations out in late 2012 that first effected tax years that begun in 2013 and are the basis of two additional parts of Schedule A that debuted with the 2014 Form. As discussed at the end of this chapter, a key need of supporting organizations is to know their type. As shown in the full reprint of Line 12 from Schedule A, Part I, there are complicated information requests at sub-lines a-g, including prompts to also complete the Schedule's Parts IV and V:

12	☐	An organization organized and operated exclusively for the benefit of, to perform the functions of, or to carry out the purposes of one or more publicly supported organizations described in **section 509(a)(1)** or **section 509(a)(2)**. See **section 509(a)(3)**. Check the box in lines 12a through 12d that describes the type of supporting organization and complete lines 12e, 12f, and 12g.
a	☐	**Type I.** A supporting organization operated, supervised, or controlled by its supported organization(s), typically by giving the supported organization(s) the power to regularly appoint or elect a majority of the directors or trustees of the supporting organization. **You must complete Part IV, Sections A and B.**
b	☐	**Type II.** A supporting organization supervised or controlled in connection with its supported organization(s), by having control or management of the supporting organization vested in the same persons that control or manage the supported organization(s). **You must complete Part IV, Sections A and C.**
c	☐	**Type III functionally integrated.** A supporting organization operated in connection with, and functionally integrated with, its supported organization(s) (see instructions). **You must complete Part IV, Sections A, D, and E.**
d	☐	**Type III non-functionally integrated.** A supporting organization operated in connection with its supported organization(s) that is not functionally integrated. The organization generally must satisfy a distribution requirement and an attentiveness requirement (see instructions). **You must complete Part IV, Sections A and D, and Part V.**
e	☐	Check this box if the organization received a written determination from the IRS that it is a Type I, Type II, Type III functionally integrated, or Type III non-functionally integrated supporting organization.
f		Enter the number of supported organizations . . . . [____]
g		Provide the following information about the supported organization(s).

(i) Name of supported organization	(ii) EIN	(iii) Type of organization (described on lines 1–10 above (see instructions))	(iv) Is the organization listed in your governing document?		(v) Amount of monetary support (see instructions)	(vi) Amount of other support (see instructions)
			Yes	No		
(A)						

The filing organization should check the box on Lines 12a–d for the type of supporting organization it has either received a determination letter from the IRS for or for which it has made a reasoned determination it qualifies as.

If the organization has a written determination, or if it can find the IRS has made a determination in the IRS Master Business File on its supporting organization type, it should check the box on Line 12e. If the organization does not check the box on Line 12e it should explain on Part VI how it has determined it qualifies for the type of supporting organization it has checked on Line 12a–d.

Things sometimes change. If the organization has a determination letter from the IRS but the organization has changed its organizational structure or operations such that it still qualifies as a supporting organization but not the same type as the type indicated on the determination letter issued by the IRS. The organization should check the box (12a–d) that most accurately reflects its current facts, also check box 12e, and explain Part VI.

Line 12f is a numerical count of the organizations which the supporting organization is claiming to support. The number should include all organizations the supporting organization supported whether or not they provided support during the current tax year.

Line 12g is a table for providing details for all supported organizations from Line 12f (whether supported in the current tax year or not). Complete all details for the columns as requested. Use additional pages as needed. Column (vi) is optional and estimates may be used. If amounts are entered in this column describe the goods, services or use of facilities provided to the supported organization and how the value was estimated on Part VI of Schedule A.

THREE NON-IDENTITY CATEGORIES OF PUBLIC CHARITY STATUS MANDATE USE OF THE TWO PUBLIC SUPPORT TESTS

Assuming a filer does not fall within one of the already-addressed six identity categories, there are three public support test categories by which public charity classification can still be obtained:

- **Section 509(a)(1)'s referencing of Section 170(b)(1)(A)(vi)— Groups qualifying based upon contributed revenue.**
- Section 509(a)(1)'s referencing of Section 170(b)(1)(A)(iv)— Groups support governmental colleges but must also demonstrate contributed revenue.[6]
- **Section 509(a)(2)—Groups qualifying based upon both contributed and earned revenue.**

Each of these three categories has their own check-boxes on Schedule A's Part I:

- ***Public Support Test 1*** (= 509(a)(l)/170(b)(l)(A)(vi) 'test'). This test, when met, establishes that the filer normally receives – measured over the most recently-completed five years – a substantial part of their support from grants or gifts from governmental units or the general public.

    Filers claiming such status as primary check Schedule A's Part I, Boxes 7 or 8 [each refer to the same test] and must successfully complete the test performed upon this 990 **at Part II**:

7	☐ An organization that normally receives a substantial part of its support from a governmental unit or from the general public described in **section 170(b)(1)(A)(vi)**. (Complete Part II.)
8	☐ A community trust described in **section 170(b)(1)(A)(vi)**. (Complete Part II.)

---

[6] This category is NOT shown in bold as it is relatively rare. Those falling within it will find themselves reporting under the same public support test as that referenced in the preceding category shown, that is, Public Support Test 1

- **Public Support Test 2** (509(a)(2) 'test'). This test, when met, establishes that the filer normally receives—measured over the most recently-completed five years—(1) more than one-third of their support from both grants or gifts and fees for service or payments for provision of goods in activities that provide same in contexts related to the organization's exempt purposes; and (2) not more than one-third of their support from gross investment income (not including capital gains) plus true net from unrelated business income-taxable revenues.

    Filers claiming such status as primary check Schedule A's Part I, Box 10 and must successfully complete the test performed upon this 990 **at Part III**:

10	☐ An organization that normally receives: (1) more than 33⅓% of its support from contributions, membership fees, and gross receipts from activities related to its exempt functions—subject to certain exceptions, and (2) no more than 33⅓% of its support from gross investment income and unrelated business taxable income (less section 511 tax) from businesses acquired by the organization after June 30, 1975. See **section 509(a)(2)**. (Complete Part III.)

    2. Filers operating to benefit governmental college or university – IRS requires these entities to have diverse public support as measured in line with **Public Support Test Part II** and their public support testing needs will be addressed in the discussion of that 'test'.

    Filers claiming such status as primary check Schedule A's Part I, Box 5:

5	☐ An organization operated for the benefit of a college or university owned or operated by a governmental unit described in **section 170(b)(1)(A)(iv)**. (Complete Part II.)

PREPARING PARTS II AND III: PUBLIC SUPPORT TESTING METHODOLOGY

Each part's distinct public support (Part II for *Public Support Test 1* and Part III for *Public Support Test 2*) are independent and different from the other. This is most clearly evident when one notes that each of the tests applies its own definition of what constitutes public support (which is the good amount totaled in each Part's Section A) and total support (which is the overall denominator that is totaled in each part's Section B). Test 1 ignores program service revenue (when it is related to exempt function or statutorily not subject to unrelated trade or business characterization) and thus does not include same in either public support or total support. Test 2, however, takes that revenue into account. All these differences are confusing, and added into the mix is the fact that information represented on each part's lines do not tie perfectly (or sometimes at all) to specific Form 990/ 990-EZ revenue categories.

Another key difference is that each Test excludes or limits from public support receipts coming from certain payers, and the payers subject to such limitations (and the limits themselves) differ.

As to methodology:

- each test uses a five year test period to certify the organization's normal receipts (covering the current year and the prior four years; taxpayers use the prior 4 tax periods even if one or more is a short year)
- neither test factors in capital gains
- in both tests, the method of accounting the filing organization normally keeps its books and records upon is the basis of reporting (thus, cash basis taxpayers prepare these parts on that basis, while accrual basis taxpayers do so on the accrual basis of accounting)

Learning about the tests is not easy since Test 1 (the Section 509(a)(1)/ 170(b)(1)(A)(vi) test employed in Schedule A's Part II) applies most often to 501(c)(3) organizations that find themselves outside of an identity category of public charity status.

509(a)(1)/ 170(b)(1)(A)(vi)—The First Test Versus 509(a)(2)—The Second Test

Organizations checking Box 7 or 8 on Part I complete the Part II of Schedule A. The reason for completing the public support test here is to prove the organization does (or could) qualify under this 509(a)(1) public support test

> Note: The "could" refers to an entity wanting to use the special rule on Schedule B regardless of whether this test is the primary basis of their non-private foundation status.[7]

Organizations checking Box 9 on Part I complete Part III of Schedule A.

Each test of the two public support tests has its own eccentricities. The first test ignores earned revenues in the form of gross receipts from related activities (that is, revenues normally reported on Core Form Part VIII, Line 2 and classified as exempt function). Such revenues are omitted for testing purposes on Part II of Schedule A (although there is a line to input the omitted amounts on Line 12. The input there is solely as a memo disclosure as these amounts are neither calculated into total public support (the test's resulting numerator) nor total support (the test's resulting denominator).

Furthermore, as the annotated snapshots following reflect, both tests allow some good support (public support) from revenue streams that would not be reported on the 990/ 990-EZ—this in the case of donated use of facilities or donated services from governmental units. *Part II* records these at Line 3, *Part III* records these at Line 5.

Finally, the remittances from certain payers face limitations in each test. The amounts received from excess contributors will be limited in inclusion in public support calculations, but these limits apply differently in each of the two tests. In the first test, it is only contributions from those payers in excess of 2 percent of total support who are excluded from public support. In the second test, it is all contributions and program service revenue paid from parties who would be disqualified persons if the entity was a private foundation (that is, using the Section 4946 rules), a group which includes substantial contributors that are excluded from public support. Furthermore, in the second test remittances by larger purchasers of program services or goods will also on a year-by-year basis have excess amounts (the greater of $5,000 or 1 percent) excluded.

An illustration of each part follows.

---

[7] As of the 2013 Form 990 instructions, the Schedule B Special Rule for reporting donors at an amount exceeding the normal > $5,000 threshold is only available to organizations passing the Part II public support test with a 33.33 percent result or greater. Accordingly, completion of Schedule A, Part II is required to show such result.

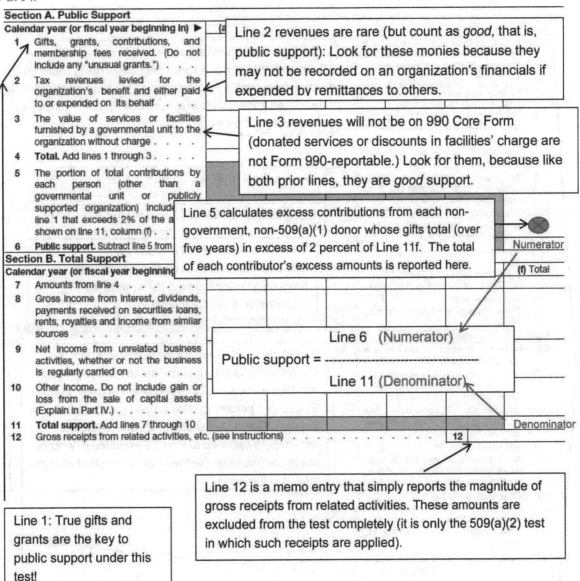

Section A. Public Support

Calendar year (or fiscal year beginning in) ▶

1. Gifts, grants, contributions, and membership fees received. (Do not include any "unusual grants.")

2. Tax revenues levied for the organization's benefit and either paid to or expended on its behalf

3. The value of services or facilities furnished by a governmental unit to the organization without charge

4. **Total.** Add lines 1 through 3

5. The portion of total contributions by each person (other than a governmental unit or publicly supported organization) included on line 1 that exceeds 2% of the amount shown on line 11, column (f)

6. **Public support.** Subtract line 5 from

Section B. Total Support

Calendar year (or fiscal year beginning

7. Amounts from line 4

8. Gross income from interest, dividends, payments received on securities loans, rents, royalties and income from similar sources

9. Net income from unrelated business activities, whether or not the business is regularly carried on

10. Other income. Do not include gain or loss from the sale of capital assets (Explain in Part IV.)

11. **Total support.** Add lines 7 through 10

12. Gross receipts from related activities, etc. (see instructions) 12

Line 2 revenues are rare (but count as *good*, that is, public support): Look for these monies because they may not be recorded on an organization's financials if expended by remittances to others.

Line 3 revenues will not be on 990 Core Form (donated services or discounts in facilities' charge are not Form 990-reportable.) Look for them, because like both prior lines, they are *good* support.

Line 5 calculates excess contributions from each non-government, non-509(a)(1) donor whose gifts total (over five years) in excess of 2 percent of Line 11f. The total of each contributor's excess amounts is reported here.

Numerator

(f) Total

$$\text{Public support} = \frac{\text{Line 6 (Numerator)}}{\text{Line 11 (Denominator)}}$$

Denominator

Line 12 is a memo entry that simply reports the magnitude of gross receipts from related activities. These amounts are excluded from the test completely (it is only the 509(a)(2) test in which such receipts are applied).

Line 1: True gifts and grants are the key to public support under this test!

Cash versus accrual matters (report based on how books are kept): Those subject to FASB Statement No. 116, *Accounting for Contributions Received and Contributions Made*, report multiyear grants at present value when an unconditional promise to give is received (and in each successive year, report the incremental increase in the to-come total gift's present value)

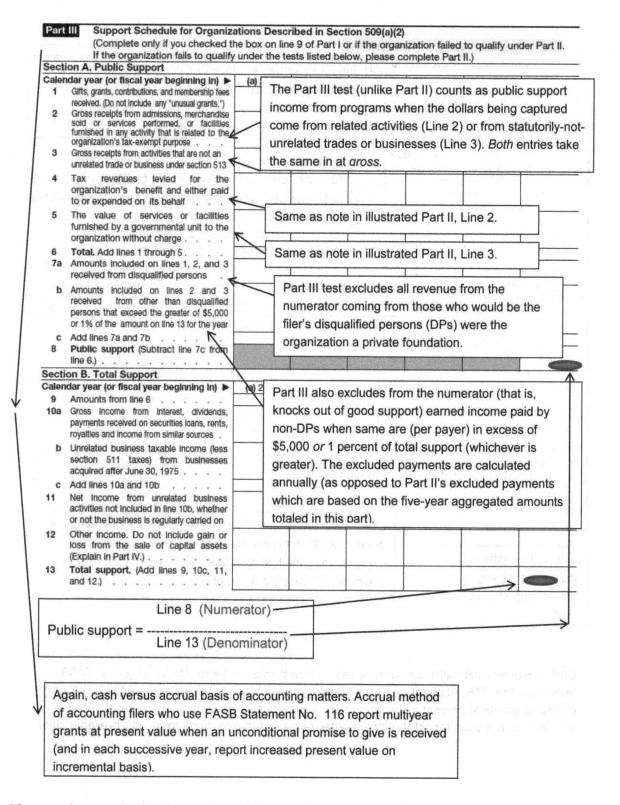

Part III   Support Schedule for Organizations Described in Section 509(a)(2)
(Complete only if you checked the box on line 9 of Part I or if the organization failed to qualify under Part II.
If the organization fails to qualify under the tests listed below, please complete Part II.)

Section A. Public Support

Calendar year (or fiscal year beginning in) ▶   (a)

1   Gifts, grants, contributions, and membership fees received. (Do not include any "unusual grants.")

2   Gross receipts from admissions, merchandise sold or services performed, or facilities furnished in any activity that is related to the organization's tax-exempt purpose . . .

3   Gross receipts from activities that are not an unrelated trade or business under section 513

> The Part III test (unlike Part II) counts as public support income from programs when the dollars being captured come from related activities (Line 2) or from statutorily-not-unrelated trades or businesses (Line 3). *Both* entries take the same in at *gross.*

4   Tax revenues levied for the organization's benefit and either paid to or expended on its behalf . . .

> Same as note in illustrated Part II, Line 2.

5   The value of services or facilities furnished by a governmental unit to the organization without charge . . . .

> Same as note in illustrated Part II, Line 3.

6   **Total.** Add lines 1 through 5 .

7a   Amounts included on lines 1, 2, and 3 received from disqualified persons

b   Amounts included on lines 2 and 3 received from other than disqualified persons that exceed the greater of $5,000 or 1% of the amount on line 13 for the year

> Part III test excludes all revenue from the numerator coming from those who would be the filer's disqualified persons (DPs) were the organization a private foundation.

c   Add lines 7a and 7b . . . .

8   **Public support** (Subtract line 7c from line 6.) . . . .

Section B. Total Support

Calendar year (or fiscal year beginning in) ▶   (a)

9   Amounts from line 6 . . . . .

10a   Gross income from interest, dividends, payments received on securities loans, rents, royalties and income from similar sources .

b   Unrelated business taxable income (less section 511 taxes) from businesses acquired after June 30, 1975 . . . .

c   Add lines 10a and 10b . . . .

11   Net income from unrelated business activities not included in line 10b, whether or not the business is regularly carried on

> Part III also excludes from the numerator (that is, knocks out of good support) earned income paid by non-DPs when same are (per payer) in excess of $5,000 *or* 1 percent of total support (whichever is greater). The excluded payments are calculated annually (as opposed to Part II's excluded payments which are based on the five-year aggregated amounts totaled in this part).

12   Other income. Do not include gain or loss from the sale of capital assets (Explain in Part IV.) . . . . .

13   **Total support.** (Add lines 9, 10c, 11, and 12.) . . . .

$$\text{Public support} = \frac{\text{Line 8 (Numerator)}}{\text{Line 13 (Denominator)}}$$

> Again, cash versus accrual basis of accounting matters. Accrual method of accounting filers who use FASB Statement No. 116 report multiyear grants at present value when an unconditional promise to give is received (and in each successive year, report increased present value on incremental basis).

The second test applies less frequently to (c)(3)s than the first test. It is the more complicated of the two, and has far more eccentricities. As noted earlier, and as evidenced in Lines 2 and 3, this test includes as public support earned revenues that the prior test excludes:

- All gross receipts from admissions, merchandise sold or services performed, or facilities furnished in any activity that is related to the organization's exempt purpose are entered on Line 2; and
- All gross receipts from activities that are not an unrelated trade or business under Section 513 are entered on Line 3.

Finally, the second test specifically excludes all remittances from public support (but not from total support) received from parties who are disqualified persons (applying the same definition that would apply if the entity was a private foundation, that found in Section 4946) or when the remittances are of a type reported on Lines 2 and 3 (earned income) and a payer's total payment of such amounts—in any of the years included in the test period—was the greater of 1 percent of the year's total support, or $5,000, exclude the payments that exceed the greater of $5,000 or 1 percent.

KNOWLEDGE CHECK

4. Which statement as to the organization's reporting under the first versus second test is accurate?

   a. The presence of in-kinds from government payers only matters under the first test.
   b. The presence of program service revenue in the test period constitutes good that is, public, support in both tests.
   c. Larger contributors in the first test will need be evaluated with respect to the calculated dollar limitation that applies to certain donors' aggregated gifts across the test period.
   d. The presence of larger contributors in the second test is not a factor unless the contributors have also remitted program service amounts.

PUBLIC SUPPORT TESTING: A LINE-BY-LINE-REVIEW OF THE INSTRUCTIONS FOR PARTS II AND III

First, the statute:

What counts as support for both tests' denominator is set out in Section 509(d). That section states that support for both the 509(a)(1)/ 170(b)(1)(A)(vi) and 509(a)(2) tests incorporates only these items:

- **gifts, grants, contributions, or membership fees**
- **gross receipts from admissions, sales of merchandise, performance of services, or furnishing of facilities in any activity which is not an unrelated trade or business** (within the meaning of Section 513) [these are of course then omitted from the 509(a)(1)/ 170(b)(1)(A)(vi) test]
- **net income** from unrelated business activities, whether or not such activities are carried on regularly as a trade or business
- **gross investment income** (as defined in subsection (e))
- tax revenues levied for the benefit of an organization and either paid to or expended on behalf of such organization
- the value of services or facilities (exclusive of services or facilities generally furnished to the public without charge) furnished by a governmental unit referred to in Section 170(c)(1) to an organization without charge.

Such term does not include any gain from the sale or other disposition of property which would be considered as gain from the sale or exchange of a capital asset, or the value of exemption from any federal, state, or local tax or any similar benefit.

(bold font in the excerpt has been added for emphasis)

SCHEDULE A, PART II (FIRST TEST), SECTIONS A AND B: INPUTTING SUPPORT

Line 1—Gifts, grants, contributions, and membership fees received.

In getting these measures accomplished, these all register as good support unless coming in the form of an unusual grant). Specific definitional imperatives rule the pertinent lines upon which material public support registers:

- gift, grant, or contribution
- membership fees
- unusual grants (these are omitted from Line 1 and from test denominator overall)

Line 1's gift, grant, contribution applies the same meaning as that used in Core Form Part VIII, Line 1. The nuances applicable there apply here as well, with one exception. The four key points are as follows:

1. Having the government call a payment a grant does not make it a true grant.
2. Rules with respect to what comprises an includible (in 990 revenue) noncash contribution[8] remain intact (indeed, for Schedule A purposes, the Regulations have long noted that contributions of services for which a deduction is not allowable are not includible in either total support or public support in the case of non-governmental donors[9]).
3. Loss on uncollectible pledge – on the Core Form, such losses do not decrease year's gift revenues but instead are reported as an adjustment to net assets. On Schedule A, the instructions state that loss is to be deducted from the contribution amount for the year in which the filer originally counted that contribution as revenue.
4. Sometimes a member pays dues/fees that qualify as a gift.

---

[8] As with Core Form Part VIII, Line 1, noncash contributions are to be recorded using a reasonable method of determining their value at date of contribution. Furthermore, donations of services (such as the value of donated advertising space or broadcast air time) or *donations of use of* (but not title to) materials, equipment, or facilities are not included. That absolute for purposes of Core Form Part VIII, Line 1 and Schedule A, Part II, Line 1 does not reach donated and services from a governmental unit for Schedule A purposes (these are reported on Part II, Line 3).

[9] This is set out in Regulations Section 1.170A-9(f)(7)(i)(B):
Definition of support [for purposes of 170(b)(1)(A)(vi)]. For purposes of this paragraph (f), the term support shall be as defined in section 509(d) [reprinted on prior page] (without regard to section 509(d)(2)). **The term support does not include** (A) Any amounts received from the exercise or performance by an organization of its charitable, educational, or other purpose or function constituting the basis for its exemption under section 501(a). In general, such amounts include amounts received from any activity the conduct of which is substantially related to the furtherance of such purpose or function (other than through the production of income); **or (B) Contributions of services for which a deduction is not allowable.** *Emphasis added.*

Regarding (1), a governmental unit's true grants and contributions go on Line 1, as do amounts received in connection with a contract entered into with a governmental unit for the performance of services or in connection with a government research grant, unless the amounts are received from exercising or performing the organization's tax-exempt purpose or function and the purpose of the payment is primarily to serve the direct and immediate needs of the payer governmental unit. The instructions state:

> *An* amount received from a governmental unit is treated as gross receipts from exercising or performing the organization's tax-exempt purpose or function if the purpose is primarily to serve the direct and immediate needs of the payer governmental unit, and is treated as a contribution, if the purpose is primarily to provide a direct benefit to the public. For example, a payment to maintain library facilities that are open to the public should be treated as a contribution. See Regs. Sec. 1.170A-9(f)(8) and Rev. Rul. 81-276. Refer to the instructions for Form 990, Part VIII, Lines 1e and 2 for more examples addressing the distinction between government payments that are contributions and government payments that are gross receipts from activities related to the organization's tax-exempt purpose or function. Medicare and Medicaid payments are treated as gross receipts from patients rather than as contributions from the government payer for purposes of the public support test. See Rev. Rul. 83-153.

Regarding item (4) of the previous page, Line 1's membership fees received are defined in Regulations Section (Regs. Sec.) 1.170A-9(f)(7)(iv). The instructions specify that these are to provide support for the organization rather than to purchase admissions, merchandise, services, or the use of facilities. In other words, these are gifts, regardless of the fact that they are cast—via the mode of solicitation—as membership fees.

a. Were membership fees payments to purchase . . . (as mentioned), in modes related to the organization's exempt purpose, the receipts would be reported on Line 12.
b. Were membership fees payments to purchase . . . (as mentioned), in modes unrelated to the organization's exempt purpose (whether or not susceptible to unrelated business income tax), the receipts factor into Line 9.

The third definitional imperative for Part II, Line 1 relates to unusual grants. These are excluded from Line 1 (and do not factor into total support at all.) Note that characterizing any contributions or grants as unusual requires the filer to narrate the circumstances of same in Part IV. (Furthermore, such narration is not to include the grantors' names). A short-hand definition of the term, and a note not to include grantors names, from the instructions follows:

Do not include the names of the grantors because Part IV will be made available for public inspection.

Unusual grants generally are substantial contributions and bequests from disinterested persons and are:

1. Attracted because of the organization's publicly supported nature,

2. Unusual and unexpected because of the amount, and

3. Large enough to endanger the organization's status as normally meeting either the 33⅓% public support test or the 10% facts and circumstances test.

For a list of other factors to be considered in determining whether a grant is an unusual grant, see Regulations section 1.509(a)-3(c)(4).

An unusual grant is excluded even if the organization receives or accrues the funds over a period of years.

As to what comprises an unusual grant, it helps to know that the question is only asked by those who are concerned that a donor's big gift is going to blow them out of the public support test. Keep in mind that such possibility is the issue when evaluating whether there are (or are not) a predominant number of positive factors setting out such a grant as explained in IRS Publication 557:

In applying the 2 percent limit to determine whether the one-third support test or the 10-percent-of-support requirement is met, exclude contributions that are considered unusual grants from both the numerator and denominator of the appropriate percent-of-support fraction. Generally, unusual grants are substantial contributions or bequests from disinterested parties if the contributions: 1) Are attracted by the publicly supported nature of the organization, 2) Are unusual or unexpected in amount, and 3) Would adversely affect, because of the size, the status of the organization as normally being publicly supported.

Characteristics of an unusual grant. A grant or contribution will be considered an unusual grant if the previous three factors apply and if it has all of the following characteristics. If these factors and characteristics apply, then even without the benefit of an advance ruling, grantors or contributors have assurance that they will not be considered responsible for substantial and material changes in the organization's sources of support.

1. *The grant or contribution is not made by a person (or related person) who created the organization or was a substantial contributor to the organization before the grant or contribution.*
2. *The grant or contribution is not made by a person (or related person) who is in a position of authority, such as a foundation manager, or who otherwise has the ability to exercise control over the organization. Similarly, the grant or contribution is not made by a person (or related person) who, because of the grant or contribution, obtains a position of authority or the ability to otherwise exercise control over the organization.*

3. The grant or contribution is in the form of cash, readily marketable securities, or assets that directly further the organization's exempt purposes, such as a gift of a painting to a museum.
4. The donee-organization has received either an advance or final ruling [author's note: that language is obsolete.] or determination letter classifying it as a publicly supported organization and the organization is actively engaged in a program of activities in furtherance of its exempt purpose.
5. No material restrictions or conditions have been imposed by the grantor or contributor upon the organization in connection with the grant or contribution.
6. If the grant or contribution is intended for operating expenses, not capital items, the terms and amount of the grant or contribution are expressly limited to one year's operating expenses.

Ruling request. Before any grant or contribution is made, a potential grantee organization may request a ruling as to whether the grant or contribution may be excluded. *** The following factors may be considered by the IRS ***:

1. Whether the contribution was a bequest or a transfer while living. A bequest will be given more favorable consideration than a transfer while living.
2. Whether, before the receipt of the contribution, the organization has carried on an active program of public solicitation and exempt activities and has been able to attract a significant amount of public support.
3. Whether, before the year of contribution, the organization met the one-third support test or the 10-percent-of-support requirement without benefit of any exclusions of unusual grants.
4. Whether the organization may reasonably be expected to attract a significant amount of public support after the contribution. Continued reliance on unusual grants to fund an organization's current operating expenses (as opposed to providing new endowment funds) may be evidence that the organization cannot reasonably be expected to attract future support from the general public.
5. Whether the organization has a representative governing body.

Final Line 1 reporting issue: **Agency Funds** (Community foundations take note.)

When an organization acts as an agent for another organization there is a public support entry in Schedule A, Part II even though those amounts are excluded from reported as revenue of the organization in Core Form Part VIII. This is the case when agency funds are transferred to a filer by other public charities (which is frequently the case with community foundations in managing so-called Agency Funds), as set out in the Schedule A, Part II, Line 1 instruction. In this instance, include the transfers of agency funds during the year on Line 1 and provide an explanation on Part VI of Schedule A explaining the difference in reporting these amounts in Core Form, Part VIII, Line 1 versus Schedule A, Part II, Line 1 on Part VI.

Note: The situation addressed here is not that of a fiscal sponsor/sponsored relationship. In an appropriately configured fiscal sponsor arrangement, the fiscal sponsor is the legal recipient of funds in favor of the programs being conducted by the sponsored organization and the programs being conducted (or dollars paid in favor of someone else's conduct) are those of the filing organization and ARE included in both Core Form Parts VIII and IX as revenues and expenses of the filer, respectively.

> **Reporting contributions not reported as revenue.** If the organization reports any **contributions** on line 1 of Schedule A (Form 990 or 990-EZ), *Part II*, that it does not report on Form 990, as revenue in Part VIII or as assets in Part X, or as revenue or assets on Form 990-EZ, explain in *Part VI* the basis for characterizing such transfers as contributions but not as revenue or assets. For example, if an organization is a community foundation that receives and holds a cash transfer for another tax-exempt organization and reports contributions of such property on Schedule A (Form 990 or 990-EZ), *Part II*, line 1, without reporting it on Form 990, as revenue in Part VIII or assets in Part X, explain the basis for characterizing the property as contributions but not as revenue or assets.

KNOWLEDGE CHECK

5. Which would not be considered a helpful factor in determining a grant is an unusual grant?

   a. That the organization would fail to meet the public support test if the grant is not treated as an unusual grant.
   b. The donor has a prior longstanding relationship of support with the organization.
   c. No material restrictions are being imposed by the grantor.
   d. The grant is intended for general operating support of the organization.

Line 2, tax revenues levied for the organization's benefit and either paid to or expended on its behalf, is the second of three public support elements. The tax revenues that are reported upon this line, per the Instructions, are includible whether or not the organization includes [the] amount as revenue on its financial statements or elsewhere on Form 990 or 990-EZ. That is an important point to appreciate as it is not uncommon to have financial statements (and the Form 990 financial reporting flowing from them) not report such in-flows when they were not paid to, but were instead expended to the benefit of the filer, in which case no remittance was made. (An example would be the government building a highway exchange serving a scientific laboratory's new building.)

Line 3, the value of services or facilities furnished by a governmental unit to the organization without charge, is the third element that constitutes public support. Though Line 1 does not include amounts attributable to donated services or discounts provided for accessing use of facilities, equipment, or materials, Line 3 will include value of donated services or use of facilities when these are provided by a governmental unit (except if generally furnished to the public without charge). The pertinent complete instruction states:

> **Line 3.** Enter the value of services or facilities furnished by a **governmental unit** to the organization without charge. Do not include the value of services or facilities generally furnished to the public without charge. For example, include the fair rental value of office space furnished by a governmental unit to the organization without charge but only if the governmental unit does not generally furnish similar office space to the public without charge. Report these amounts whether or not the organization includes these amounts as revenue on its financial statements or elsewhere on Form 990 or 990-EZ.

Line 4 calls for computation – total of Lines 1-3 (that is, all elements of public support prior to limitation being applied via Line 5).

Line 5, the portion of total contributions by each person (other than a governmental unit or publicly supported organization) included on Line 1 that exceeds 2 percent of [the five-year test period's total support], factors in the 509(a)(1)/170(b)(l)(A)(vi) test's specific limitation on public support gifts when same come from certain large donors. The affected donors are those other than governmental grantors and most publicly supported organizations. Two important items rule this line: (1) defining who is not subject to the 2 percent limitation; and (2) when certain donors need be linked.

Who is not subject to the 2 percent limitation?

The instructions summarize the relevant reach of the Regulations, explaining that the limit does not apply to contributions from:

1. Organizations qualifying under Section 170(b)(1)(A)(vi)
2. Governmental units described in 170(b)(1)(A)(v)
3. Other organizations (such as the following) but only if they also qualify as a publicly supported organization under Section 170(b)(1)(A)(vi)
   a. Churches described in Section 170(b)(1)(A)(i)
   b. Educational institutions described in Section 170(b)(1)(A)(ii)
   c. Hospitals described in Section 170(b)(1)(A)(iii)
   d. Organizations operated for the benefit of a college or university owned by or operated by a governmental unit (and thus) described in Section 170(b)(1)(A)(iv)

Need to connect parties together for pooled application of the 2 percent limitation in certain cases

Requisite linking of large donors for purposes of the 2 percent limitation is mandated by Regs. Sec. 1.170A- 9(f)(6)(i). That Regulation states:

In determining whether the 33-1/3 percent support test or the 10 percent support limitation [for purposes of then meeting the facts and circumstances test] is met, contributions by an individual, trust, or corporation shall be taken into account as support ... from the general public only to the extent that the total amount of contributions by any such [person] does not exceed 2 percent of the organization's total support for such *period. . . . In applying the 2 percent limitation, all contributions made by a donor and by any person or persons standing in a relationship to the donor that is described in Section 4946(a)(1)(C)-(G) and [its Regulations] shall be treated as made by one person.* (Italics added in emphasis)

The 'persons' picked up by Section 4946(a)(1)(C)-(G) are:

- a family member (spouse, ancestors, children through great grandchildren and spouses of children through great grandchildren)
- > 20 percent owner of total combined voting power of a corporation
- > 20 percent owner of profits interests of a partnership
- > 20 percent owner of beneficial interest of a trust or unincorporated enterprise
- corporations in which persons described previously are > 35 percent owners of total combined voting power
- partnerships in which persons described previously own > 35 percent profits interest
- trusts or estates in which persons described previously own > 35 percent beneficial interest

Line 6, calls for computation – total here calls for subtracting from Line 4f's five year public support before limitation, the result at 5. Result is the pertinent numerator for the public support test, and concludes Part II's Section A.

Line 7 calls for repeat of all Line 4 entries (that is, input of public support receipts without Line 5 limit applied)

Thereafter, Lines 8-10 calls for input of three non-public support items.

Line 8, gross income from interest, dividends, payments received on securities loans, rents, royalties and income from similar sources, reaches the specified passive income sources only. Note that capital gains are not to be included (they are not specified for this line and indeed, are omitted from the test completely.) Also not included are payments that result from activities of the organization that further its exempt purpose (these go on Line 12). Note that income from program-related investments would thus be omitted from Line 8.

Line 9, net income from unrelated business activities, whether or not the business is regularly carried on, reaches net income from carrying on any and all unrelated business activities, regardless of whether they are taxed under the unrelated business income tax scheme. The instructions continue the longstanding rule that picks up (as this test's total support) activities that fall within Section 513's characterization as an unrelated business, regardless of whether they are regularly carried on and thus subjected to tax under Section 512(b)'s general rule that sets out the calculation of unrelated business taxable income. The inclusion of receipts here is always at net (pursuant to Section 509(d), reprinted earlier at page 21). No specifics in the Instructions address inputs to net, but Sections 512 and 513 (and their Regulations) are cited. Activities that fall outside of unrelated trade/ business characterization due to a Section 513 exception (for example, volunteer labor exception or lawfully-conducted bingo) do not get reported on Line 9. (They are included in the memo-entry at Line 12, which does not factor into the test.)

IMPORTANT: PER INSTRUCTIONS, ANY NET LOSS MUST BE REPORTED AS -0- .

Line 10, other income (note the annotation upon the Form to not include capital gain or loss), any entry here must be explained in Part IV. (As Section B's lines record all support, the only basis for input on Line 12 would be a revenue stream not included on Lines 7-9 that was otherwise within Section 509(d) (that section was reprinted on page 21).

Line 11, computation made here, adding Column (f) amounts for Lines 7-10. Result equates to the five-year test period's total support and will thus be the denominator for the 509(a)(l)/170(b)(l)(A)(vi) test being performed in this part.

Line 12 captures all of the filer's gross receipts received from related activities for all years reported in Part II. The reason for memo-ing such receipts is to flag organizations who do not qualify for Part II testing under Regs. Sec. 1.170A-9(f)(7)(iii) (because they receive only an insignificant amount of gifts and grants income and thus have almost all of their support (as defined in Section 509(d), reprinted earlier at page 21) coming from related activities). The instructions detail what is to be included on this line:

509(d)(2). Include membership fees to the extent they are payments to purchase admissions, merchandise, services, or the use of facilities in a related activity. For example, include on this line gross receipts from:
- A trade or business in which substantially all work is performed by **volunteers** (such as book fairs and sales of gift wrap paper). See section 513(a)(1).
- A trade or business carried on by the organization primarily for the convenience of its members, students, patients, **officers**, or **employees**. See section 513(a)(2).
- A trade or business which is the selling of merchandise, substantially all of which the organization received as gifts or **contributions**. See section 513(a)(3).

- "Qualified public entertainment activities" or "qualified convention and trade show activities" of certain organizations. See section 513(d).
- Furnishing certain hospital services. See section 513(e).
- A trade or business consisting of conducting **bingo** games, but only if the conduct of such games is lawful. See section 513(f).
- Qualified pole rentals by a mutual or cooperative telephone or electric company. See section 513(g).
- The distribution of certain low cost articles and exchange and rental of members lists. See section 513(h).

Include on line 12 gross receipts from admissions, sales of merchandise, performance of services, or furnishing of facilities in any activity which is not an unrelated trade or business (within the meaning of section 513). See section

SCHEDULE A, PART III (SECOND TEST), SECTIONS A AND B: INPUTTING SUPPORT

Line 1, gifts, grants, contributions, and membership fees received.

The entire discussion with respect to Part II, Line 1 (pages 22-24), is appropriate here as well, although each part's discussion of what makes a government grant emphasizes the relevant test's regulatory inputs. In both cases, a governmental unit's true grants and contributions go on Line 1, as do amounts received in connection with a contract entered into with a governmental unit for the performance of services or in connection with a government research grant, unless the amounts are gross receipts from exercising or performing the organization's tax-exempt purpose or function [in] which [case they] should be reported on Line 2. (Quote is from the Part III Instructions, the complete Schedule A instruction for this line is as follows):

> **Support from a governmental unit.**
> Include on line 1 support received from a **governmental unit**. This includes **contributions**, but not gross receipts from exercising or performing the organization's tax-exempt purpose or function, which should be reported on line 2. Contributions are sometimes difficult to distinguish from such gross receipts—the label on the agreement is not controlling. An amount received from a governmental unit is treated as gross receipts from exercising or performing the organization's tax-exempt purpose or function if the purpose of the payment is primarily to serve the direct and immediate needs of the payor governmental unit, and is treated as a contribution if the purpose is primarily to provide a direct benefit to the public. For example, if a state government agency pays an organization to operate an institute to train agency employees in the principles of management and administration, the funds received should be included on line 2 as gross receipts. See Regulations section 1.509(a)-3(g). Refer to the instructions for Form 990, Part VIII, lines 1e and 2 for more examples addressing the distinction between government payments that are contributions and government payments that are gross receipts from activities related to the organization's tax-exempt purpose or function. Medicare and Medicaid payments are treated as gross receipts from patients rather than as contributions from the government payor for purposes of the public support test. See Rev. Rul. 83-153, 1983-2 C.B. 48.

Line 2, gross receipts from admissions, merchandise sold or services performed, or facilities furnished in any activity that is related to the organization's tax-exempt purpose.

This is the second of five public support elements allowed under the 509(a)(2) test Part III reports upon. Accordingly, this line solely reports related program service revenues. The instruction's only example of type says: to the extent that membership fees are payments to purchase admissions, merchandise, services, or the use of facilities in a related activity, include the membership fees on this Line 2. The author notes that fee-for-service revenues from exempt functions and program-related investment income are to be reported here as well.

Note: unrelated activities that are statutorily (that is, under Section 513) not treated as an unrelated trade or business are to be reported on Line 3.

Line 3, gross receipts from activities that are not an unrelated trade or business under Section 513.

This is the third of five public support elements within the 509(a)(2) test Part III reports upon. This line reports receipts from activities that fall into any of the Section 513 exceptions. Major examples include: unrelated activities where substantially all the work is performed by volunteers; lawfully conducted bingo; qualified sponsorship payments; selling merchandise substantially of which has been donated.

Line 4, tax revenues levied for the organization's benefit and either paid to or expended on its behalf.

This is the fourth of five public support elements within the 509(a)(2) test Part III reports upon. See the discussion with respect to Part II, Line 2, as same addresses this term which applies to both parts.

Line 5, the value of services or facilities furnished by a governmental unit to the organization without charge.

This is the fifth of five public support elements within the 509(a)(2) test Part III reports upon. The entire discussion with respect to Part II, Line 3 (page 25), addressing the same term, is appropriate here as well.

Line 6 performs computation only—totaling all receipts across the five years reported upon Lines 1-5, which thus make up public support without the limitations of Line 7.

Line 7's subparts then impose the two limitations on public support:

> **Line 7a**, amounts included on Lines 1, 2, and 3 from disqualified persons. That last term is meant within the private foundation definition (that is, Section 4946) with one reporting convention for Part III of the Schedule A, both set out in the Core Form Glossary:

B. Under Section 4946, a disqualified person includes:

1. A substantial contributor, which is any person who gave an aggregate amount of more than $5,000, if that amount is more than 2 percent of the total contributions the foundation or organization received from its inception through the end of the year in which that person's contributions were received. If the organization is a trust, a substantial contributor includes the creator of the trust (without regard to the amount of contributions the trust received from the creator and related persons). Any person who is a substantial contributor at any time generally remains a substantial contributor for all future periods even if later contributions by others push that person's contributions below the 2 percent figure discussed previously. Gifts from the contributor's spouse are treated as gifts from the contributor. Gifts are generally valued at FMV as of the date the organization received them.

2. A foundation manager, defined as an officer, director, or trustee of the organization or any individual having powers or responsibilities similar to those of officers, directors, or trustees.

3. An owner of more than 20 percent of the voting power of a corporation, profits interest of a partnership, or beneficial interest of a trust or an unincorporated enterprise that is a substantial contributor to the organization.

4. A family member of an individual in the first three categories. For this purpose, family member includes only the individual's spouse, ancestors, children, grandchildren, great-grandchildren, and the spouses of children, grandchildren, and great-grandchildren.
[PRACTICE POINTER: NO SIBLINGS]

5. A corporation, partnership, trust, or estate in which persons described in (1) through (4) own more than 35 percent of the voting power, profits interest, or beneficial interest.

For purposes of Section 509(a)(2), as referenced in Schedule A (Form 990 or 990-EZ), Public Charity Status and Public Support, a disqualified person is defined in Section 4946, except that it does not include an organization described in Section 509(a)(1).

Line 7a thus excludes from public support receipts from any and all disqualified persons and thus factors out from public support any remittances of: gifts, grants, contributions; related program services; and revenues captured in activities excepted-from-unrelated-trade/ business-characterization when paid by foundation managers, substantial contributors, their family members, or 35 percent-controlled entities connected to any of the former.

KNOWLEDGE CHECK

6. Disqualified persons whose contributions must be tracked in light of such amounts being excluded from Part III, Line 7a do NOT include:

   a. Current (to the filing year) members of the governing board
   b. Legal spouses of the current members of the governing board
   c. The father or mother of the executive director's father
   d. A company under 51 percent ownership of those who are brothers or sisters of other disqualified persons, one of whom is a sibling of a substantial contributor and that sibling's stake is 21 percent.

Line 7b, amounts included on Lines 2 and 3 received from other than disqualified persons that exceed the greater of 1 percent of the total of Lines 9, 10c, 11, and 12 for the year or $5,000. This line imposes set annual limits (in measuring public support) with respect to certain purchaser's payments made to access the filer's services provided that are: related to the filer's exempt purposes; or unrelated but falling within a Section 513 statutory exception from unrelated trade or business characterization.

Line 7b thus factors out of public support such remittances when made by a payer (who is NOT a disqualified person, such payers already captured on Line 1a) to the extent that same exceed significant levels for the year (defined as the greater of $5,000 or 1 percent of the filer's total support [Line 13 as that line = 9+ 10c+ 11+ 12] for each year)

Line 7c, math only: total Lines 7a + 7b

Line 8, calculate Line 6f minus Line (7c)

Line 9 calls for repeat of all Line 6 entries (that is, input of public support receipts without Line 7c's total limits applied)

Section B's Lines 10a, 10b, 11 and 12 then input four non-public support items to the end of arriving at total support (= Line 13) across the five-year test period –

Line 10a: gross income from interest, dividends, and payments received on securities loans, rents, royalties, and income from similar sources. This line includes only these passive income sources. When same come from activities of the organization furthering its exempt purpose (for example, interest on low-interest scholarship loans), the amounts would be reported on Line 2.

Line 10b: unrelated business taxable income (less Section 511 taxes) from businesses acquired after June 30, 1975 (this date limitation reflects off-Code Congressional enactment in favor of protecting non-private foundation classification for at least one known taxpayer, Colonial Williamsburg). This line includes excess of 990-T taxable income (= unrelated business taxable income as determined following the Section 512 rules) less taxes computed on that amount (but only on unrelated trade or business activities acquired or initiated after the specified date). **Note: any net loss must be reported at $-0-.**

Line 11: net income from unrelated business activities, whether or not the business is regularly carried on. This line reports net income from unrelated business activities not included on Line 10b, regardless of whether or not they are regularly carried on. **Note: any net loss must be reported at $-0-.**

Line 12: other income (note the annotation on this line to not include capital gain or loss – as was the case with the 509(a)(1)/ 170(b)(1)(A)(vi) test, this test does NOT factor in to support gain from the sale or disposition of property which would be considered as gain from the sale or exchange of a capital asset). Any entry upon Line 12 here must be explained in Part IV. (As the immediately preceding lines attempt to pick up ALL support, the only basis for input on Line 12 would be Section 509(d), reprinted in these materials at page 22).

Line 13: total support. This line performs a computation only, adding col. (f) amounts for Lines 9-12, arriving at the five year test period's total support which is thus the denominator for the upcoming 509(a)(2) tests to be performed in Sections C and D of this part.

Knowledge Check

7. All organizations, regardless of whether they are completing Part II or III of Schedule A, will exclude which from the calculation?

    a. All passive revenue as defined under Section 512(b)(1): interest, dividends, payments with respect to securities loans, and annuities.

    b. Free use of space and donated services they receive from the city.

    c. Net unrelated business income whether the activity generating the income is regularly carried on or not.

    d. Capital gain from the disposal of exempt use or investment assets.

8. A 501(c)(3) organization is not sure which of the two public support tests it will meet. Which is a correct statement as to the data the organization should be anticipating it may need access if it is to report under the Second Test?

    a. List of contributions from all persons with whom the organization conducts insider transactions.

    b. List of contributions from all persons who stand in relationship to the filer as disqualified persons under the private foundation rules.

    c. List of program service revenue receipts from all persons with whom the organization conducts insider transactions.

    d. List of program service revenue receipts from all persons if those persons have also provided potentially significant contributions.

Testing Results of Public support Calculations
Testing is POSTPONED in First Five Years of 501(c)(3) Exemption

Regulations issued for the redesign of Form 990 (first applicable for the 2008 form), allow 501(c)(3)-applicants who have not sought an identity basis for non-private foundation classification to be automatically accorded public charity status for their first five tax years. This means they are not to be tested over a five year period until the end of their sixth year of operation. Note how the last lines of both Part II, Section B and Part III, Section B (Part II, Line 13 and Part III, Line 14) reflect this:

Part II:

13	First five years. If the Form 990 is for the organization's first, second, third, fourth, or fifth tax year as a section 501(c)(3) organization, check this box and **stop here** . . . . ▶ ☐

Part III:

14	First five years. If the Form 990 is for the organization's first, second, third, fourth, or fifth tax year as a section 501(c)(3) organization, check this box and **stop here** . . . . ▶ ☐

PERCENTAGE RESULTS THAT MATTER IN PARTS II AND III

Filers who have concluded more than six tax years overall compute a result to determine whether they pass the public support test set out in the part they have chosen. A pass of the public support test is determined in reference to the filer's computed public support percentage (for the second test, which is one of two percentage calculations that matter). The public support percentage is calculated in both Parts' Section C, at that section's first line:

Part II:

14	Public support percentage for 2016 (line 6, column (f) divided by line 11, column (f))	14		%
15	Public support percentage from 2015 Schedule A, Part II, line 14	15		%

Part III:

15	Public support percentage for 2016 (line 8, column (f) divided by line 13, column (f))	15		%
16	Public support percentage from 2015 Schedule A, Part III, line 15	16		%

> **Note regarding requirement to include the percentage from the prior year's form:** Regardless of the test the filer uses, a pass on one year covers the next year. Thus, a pass on the 2015 form covered the filer for year to be reported on its 2016 form (and a pass on the 2016 form will cover the filer for the 2017 form year as well.)

PART II PUBLIC SUPPORT TESTING: APPLICATION OF PERCENTAGE RESULTS

This part's testing is based on 509(a)(l)/170(b)(l)(A)(vi)'s mandates. They call for a public support percentage to be achieved at either 33.33 percent, a level at which qualification under this test vests automatically, or with a public support percentage of no less than 10 percent and qualification then in place if the filer's facts and circumstances are appropriate.

Section C. Computation of Public Support Percentage			
14	Public support percentage for 2016 (line 6, column (f) divided by line 11, column (f))	**14**	%
15	Public support percentage from 2015 Schedule A, Part II, line 14	**15**	%
16a	**33¹/₃% support test—2016.** If the organization did not check the box on line 13, and line 14 is 33¹/₃% or more, check this box and **stop here.** The organization qualifies as a publicly supported organization . . . . ▶ ☐		
b	**33¹/₃% support test—2015.** If the organization did not check a box on line 13 or 16a, and line 15 is 33¹/₃% or more, check this box and **stop here.** The organization qualifies as a publicly supported organization . . . . ▶ ☐		
17a	**10%-facts-and-circumstances test—2016.** If the organization did not check a box on line 13, 16a, or 16b, and line 14 is 10% or more, and if the organization meets the "facts-and-circumstances" test, check this box and **stop here.** Explain in Part VI how the organization meets the "facts-and-circumstances" test. The organization qualifies as a publicly supported organization . . . . ▶ ☐		
b	**10%-facts-and-circumstances test—2015.** If the organization did not check a box on line 13, 16a, 16b, or 17a, and line 15 is 10% or more, and if the organization meets the "facts-and-circumstances" test, check this box and **stop here.** Explain in Part VI how the organization meets the "facts-and-circumstances" test. The organization qualifies as a publicly supported organization . . . . ▶ ☐		
18	**Private foundation.** If the organization did not check a box on line 13, 16a, 16b, 17a, or 17b, check this box and see instructions . . . . ▶ ☐		

Part II evaluates each of the subpart tests (33.33 percent versus 10 percent, plus facts and circumstances) for the current and the prior year, in this order on Lines 14–18:

1. Testing first for a result of 33.33 percent or more this year (certifying on Line 16a that Line 14 has such percentage);

2. If not, asking if the prior year's Schedule A result (under this test) was 33.33 percent or more (that certification on Line 16b);

3. If not, testing if a result of 10 percent or more was achieved this year along with activities and operations in place this year sufficient to meet the so-called facts-and-circumstances test (disclosures required of those meeting this test are addressed in the following text; also see the Regulation[10] — certification of this result occurs on Line 17a);

4. If not, asking if the prior year's Schedule A result (under this test) was 10 percent or more and that the prior year's activities and operations in place would meet the so-called facts-and-circumstances test (that certification occurring on Line 17b).

---

[10] The 'facts and circumstances' test is set out in Regulations Section 1.170A-9(f)(3)(ii)-(iii) to apply to 501(c)(3)s:

(ii) Organized and operated as to attract new and additional public or governmental support on a continuous basis. An organization will be considered to meet this requirement if it maintains a continuous and bona fide program for solicitation of funds from the general public, community, or membership group involved, or if it carries on activities designed to attract support from governmental units or other organizations described in Section 170(b)(1)(A)(i) through (vi).

(iii) In determining whether an organization maintains a continuous and bona fide program for solicitation of funds from the general public or community, consideration will be given to whether the scope of its fundraising activities is reasonable in light of its charitable activities. Consideration will also be given to the fact that an organization may, in its early years of existence, limit the scope of its solicitation to persons deemed most likely to provide seed money in an amount sufficient to enable it to commence its charitable activities and expand its solicitation program.

FACTS and CIRCUMSTANCES—Disclosures required (in Schedule A's blank lines Part VI):

If this box is checked, explain in *Part IV* how the organization meets the "facts and circumstances" test in Regulations section 1.170A-9(f)(3). Include the following information.
* Explain whether the organization maintains a continuous and *bona fide* program for solicitation of funds from the general public, community, membership group involved, **governmental units** or other **public charities**.
* List all other facts and circumstances, including the sources of support, whether the organization has a **governing body** which represents the broad interests of the public, and whether the organization generally provides facilities or services directly for the benefit of the general public on a continuing basis.
* If the organization is a membership organization, explain whether the solicitation for dues-paying members is designed to enroll a substantial number of persons from the community, whether dues for individual members have been fixed at rates designed to make membership available to a broad cross-section of the interested public, and whether the activities of the organization will likely appeal to persons having some broad common interest or purpose.

It is not enough to just check box 17a indicating that the organization is asserting it meets the facts and circumstances test. It must provide specific evidence on Part IV.

Remember that the 10 percent is a minimum threshold. If the organization does not have 10 percent public support it cannot assert it meets facts and circumstances.

The organization must list *all of the facts and circumstances* indicating that it qualifies as a public charity given its striving to achieve diverse support (for purposes of this test, support relates to gift and contribution income from the government and the public.)

KNOWLEDGE CHECK

9. Which accurately describes a requirement that must be achieved to meet the facts and circumstances test?

   a. The filer must have a public support percentage of at least 10 percent.
   b. The filer must be conducting fundraising events of sufficient magnitude to require completion of Form 990's Schedule G, Part II.
   c. The governing board of the filer must have no less than 5 independent board members.
   d. The filer must have a physical presence in the community.

FAIL PART II? GO ONTO PART III.

Filers who complete the entries at Part II, but fail its test (find themselves ready to check the box at Line 18) will find that the instructions tell them to file the Form 990-PF unless they can pass the test in Part III. This result demonstrates that fluidity each year between the two tests is permitted under the regulations.

PART III PUBLIC SUPPORT TESTING: APPLICATION OF PERCENTAGE RESULTS

This part's testing is based on 509(a)(2)'s mandates. The standard for the 509(a)(2) public support test is dual, requiring two testing points, both of which must be met:

1. Across the aggregated 5 years, the filer must achieve a public support percentage of 33.33 percent minimum (there is no alternative facts and circumstances testing under IRC Section 509(a)(2)); and
2. Across the aggregated 5 years, the filer must show that its investment and unrelated business income net combined do not exceed 33.33 percent.

Part III employs both Section C (to the same end as its analogue Section C in Part II), testing overall public support under the specifics of this part's test, and Section D. The latter section enters the filer's investment income percentage measuring the part's reported investment revenues (non-capital gain passive income - interest, dividends, rents, royalties, + unrelated business taxable income off of the 990-T less the taxes paid on such amounts) against total support. To pass this test, the result can be no greater than 33.33 percent.

After the percentage results are calculated for the filing year, Part III's results are determined by looking at those results, and the prior year's results, to see if:

- A public support percentage result of 33.33 percent or more has been achieved across the 5-year test period, and no more than 33.33 percent investment income calculated (Line 19a a "Yes" if Line 15 reports a favorable public support percentage and Line 17 satisfies the investment income limitation).

- If not, Line 19b tests the prior tax year's Schedule A public support percentage and investment income limitation percentage.

Section C. Computation of Public Support Percentage			
15	Public support percentage for 2016 (line 8, column (f) divided by line 13, column (f))	15	%
16	Public support percentage from 2015 Schedule A, Part III, line 15	16	%
Section D. Computation of Investment Income Percentage			
17	Investment income percentage for 2016 (line 10c, column (f) divided by line 13, column (f)) . . .	17	%
18	Investment income percentage from 2015 Schedule A, Part III, line 17	18	%
19a	33¹/₃% support tests—2016. If the organization did not check the box on line 14, and line 15 is more than 33¹/₃%, and line 17 is not more than 33¹/₃%, check this box and **stop here**. The organization qualifies as a publicly supported organization . ▶ ☐		
b	33¹/₃% support tests—2015. If the organization did not check a box on line 14 or line 19a, and line 16 is more than 33¹/₃%, and line 18 is not more than 33¹/₃%, check this box and **stop here**. The organization qualifies as a publicly supported organization ▶ ☐		
20	**Private foundation.** If the organization did not check a box on line 14, 19a, or 19b, check this box and see instructions ▶ ☐		

Fail Part III? Go back and try Part II.

Filers who try the Part III test, but fail it (find themselves ready to check the box at Line 20) will find that the instructions tell them to file the Form 990-PF unless they can pass the test in Part II (the reverse of what we noted for Part II's Line 18; again, note the fluidity each year between these two tests).

KNOWLEDGE CHECK

10. Which is the most appropriate statement as to how a filer is required to confirm meeting the First Test (509(a)(1)/ 170(b)(1)(A)(vi)) by appropriate Part II completion?

    a. Across the five-year test period reported on the current year's return or upon the immediately prior year's return, the filer has a percentage result of 45 percent.

    b. Across the five-year test period reported on the current year's return and/ or upon the immediately prior year's return or either, the filer has a percentage result 33.33 percent or higher, and has in the year in which such result is achieved made the required disclosures in support of classification under the facts and circumstances test.

    c. Across both the five-year test period reported on the current year's return and upon the immediately prior year's return, the filer has a percentage result calculated at 8 percent and 9.9 percent, respectively, plus has made the required disclosures which support classification under the facts and circumstances test on one or both years' returns.

    d. Across the five-year test period reported on the current year's return or upon the immediately prior year's return, the filer has a percentage result of >10 percent but less than 20 percent and explains that the percentage is due to contributions being included that are unusual grants.

11. A filer is in year six of 501(c)(3) status and is completing Part II's percentage calculations for the first time. If the filer does NOT achieve percentage results allowing automatic or facts and circumstances test results in favor of 509(a)(1)/ 170(b)(1)(A)(vi) classification, which most accurately describes what the filer should do?

    a. Seek permission from the IRS to file a new exemption application.

    b. File a Form 990-PF if Part III testing under the second test (509(a)(2)) fails.

    c. File a corporate or trust income tax return.

    d. Access the prior year's return Part II and compute test results on tax years 1–5 as successful percentage result there need be inputted on the current years' Part II.

12. For a 501(c)(3) filer that has been classified by the IRS as a non-private foundation which sentence completion is incorrect: If an organization _____

    a. meets the Part II public support test in one year, it is not necessary to meet the same test the next year in order to qualify that next year as a public charity.

    b. fails the Part II public support test two years in a row, it may try the other test on the second year, and if it passes there, it will have public charity for that second year.

    c. is failing its public support test using the cash method of accounting, it can file a Form 3115, Change of Accounting Method, to switch its method of accounting to the accrual method and redo its public support test.

    d. fails both the Part II and Part III public support tests for two years in a row, it will lose its public charity status effective for the second of the two years and be required to complete Form 990-PF instead of Form 990 on the second year.

SCHEDULE A'S FINAL TWO SUBSTANTIVE PARTS, IV AND V, APPLY ONLY TO SUPPORTING ORGANIZATIONS. UNLIKE MUCH OF THE FORM 990 AND MOST OF ITS SCHEDULES, THEIR INQUIRIES ARE BASED DIRECTLY ON THE LEGAL PRECEPTS BY WHICH SUPPORTING ORGANIZATIONS ARE ENTITLED TO STATUS AS NON-PRIVATE FOUNDATIONS.

Supporting Organization TYPES

Supporting organizations must meet three general tests in light of the interaction between Sections 501(c)(3) and 509(a)(3). Per these, a supporting organization must be

1. organized and operated exclusively for the benefit of, to perform the functions of, or to carry out the purposes of one or more publicly supported charities;
2. operated, supervised or controlled by (or in connection with) one or more publicly supported charities; and
3. not under the control of or by a disqualified person (as such term is set out in Section 4946) other than those who are foundation managers or publicly supported charities.

We will approach Schedule A, Parts IV and V from the perspective of the four types of supporting organizations that complete the Schedule: Type I, Type II, Type III (functionally integrated), and Type IV (non-functionally integrated—sometimes referred to as Type IV: Other.)

FIRST: TYPE I SUPPORTING ORGANIZATIONS

Type I supporting organizations must be operated, supervised or controlled by its supported organization(s), typically by giving the supported organization(s) the power to regularly appoint or elect a majority of the directors or trustees of the supporting organization. The relationship between the supported organization(s) and the supporting organization is akin to a parent-subsidiary relationship.

Type I organizations' boards are controlled by the parent organization.

Type I supporting organizations meet the definition of control by having the board controlled by the supported organization(s). In this way, the supported organization(s) substantially direct (by act or right to act) the supporting organization's policies, programs, and activities.

Type I Supporting Organizations are required to complete Part IV, Sections A and B.

Section A.

Section A applies to all types of supporting organizations. There are 11 questions. All questions are intended to remind filers that although Type III supporting organizations have specific notification, responsiveness or integral part requirements, all supporting organizations must demonstrate they are responsive to the needs or demands of one more organizations they to exist to support. The Section A questions are designed to uncover any potential policies or practices which would disqualify any type of supporting organization from qualifying as a supporting organization. The questions are difficult because the rules are different for different types of supporting organizations. The questions can be traced to specific legislative and regulatory requirements for qualification as a supporting organization. It is important to understand what the question is asking and what the compliant response to each question is for the type of supporting organization for which you are preparing the Schedule A.

Question one is a good example of why it is important to understand the question and the type of supporting organization for which you are completing Schedule A:

Question 1—For a Type I or II Supporting Organization a "No" response is fine. These organizations are allowed to designate supported organizations by name, purpose, or class.

1 Are all of the organization's supported organizations listed by name in the organization's governing documents? *If "No" describe in* **Part VI** *how the supported organizations are designated. If designated by class or purpose, describe the designation. If historic and continuing relationship, explain.*	**1**	

Question 4 is interesting for supporting organizations established as friends of supporting organizations to foreign charities. A Type I or Type II supporting organization can qualify for exemption however, the issues of governance control versus control over distributing funds becomes an issue that must be explained. From a governance perspective these organizations are a subsidiary of a foreign charity or commonly controlled by the same people who control the foreign charity. Question 4b and c are digging into how the supporting organization preserve the deductibility of U.S. donors' charitable contributions. Does the supporting organization have discretion and control over the funds granted to it and when funds are granted to the foreign organization even though it is a Type I or Type II supporting organization. These organizations must have a good answer to these questions and explain on Part VI.

4a Was any supported organization not organized in the United States ("foreign supported organization")? *If "Yes," and if you checked 12a or 12b in Part I, answer (b) and (c) below.*	**4a**	
b Did the organization have ultimate control and discretion in deciding whether to make grants to the foreign supported organization? *If "Yes," describe in* **Part VI** *how the organization had such control and discretion despite being controlled or supervised by or in connection with its supported organizations.*	**4b**	
c Did the organization support any foreign supported organization that does not have an IRS determination under sections 501(c)(3) and 509(a)(1) or (2)? *If "Yes," explain in* **Part VI** *what controls the organization used to ensure that all support to the foreign supported organization was used exclusively for section 170(c)(2)(B) purposes.*	**4c**	

Question 11 is a "gotcha" question for Type I or Type III supporting organizations. Accepting a gift from a donor that controls the governing body of the supported organization would cause a Type I or Type III to fail to qualify for supporting organization status. Unless the supporting organization could qualify under some other public support or as a Type II supporting organization, it would be re-categorized as a private foundation.

11 Has the organization accepted a gift or contribution from any of the following persons?		
a A person who directly or indirectly controls, either alone or together with persons described in (b) and (c) below, the governing body of a supported organization?	**11a**	
b A family member of a person described in (a) above?	**11b**	
c A 35% controlled entity of a person described in (a) or (b) above?*If "Yes" to a, b, or c, provide detail in Part VI.*	**11c**	

Section B.

Section B. Type I Supporting Organizations		Yes	No
1	Did the directors, trustees, or membership of one or more supported organizations have the power to regularly appoint or elect at least a majority of the organization's directors or trustees at all times during the tax year? *If "No," describe in* **Part VI** *how the supported organization(s) effectively operated, supervised, or controlled the organization's activities. If the organization had more than one supported organization, describe how the powers to appoint and/or remove directors or trustees were allocated among the supported organizations and what conditions or restrictions, if any, applied to such powers during the tax year.* **1**		
2	Did the organization operate for the benefit of any supported organization other than the supported organization(s) that operated, supervised, or controlled the supporting organization? *If "Yes," explain in* **Part VI** *how providing such benefit carried out the purposes of the supported organization(s) that operated, supervised, or controlled the supporting organization.* **2**		

If the parent organization relies on other means than the power to appoint and remove a majority of the Type I supporting organization's board of directors, check Line 1, "no" and explain how control is exercised on Part VI.

Question 2 is another area where Type I supporting organizations must understand the law. There is both an organizational and operational test. As noted in Section A, the organization may denote its supported organization by name, class or purpose (most designate by name). The method has significance for meeting the operational test as a Type I supporting organization with one or more named supported organizations is statutorily limited to making grants to the supported organizations or to individuals in the beneficial class served by the supported organizations. See Treasury Regulation 1.509(a)-4(e)(1) reprinted here for the permissible beneficiaries rules for Type I supporting organizations. A Type I supporting organization with a named supported organization may only make grants to the named supported organization or to individuals in the beneficial class supported by that supported organization; not to other public charities supported by that supported organization.

Reprint of Treasury Regulation 1.509(a)-4(e)(1): *Permissible beneficiaries.* A supporting organization will be regarded as operated exclusively to support one or more specified publicly supported organizations (hereinafter referred to as the operational test) only if it engages solely in activities which support or benefit the specified publicly supported organizations. Such activities may include making payments to or for the use of, or providing services or facilities for, individual members of the charitable class benefited by the specified publicly supported organization. A supporting organization may also, for example, make a payment indirectly through another unrelated organization to a member of a charitable class benefited by the specified publicly supported organization, but only if such a payment constitutes a grant to an individual rather than a grant to an organization.

The authors are aware of this statutory rule's language (which does not allow grants to organizations) not defeating ruling requests obtained by community foundations in seeking exemption determination rulings with Type I status via Form 1023 exemption application. These applications have stated that the supporting organization would make grants directly to public charities supported by the community foundation, with such grants made under the direction and control of the community foundation (the reason for direct grants this way was cited as ease of administration, the alternative would be granting to the community foundation and then the community foundation re-granting the funds). In addition, the authors have seen an audit of a community foundation in which the IRS issued a no-change letter to a taxpayer who employed this methodology. This information is, of course, anecdotal and such results by taxpayers is not precedential guidance that other taxpayers may rely upon.

SECOND: TYPE II SUPPORTING ORGANIZATIONS

A Type II supporting organization must be supervised or controlled in connection with its supported organization(s). Such a relationship is evidenced by common control of both entities situated in the same individuals or parties. Thus, Type II supporting organizations typically have more than half of their boards (that is, a majority) overlapped with their supported organization(s) boards. The structure here effects the requirement that there be sufficient common supervision or control so that the supporting organization will be responsive to the needs and requirements of the supported organization.

As noted, the requirement of common control is met when a majority of the directors or trustees of the supported organization(s) serve as a majority of the trustees or directors of the supporting organization. Such a structure is akin to a brother/ sister relationship.

TYPE II SUPPORTING ORGANIZATIONS MUST COMPLETE PART IV'S SECTIONS A AND C.

Section A

As discussed earlier, Section A is required of all types of supporting organizations. Type I and Type II supporting organizations face many of the same challenges with qualification. See previous discussion of Lines 1 and 4 as they apply to Type II supporting organizations as well Type I.

Type II supporting organizations will want to pay particular attention to Section A, Question 10a. If the organization accepts a contribution from a donor that controls the supported organization (or a family member of such person or an entity that such persons control a great than 35 percent interest in), the Type II supporting organization is subject to the excess business holding rules under 4943(f) which normally only apply to private foundations. These rules generally limit the holdings the organization may own in a business enterprise to 20 percent combined with the holdings of all disqualified persons.

10a	Was the organization subject to the excess business holdings rules of section 4943 because of section 4943(f) (regarding certain Type II supporting organizations, and all Type III non-functionally integrated supporting organizations)? *If "Yes," answer 10b below.*	10a
b	Did the organization have any excess business holdings in the tax year? *(Use Schedule C, Form 4720, to determine whether the organization had excess business holdings.)*	10b

Section C

If the Type II supporting organization relies on other means than a majority of the governance board of the supported and supporting organizations consisting of the same individuals, check Line 1, "No" and explain how common control is exercised on Part VI.

Section C. Type II Supporting Organizations			
		Yes	No
1 Were a majority of the organization's directors or trustees during the tax year also a majority of the directors or trustees of each of the organization's supported organization(s)? *If "No," describe in **Part VI** how control or management of the supporting organization was vested in the same persons that controlled or managed the supported organization(s).*	**1**		

THIRD: TYPE III SUPPORTING ORGANIZATIONS (FUNCTIONALLY INTEGRATED)

Type III supporting organizations who are functionally integrated must complete Part IV's Sections A, D and E.

A Type III supporting organization must be operated in connection with one or more publicly supported organizations. All supporting organizations must be responsive to the needs and demands of, and must constitute an integral part of or maintain significant involvement in, their supported organizations. As set out in the preceding sections, Type I and Type II supporting organizations are deemed to accomplish these responsiveness and integral part requirements by virtue of their control relationships. **Because a Type III supporting organization is not subject to the same level of control by its supported organization(s), Type III supporting organizations must pass separate responsiveness and integral part tests.**

Type III supporting organizations have additional requirements not imposed on the Type I and Type II supporting organizations:

- They must support a domestic organization;
- They have (and must meet) an annual notification requirement;
- They must demonstrate that they are meeting a responsiveness test; and
- They must demonstrate they are meeting an integral part test. It is this last test where the Type III supporting organizations divide into:
  - Functionally Integrated or
  - Non-Functionally Integrated.

The Type III tests (responsiveness and integral part) are described on the IRS website as follows:

Responsiveness test

A Type III supporting organization must be responsive to the needs or demands of a supported organization. An organization meets this test with regard to a particular supported organization if:

1. The supported organization is adequately represented in the governing body of the supporting organization because:

   - The supported organization may appoint at least one officer, director or trustee of the supporting organization
   - At least one member of the governing body of the supported organization also serves as an officer, director or trustee of a supporting organization, or
   - The officers, directors, or trustees of the supporting organization and of the supported organization maintain a close and continuous working relationship; *and*

2. Because of this relationship, the supported organization has a significant *voice* in how the supporting organization manages and uses its assets.

Integral part test

A Type III supporting organization may be functionally integrated (FISO) or non-functionally integrated (non-FISO) depending on the manner in which it meets the integral part test. Type III FISOs are subject to fewer restrictions and requirements than non-FISOs. In particular, distributions from private foundations to Type III non-FISOs are not qualifying distributions for purposes of satisfying a private foundation's required annual distributions under Section 4942, and may be taxable expenditures under Section 4945. In addition, Type III non-FISOs are subject to excess business holding rules under Section 4943 and must meet annual payout requirements.

Functionally integrated—A Type III organization must satisfy one of three alternative integral part tests.

- **Alternative 1: Activities test (two prongs):**
  "Direct furtherance" prong. Substantially all of the supporting organization's activities must be *direct furtherance* activities.
  Direct furtherance activities are conducted by the supporting organization itself, rather than by a supported organization.
  Fundraising, managing non-exempt-use assets, grant making to organizations, and grant making to individuals (unless it meets certain requirements) are not direct furtherance activities.

"But for" prong. In addition, substantially all of such activities must be activities in which, but for the supporting organization's involvement, the supported organization would normally be involved.

Examples include holding and managing facilities used by a church for its religious purposes, operating food pantries for a group of churches that normally would operate food pantries themselves, and maintaining local parks for a community foundation that otherwise would maintain those parks.

- **Alternative 2: It is the PARENT of the supported organizations**

  Governance. The supporting organization must have the power to appoint a majority of the officers, directors or trustees of each of its supported organizations.

  Substantial degree of direction. In addition, the supporting organization must perform parent-like activities by exercising a substantial degree of direction over the policies, programs and activities of the supported organizations.

- **Alternative 3: It is supporting a governmental entity**

Section A

All questions on Section A must be completed. Of particular importance for Type III supporting organizations:

Section A, Question 1 for a Type III, a "No" response could be problematic. A Type III supporting organization must designate the supported organization by name unless there is a historic and continuing relationship between the organizations. Any "No" answer will require an explanation on Part VI but for a Part III the answer will only be accepted if it meets the historic and continued relationship exception.

1	Are all of the organization's supported organizations listed by name in the organization's governing documents? *If "No" describe in Part VI how the supported organizations are designated. If designated by class or purpose, describe the designation. If historic and continuing relationship, explain.*			
		1		

Section A, Question 4 is a trap for the unwary. A Type III supporting organizations must support an organization formed in the United States to qualify for exempt status. A "Yes" answer is fatal for a Type III supporting organization.

4a	Was any supported organization not organized in the United States ("foreign supported organization")? *If "Yes," and if you checked 12a or 12b in Part I, answer (b) and (c) below.*	4a		
b	Did the organization have ultimate control and discretion in deciding whether to make grants to the foreign supported organization? *If "Yes," describe in Part VI how the organization had such control and discretion despite being controlled or supervised by or in connection with its supported organizations.*	4b		
c	Did the organization support any foreign supported organization that does not have an IRS determination under sections 501(c)(3) and 509(a)(1) or (2)? *If "Yes," explain in Part VI what controls the organization used to ensure that all support to the foreign supported organization was used exclusively for section 170(c)(2)(B) purposes.*	4c		

Question 11 is a "gotcha" question for Type I or Type III supporting organizations. Accepting a gift from a donor that controls the governing body of the supported organization would cause a Type I or Type III to fail to qualify for supporting organization status. Unless the supporting organization could qualify under some other public support or as a Type II supporting organization, it would be re-categorized as a private foundation.

11	Has the organization accepted a gift or contribution from any of the following persons?			
a	A person who directly or indirectly controls, either alone or together with persons described in (b) and (c) below, the governing body of a supported organization?	11a		
b	A family member of a person described in (a) above?	11b		
c	A 35% controlled entity of a person described in (a) or (b) above? *If "Yes" to a, b, or c, provide detail in* **Part VI.**	11c		

Section D

The three questions of Section D are addressing the Type III supporting organization requirements of notification, responsiveness to the needs of the supported organization(s). It does this by ensuring the supported organization has a significant voice in the supporting organization.

At this point the Type III supporting organizations divide into functionally integrated and non-functionally integrated organizations. A functionally integrated organization demonstrate how they are an integral part of the organization.

Section D. All Type III Supporting Organizations

			Yes	No
1	Did the organization provide to each of its supported organizations, by the last day of the fifth month of the organization's tax year, (i) a written notice describing the type and amount of support provided during the prior tax year, (ii) a copy of the Form 990 that was most recently filed as of the date of notification, and (iii) copies of the organization's governing documents in effect on the date of notification, to the extent not previously provided?	1		
2	Were any of the organization's officers, directors, or trustees either (i) appointed or elected by the supported organization(s) or (ii) serving on the governing body of a supported organization? *If "No," explain in* **Part VI** *how the organization maintained a close and continuous working relationship with the supported organization(s).*	2		
3	By reason of the relationship described in (2), did the organization's supported organizations have a significant voice in the organization's investment policies and in directing the use of the organization's income or assets at all times during the tax year? *If "Yes," describe in* **Part VI** *the role the organization's supported organizations played in this regard.*	3		

Section E

Type III functionally integrated supporting organizations must complete Section E to demonstrate their significant involvement in the supported organization (that is, the fact of their functional integration with the supported organization). Here, requirements of statute must be evidenced: the filer must pass the activities test, be the parent of its supported organization(s), support a governmental organization(s), or show that its operations and activities are an integral part of the supported organization.

FOURTH: TYPE III SUPPORTING ORGANIZATIONS (NON-FUNCTIONALLY INTEGRATED)

Type III non-functionally integrated supporting organizations must complete Part IV's Sections A and D (which are also completed by Type III functionally integrated supporting organizations, as addressed in the immediately preceding section), and Part V, which is unique to groups here.

The Type III tests for responsiveness and integral part as described on the IRS website were reprinted in the immediately preceding section on Type III functionally integrated supporting organizations. For supporting organizations not meeting the integral part test, the IRS website describes both the distribution requirement and attentiveness requirements that apply (these inform the Schedule A Part V reporting requirements and are discussed in these materials related to reporting at Part V's D, Line 8):

Distribution Requirement. A Type III non-FISO must distribute its distributable amount each year to one or more of its supported organizations.

- The distributable amount equals the greater of (1) 85 percent of the organization's adjusted net income for the prior taxable year and (2) 3.5 percent of the aggregate fair market value of the organization's non-exempt use assets, with certain adjustments.
- Certain excess amounts may reduce the distributable amount in subsequent years (for up to five years after the excess amount is generated).

Attentiveness Requirement. It is not enough for a Type III non-FISO to maintain a certain level of distributions to a supported organization. Those distributions must be sufficiently important to the supported organization to ensure that the supported organization has sufficient reason to pay attention to the supporting organization's role in its operations. Distributions to a particular supported organization are sufficient to ensure such attentiveness if the amount of support:

- Equaled at least 10 percent of the supported organization's total support for the supported organization's prior year;
- Was necessary to avoid interruption of the carrying on of a particular substantial function or activity of the supported organization; or
- Based on all facts and circumstances (including actual evidence of attentiveness) was sufficient to ensure attentiveness.

At least one-third of the supporting organization's distributable amount must be distributed to supported organizations (1) that meet this attentiveness requirement and (2) to which the supporting organization is responsive.

Failure by a Type III non-functionally integrated supporting organization to meet either the distribution amount payout requirement (having distributed the greater of > 85 percent of the prior year's adjusted net income or 3.5 percent of FMV of specified assets, within the parameters of the statute) or the attentiveness requirement (which, as a first step requires distribution of 1/3 of the payout amount to have gone to certain supported organizations) results in private foundation classification. Part V's reporting scheme calculations related to determining the distribution amount payout is very similar to the calculations required to be made by private foundations under Section 4942.

Part V's Section A calculates the organization's adjusted net income, including recoveries of qualified distributions made in a prior period.

Line 1 Net Short-term capital gain, report the filing organization's net short-term capital gain, if any on Line 1. Long-term capital gains and losses from the sale or disposition of property. The distinction between short term and long term is a 12-month holding period. If the assets are donated the holding period from the donor is tacked onto the holding period of the filing organization. Because public charities rarely obtain this information from donors or the donor's basis information, this can be problematic for public charities. Type III supporting organizations will have to start acting more like private foundations in obtaining donor information when accepting gifts of appreciated stock.

Section A - Adjusted Net Income		(A) Prior Year	(B) Current Year (optional)
1 Net short-term capital gain	1		
2 Recoveries of prior-year distributions	2		
3 Other gross income (see instructions)	3		
4 Add lines 1 through 3	4		
5 Depreciation and depletion	5		
6 Portion of operating expenses paid or incurred for production or collection of gross income or for management, conservation, or maintenance of property held for production of income (see instructions)	6		
7 Other expenses (see instructions)	7		
8 Adjusted Net Income (subtract lines 5, 6 and 7 from line 4)	8		

The following should be considered in relation to short term capital gains:

- Net short-term capital losses cannot be carried back or forward to other tax years.
- Amounts treated as long-term capital gains include capital gain dividends from a regulated investment company are excluded from this calculation.
- Net Section 1231 gains are capital gains and considered depending upon the holding period (net Section 1231 losses are treated as ordinary losses and not considered).
- If an organization makes charitable distributions using appreciated assets, the difference between the fair market value of the distributed asset and the basis in the asset is not includable in adjusted net income.

The adjusted basis for determining gain from the sale or other disposition (other than charitable dispositions) of property is the greater of:

1. The fair market value of such property on August 17, 2006, plus or minus all adjustments thereafter and before the date of disposition under Sections 1011–1023, if the property was held continuously from August 17, 2006, to the date of disposition; or
2. The adjusted basis under Sections 1011-1023, without regard to Section 362(c). If assets acquired before August 17, 2006, were subject to depreciation or depletion, to determine the adjustment to basis between the date of acquisition and August 17, 2006, straight line depreciation or cost depletion must be considered. Any other adjustment made during such period (such as a change in useful life based upon additional data or a change in facts) must also be considered.

The adjusted basis to determine loss is only the amount described in item 2.

Line 2 Recoveries of Prior Year Distributions. These amounts may also reported on Form 990, Part XI, Line 9. They include:

- Repayments grants made in prior years;
- Proceeds from the sale or disposition of property if such acquisition of property was considered as a charitable use asset or
- An amount set aside and considered as a distribution counting toward the distribution requirement in a prior tax year to the extent it is determined that such amount is unnecessary for the purposes for which it was set aside (Schedule A, Part V, Section D, Line 5).

Line 3 Other Gross Income, report all other gross income. Gross income includes:

- All amounts derived from, or in connection with, property held by the organization (except as specified otherwise in the instructions for Line 1).
- Income from any related or unrelated trade or business.
- Income from tax-exempt bonds.

Gross income does not include:

- Gifts, grants or contributions received.
- Long-term capital gains or losses and net short-term capital gains and losses.
- Income received from an estate, unless the estate is terminated due to a prolonged period of administration.
- Distributions from a trust created and funded by another person.

Certain amounts received by an organization in the redemption of stock in a corporate disqualified person to avoid excess business holdings, which are treated as not equivalent to a dividend under Section 302(b)(1) (and as amounts received in exchange for the stock, giving rise to long-term capital gain or loss) if the conditions or Section 53.4942(a)-2(d)(2)(iv) are met.

Line 5 Depreciation and Depletion. The deduction for deprecation under Section 167 is allowed, but only on the basis of the straight-line method. The deduction for depletion under Section 611 is also allowed, but without regard to Section 613 (percentage depletion).

Line 6 Operating Expenses. The portion of ordinary and necessary operating expenses paid or incurred for production or collection of gross income or for management, conservation, or maintenance of property held for production of income is reported on Line 6.

Such expenses include:

- Compensation of officers, and employees;
- Interest;
- Rent;
- Expenses and interest relating to tax-exempt income under Section 265; and
- Taxes

Where only a portion of the assets are held for the production of income and a portion is used for charitable purposes, shared expenses may be allocated on a reasonable and consistently applied basis.

These expenses may not be deducted in arriving at adjusted net income:

- Net losses from a related business or other charitable activity that produces gross income (no deduction over the income from such activity)
- Charitable contributions under Sections 170 or 642
- Net operating loss carrybacks and carryovers under Section 172
- Dividends under Section 241 and the sections following it (the dividends-received deductions for corporations)
- Net capital losses (short-term or long-term)

Adjusted Net Income. The prior year amount is calculated on Line 8, Column (A) and is carried down to Part V, Section C, Line 1.

The current year amount is not factored into current year compliance and is thus not required to be completed. However the table allows you to calculate the amount for the current year and thus have it readily obtainable for use in the subsequent tax year's Form 990.

Part V's Section B values the filer's non-charitable use assets to calculate the amount that must be distributed. There are very specific rules for valuing different classes of assets. At the simplest level cash is valued on an average monthly basis and then the monthly values are averaged, marketable securities are valued monthly on any reasonable basis, land is valued no less than every five years, and all other assets must be valued annually. There are special rules for assets held less than a year and allowances blockage, acquisition indebtedness, and cash held for charitable purposes. The resulting value is then multiplied by 3.5 percent. The resulting amount is then reduced by any prior period distributions recovered in current year to arrive at the current year Minimum Asset Amount. This amount is utilized to determine the Distributable Amount.

Section B - Minimum Asset Amount		(A) Prior Year	(B) Current Year (optional)
1 Aggregate fair market value of all non-exempt-use assets (see instructions for short tax year or assets held for part of year):			
a Average monthly value of securities	1a		
b Average monthly cash balances	1b		
c Fair market value of other non-exempt-use assets	1c		
d Total (add lines 1a, 1b, and 1c)	1d		
e Discount claimed for blockage or other factors (explain in detail in **Part VI**):			
2 Acquisition indebtedness applicable to non-exempt-use assets	2		
3 Subtract line 2 from line 1d	3		
4 Cash deemed held for exempt use. Enter 1-1/2% of line 3 (for greater amount, see instructions).	4		
5 Net value of non-exempt-use assets (subtract line 4 from line 3)	5		
6 Multiply line 5 by .035	6		
7 Recoveries of prior-year distributions	7		
8 **Minimum Asset Amount (add line 7 to line 6)**	8		

Columns (A) and (B)—Prior Year and Current Year. The filer's minimum asset amount for the prior tax year is used in determining the organization's distributable amount for the current tax year. The schedule also calculates the minimum asset amount for the current tax year for next year's calculations. This reporting is optional but may be helpful if the organization anticipates being required to complete Part V in the subsequent tax year.

In defining minimum asset amount, only non-charitable use assets are included in the calculation of the minimum asset amount. This is similar to the concept of the minimum investment return for private foundations. Non-charitable use assets are assets that are not used or held for use by the supporting organization to carry out the exempt purposes of the supported organization(s). This also includes assets held by the supported organization if the supporting organization provides the asset free or at a nominal rent to the supported organization.

Assets held for the production of income or for investment are not considered used directly for charitable functions even though the income from the assets is used for charitable functions.

Whether an asset is a charitable use asset or a non-charitable use asset is a factual question. An illustrative example in the instructions includes an office building used to provide offices for employees engaged in managing endowment funds for the supporting organization or supported organization. This building is not considered an asset used for charitable purposes.

Dual Use Property. When property is used for both charitable and non-charitable purposes, the property is considered used entirely for charitable purposes if 95 percent or more of its total use is for charitable purposes. If less than 95 percent of its total use is for charitable purposes, a reasonable allocation must be made between charitable and non-charitable use. Use is not defined in the instructions. Two common factors of use are square footage for exclusive use property or time if the same property is used at different times for different purposes.

Excluded Property. Besides charitable use property, certain assets are excluded entirely from the computation of the minimum asset amount. These include charitable pledges and interests in an estate or trust created and funded by another person prior to the distribution to the supporting organization.

Line 1 Aggregate Fair Market Value of All Non-exempt Use Assets

1a. Average monthly value of securities. A supporting organization may use any reasonable method for determining the fair market value of marketable securities if it is consistently applied and valued at least monthly. Common examples are to pick a day each month and then average the monthly values for the year to determine the fair market value of marketable securities. A supporting organization could average the beginning and ending value each month and then average these average values. Marketable securities include common or preferred stock, bonds, mutual fund shares, and any other financial instruments traded on a domestic or foreign exchange or over-the-counter (OTC).

The exchange or market can be on a local, regional, or national recognized market. Market quotations are considered readily available if a security is any of the following:

- Listed on the New York or American Stock Exchange or any city or regional exchange in which quotations appear on a daily basis, including foreign securities listed on a recognized foreign national, or regional exchange;
- Regularly traded in the national or regional over-the-counter market for which published quotations are available; or
- Locally traded, for which quotations can be readily obtained from established brokerage firms.

If securities are held in trust for, or on behalf of, a supporting organization by a bank or other financial institution that values those securities periodically using a computer pricing system, the organization may use that system to determine the value of the securities. The system must be acceptable to the IRS for federal estate tax purposes.

1b. Average monthly cash balances. To determine the average fair market value of cash, take the value at the beginning and end of each the month and average these amounts for each month. The next step is to averages the average cash for each month in the year. Include all the cash held by the organization even if it is a set aside for qualifying distributions (See Section D, Line 5) or the cash is deemed to be held for charitable purposes (see the following passage on "Line 4 Cash Deemed Held for Exempt Use").

1c. Fair market value of other non-exempt-use assets. If a non-charitable use asset has been determined not to be cash or a marketable security then it should be included on Line 1c. Other assets commonly include privately held investments and real estate held for investment. To determine the fair market value of other assets the supporting organization should value them annually. The supporting organization should remain consistent in the valuation process. The supporting organization should choose a date each year to value its other assets and that date should remain the same for future years. The valuation may be made by supporting organization employees or any other person even if that person is a disqualified person. If the IRS accepts the valuation, it is valid only for the tax year for which it is made. A new valuation is required for the next tax year. For investment real estate, the supporting organization may value the property once every five years instead of annually. If the supporting organization chooses the five-year method, it must obtain a written, certified and independent appraisal on the property. The appraiser cannot be a disqualified person or an employee of the supporting organization and should be qualified to give such an appraisal. The appraisal must have the following elements to be accepted by the IRS:

1. Prepared by a qualified appraiser.
2. Include a closing statement that indicates, in the appraiser's opinion, the real estate is valued in accordance to the valuation principles regularly employed in making appraisals of such property, using all reasonable valuation methods.
3. The supporting organization must maintain a copy of the valuation for the remaining four years.

The appraisal need not be performed on the same date of the other assets valued annually. It can be dated anytime in the first year it applies.

If the other investment is held for less than the full tax year, then the value should be adjusted for the days the supporting organization held the investment during the year. For assets sold during the year, take the value of the asset on the last valuation date and multiple by days held divided by 365 days (366 in a leap year). For assets purchased during the year, take the purchase price and multiply by the days held divided by 365 days (366 in a leap year). The calculated amount should be included in Line 1c instead of the full amount valued on the last valuation date.

1e. Discount claimed for blockage or other factors. If the fair market value of certain assets determined for Lines 1a and 1c are not accurate due to other factors, Line 1e can reduce such values to reflect the true value. Items reported on this line may include reductions or discounts allowed when there is a lack of marketability due to the size of the block of securities held, closely held shares, or the sale of the asset would cause a distress sale. Provide an explanation in Part VI that includes the following information for each asset or group of assets for with a discount is taken:

- A description of the asset including number of shares, name of stock and type of shares (for example, common or preferred shares);
- If the asset is a security, the percentage of the total issued and outstanding securities of the same class represented by the supporting organization's holdings;
- The fair market value of the asset or asset group before any claimed blockage discount or other reduction;
- The discount claimed; and
- An explanation of the reason for the discount.

If the asset the supporting organization is claiming a discount on is a security, there are certain limitations on the size of the reduction in value that can be claimed. The organization may reduce the fair market value of securities only if it can establish that the securities could only be liquidated in a reasonable period of time at a price less than the fair market value for one of these reasons:

- The securities are such a large block that liquidation would depress the market;
- The securities are in a closely held corporation; or
- The sale would cause a forced or distress sale.

Any reduction in value of securities may not exceed 10 percent of the fair market value, determined without regard to any reduction in value.

Line 2 Acquisition Indebtedness Applicable To Non-Exempt Use Assets. If an investment is purchased or acquired using borrowed funds it is considered to have acquisition indebtedness. The acquisition indebtedness related to any investments reported on Lines 1a and 1c should be reported on Line 2. Acquisition indebtedness is defined in Section 514(c)(1) as debt acquired to purchase an asset. This includes debt acquired before (the "but for" test) or after (the reasonable foreseeable test) the purchase of the asset. There are multiple exceptions to acquisition indebtedness. Review the transaction thoroughly to determine if an exception applies. The following are exceptions to the debt acquisition rules:

- Certain debt related to property received by a bequest or a gift (see the IRC and regulations for details)
- Taxes or assessments that attach to the property before the payment date
- Extension, renewal, or refinancing of a preexisting indebtedness
- Debt related to property used for the exempt purpose of the foundation
- Annuities
- Certain federal debt

- Securities lending collateral
- Debt used by qualified organizations for real property

If real estate has a mortgage, or securities are purchased on margin, then the acquisition indebtedness is relatively straightforward. It can be problematic determining if the facts and circumstances support the but for test or the reasonable foreseeable tests related to Section 514(c)(1)(B) and (C). There is unclear guidance from the Service to ensure that any debt acquired close to an investment purchase will not constitute acquisition indebtedness. In one private letter ruling the Service stated that if there is sufficient cash on hand and the debt is not considered acquisition indebtedness. Likewise, if the debt is transitory to implement the foundation's investments, the short-term debt may not be acquisition indebtedness. In both cases, a supporting organization should document the facts and circumstances that would connect the investment to the debt.

Line 4 Cash Deemed Held for Exempt Use. Supporting organizations may exclude from the minimum assets amount the reasonable cash balances necessary to cover current administrative expenses and other normal and current disbursements directly connected with the charitable, educational, or other similar activities. Charitable use assets include a portion of the cash reserved to cover current administrative expenses and other normal and current disbursements directly connected to the supporting organization's charitable activities. The amount of charitable use cash reduces the value of non-charitable use assets in determining the minimum asset amount. In general the amount of cash needed for charitable activities is deemed to be equal to 1.5 percent of the value of the non-charitable assets less any acquisition indebtedness. If the supporting organization can justify the need for additional cash for charitable purposes it can take an amount larger than the 1.5 percent. The supporting organization must document the facts and circumstances for the need and include an explanation in Part VI.

Line 7 Recoveries of Prior-Year Distributions. Report any recoveries entered on Section A, Line 2. This amount increases the minimum asset amount.

Line 8 Minimum Asset Amount. The Minimum Asset Amount from the prior year in Column (A) is carried down to Part VI, Section C – Distributable amount, Line 3. The current year amount is optional but will be used in the subsequent year's tax return.

Part V's Section C takes the result from Section A (adjusted net income from the prior year) and calculates 85 percent of that amount, which is then compared to the result from Section B (minimum asset amount from the prior tax year). The **greater** of these two amounts is reduced by any income tax imposed on the filing organization in the prior year and the result is the filer's distributable amount.

Section C - Distributable Amount			Current Year
1 Adjusted net income for prior year (from Section A, line 8, Column A)	1		
2 Enter 85% of line 1	2		
3 Minimum asset amount for prior year (from Section B, line 8, Column A)	3		
4 Enter greater of line 2 or line 3	4		
5 Income tax imposed in prior year	5		
6 **Distributable Amount.** Subtract line 5 from line 4, unless subject to emergency temporary reduction (see instructions)	6		
7 ☐ Check here if the current year is the organization's first as a non-functionally-integrated Type III supporting organization (see instructions).			

Line 7 The First Tax Year, the distributable amount for the first tax year that an organization is treated as a Type III non-FISO is zero rather than the amount as ordinarily determined. If this is the organization's first year, check the box on Line 7.[11] The distributable amount, as ordinarily determined, applies to every non-functionally integrated Type III supporting organization for purposes of determining whether the organization has an excess distribution in its tax year that can be carried over to future years. This includes an organization that checks the box on Line 7 for the current year. The distributable amount, as ordinarily determined, is reported in Sections C and E.

Emergency temporary reduction. In cases of disaster or emergency, the IRS may provide for temporary reduction in the distributable amount by publication in the Internal Revenue Bulletin. In these cases, the reduced amount should be reported on Line 6 and the reduction noted in Part VI.

Part V's Section D then reports how much the organization distributed in the current year to support its supported organization(s). This includes amounts paid directly over to the supported organization, amounts otherwise paid to further the exempt purposes of the supported organization, specified administrative expenses supporting both prior amounts, amounts paid to acquire exempt-purpose assets, qualified set-asides, and other distributions. The result here represents whether the attentiveness requirement is met.

Section D - Distributions	Current Year
1 Amounts paid to supported organizations to accomplish exempt purposes	
2 Amounts paid to perform activity that directly furthers exempt purposes of supported organizations, in excess of income from activity	
3 Administrative expenses paid to accomplish exempt purposes of supported organizations	
4 Amounts paid to acquire exempt-use assets	
5 Qualified set-aside amounts (prior IRS approval required)	
6 Other distributions (describe in **Part VI**). See instructions.	
7 **Total annual distributions.** Add lines 1 through 6.	
8 Distributions to attentive supported organizations to which the organization is responsive (provide details in **Part VI**). See instructions.	
9 Distributable amount for 2015 from Section C, line 6	
10 Line 8 amount divided by Line 9 amount	

Line 1 Amounts paid to supported organizations to accomplish exempt purposes. The amount of a distribution made to a supported organization is the cash or fair market value of property on the date of distribution. The organization must use the cash method of accounting for this purpose regardless of the method of accounting on which the organization keeps its books and records. Report amounts paid to supported organizations to accomplish their exempt purposes. Distributions furthering the exempt purposes of supported organizations not described in Section 501(c)(3) refer solely to distributions for Section 501(c)(3) purposes.

Line 2 Amounts Paid to Perform Activity That Directly Furthers Exempt Purposes of Supported Organization(s). Report amounts paid to perform any activity that directly furthers exempt purposes of supported organizations and that would otherwise normally be engaged in by the supported organizations, but only if expenses from the activity exceed income from the activity. See Schedule A, Part IV, Section E, regarding direct furtherance of supported organization's activities.

---

[11] However, an organization that was a Type III non-FISO in its tax year beginning in 2012 or 2013 (or was treated as meeting such requirements because it met the requirements of Treas. Reg. 1.509(a)-4(i)(3)(iii) before Temp. Regs. released December 28, 2012) <u>cannot</u> check the box on Line 7.

Line 3 Administrative Expenses Paid to Accomplish Exempt Purposes of Supported Organizations. Report reasonable and necessary administrative expenses paid to accomplish exempt purposes of supported organizations. Do not include expenses in production of investment income.

Line 4 Amounts Paid to Acquire Exempt Use Assets. Report cash distributions made to purchase exempt-use assets. Such assets must be used (or held for use) to carry out the exempt purposes of the supported organization(s). The assets may be used or held by either the supporting organization or one or more supported organizations; if the latter, the supporting organization must make the asset available to the supported organization(s) free of charge or for nominal rent.

Line 5 Qualified Set-Aside Amounts. Qualified set-asides must be for a specific project that accomplishes the exempt purpose of a supported organization to which the supporting organization is responsive. A qualified set-aside counts toward the distribution requirement in the tax year set aside but not again when paid. In addition, advance written approval both from the pertinent supported organization(s) and from the IRS is required to create a qualified set-aside.

The supporting organization must submit Form 8940 to the IRS and pay the user fee before the end of the tax year in which it wants to create a qualified set-aside. The supporting organization must establish to the satisfaction of the IRS that the amount will be paid for the specific project within 60 months from the date of the set-aside and the project can be better accomplished by a set-aside than by the immediate payment of funds. This is known as the suitability test. The cash distribution test is only available for use by private foundations.

The application must contain all of the following information:

- The nature and purposes of the specific project and the amount of the set-aside for which approval is requested;
- The amounts and approximate dates any planned additions to the set-aside after its initial establishment;
- The reasons the project can be better accomplished by the set-aside than by the immediate payment of funds;
- A detailed description of the project, including estimated costs, sources of any future funds expected to be used for completion of the project, and the location(s) (general or specific) of any physical facilities to be acquired or constructed as part of the project; and
- A statement of an appropriate supporting organization manager that the amounts set-aside will be paid for the specific project within a specified period of time ending within 60 months after the date of the set-aside. Alternatively, the application must contain a statement explaining why the period for paying the amount set aside should be extended and indicating the extension of time required. Include in this statement the reason the proposed project could not be divided into two or more projects covering periods of no more than 60 months each.

If the organization obtains the permission of the appropriate supported organizations and the IRS, it must explain on Part VI whether the organization has requested and obtained the approvals for the set-aside.

Line 6 Other Distributions. Report any other distributions not described previously that the organization claims are for its supported organization(s), and describe such distributions in Part VI.

Line 8 Distributions to Attentive Supportive Organizations to Which the Organization is Responsive. Lines 8 through 10 should report on the supporting organization's responsiveness to its supported organization(s). A Type III non-FISO must distribute at least one-third of its distributable amount, calculated in Section C, each tax year to one or more supported organization that are attentive to its operations and to which the supporting organization is responsive; the Line 10 amount, following, must be at least 33.33 percent. Carryovers of excess distributions from prior years do not count toward the attentiveness requirement.

Line 8 is a factual question. The organization should report the distributions to supported organizations which meet the attentiveness test and to which the supporting organization is responsive.

Attentiveness Test. A supported organization is attentive to the operations of the supporting organization if, during the tax year, at least one of these requirements is satisfied:

1. The supporting organization distributes to the supported organization at least 10 percent of the supported organization's total support in its tax year ending before the beginning of the supporting organization's tax year.

    When a supporting organization supports a particular department or school of a university, hospital, or church the department's or school's total support is considered instead of the entire organization.

2. The amount of support received from the supporting organization is necessary to avoid the interruption of a particular function or activity of the supported organization.
3. The amount of support received from the supporting organization is a sufficient part of the supported organization's total support to ensure attentiveness, based on all facts, including the number of supported organizations, the length and nature of the relationship between the supporting and supported organization(s), and the purpose to which the funds are put.

The attentiveness of a supported organization is normally influenced by the amounts received from the supporting organization, but evidence of actual attentiveness to the operations (including investments) of the supporting organization is of almost equal importance.

Amounts received from a supporting organization held in a donor advised fund of the supported organization are disregarded in determining attentiveness.

See Regulations Section 1.509(a)-4(i)(5)(iii)(D) for more examples of the Attentiveness Test.

Responsiveness Test. A supporting organization is responsive to the needs and demands of a supported organization if it meets the responsiveness test set forth in the instructions for Part IV, Section D, Lines 2 and 3, regarding the supported organization(s).

In Part VI, identify each of the supported organization in Schedule A, Part I, Line 11g, Column (i) that met both of the following conditions for the tax year:

1. The supporting organization was responsive to the supported organization and
2. The supported organization was attentive to the supporting organization.

For each organization, detail the facts that demonstrate how both the attentiveness test and the responsiveness test were met by the supporting organization and each of the supported organizations.

Line 10 Results. If the amount on Line 10 is less than 33.33 percent—that is, the amount of distributions to supported organizations that met the attentiveness test and responsiveness test is less than one-third of the distributable amount – then the organization does not qualify as a Type III non-FISO for the tax year. As a result, unless the organization has another basis upon which to qualify as a public charity in the tax year, the organization is a private foundation and must file Form 990-PF for the tax year.

Part V's Section E then takes the actual distributions calculated in Section D (current year distributions) and applies them first to the distributable amounts calculated on the prior year and then to the distributable amount related to the current year as calculated in Sections A through C. Note that the ordering for distributions for supporting organization differs from the ordering required of private foundations under IRC Section 4942. Carryovers of excess distributions from prior years are always applied in full before current year distributions, and any older carryovers are applied before newer carryovers. However, Similar to private foundations, excess distributions of a year cannot be carried over for more than five years. But, because the organization is always using the oldest distributions first, expiring distributions are less problematic for supporting organizations than for private foundations.

Several lines in Section E are not yet applicable during the phase-in period of the new regulations for Type III non-FISO. Those lines are grayed out in Section E.

In completing Section E there are three basic steps:

1. Apply distributions to eliminate any under distribution for reasonable cause in a prior tax year;
2. Apply distributions to satisfy the distributable amount for the current year;
3. Carry over any excess distributions to future years.

There is no need for a line by line walk through because the numbers all come from elsewhere and the form is self-explanatory.

	Section E - Distribution Allocations (see instructions)	(i) Excess Distributions	(ii) Underdistributions Pre-2016	(iii) Distributable Amount for 2016
1	Distributable amount for 2016 from Section C, line 6			
2	Underdistributions, if any, for years prior to 2016 (reasonable cause required—explain in Part VI). See instructions.			
3	Excess distributions carryover, if any, to 2016:			
a				
b				
c	From 2013			
d	From 2014			
e	From 2015			
f	Total of lines 3a through e			
g	Applied to underdistributions of prior years			
h	Applied to 2016 distributable amount			
i	Carryover from 2011 not applied (see instructions)			
j	Remainder. Subtract lines 3g, 3h, and 3i from 3f.			
4	Distributions for 2016 from Section D, line 7: $			
a	Applied to underdistributions of prior years			
b	Applied to 2016 distributable amount			
c	Remainder. Subtract lines 4a and 4b from 4.			
5	Remaining underdistributions for years prior to 2016, if any. Subtract lines 3g and 4a from line 2. For result greater than zero, explain in Part VI. See instructions.			
6	Remaining underdistributions for 2016. Subtract lines 3h and 4b from line 1. For result greater than zero, explain in Part VI. See instructions.			
7	Excess distributions carryover to 2017. Add lines 3j and 4c.			
8	Breakdown of line 7:			
a				
b	Excess from 2013			
c	Excess from 2014			
d	Excess from 2015 . . .			
e	Excess from 2016 . . .			

Part VI—Supplemental Information

There are numerous disclosures required to be made and many that may more than be elected. This clip provides some of the required disclosures.

Part VI	**Supplemental Information.** Provide the explanations required by Part II, line 10; Part II, line 17a or 17b; Part III, line 12; Part IV, Section A, lines 1, 2, 3b, 3c, 4b, 4c, 5a, 6, 9a, 9b, 9c, 11a, 11b, and 11c; Part IV, Section B, lines 1 and 2; Part IV, Section C, line 1; Part IV, Section D, lines 2 and 3; Part IV, Section E, lines 1c, 2a, 2b, 3a and 3b; Part V, line 1; Part V, Section B, line 1e; Part V, Section D, lines 5, 6, and 8; and Part V, Section E, lines 2, 5, and 6. Also complete this part for any additional information. (See instructions.)

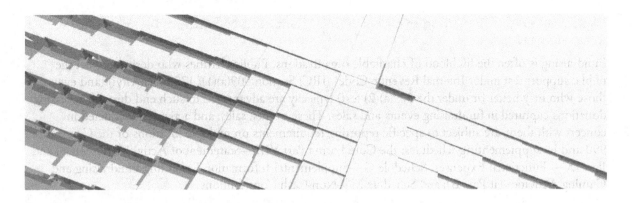

Chapter 4

OTHER REVENUE DISCLOSURES IMPORTANT TO FUNDRAISING (SCHEDULES G-II AND M)

LEARNING OBJECTIVES

After completing this chapter, you should be able to do the following:

- Recognize the correct tax reporting fundraising revenue related to special events by its separate parts both by time and character.
- Identify the need to report all costs associated of fundraising events on Part VIII and Schedule G to get a complete and accurate disclosure of fundraising activities conducted by the filing organization.
- Recognize which noncash contributions (a term used in reference to gifts of goods, services, and <u>use</u> of a donor's property at no charge or at charge below fair market) are to be reported by dollar amounts within revenue and expense parts of the 990 organization and when they are not reported in such parts but may be noted narratively in Part III.
- Identify required reporting on Schedule M triggered by receipts of noncash contributions.
- Recognize the reporting (and internal inconsistencies therefrom) relating to *quid pro quo* fundraising events and the donor acknowledgment disclosures that result.

Fundraising is often the lifeblood of charitable organizations. Public charities who desire to meet the public support test under Internal Revenue Code[1] (IRC) Section 509(a)(1)/ 170(b)(1)(A)(vi) (and even those who may better fit under the 509(a)(2) test) typically are advantaged to such end through accessing donations captured in fundraising events and sales. These events, sales, and activities conducted in concert with them, are subject to specific reporting requirements on multiple locations of the Core Form 990 and its supplementing schedules: the Core Form's Part VIII—Statement of Activities (Revenue) and Part IX— Functional Expenses; Schedule G—Supplemental Information Regarding Fundraising and Gaming Activities (at Part II); and Schedule M—Non-Cash Contributions.

Fundraising activities overall are almost always characterized as unrelated business activities, but they usually avoid unrelated business income taxation because they are not regularly carried on. Even if they were subjected to unrelated business income tax, the way such activities' sales of goods or services are reported for Form 990 purposes typically leads to a net loss upon Part VIII of the Core Form (a result that carries over to the Form 990-T). Accordingly, the impact of such activities on an organization's public support usually only comes from two places: (1) the value of noncash contributions of property achieved prior to the fundraising event in support of the event (such donations reported on Part VIII's Line 1g); and (2) generous over-payment related to purchasing of goods or services (equivalent to donations reported on Part VIII's Line 1c). Any net loss from these events or sales activities is negated (that is, rounded up to zero) and thus of no consequence to the filer's Schedule A public support testing.

A common error is for organizations to report fundraising events and sales activities as a program when reporting program accomplishments in the Core Form's Part III. However, the instructions to Part III state quite clearly that this means of raising funds does not equate to a program service:

> Do not report a fundraising activity as a program service accomplishment unless it is substantially related to the accomplishment of the organization's exempt purposes (other than by raising funds).

---

[1] Hereafter short-handed by reference to Section.

As to what is a fundraising event, the instructions to Part VIII, Line 8 of the Core Form state:

Fundraising events include:	Fundraising events do not include:
• Dinners/dances,	• Sales or gifts of goods or services of only nominal value,
• Door-to-door sales of merchandise,	• Raffles or lotteries in which prizes have only nominal value, and
• Concerts,	• Solicitation campaigns that generate only **contributions**.
• Carnivals,	
• Sports events, and	Proceeds from these activities are considered contributions and should be reported on line 1f.
• Auctions.	

Reporting Revenue from Fundraising Events and Activities—Part VIII's Line 1c (Donations from Fundraising Events) Versus Line 8 (Fundraising Events)

Those attending fundraising events (or those buying items at fundraising sales) make a payment with the expectation that they will receive goods or services in exchange for the amounts they remit. Because of that exchange of consideration (the goods or services being provided in whole or part in exchange for the payment), there is a need to bifurcate and separately report amounts a donor/ attendee/ buyer pays— separating any donation component (that is, a gift) and the purchase price component (that is, an exchange payment for goods/ services.) The former goes on Part VIII Line 1c (and is noted on the memo line accompanying Line 8a) and the latter, amounts received from sales at fundraising events or in the course of fundraising sales, is recorded on Line 8a. Handling this division properly, whenever an exchange of dollars in whole or part for goods or services is received in fundraising contexts, is key to both proper completion of Form 990's Part VIII as well as Schedule G-II (when that schedule/ part's reporting threshold is reached). See the following figure:

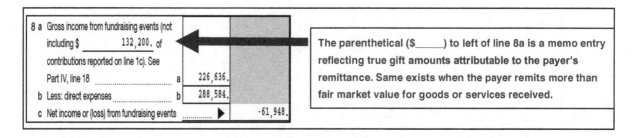

Fundraising Events: Properly Reporting the Economics

Although generally accepted accounting principles (GAAP) reporting compresses the reporting of fundraising events into a single result, the Form 990 reporting reflects that fundraising events and sales combine what are often multiple separate transactions that may occur at varying points in time. Regardless of timing, all transactional activities need be accounted for (and reported) for Form 990 purposes.

A common first transactional event occurs when the filer solicits event sponsors or donations of items or services that will either be consumed at, provided as benefits of, or auctioned off in, a fundraising event or fundraising sales. The result of such pre-fundraising event/ sales efforts come in various forms:

- In-kind contributions that are not reportable on the Form 990 as revenues because they do not fit characterization as noncash contributions (see the glossary definition that follows at its last sentence for the convention that applies here) – due to these not being reported as income, there may be a reconciling item on Change in Net Assets on Part XI;
- Cash or noncash contributions that constitute qualified sponsorship payments under Section 513(i) and because of such qualification may be reported on Part VIII Line lf (and count, regardless of where reported upon Part VIII, as contributed support on the two public support tests);[2]
- In-kind contributions that are reportable on the Form 990 as revenues due to characterization as noncash contributions (again, see glossary definition). If these donations are intended to be consumed or auctioned off at the fundraising event or through fundraising sales, that event (that is, their disbursement) is reportable as a direct fundraising event/ sales expense on Line 8b.

| Noncash contributions | **Contributions** of property, tangible or intangible, other than money. Noncash contributions include, but are not limited to, stocks, bonds, and other **securities**; real estate; **works of art**; stamps, coins, and other **collectibles**; clothing and **household goods**; vehicles, boats, and airplanes; inventories of food, medical equipment or supplies, books, or seeds; intellectual property, including patents, trademarks, copyrights, and trade secrets; donated items that are sold immediately after donation, such as publicly traded stock or used cars; and items donated for sale at a charity auction. Noncash contributions do not include **volunteer** services performed for the reporting organization or donated use of materials, facilities or equipment. |

Further transactional events occur when those attending fundraising event or purchasing fundraising sales items make their remittances. In both cases, the results need be properly reflected amounts between Lines lc (and memo'd on Line 8a's parenthetical) and Line 8:

---

[2] Section 513(i) and the underlying Regulations define a qualified sponsorship payment (QSP) as one that provides no substantial return benefit to the payer, in essence considering the benefits the sponsor receives as akin to donor acknowledgement. They also provide that a QSP counts as donative support under the public support tests.

From the line 1c instructions:

Line 1c. Enter the total amount of *contributions* received from *fundraising events*, which includes, but is not limited to, dinners, auctions, and other events conducted for the sole or primary purpose of raising funds for the organization's exempt activities. Report contributions received from *gaming* activities in line 1f, not in line 1c.

Example. An organization holds a dinner, charging $400 per person for the meal. The dinner has a retail value of $160. A person who purchases a ticket is really purchasing the dinner for $160 and making a contribution of $240. The contribution of $240, which is the difference between the buyer's payment and the retail value of the dinner, would be reported on line 1c and again on line 8a (within the parentheses). The revenue received ($160 retail value of the dinner) would be reported in the right-hand column on line 8a.

If a contributor gives more than $160, that person would be making a contribution of the difference between the dinner's retail value of $160 and the amount actually given. Rev. Rul. 67-246, 1967-2 C.B. 104, as distinguished by Rev. Rul. 74-348, 1974-2 C.B. 80, explains this principle in detail. See also the instructions for lines 8a–8c and Pub. 526, Charitable Contributions.

From the line 8/8a instructions:

Fundraising events sometimes generate both *contributions* and income, such as when an individual pays more than the retail value for the goods or services furnished. Report in parentheses the total amount from fundraising events that represents contributions rather than payment for goods or services. Treat the following as contributions.
Amounts paid in excess of retail value of goods or services furnished. See *Example* for line 1c.
Amounts received from fundraising events when the organization gives items of only nominal value to recipients. See Publication 1771.

Example: In return for a contribution of any amount, donors receive a keychain with the organization's logo. All amounts received should be reported as contributions on line 1f and all associated expenses on the appropriate lines in Part IX, column (D). In such a case, no amounts would be reported on line 8.

Line 8a. Enter in the line 8a box the gross income from fundraising events, not including the amount of contributions from fundraising events reported on line 1c. Report the line 1c amount in the line 8a parenthetical. If the sum of the amounts reported on line 1c and the line 8a box exceeds $15,000, then the organization must answer "Yes" to Part IV, line 18 and complete Schedule G (Form 990 or 990-EZ), Part II. If gaming is conducted at a fundraising event, the income and expenses must be allocated between the gaming and the fundraising event in Form 990, Part VIII; report all income from gaming in line 9a.

Compute the organization's gross income from fees, ticket sales or other revenue from *fundraising events*.

The example in the instruction reprinted is predicated on the keychain being a premium that fits within either the "token goods" or "nominal value" disregarded goods or services exceptions (see Publication 1771 for more info).

REPORTING EXCHANGED FUNDRAISING DOLLARS—LINE 8A

As the cited instructions note, filers need treat the following as contributions—amounts paid in excess of retail value of goods or services furnished. Thus, the issue in distinguishing a payment for the goods or services acquired by a buyer at a fundraising event from a true gift payment provided at the same time is whether the payment by the buyer exceeds the **fair market value** of the property or services acquired.

The tricky part here for filers selling (or otherwise disbursing) goods at a fundraising event is the need to make a good faith determination of the fair market value of the exchanged items or services as of the date the items or services are being provided (that is, sold). The result, fair market value, is then the floor above which any payment becomes a gift. It doesn't matter if the exchange/sales date occurs well after the items were purchased or contributed for purposes of ascertaining line 8a (and resulting 1c), even though the expensing out of the item at line 8b will reflect book basis (book basis generally being fair market value effective on the original date of acquisition, whether acquisition occurred via purchase by or contribution to the filer).

WARNING: A rule that is advantageous to donors when accessing statements from donee charities related to quid pro quo payments is of little assistance in the reporting tasks here. Under the quid pro quo rules of Section 6115, when the amount remitted by a payer exceeds $75, the charity is required to provide a written statement to the payer providing a good faith estimate of the value of the goods and services provided back to them in exchange for their payment. Rev. Proc. 90-12 sets out specific safe harbor rules for situations where token benefits received by a donor in the context of a fundraising campaign are treated as having such insubstantial value that they will be disregarded for Section 6115 purposes (and in such case the benefit received by the contributor is also disregarded for purposes of the contemporaneous written acknowledgment rules under Section 170(f)(8) applicable to contributions of $250 or more). However, there is a problem for filers in applying such an exception at lines 1c and 8a as the token benefits exception is measured from the payer's side and is not available if *in the aggregate* they receive items or services back whose <u>cost</u> exceeds the appropriate limit, as follows:

1. Fair market value of the benefits received does not exceed the lesser of 2 percent of the payment or $106,* or
2. The payment is at least $53,* the only items provided are so-called token goods (those bearing the organization's name or logo), and the <u>cost</u> of these items is within the limit for low-cost articles, which is $10.60.*

*The dollar amounts shown are for 2016 (amounts are adjusted for inflation annually).

Measuring Fair Market Value. The Fair Market Value measure of goods or services sold at fundraising activities or events does no more than reflect what a willing buyer and willing seller—neither under compulsion to buy or sell—would pay that day to access the goods or services. The following examples illustrate fair market valuation in varying factual contexts:

- The right to a three-course meal at the local James Beard Foundation-awarded-chefs restaurant is what that restaurant would charge the public for the same meal in its regular course of its business at the time of the fundraising event providing the meal or when the right to such a meal was purchased in a fundraising sale. (Contrast the result here to the value of catered group meals: choosing food service from a per plate menu at the same price as that charged to the public proves the fair market value of the right to eat that meal with that number of people is the per plate amount charged.)
- Rare paintings or historical artifacts are typically valued by private placement auction or bid price that the item would likely command at a fully advertised, open-to-the-buying-public event.

- Non-unique items (for instance, face-value gift card, floral gift basket) are valued at the price that local purveyors sell these items.
- Items incapable of valuation because they are unique but not auction-able in real world (for instance, right to fly in plane recreating weightlessness shots used in the movie "Apollo 13"), are valued at what someone would have to pay to recreate that opportunity (rent the plane, pay the pilots, buy the insurance, bribe the local officials to ignore the sonic boom, and so on).

KNOWLEDGE CHECK

1. A fundraising event conducted by museum Z charges a $60 entry fee (ticket price). All attendees are provided three items:

   i. A $10 gift certificate to Z's holiday season kiosk gift shop at a local high-end shopping mall;

   ii. A dinner catered by a local hotel at a non-discounted from normal to public cost-per-plate charge to Z of $25; and

   iii. One item to be chosen from items of wearing apparel, each of which bears Z's name and normally are sold to the public at a charge of $22.

   On these facts, which is correct with respect to Line 8a results?

   a. If the cost of each item of wearing apparel to Z is less than $10, the charity need not include the $22 fair market value of the item on Line 8a.

   b. If Z can document from similar facts from the prior year's event that only 20 percent of the gift certificates provided to attendees are redeemed at its kiosk gift shop, then it may reduce the gift certificates' fair market value for Line 8a purposes to $2.

   c. All three items' stated values per attendee ticket sold ($10 gift certificate + $25 per plate cost to charity + $22 apparel price tag = $57) is reported on Line 8a.

   d. Line 8a cannot be determined on the facts here, as adjustments are permitted for each of the following factors: the number of meals actually consumed at the event and the number of items of apparel distributed at the event.

REPORTING DIRECT EXPENSES OF FUNDRAISING EVENTS OR SALES—LINE 8B

Line 8b instructions state this:

Enter on this line the cost or other basis of any items sold at the events and the expenses that relate directly to the production of the revenue portion of the fundraising activity, whether incurred before, during, or after the event. In the line 1c dinner example referred to earlier, the cost of the food and beverages served and invitation to the dinner would be among the items; in the reported on Line 8b. Indirect fundraising expenses, such as certain advertising expenses associated with raising these contributions, must be reported on the appropriate lines in Part IX, Column (D) and not on Line 8b.

- The instructions explain that direct expenses may include expenses incurred before, during or after the event. Their example provided, of a fundraising dinner, states that the cost of the invitation to the dinner is a direct expense. That directive is potentially misleading as it relates to the cost of printing the invitation. In line with the long-standing principle followed by state regulators (as well as the IRS) that solicitation expenses constitute fundraising expenses (that is, costs reported in Part IX, Column (D)), the authors note that this example likely does not apply to some or all of the mailing costs of the invitation. In general, asks or prompts to support the organization via attendance at fundraising events or otherwise are considered fundraising expense and not direct event expense. Further explication by the IRS about the language used in their example to clear up this confusion would be helpful.
- Further issues arise in confronting the second task of proper reporting at Line 8b when items being sold were originally donated to the filer:

> For such items, there was an initial revenue item: the contribution of the goods (or services, which indeed has reportable/recordable (for 990 purposes) value if the right to service now being sold equates to intangible right to property or services)—such goods and service-certificates need be recorded at the item's fair market value *at time of the original gift* as contributed _income_ upon Part VIII, Line 1.
>
> Thereafter, at the disposal of the goods or service-certificate by sale *at a fundraising event*, such items' corresponding value at the time they were gifted to the filer need be expensed out as an *event expense* upon Part VIII, Line 8b (and corresponding G-II disclosure).

- As the preceding box notes, the cost or then-existing asset value of items sold at fundraising events (for example, donated candlesticks being sold at auction, or the cost of dinner being provided to each attendee) is a direct expense (as are all costs of disbursing goods (whether donated or not to the filer)) that are disposed of at the event.

REPORTING RESULTS: LINE 8A RECEIPTS MINUS LINE 8B DIRECT EXPENSES = LINE 8C

Filers record on Line 8c the net between the exchange-portion they have received from fundraising sales (for example, the amounts on Line 8a) and the direct expenses/cost of those sales. This leads oftentimes to a perceived conundrum in the case of donated goods being sold. When a buyer purchases donated items at a fundraising event [for example, candlesticks] and pays less than their expensed value in the hands of the filer plus the costs of the sale attributable to the event, the result may well be break-even or even a loss. (Addressing the fact of such loss is returned to later in these materials in addressing Schedule G-II completion.) Either way, the organization has converted the contributed item to cash—and the purchaser who has paid more than their then-fair market value has made a gift for the excess amount they paid, or if they paid less than fair market value, got the benefit of a bargain.

Note the result in the following fundraising auction liquidation scenarios in which the same pair of donated candlesticks sell for $140 OR $65 at auction:

Ugly candlesticks "worth" $100 donated/book them in upon Lines 1f & 1g (at $100). Dispose at silent auction,$100 now is amount on Line 8b

A. Silent Auction A: candlesticks "sell" at $140 – Line 8 result -- $40 on Line 1c (and parenthetical preceding Line 8a); $100 on Line 8a

B. Line 8c is $-0-. Line 1, however, has gifts of $100 (from donation of candlesticks) + $40 (from "overpay" at silent auction's sale!)

C. Results: $140 on Line 1 in total; $0 on Line 8. Total thus $140.

A. Silent Auction B: candlesticks "sell" at $65 – Line 8 result -- $0 on Line 1c (and parenthetical preceding Line 8a); $65 on Line 8a

B. Line 8c is NEGATIVE $35. Line 1, however, has gifts of $100 (from donation of candlesticks) but NO gift from "overpay" at sale!

C. Results: $100 on Line 1 in total; –$35 on Line 8c. Total thus $65.

The preceding text comports with the Form 990 instructions' auction example:

Example 1. If an organization receives a donation of a home theater system with a FMV of $5,000 at the time of donation; sells the system for $7,500 at an auction, after having displayed the system and its FMV (which remains $5,000) at and before auction so that its value was known to the bidders; and incurs $500 in costs related to selling the system at auction, it should report the following amounts in Part VIII:

Line 1c (**contributions** from fundraising events):	$2,500
Line 1f (all other contributions):	$5,000
Line 1g (noncash contributions):	$5,000
Line 8a (gross income from fundraising events):	$5,000
Line 8a parenthetical (contributions reported on line 1c):	$2,500
Line 8b (direct expenses: $5,000 FMV on donation date + $500 in auction costs)	$5,500
Line 8c (net income from fundraising event, line 8a minus line 8b):	($500)

Example 2. If the home theater system in Example 1 sold at auction for $2,500 instead of $7,500, and all other facts in Example 1 remain the same, then the organization should report the following amounts in Part VIII:

Line 1c (**contributions** from fundraising events):	$0
Line 1f (all other contributions):	$5,000
Line 1g (noncash contributions):	$5,000
Line 8a (gross income from fundraising events):	$2,500
Line 8a parenthetical (contributions reported on line 1c):	$0
Line 8b (direct expenses: $5,000 FMV on donation date + $500 in auction costs)	$5,500
Line 8c (net income from fundraising event, line 8a minus line 8b):	($3,000)

Treatment of Donated Services and Use of Contributors' Facilities or Property

As noted earlier, it is often the case that organizations embarking on a significant fundraising event or sales activity undertake two major efforts before the main fundraising event: 1) solicitation of event sponsors to contribute both cash and noncash sponsorships; and 2) procurement of noncash contributions to be auctioned off or consumed at the event.

It is important to properly characterize all contributions and who they came from. This is because donated services and use of facilities (or use of other property) provided by the underlying owner of the facility/ property are excluded from revenue and expenses on Form 990 Core Form reporting of revenue on Part VIII and expenses on Part IX. If the donative value of these types of contributions are recorded on the filer's books and records (as would be the case if the financial statements are presented in line with GAAP), this disjuncture between 990 reporting and book recording will lead to reporting on Part XI—Other changes in Net Assets unless the amounts net to zero (as is often the case.) Note that the Form 990 reporting convention noted here is not applicable when a donor of services or use of facilities/ property donates their entire property right. This is the case definitively when a party who donates a certificate for services has purchased the certificate and transfers it to the organization (see

---

further address on the topic as follows, with respect to the IRS having concerns when the certificate comes directly from the service-provider such as hotel companies or airlines) – here, the value is recorded both as a contribution to, and when the property is disbursed out, an expenditure of, the organization.

Although fundraising is not a program activity, Core Form Part III—Program Service Accomplishments, is an appropriate place to denote the application of donated services or use of facilities/ property which otherwise are not reflected on the 990's presentation of financial statements. This is especially useful for organizations who receive large donations of donated gifts of services or use of facilities. For example, charities commonly known as wish granting organizations receive large donations of hotel rooms, airline tickets, cruises, and tickets to attend games or concerts and typically utilize most of these in their exempt programs, but may also sell them at fundraising events. Because of these items' characterization as donated services or goods their value is omitted from Part IX expenditure reporting (and in program service expenditures reported on Part Ill's Line 4 program lines), but the instructions note that their description and good faith valuation can be included in Part III's Line 4 narratives:

> **Donated services or use of equipment, materials, or facilities.** The organization can report the amount of any donated services, or use of materials, equipment, or facilities it received or used in connection with a specific program service, on the lines for the narrative description of the appropriate program service. However, do not include these amounts in revenue, expenses, or grants reported on Part III, lines 4a–4e, even if prepared according to **generally accepted accounting principles**.

KNOWLEDGE CHECK

2. In reporting on fundraising events, what is not a direct event expense of an annual dinner or dance?

   a. Cost of catering and facility rental.
   b. Value of volunteer hours undertaken in support of, and at, the event.
   c. Entertainment (for example, the musicians).
   d. Value of donated items auctioned at the event.

3. How is direct event expense measured with respect to the disbursement of a donated item that is sold at a fundraising event?

   a. The donor's basis in the item is a cap on the amount.
   b. The item's fair market value at the time of donation to the organization.
   c. The greater of the item's fair market value at the time of donation versus the time of sale.
   d. The sales price is a cap on the amount.

As discussed, the IRS is not (yet) comfortable treating certain certificates for right to access goods/services as 990-reportable donated property when the certificate comes from the owner of property or an employer whose goods or services are the basis of the donation. In such cases, the IRS wants same handled as a use donation (such as when a hotel owner gives the right to the use of its rooms). Accordingly, the 990 instructions assign different results in reporting contributed income from gift certificates depending on who donates them – the service provider (in their example, a hotel operator) versus someone who has already paid the service provider for the certificates, as the instructions' excerpts that follow reflect. The authors' position is that irrespective of the relationship of the donor to the promised goods/services, a <u>transferable</u> certificate to access services (or right to use another's property) that is not put to use by the recipient in its exempt function but is procured for sale to others constitutes an intangible property right and as such is within the definition of a noncash contribution. To this end, the authors note that the IRS' contrary posture is driven by public support test mandates under the Regulations, which are dissonant from the principles by which contributions are defined. The latter principles not only contradict the IRS' posture here, but as not supported by the IRS' instructions for Core Form Part VIII, Line 1, where it is stated: Contributions are reported on Line 1 regardless of whether they are deductible by the contributor.

• Donations of services such as the value of donated advertising space, broadcast air time (including donated public service announcements), or discounts on services or donations of use of materials, equipment, or facilities, even though reporting donated services and facilities as items of revenue and expense is called for in certain circumstances by generally accepted accounting principles. The optional reporting of donated services and facilities is discussed in the instructions for Form 990, Part III.

Example 1. A hotel in a city's entertainment district donates 100 "right to use" certificates covering 15 hotel rooms a night to disaster relief organization B. B then uses these certificates as emergency housing in furtherance of its exempt purposes. B should not report the value of this contribution on line 1 (or on any other line in Part VIII), because this is a donation of services and use of facilities to B. Similarly, if B were to auction off the certificates as part of a fundraising event, B should not report the value of the contributed certificates on line 1 (or on any other line in Part VIII). Rather, it should report gross income from the auction on Part VIII, line 8a.

Example 2. Organization C purchases 100 "right to use" certificates (as described in Example 1) from the hotel, then contributes them to disaster relief organization B and designates that they be used for disaster relief purposes. B should report the FMV of these certificates on line 1. If B were to auction off the certificates as part of a fundraising event, then use the proceeds for disaster relief purposes, B should report the gross income from the auction on Part VIII, line 8a, report the FMV of the contributed certificates in line 8b, and report the difference between lines 8a and 8b on line 8c.

---

4. Ignoring Example 1 in the preceding IRS instruction, what properly reflects a donation that is reportable for 990 purposes as revenue when received by a filer?

   1. A promise by a professional photography studio to provide the filer with 3 hours of custom studio services before the tax year ends.
   2. A transferable certificate from a professional photography studio, procured for auction use at the filer's fundraising event upcoming in the tax year, by which the holder gets 3 hours of custom studio services.
   3. A professional photography studio's write-down of a bill to the filer of 3 hours of custom studio services by 50percent.
   4. A professional photography studio's provision this tax year of a staffed photo-shop booth at filer's fundraising event where attendees create photos of themselves and co-participants to take home.

      a. all
      b. 1 and 3.
      c. 3 and 4.
      d. 2 only.

GAAP versus 990

Devotees of GAAP standards will note that the 990 instructions override GAAP-financial statement reporting with respect to reporting donated goods sold at auction. The GAAP rule requires an adjustment to in-kind property's donated value when such property is sold at fundraising events for a loss. (See following reprint of FASB Accounting Standards Codification (ASC) 958-605-25-20, which effectively moots any loss from auction result by requiring that the donated good's fair market value at time of contribution be adjusted [that is, written down] to the amount realized at sale.)

> It should be noted that sloppy tax-preparation (particularly, entering GAAP-audited financial statement's net results from fundraising events or sales upon Form 990) was behind the IRS' vocal calls for proper reporting related to fundraising events that Core Form Part VIII, Line 1c and Lines 8a-c and Schedule G-II now implement.

It should be emphasized that regardless of the previously-noted controversies or issues, the instructions to Line 1 require that donated goods be reported at fair market value at time of donation:

> Report the value of **noncash contributions** at the time of the donation. For example, report the fair market value of a donated car at the time the car was received as a donation.

Accordingly, 990 preparers may not apply FASB ASC 958 financial statement results (highlighted in the following text box) for 990 reporting of fundraising sales of donated goods.

14.227 *Items used for fund-raising Purposes:* Organizations may receive contributions of gifts-in-kind to be used for fund-raising purposes. (For example, an organization may receive tickets, gift certificates, or merchandise from donors to be sold to others during a fund-raising event such as an auction.) An organization should recognize a donated item to be used for fund-raising purposes as a contribution and measure it as fair value. Any difference between the item's fair value and the ultimate amount received for the item should be recognized as an adjustment to the original contribution amount (FASB ASC 958-605-25-20)

Schedule M Required Reporting of Noncash Contributions

The text to this point has addressed the reporting rules concerning receipt and later sale of noncash contributions related to fundraising activities as same are reported on Core Form Part VIII, Lines 1 and Line 8. We now examine when the supplemental schedule for reporting noncash contributions (if noncash contributions are over the reporting thresholds). Schedule M both reports details related to noncash contributions and requires disclosures related to donor acknowledgment and gift acceptance policies.

Schedule M is triggered by 990 filers who answer "Yes" to Core Form Part IV Q 29 or 30:

29	Did the organization receive more than $25,000 in non-cash contributions? *If "Yes," complete Schedule M*	29	✓	

Schedule M's first trigger is reached if the total amount of noncash contributions received in the filing year exceeds $25,000 (per memo line at Core Form Part VIII, Line 1g). Note that what is done with such contributions (for example, if the donated items are sold immediately after donation), does not matter as for 990-reporting purposes, it is their <u>receipt</u> that matters.

PRACTICE POINTER: The preceding passage is especially important in the case of receipt of marketable securities, as for GAAP purposes marketable securities are not treated as in-kind contributions if the organization's policy is to sell such assets immediately upon receipt.

Line 29. The organization is required to answer "Yes" to Line 29 if it received during the year more than $25,000 in *fair market value (FMV)* of donations, gifts, grants or other *contributions* of property other than cash, regardless of the manner received (such as for use in a charity auction—for example, donated centerpieces for the tables). Do not include *contributions* of services or use of facilities.

As with Core Form Part VIII, Lines 1 and 8 principles previously noted, the key to proper Schedule M triggering (and completion) is understanding the glossary definition of noncash contributions:

Noncash contributions	**Contributions** of property, tangible or intangible, other than money. Noncash contributions include, but are not limited to, stocks, bonds, and other **securities**; real estate; **works of art**; stamps, coins, and other **collectibles**; clothing and **household goods**; vehicles, boats, and airplanes; inventories of food, medical equipment or supplies, books, or seeds; intellectual property, including patents, trademarks, copyrights, and trade secrets; donated items that are sold immediately after donation, such as publicly traded stock or used cars; and items donated for sale at a charity auction. Noncash contributions do not include **volunteer** services performed for the reporting organization or donated use of materials, facilities or equipment.

When amount on 1g is greater than $25,000, Schedule M reporting obligation follows. (Note: Part IV's Line 29 trigger question for Schedule M reminds filers that items taken for resale in fundraising events are to be recorded and reported as noncash contributions; as noted earlier in this text, for those who prepare financial statements according to GAAP, this may result in a GAAP-tax difference.)

Contributions, Gifts, Grants and Other Similar Amounts	**1a** Federated campaigns . . .	**1a**	68,441.	
	b Membership dues	**1b**		
	c Fundraising events	**1c**	132,200.	
	d Related organizations . . .	**1d**		
	e Government grants (contributions)	**1e**		
	f All other contributions, gifts, grants, and similar amounts not included above	**1f**	38,585,846.	
	g Noncash contributions included in lines 1a-1f: $		9,884,988.	
	h Total. Add lines 1a–1f . . . . ▶			38,786,487.

There is a second trigger question for Schedule M, at Core Form's Part IV, Q. 30 that is generally unrelated to fundraising activities:

30	Did the organization receive contributions of art, historical treasures, or other similar assets, or qualified conservation contributions? *If "Yes," complete Schedule M*	**30**	

Note that there is no dollar threshold to this question. A donation of any value of these types of noncash contributions triggers a Schedule M filing requirement.

Line 30. The organization is required to answer "Yes" to Line 30 if during the year it received as a donation, gift, grant, or other *contribution*:

1. Any *work of art, historical treasure*, historical artifact, scientific specimen, archeological artifact, or similar asset, including a fractional interest, regardless of amount or whether the organization maintains collections of such items
2. Any *qualified conservation contributions* regardless of whether the contributor claimed a charitable contribution deduction for such *contribution*

SCHEDULE M—PREPARATION

Part I	Types of Property	(a) Check if applicable	(b) Number of contributions or items contributed	(c) Noncash contribution amounts reported on Form 990, Part VIII, line 1g	(d) Method of determining noncash contribution amounts
1	Art—Works of art				
2	Art—Historical treasures				
3	Art—Fractional interests				
4	Books and publications				
5	Clothing and household goods				
6	Cars and other vehicles				
7	Boats and planes				
8	Intellectual property				
9	Securities—Publicly traded				
10	Securities—Closely held stock				
11	Securities—Partnership, LLC, or trust interests				
12	Securities—Miscellaneous				
13	Qualified conservation contribution—Historic structures				
14	Qualified conservation contribution—Other				
15	Real estate—Residential				
16	Real estate—Commercial				
17	Real estate—Other				
18	Collectibles				
19	Food inventory				
20	Drugs and medical supplies				
21	Taxidermy				
22	Historical artifacts				
23	Scientific specimens				
24	Archeological artifacts				
25	Other ▶ (_____)				
26	Other ▶ (_____)				
27	Other ▶ (_____)				
28	Other ▶ (_____)				

The highlighted lines are, in general, those within the second trigger (leading to requirement to file Schedule M regardless of value of such items).

Once Schedule M reporting is triggered, reporting by types of property is made (as shown in the preceding image). Lines 1–28 instructions require the following details:

- Check Column (a) if the filing organization received any contributions within each denoted category type.
- Report a contributions count for each type in Column (b)—either the number of contributions of such type, or the number of items contributed within such type (further, use Schedule M's blank line part, Part II, to explain which method is applied). Note that with respect to contributions of stock, each separate gift (of shares) is to be reported, not the number of shares.
- Column (b) instructions also set out an exception for Lines 4 and 5 as to the need to count contributions or items, and explain how contribution of securities should be reported by number of gifts, not by amount of shares.
- Columns (c)–(d) instructions are self-explanatory, with helpful valuation examples (these are reprinted several pages after this text): example (1) addresses the valuation of a donated car, and example (2) speaks to the types of filers who benefit from the exception for Lines 4 and 5, filers receiving contributions of books, publications, clothing, and household goods, when these contributions are intended for resale.

Column (b): For each type of property received during the year, enter the number of *contributions* or the number of items contributed, determined in accordance with the organization's recordkeeping practices. Explain in Part II of this schedule whether the organization is reporting the number of contributions or the number of items received, or a combination of both methods. As subsequently described, for contributions of securities, such as publicly traded stock, treat each separate gift (rather than each share received) as an item for this purpose. Organizations that receive contributions of books, publications, clothing, and household goods are not required to complete Column (b) for those items reported on Lines 4 and 5.

Columns (c)–(d): In Column (c), enter the revenues reported on Form 990, Part VIII, Line 1g, for the appropriate property type. If none were reported, enter 0. In Column (d), describe the method used to determine the amount reported on Form 990, Part VIII, Line 1g (for example, cost or selling price of the donated property, sale of comparable properties, replacement cost, opinions of experts, and so on). See Publication 561, *Determining the Value of Donated Property*, for more information.

The instructions discuss how to report receipts of art and historical treasures by museums or similar organizations:

Museums and other organizations that do not report contributions of art, historical treasures, and other similar items as revenue, as permitted under GAAP, enter 0 in Column (c) and leave Column (d) blank. The organization can explain in Part II that a zero amount was reported on Form 990, Part VIII, Line 1g, because the museum did not capitalize its collections, as allowed under FASB ASC 958-360-25.

In addition, conservation easements are also to be reported consistent with the valuation on the organization books and records:

An organization that received **qualified conservation contributions** or **conservation easements** must report column (c) revenue consistent with how it reports revenue from such contributions in its books, records, and financial statements. The organization must also report revenue from such qualified conservation contributions and conservation easements consistently with how it reports such revenue in Form 990, Part VIII.

The helpful examples for Columns (c) and (d) regarding valuation for difficult property types are as follows:

Example 1: A used car in poor condition is donated to a local high school for use by students studying car repair. A used car guide shows the dealer retail value for this type of car in poor condition is $1,600. However, the guide shows the price for a private party sale of the car is only $750. The fair market value of the car is considered to be $750, which is the amount the organization reported on Form 990, Part VIII, line 1g. In column (c), the organization should enter $750. In column (d), the organization should enter "sale of comparable properties or opinion of expert" as the method used to determine fair market value.	*Example 2:* An organization primarily receives bulk donations of clothing, household goods, and other similar items, intended for resale. Under its permitted financial reporting practices, it does not recognize or record revenue at the time of receipt of the contribution, but instead records such items in inventory and reports contribution revenues at the time of sale based on prior inventory turnover experience. In column (c), the organization can enter the amount that represents the total estimated amount of annual sales revenue for each type of property received under its permitted financial reporting method, and in column (d), enter "resale value or annual sales revenue" as the method of determining revenue.

Definitions for each of the types of property listed in Part I are provided in the instructions. If you are uncertain as to what is included in each asset class, refer to the detailed instructions for each of Schedule M's lines. Items contributed for sale at auction by the filer are to be included on their specific type line, in accordance with the command that noncash contributions must also be reported as revenue for Form 990 purposes regardless of their disposition.

Auction Items as a class of donated goods: The instructions indicate auction items should be reported by class of items donated on Lines 1–24. However, most organizations find that by reporting all auction items on one of the supplemental reporting Lines 25 through 28, they actually have better transparency on the Form 990 and Schedule M.

To-be-auctioned items are to be included in the specific lines (1–24). However, the authors' experience is that many organizations do report "auction items" on lines 25–28.	Donations of items used by the organization at a charitable auction (other than goods sold by the charity at the auction, which should be reported on lines 1 through 24, as appropriate), such as food served at the event or floral centerpieces, can be reported separately on lines 25 through 28. **Noncash contributions** do not include donations of services or donated use of materials, equipment, or facilities, which may be reported in the narrative section of Form 990, Part III, line 4.

If the types of noncash assets reflected on Lines 1–24 are not applicable, Lines 25–28 are to be used to provide descriptions of the contributed property. The instructions provide examples of the types of noncash assets that may be reported on lines 25–28:

> Lines 25–28. Use Lines 25–28 to separately report other types of property not previously described or reported on previous lines. These include items that did not satisfy specific charitable deduction requirements applicable to the contribution of such type of property, but which were contributed to the organization, such as clothing and household goods that were not in good used or better condition, and conservation easements that the organization knows do not constitute qualified conservation contributions.

> Self-created items, such as personal papers and manuscripts, including archival records, are to be listed separately as a type. Archival records are materials of any kind created or received by any person, family, or organization in the conduct of their affairs that are preserved because of the enduring value of the information they contain or as evidence of the functions and responsibilities of their creator.

Schedule M, Lines 29—33 address the filer's policies and procedures with respect to the capture of noncash contributions. These questions are similar in nature to those found on the Core Form's governance part (Part VI) or the compliance part (Part V). They appear on Schedule M because they are specific only to filers who receive noncash contributions.

Question 29 is a compliance question that asks how many Form 8283s were provided for completion (by donors). Its presence is a helpful reminder of the need donees have, in certain instances, to complete that Form's Part IV in order to protect the donor's eligibility for a tax deduction associated with noncash charitable contributions of a magnitude of $5,000 or greater.

| 29 | Number of Forms 8283 received by the organization during the tax year for contributions for which the organization completed Form 8283, Part IV, Donee Acknowledgement . . . . . | 29 | |

Questions 30a and b follow with questions about whether the donor restricted contributed property with a provision that it be held for three years. If the property is restricted by the donor from being sold for three years, and the restriction does not also include a restriction that the property must be used for an exempt purpose, the terms of the gift must be explained in Part II. Note that dispositions of noncash contributions that were subject to a Form 8283 filing must be noticed by the donee organization to the IRS using Form 8282 (to disclose the proceeds from the disposed-of property).

			Yes	No
30a	During the year, did the organization receive by contribution any property reported in Part I, lines 1–28 that it must hold for at least three years from the date of the initial contribution, and which is not required to be used for exempt purposes for the entire holding period?	30a		
b	If "Yes," describe the arrangement in Part II.			

Questions 31 and 32 ask additional questions about policies the filing organization has regarding gift acceptance and require those policies (if in place) to be described in Part II.

31	Does the organization have a gift acceptance policy that requires the review of any non-standard contributions?	31		
32a	Does the organization hire or use third parties or related organizations to solicit, process, or sell noncash contributions?	32a		
b	If "Yes," describe in Part II.			

Question 33 provides a reminder of additional disclosures required in Part II related to Part I.

33	If the organization did not report an amount in column (c) for a type of property for which column (a) is checked, describe in Part II.			

Part II of Schedule M consists of blank lines provided for filers to make additional disclosures related only to Schedule M. These may include anything, but the header to Part II and instructions specifically request the following language:

Schedule M (Form 990) (2013)	Page 2
Part II **Supplemental Information.** Provide the information required by Part I, lines 30b, 32b, and 33, and whether the organization is reporting in Part I, column (b), the number of contributions, the number of items received, or a combination of both. Also complete this part for any additional information.	

KNOWLEDGE CHECK

5. Which statement accurately reflects what is required to be disclosed on Schedule M to satisfy the reporting requirement with respect to receipt of noncash contributions?

    a. In the case of donations of stock or securities, only stock or securities that are not immediately converted to cash upon receipt (for example, under instructions to one's broker requiring immediate sale of stock or securities when transferred in) must be disclosed as noncash contributions and reported on Schedule M.

    b. The number of items received, rather than the number of donations, of a specific type of noncash item separately reported upon Schedule M must be disclosed on each line.

    c. The total value of contributions reported on Core Form Part VIII, Line 1g is to be reflected in reporting amounts on Schedule M.

    d. Separate fair market value enunciation of the value of art, historical treasures and other similar items need be disclosed, regardless of whether the organization follows FASB ASC 958-360-25 or whether income was reported in line with such amounts on Core Form Part VIII.

BACK TO PART VIII'S LINE 8 AND THE CORRESPONDING REPORTING ALMOST ALWAYS REQUIRED AT SCHEDULE G, PART II

Schedule G's Part II details result from special events or activities income. The current Forms 990 and 990-EZ refer to same as fundraising events. The 990 glossary details that term as comprising the following:

> Dinners and dances, door-to-door sales of merchandise, concerts, carnivals, sports events, auctions, casino nights (in which participants can play casino-style games but the only prizes or auction items provided to participants are noncash items that were donated to the organization), and similar events not regularly carried on that are conducted for the primary purpose of raising funds. Fundraising events do not include the following:
>
> 1. The conduct of a trade or business that is regularly carried on
> 2. Activities substantially related to the accomplishment of the organization's exempt purpose (other than by raising funds)
> 3. Solicitation campaigns that generate only contributions, which may involve gifts of goods or services from the organization of only nominal value, or sweepstakes, lotteries, or raffles in which the names of contributors or other respondents are entered in a drawing for prizes of only nominal value
> 4. Gaming

The reporting accomplished on Schedule G's Part II had long been required to be provided by attachment to the pre-redesigned Form 990 (the version in place through tax years started in 2007). Unfortunately, what was required by that attachment was not well-understood and what filers provided typically failed to comply with the instructions' requirements. The reaction from the IRS, evidenced on the current Form, was to enforce standardization in such reporting upon Schedule G-II.

The format requires virtually all filers to make appropriate disclosure of what these events and activities generate in dollars, in line with the same mandates the text has earlier described for Core Form Part VIII Lines 8 and 1(c) reporting. That is, some portion of the dollars captured reflect fair market value *exchange* amounts, and the balance above such amounts (if any) comprises a true gift amount. It cannot be overemphasized that no gift amount exists until the payer makes a payment exceeding the fair market value (glossary definition is reprinted in following text box) of items or services they receive back. Furthermore, regardless of whether any such excess payments are captured, Form 990 at both Core Form Part VIII, Line 8b and on Schedule G-II requires reporting the direct expenses paid or incurred associated with such exchanges.

Fair Market Value (FMV)	The price at which property, or the right to use property, would change hands between a willing buyer and a willing seller, neither being under any compulsion to buy, sell, or transfer property or the right to use property, and both having reasonable knowledge of relevant facts.

The trigger question by which Schedule G's Part II is invoked ties to the gross amounts received from the conduct of fundraising events and sales; the Core Form Part IV trigger question sets out that gross receipts of greater than $15,000 is the trigger.

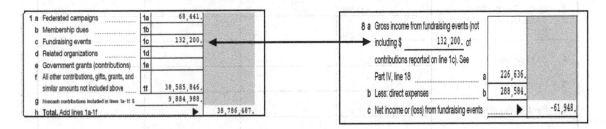

| 18 | Did the organization report more than $15,000 total of fundraising event gross income and contributions on Part VIII, lines 1c and 8a? If "Yes," complete Schedule G, Part II . . . . | 18 | ✓ | |

The reporting accomplished at the first line of Line 8 (8a plus its parenthetical memo'd amount of gifts) reflects the amounts of gross income from fundraising events, the subject of the trigger question for G-II. That trigger question highlights that Line 8a's parenthetical amount (a memo entry there) corresponds to Line 1c—a result evidenced in the following example:

1 a	Federated campaigns	1a	68,441			8 a	Gross income from fundraising events (not		
b	Membership dues	1b					including $ 132,200. of		
c	Fundraising events	1c	132,200				contributions reported on line 1c). See		
d	Related organizations	1d					Part IV, line 18	a	226,636
e	Government grants (contributions)	1e				b	Less: direct expenses	b	288,584
f	All other contributions, gifts, grants, and similar amounts not included above	1f	38,585,846			c	Net income or (loss) from fundraising events	▶	-61,948
g	Noncash contributions included in lines 1a-1f: $		9,884,988						
h	Total. Add lines 1a-1f		▶	38,786,487					

In this example, the exchange portion of goods or services sold at fundraising events totaled $226,636, while contributions achieved in the course of exchanging those goods or services totaled $132,200, for total gross receipts of $358,838. (Note: Although the events' direct expenses of $228,584 exceeded the $226,636 sales results by $61,948, that loss is less than the $132,000 of contributions brought in in the course of achieving those sales, so actually the event's true result yields a monetary gain.)

The function of Schedule G-II is to provide a look behind Line 8a (including its memo parenthetical), as well as Lines 8b and 8c, allowing us to see what is behind those totals with respect to all the year's fundraising events that brought in $5k or more.

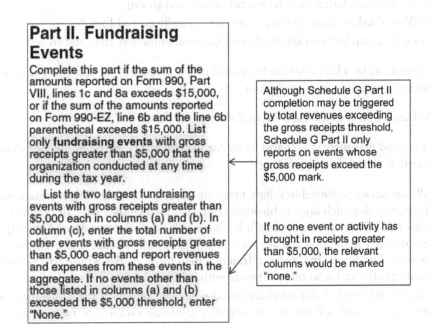

Part II. Fundraising Events

Complete this part if the sum of the amounts reported on Form 990, Part VIII, lines 1c and 8a exceeds $15,000, or if the sum of the amounts reported on Form 990-EZ, line 6b and the line 6b parenthetical exceeds $15,000. List only **fundraising events** with gross receipts greater than $5,000 that the organization conducted at any time during the tax year.

List the two largest fundraising events with gross receipts greater than $5,000 each in columns (a) and (b). In column (c), enter the total number of other events with gross receipts greater than $5,000 each and report revenues and expenses from these events in the aggregate. If no events other than those listed in columns (a) and (b) exceeded the $5,000 threshold, enter "None."

Although Schedule G Part II completion may be triggered by total revenues exceeding the gross receipts threshold, Schedule G Part II only reports on events whose gross receipts exceed the $5,000 mark.

If no one event or activity has brought in receipts greater than $5,000, the relevant columns would be marked "none."

Schedule G-II requires reporting of detail on revenue capture and expenses for

- The two largest events where total receipts (including gifts) exceeded $5,000; and
- In the aggregate, all other events where total receipts (including gifts) exceeded $5,000.

Note: Because events with total receipts of $5,000 or less do not need be reported on this Part, G-II's total numbers may not tie to the totals on Core Form Line 8c.

		(a) Event #1 Sky School Auction (event type)	(b) Event #2 _____ (event type)	(c) Other events None (total number)	(d) Total events (add col. (a) through col. (c))
1	Gross receipts	358,836.			358,836.
2	Less: Contributions . .	132,200.			132,200.
3	Gross income (line 1 minus line 2)	226,636.			226,636.
4	Cash prizes				
5	Noncash prizes . . .				
6	Rent/facility costs . . .	7,154.			7,154.
7	Food and beverages . .	10,200.			10,200.
8	Entertainment				
9	Other direct expenses .	271,230.			271,230.
10	Direct expense summary. Add lines 4 through 9 in column (d) . . . . ▶				288,584.
11	Net income summary. Subtract line 10 from line 3, column (d) . . . . ▶				-61,948.

Overall results per event can be calculated:

- Line 3 Gross Income from sales less the contributed revenue reflects FMV assigned by the organization to items purchased (tickets, auction items, and so on)
- With that FMV established; Line 10 direct expenses typically exceed Line 3
- Remember Line 10 often includes donated items (auction items, catering, and so on)

Although there appears to be a loss (that has happened in the preceding situation) in reality there was not when you take into account the related donations.

Doing the math (Line 3 minus Lines 4–9), we find the loss of almost $62,000.

It should be emphasized that there is no harm or shame in such losses, either by any one event or by all events here reported, for the following reasons:

- Filers typically are not experienced in selling meals or candy or any other items commercially, and are unlikely to be conducting such sales in business contexts in which they have the ability to maximize profit potential (for example, what for-profit business sells items door to door? Similarly, charity auctions are not widely publicized and are subject to vagaries of audience and even that evening's weather.) Overall, charities are motivated differently than those parties whose sole rationale for such sales is to realize profits and who must compete with others who are similarly inclined.
- Magnitude of gifts achieved (dollar-wise) and good-will enhancement is the actual measure of the charity event's success (and as illustrated in preceding common sample, for many or most events the

payments in excess of FMV for items procured by buyers [equivalent to gifts] will well exceed the loss amount).

- Some sales (for example, goods at silent auction) are necessary to the conversion (to cash) of what was solicited. The real value (to the charity) of acquiring such goods in the first place is their ability to yield cash and entice people to the fundraising event. In such scenarios, the charity achieves cash from buyers urging them to pay at least (and hopefully more than) fair market value. The authors believe the GAAP-rule write down of such contributed goods' value to the dollars achieved at their sale is a distortion of fair market value and is not countenanced by 990 reporting rules.

Note that the breakout of Direct Expenses in Schedule G-II (which are otherwise noted on the Core Form's Part VIII, Line 8b) is more detailed than that reflected upon the Core Form, as evidenced by the instructions for that Schedule:

Direct Expenses	Line 8.
Enter the expense amount in the appropriate column (a through c) for events with gross receipts greater than $5,000 each. Enter the total of columns (a), (b), and (c) in column (d).	**Line 8.** Enter the expenses paid or incurred for entertainment, including direct expenses for labor and wages.
Line 4. Enter the total amount paid out as cash prizes.	**Line 9.** Enter the amount of other direct expense items not included in Part II, lines 4 through 8. The organization should retain in its records an itemized list of all other direct expenses not included on lines 4 through 8. For labor costs and wages, include the total amount of compensation paid to **fundraising event** workers or paid independent contractors for labor costs.
Line 5. Enter the **fair market value** of the noncash prizes paid or given out for each **fundraising event**.	
Line 6. Enter the expenses paid or incurred for the rent or lease of property or facilities.	
Line 7. Enter the expenses paid or incurred for food and beverages. Include all direct expenses such as catering.	**Line 10.** Add lines 4 through 9 in column (d).

Glossary term review:

Fair market value (FMV)	The price at which property, or the right to use property, would change hands between a willing buyer and a willing seller, neither being under any compulsion to buy, sell, or transfer property or the right to use property, and both having reasonable knowledge of relevant facts.

Additional Compliance Check on Part V Associated with Fundraising in *Quid Pro Quo*[3] Contexts

7	Organizations that may receive deductible contributions under section 170(c).			
a	Did the organization receive a payment in excess of $75 made partly as a contribution and partly for goods and services provided to the payor?	7a	X	
b	If "Yes," did the organization notify the donor of the value of the goods or services provided?	7b	X	

Line 7. Line 7 is directed only to organizations that can receive deductible charitable **contributions** under section 170(c). See Pub. 526, Charitable Contributions, for a description of such organizations. All other organizations should leave lines 7a through 7h blank and go to line 8.

Lines 7a and 7b. If a donor makes a payment in excess of $75 partly as a contribution and partly in consideration for goods or services provided by the organization, the organization generally must notify the donor of the value of goods and services provided.

Example. A donor gives a charity $100 in consideration for a concert ticket valued at $40 (a quid pro quo **contribution**). In this example, $60 would be deductible. Because the donor's payment exceeds $75, the organization must furnish a disclosure statement even though the taxpayer's deductible amount does not exceed $75. Separate payments of $75 or less made at different times of the year for separate fundraising events will not be aggregated for purposes of the $75 threshold.

If an organization completes Schedules G-II and Core Form Part VIII, Line 8 fundraising activities reflecting capture of amounts bifurcated between contributions and fair market value purchases, Part V line 7 needs completion. The tax compliance inquiry here relates to Sections 6115 and 6714, the latter imposes a $10 per contribution penalty, capped at $5,000 per fundraising event or sales activity, for failure to provide appropriate ***quid pro quo*** donor acknowledgment letters.

Knowledge Check

6. A fundraising event conducted by charity AJ charges a $30 entry fee, and each attendee receives a catered dinner that AJ pays for at $18 per plate (this is non-discounted cost from the caterer's normal commercial price). Based on these facts, which is a correct statement?

   a. No *quid pro quo* donor acknowledgment letter will be required because the entry fee does not exceed $75.

   b. No *quid pro quo* donor acknowledgment letter will be required unless a party buys one or two tickets and the total fee here ($30 or $60, respectively) plus the party's other payments for AJ's fundraiser events/sales in the year exceed $45 or $15, respectively.

   c. A *quid pro quo* donor acknowledgment letter will be required for any payer who buys three or more tickets unless right to the dinner meals are renounced, because at that point a payment of greater than $75 will have been made.

   d. A *quid pro quo* donor acknowledgment letter will be required for any payer who buys five or more tickets and has not renounced rights to the dinner meals, because at that point a payment for goods or services of greater than $75 (5 x $18 = $90) will have been made.

---

[3] The text earlier, in addressing proper completion of Part VIII, line 1c versus 8a, noted via a warning the reach of the *quid pro quo* rules which have exceptions for certain *de minimis* provision of goods or services.

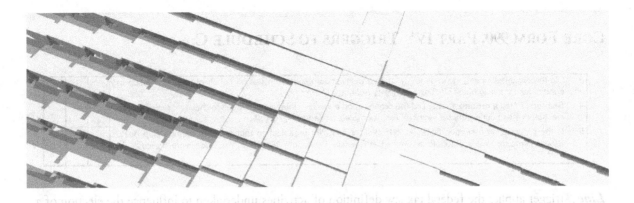

Chapter 5

PUBLIC POLICY, POLITICAL ACTIVITY, AND LOBBYING DISCLOSURES ON SCHEDULE C

LEARNING OBJECTIVES

After completing this chapter, you should be able to do the following:

- Differentiate the reporting obligations of 501(c)(3) organizations as they relate to whether the filer has made the 501(h) election or not
- Recognize that reporting of all political campaign activity expenses is required of 501(c) entities, regardless of whether their conduct is in accord with tax-exemption or other federal, state, or local law.
- Evaluate the application of IRC Section 6033(e) proxy tax and notice and reporting requirements as rules that apply a tax if a subject organization chooses to not issue notices to members of the nondeductible portion of their dues payments.

CORE FORM 990, PART IV'S TRIGGERS TO SCHEDULE C:

3	Did the organization engage in direct or indirect political campaign activities on behalf of or in opposition to candidates for public office? *If "Yes," complete Schedule C, Part I*	**3**		
4	**Section 501(c)(3) organizations.** Did the organization engage in lobbying activities, or have a section 501(h) election in effect during the tax year? *If "Yes," complete Schedule C, Part II*	**4**		
5	Is the organization a section 501(c)(4), 501(c)(5), or 501(c)(6) organization that receives membership dues, assessments, or similar amounts as defined in Revenue Procedure 98-19? *If "Yes," complete Schedule C, Part III*	**5**		

Line 3 trigger applies the federal tax law definition of activities undertaken to influence the election of a candidate for elective public office or for selecting the officers of a political party. Such efforts are those set out in IRC Section 527, and although 501(c)(3)s have an electioneering proscription that forbids their participation in such activities, the reach and direction of this inquiry goes beyond interpreting that proscription. Many non-501(c)(3) exempt organizations will be reached by this trigger.

> A "Yes" answer to Part IV's Line 3 yields the need for any 501(c) exempt organization or 527 political organization to, at Schedule C-I[1], narrate its political campaign activities, make certain expenditure disclosures, and state the number of volunteer hours undertaken to such ends.

Tip: Regardless that these types of activities are impermissible to 501(c)(3) organizations, Schedule C-I applies if a filer has engaged in these activities.

Line 4 trigger is specific solely to 501(c)(3) entities. It invokes the mandate that (c)(3)s report on their lobbying efforts, a term that relates solely to attempts to influence the passage of legislation (on any level). Such efforts are permissible to (c)(3)s if they are not substantial. Completion of Schedule C-II is required by filers who either

- have in the reporting year conducted any lobbying efforts (including ones at no cost other than volunteered time) if they are not covered by the 501(h) election; or
- have the 501(h) election in effect during the reporting year, regardless of whether they have expended any dollars on lobbying efforts as same are measured under Section 501(h).

Line 5 trigger is specific solely to 501(c)(4), (5), or (6) organizations. It is there to assure that membership-benefit organizations, exempt under any of these three noted 501(c)-subsections, properly calculate potential liability from revenues paid by their dues-paying members under the Section 6033(e) proxy tax. Self-assessment of this tax (or the fact of circumstances leading to the filer's exception from that tax) is accomplished by completion of Schedule C-III.

---

[1] Schedule letter followed by Roman numeral is a reference to that schedule's PART.

COMPLETION OF SCHEDULE C, PART II

As the most common application of Schedule C applies to 501(c)(3) organizations' reporting on their lobbying efforts, we address that part first. Here, the purpose of reporting is to enforce compliance by 501(c)(3) organizations with the Section limitation on such efforts:

> (c)(3)s other than those classified as private foundations may undertake activities to influence legislation (that is, promoting or opposing the adoption of laws on any level—federal, state, local, international), but such activities must not be a substantial part of their activities overall.

Because of this limit, Part II of Schedule C requires (c)(3)s to make specified disclosure on their conduct of lobbying activities.

The Section's "no substantial part" language by which lobbying is limited for 501(c)(3) organizations will apply to a filer in one of two ways, as filers are either

- under the so-called "no substantial part" test (which is both broadly defined and purely subjective to each taxpayer's facts); or
- under the expenditure-based limits (and excise tax penalties) set out in Section 501(h)—but these only apply to a taxpayer who has elected that code's provisions by filing of Form 5768.

SCHEDULE C, PART II-A

Schedule C, Part II-A is completed by filers who have elected to be covered by 501(h)'s provisions.

Per the Schedule C instructions:

> Part II-A provides a reporting format for any Section 501(c)(3) organization for which the 501(h) lobbying expenditure election was valid and in effect during the [201X] tax year, whether or not the organization engaged in **lobbying activities** during the tax year. A public charity that makes a valid 501(h) election may spend up to a certain percentage of its exempt purpose expenditures to influence **legislation** without incurring tax or losing its tax exempt status.
>
> Pertinent glossary definitions (in bold) are reprinted here.

> **Lobbying activities**—All activities intended to influence foreign, national, state, or local **legislation**. Such activities include direct lobbying (attempting to influence the legislators) and grassroots lobbying (attempting to influence legislation by influencing the general public.

> **Legislation**—Includes action by Congress, any state legislature, any local council, or similar governing body about acts, bills, resolutions, or similar items, or action by the public in referenda, ballot initiatives, constitutional amendments or similar procedures. It does not include actions by executive, judicial, or administrative bodies.

The standard set out for organizations under 501(h) applies an expenditure test whereby the filer measures its permissible lobbying solely on the basis of its expenses (the Schedule C instructions start with a "Definitions" section in which Part II's terms are provided). The several benefits of the 501(h) election are

- known punishment for exceeding the lobbying limits (chiefly a 25 percent excise tax on amounts expended above the lobbying limits calculated each year); and
- known definitions as to what constitutes instances of lobbying and how to calculate costs of such efforts; and no requirement to narrate activities.

The only disclosure each year is tabbed to the dollars expended as grass roots lobbying or (overall) lobbying.

Note: Part II-A is completed for every year in which the organization has the h-election in place regardless of whether any expenditures were made.

Lines 1a and Line 1b require entry of the specific dollar amounts that the filer spent on grass roots lobbying (Line 1a) and direct lobbying (Line 1b). Both categories apply the 501(h) definitions set out via Regulations under Section 4911 set out in Schedule C's "Definitions" section). *Line 1c* totals those lines.

Line 1d reports all other exempt purpose expenditures made during the year, including all of the organization's non-lobbying expenditures except those associated with the filer's separate fundraising unit, non-employee fundraising counsel, capital expenses, and expenses to pay unrelated business income tax or to produce income not substantially related to its exempt purpose. *Line 1e* totals Lines 1c and 1d, and is the result by which the 501(h)'s lobbying limit(s) for the year will be measured.

The table at 1f is applied to the 1e amount to determine the filer's (for the reporting year) overall lobbying limit (at 1f) and then (by multiplying that limit by ¼) the filer's grassroots limit (at 1g). Actual total lobbying expenditures for the year (1c) are compared to 1f's overall limit at 1i; actual grassroots lobbying expenditures for the year (1a) are compared to 1g's grassroots limit at 1h. If an excess amount for the year resulted (amounts on 1i or 1h), excise tax is due, and 1j accordingly asks if the organization filed the Form 4720 to self-assess such tax.

Part II-A	Complete if the organization is exempt under section 501(c)(3) and filed Form 5768 (election under section 501(h)).		
A	Check ▶ ☐ if the filing organization belongs to an affiliated group (and list in Part IV each affiliated group member's name, address, EIN, expenses, and share of excess lobbying expenditures).		
B	Check ▶ ☐ if the filing organization checked box A and "limited control" provisions apply.		
	Limits on Lobbying Expenditures (The term "expenditures" means amounts paid or incurred.)	(a) Filing organization's totals	(b) Affiliated group totals
1a	Total lobbying expenditures to influence public opinion (grass roots lobbying)		
b	Total lobbying expenditures to influence a legislative body (direct lobbying)		
c	Total lobbying expenditures (add lines 1a and 1b)		
d	Other exempt purpose expenditures		
e	Total exempt purpose expenditures (add lines 1c and 1d)		
f	Lobbying nontaxable amount. Enter the amount from the following table in both columns.		

If the amount on line 1e, column (a) or (b) is:	The lobbying nontaxable amount is:		
Not over $500,000	20% of the amount on line 1e.		
Over $500,000 but not over $1,000,000	$100,000 plus 15% of the excess over $500,000.		
Over $1,000,000 but not over $1,500,000	$175,000 plus 10% of the excess over $1,000,000.		
Over $1,500,000 but not over $17,000,000	$225,000 plus 5% of the excess over $1,500,000.		
Over $17,000,000	$1,000,000.		

		(a)	(b)
g	Grassroots nontaxable amount (enter 25% of line 1f)		
h	Subtract line 1g from line 1a. If zero or less, enter -0-		
i	Subtract line 1f from line 1c. If zero or less, enter -0-		
j	If there is an amount other than zero on either line 1h or line 1i, did the organization file Form 4720 reporting section 4911 tax for this year? . . . . ☐ Yes ☐ No		

Part II-A concludes with a four year grid that reflects both the reporting year's expenditures and those entered on the filer's three prior tax years:

4-Year Averaging Period Under section 501(h) (Some organizations that made a section 501(h) election do not have to complete all of the five columns below. See the separate instructions for lines 2a through 2f.)					
Lobbying Expenditures During 4-Year Averaging Period					
Calendar year (or fiscal year beginning in)	(a) 2013	(b) 2014	(c) 2015	(d) 2016	(e) Total
2a Lobbying nontaxable amount					
b Lobbying ceiling amount (150% of line 2a, column (e))					
c Total lobbying expenditures					
d Grassroots nontaxable amount					
e Grassroots ceiling amount (150% of line 2d, column (e))					
f Grassroots lobbying expenditures					

This 2 grid schedule requires the filer to make the cited inputs which then are the basis of a four year calculation to determine if the filer (although subject to excise tax on any one year's over-run of lobbying limits) has overall exceeded the threshold by which lobbying is considered to comprise a substantial part of the filer's operations per Section 501(h). That statute mandates a result of automatic revocation of 501(c)(3) if across the four year averaging period a filer expends a dollar over 150 percent of their permitted amounts.

KNOWLEDGE CHECK

1. The filer made the 501(h) election in a prior tax year and has not revoked it. In the reporting year, the only possible expenditures for lobbying is $100,000 advanced by the filer to cover expenses of sending its representatives to a meeting of legislators to strategize their intended moving forward with legislation supported by the filer. Which properly reports the filer's obligation to complete Part II-A in each situation:

– the meeting goes ahead	– the meeting is cancelled and $100,000 refunded
a. Completion is required	Completion is not required
b. Completion is not required	Completion is not required
c. Completion is required	Completion is required
d. Not enough facts to know	

SCHEDULE C, PART II-B

Schedule C, Part II-B is completed by all 501 (c)(3)'s who do not have a valid 501(h) election in place for the tax year and have engaged in lobbying activities during the tax year. This part requires filers to provide information here by which the extent to which their lobbying falls within the "no substantial part" limitation can be evaluated. However, no clear legal parameters exist for such limit. There is no clear definition of what types of undertakings even comprise lobbying activities here (and the regulations state that the mere endorsement of a bill counts as lobbying activity). The instructions provide a note to this effect:

> **Note:** A non-electing organization will generally be regarded as engaging in lobbying activity if the organization either contacts, or urges the public to contact, members of a legislative body for the purpose of proposing, supporting, or opposing legislation or the government's budget process; or advocates the adoption or rejection of legislation.

Filers must report detailed description of any activities the organization engaged in (including through its volunteers) to influence legislation. That detail goes in Part IV's blank lines.

Part II-B	Complete if the organization is exempt under section 501(c)(3) and has NOT filed Form 5768 (election under section 501(h)).			
		(a)		(b)
For each "Yes," response to lines 1a through 1i below, provide in Part IV a detailed description of the lobbying activity.		Yes	No	Amount
1	During the year, did the filing organization attempt to influence foreign, national, state or local legislation, including any attempt to influence public opinion on a legislative matter or referendum, through the use of:			
a	Volunteers?			
b	Paid staff or management (include compensation in expenses reported on lines 1c through 1i)?			
c	Media advertisements?			
d	Mailings to members, legislators, or the public?			
e	Publications, or published or broadcast statements?			
f	Grants to other organizations for lobbying purposes?			
g	Direct contact with legislators, their staffs, government officials, or a legislative body?			
h	Rallies, demonstrations, seminars, conventions, speeches, lectures, or any similar means?			
i	Other activities?			
j	Total. Add lines 1c through 1i			
2a	Did the activities in line 1 cause the organization to be not described in section 501(c)(3)?			
b	If "Yes," enter the amount of any tax incurred under section 4912			
c	If "Yes," enter the amount of any tax incurred by organization managers under section 4912			
d	If the filing organization incurred a section 4912 tax, did it file Form 4720 for this year?			

> *Although all lobbying activities are to be detailed, care should be applied to ensure that the involvement of volunteers versus paid staff or management, and also in listing what comprises other activities, is noted as all such efforts will factor into the determination of whether lobbying arises to a substantial part.*

Completion of Line 1. Per the instructions:

> Organizations should answer "Yes" or "No" in Column (a) as to questions 1a through 1i **and provide in** *Part IV* **a detailed description of any activities the organization engaged in** (through employees or volunteers) to influence legislation. **The description should include all lobbying activities, whether expenses were incurred or not.** *Bold added for emphasis.*

The instructions then give these examples:

- Sending letters or publications to government officials or legislators,
- Meeting with or calling government officials or legislators,
- Sending or distributing letters or publications (including newsletters, brochures, and so on) to members or to the general public, or
- Using direct mail, placing advertisements, issuing press releases, holding news conferences, or holding rallies or demonstrations.

Note: The examples given previously only detail the activity, so presumably if one checked Lines 1c (media advertisements), 1d (mailings to members, legislators or the public), 1e (publications, or published or broadcast statements) and 1h (rallies, demonstrations, and so on), the description provided in the last bullet point would suffice.

Lines 1a/ b asks if activities are conducted with volunteers or paid staff, respectively.

Lines 1c thru 1h represent canned categories of reporting on specific activities undertaken for influencing legislation—for each the filer must reflect total expenditures. Activities not fitting into any of those lines' categories are denoted on Line 1i (and expense totals for those entered as well)—note that a "Yes" checkmark on each line should be incorporated into the required detailed description of all lobbying activities to be reported in Part IV.

Line 2a asks the filer (to self-assess or note that IRS ruled?) that its activities for influencing legislation were substantial and caused the organization to be not described in Section 501(c)(3). Any "Yes" answer there also requires organization to note excise tax liability result (to date) for both the organization and its managers on Lines 2b and 2c, and denote if it reported for the year its liability for excise tax via Form 4720 filing.

KNOWLEDGE CHECK

2. Which reporting disclosure is required of filers who have no 501(h) election in effect for a filing year but who conducted lobbying activities in the year and must report in Schedule C, Part II-B?

    1. Fact that board members participate in conduct of lobbying
    2. Types of activities undertaken
    3. Dollars expended on activities (by line)
    4. Dollars expended on activities (only to extent same is funded through donations)

        a. 2-3
        b. 1-3
        c. 2 and 4
        d. All

COMPLETION OF SCHEDULE C, PART I

All 501(c) organizations (and 527 organizations, whose filing responsibilities are otherwise not addressed in this course) complete Part I-A:

Part I-A	Complete if the organization is exempt under section 501(c) or is a section 527 organization.
1	Provide a description of the organization's direct and indirect political campaign activities in Part IV. (see instructions for definition of "political campaign activities")
2	Political campaign activity expenditures (see instructions) . . . . ▶ $ _____
3	Volunteer hours for political campaign activities (see instructions) . . . . ▶

Note: Requirement for Part IV description of political campaign activities and the number of volunteer hours.

As to the reporting by 501(c) organizations who have established Section 527(f)(3) separate segregated funds to engage in political activity, the instructions note that the separate segregated fund has its own filing responsibility, BUT also note that transfers to the fund by the 501(c) are to be reported in Parts I-A and I-C. However, if the 501(c) collects political contributions or member dues earmarked for a separate segregated fund, and promptly and directly transfers them to that fund as prescribed in Regulations Section 1.527-6(e), do not report them here [but instead] in Part I-C, Line 5e.

Key to Part I-A's Line 1 is the glossary definition of political campaign activities:

> All activities that support or oppose candidates for elective federal, state, or local public office. It does not matter whether the candidate is elected. A candidate is one who offers himself or is proposed by others for public office. Political campaign activity does not include any activity to encourage participation in the electoral process, such as voter registration or voter education, provided that the activity does not directly or indirectly support or oppose any candidate.

The overall Schedule C instructions define political expenditures (the subject of Part I-A's Line 2):

> Any expenditures made for political campaign activities [glossary term, previously defined] are political expenditures. An expenditure includes a payment, distribution, loan, advance, deposit, or gift of money, or anything of value. It also includes a contract, promise, or agreement to make an expenditure, whether or not legally enforceable.

501(c)(3) organizations ALSO complete Part I-B:

Part I-B is additionally completed by (c)(3) filers to report the fact that their conduct of political activities has violated the absolute proscription against such involvement that is a condition of their Section 501(c)(3) exemption. Excise tax liability may attach to both the organization and to managers of the organization when this proscription is violated; for public charities there is a penalty excise tax set out in Section 4955 (reported upon Form 4720), and it is that subject which drives Lines 3 and 4. Violation of this prohibition may cause denial or revocation of tax-exempt status, and correction (to be detailed on Part IV) may preserve the right to exemption.

Part I-B	Complete if the organization is exempt under section 501(c)(3).		
1	Enter the amount of any excise tax incurred by the organization under section 4955 . . . . ▶ $		
2	Enter the amount of any excise tax incurred by organization managers under section 4955 . . ▶ $		
3	If the organization incurred a section 4955 tax, did it file Form 4720 for this year?	☐ Yes	☐ No
4a	Was a correction made?	☐ Yes	☐ No
b	If "Yes," describe in Part IV.		

Non-501(c)(3) organizations ALSO complete Part I-C:

Part I-C	Complete if the organization is exempt under section 501(c), except section 501(c)(3).

1 Enter the amount directly expended by the filing organization for section 527 exempt function activities . . . . ▶ $ _____

2 Enter the amount of the filing organization's funds contributed to other organizations for section 527 exempt function activities . . . . ▶ $ _____

3 Total exempt function expenditures. Add lines 1 and 2. Enter here and on Form 1120-POL, line 17b . . . . ▶ $ _____

4 Did the filing organization file **Form 1120-POL** for this year? . . . . ☐ Yes ☐ No

5 Enter the names, addresses and employer identification number (EIN) of all section 527 political organizations to which the filing organization made payments. For each organization listed, enter the amount paid from the filing organization's funds. Also enter the amount of political contributions received that were promptly and directly delivered to a separate political organization, such as a separate segregated fund or a political action committee (PAC). If additional space is needed, provide information in Part IV.

(a) Name	(b) Address	(c) EIN	(d) Amount paid from filing organization's funds. If none, enter -0-.	(e) Amount of political contributions received and promptly and directly delivered to a separate political organization. If none, enter -0-.
(1)				
(2)				

Lines 1-4 are directed to Section 527 exempt function activities. These are set out in the statutory framework relating to 527 political organizations and on the tax imposed under 527(f) on 501(c) entities conducting exempt functions. The overall Schedule C instructions define such activities:

Section 527 exempt function activities include all functions that influence or attempt to influence the selection, nomination, election, or appointment of any individual to any federal, state, or local public office or office in a political organization, or the election of Presidential or Vice-Presidential electors, whether or not such individual or electors are selected, nominated, elected, or appointed.

Note that Line 1 refers to direct expenditures, and Line 2 refers to contributions to other organizations. When such other organization is a 527 organization, further information on the donee will be required on Line 5.

Line 5 Practice tip: As noted earlier, filers are directed, if they collect political contributions or member dues earmarked for a separate segregated fund, and promptly and directly transfers them to that fund as prescribed in Regulations Section 1.527-6(e) to report them at this line's Column (e).

Line 4 relates to the filing required of 501(c) organizations to report liability for Section 527(f) tax on expenditures for 527-exempt function activities. That tax vests on taxable income, defined as follows:

Per the Form 1120 instructions, *Taxable income** for an exempt organization described in Section 501(c) that is not a political organization is the smaller of:

1. The net investment income of the organization for the tax year, or
2. The amount spent for an exempt function during the tax year either directly or indirectly through another organization.

Net investment income, for this purpose, is the excess of:

1. The gross amount of interest, dividends, rents, and royalties, plus the excess, if any, of gains from the sale or exchange of assets, over the losses from the sale or exchange of assets, over
2. The deductions directly connected with the production of this income.

* *Taxable income* is figured with these three adjustments:

- A specific deduction of $100 is allowed (but not for newsletter funds),
- The net operating loss deduction is not allowed, and
- The dividends-received deduction for corporations is not allowed

KNOWLEDGE CHECK

3. A 501(c)(4) filer made multiple contributions to various candidate PACs related to upcoming state office races. After the tax year was over, it was discovered that the amounts contributed exceeded the per-recipient maximum per state law, and some recipients will be returning the overage. How should the filer report in Parts I-A, Line 2 and I-C, Lines 2 and 5 in such circumstances?

   a. Report the actual amount contributed during the tax year in both parts.
   b. Report the actual amount contributed during the tax year in Part I-A, but show only the permitted amount in Part I-C.
   c. Report only the permitted amount of the contribution in both parts.
   d. Report the actual amount contributed during the tax year in both parts' Line 2, but only show the permitted amount in Part I-C, Line 5.

COMPLETION OF SCHEDULE C, PART III

This part is where specified members organizations, if they hold exemption under 501(c)(4), (5) or (6), report their compliance with notice and reporting requirements regarding their capture of revenues from dues-paying members under the Section 6033(e) proxy tax. The tax prevents members from computing their taxable income with deductions for dues paid that may go to lobbying and political expenditures.

Self-assessment of this tax (or the fact of circumstances leading to the filer's exception from that tax) is accomplished by its Parts III-B and III-A, respectively.

Section 6033(e) requires certain 501(c)(4), (5), and (6) organizations to tell their members what portion of their membership dues were allocable to the political or lobbying activities of the organization. If an organization does not give its members this information, then the organization is subject to a proxy tax. This tax is reported on Form 990-T.

Part III-A Testing for Exception from Proxy Tax

Part III-A	Complete if the organization is exempt under section 501(c)(4), section 501(c)(5), or section 501(c)(6).		Yes	No
1	Were substantially all (90% or more) dues received nondeductible by members?	1		
2	Did the organization make only in-house lobbying expenditures of $2,000 or less?	2		
3	Did the organization agree to carry over lobbying and political campaign activity expenditures from the prior year?	3		

The 6033(e) tax does not apply if either Lines 1 or 2 are "Yes." (Line 3 is a survey question that relates to completion of Part III-B; discussion of the terms in this line is taken up there.)

Line 1. Are 90 percent or more of members' dues nondeductible (by the members) in computing their taxable income? The instructions set out seven situations by which entities are considered to have 90 percent or more of members' dues nondeductible as follows, note one correction at 4.c:

1. Local associations of employees' and veterans' organizations described in section 501(c)(4), but not section 501(c)(4) social welfare organizations.

2. Labor unions and other labor organizations described in section 501(c)(5), but not section 501(c)(5) agricultural and horticultural organizations.

3. Section 501(c)(4), section 501(c)(5), and section 501(c)(6) organizations that receive more than 90% of their dues from:

a. Organizations exempt from tax under section 501(a), other than section 501(c)(4), section 501(c)(5), and section 501(c)(6) organizations,

b. State or local governments,

c. Entities whose income is excluded from gross income under section 115, or

d. Organizations described in 1 or 2, above.

4. Section 501(c)(4) and section 501(c)(5) organizations that receive more than 90% of their annual dues from:

a. Persons

b. State or local governments,

c. Entities whose income is excluded from gross income under section 115, or

d. Organizations described in 1 or 2, earlier.

4. Section 501(c)(4) and section 501(c)(5) organizations that receive more than 90% (0.9) of their annual dues from:

a. Persons,

b. Families, or   [4c. has TYPO -- correct amt is: $111]

c. Entities, who each paid annual dues of $160 or less in 2015 (adjusted annually for inflation). See Rev. Proc. 2014-61, 2014-47 IRB 860, section 3.38 at *http://www.irs.gov/irb/2014-47 IRB/ index.html* (or latest annual update).

5. Any organization that receives a private letter ruling from the IRS stating that the organization satisfies the section 6033(e)(3) exception.

6. Any organization that keeps records to substantiate that 90% (0.9) or more of its members cannot deduct their dues (or similar amounts) as business expenses whether or not any part of their dues are used for lobbying purposes.

7. Any organization that is not a membership organization.

Note: Special affiliation rules under Rev. Proc. 98-19 require treatment of 501(c)(4), (c)(5), or (6) organizations that share a name, charter, historic affiliation or other similar characteristic and coordinate their activities as though they were one organization. In such case, if the treated-as-one meets the exception, then all the organizations making up the single organization are considered to meet the exception. Where the treated-as-one has affiliates with different tax years, the organizations may base their calculation of annual dues on any single reasonable tax year.

Line 2. Has the filer only made domestic lobbying expenditures (not foreign lobbying), and not made any political expenditures, and those lobbying expenditures are exclusively in-house and in amounts of $2,000 or less?

The instructions state:

Answer "Yes" on Line 2 if the organization satisfies the following criteria:

1. The organization did not make any political expenditures or foreign lobbying expenditures during the 2015 reporting year.
2. The organization made lobbying expenditures during the 2015 reporting year consisting only of in-house direct lobbying expenditures totaling $2,000 or less, but excluding

   a. any allocable overhead expenses, and

   b. all direct lobbying expenses of any local council regarding legislation of direct interest to the organization or its members.

If the organization's in-house direct lobbying expenditures during the 2015 reporting year were $2,000 or less, but the organization also paid or incurred other lobbying or political expenditures during the 2015 reporting year, it should answer "No" to question 2. If the organization is required to complete Part III-B, the $2,000 or less of in-house direct lobbying expenditures should not be included in the total of Part III-B, Line 2a.

Part III-B Calculation of the Proxy Tax

The proxy tax (which is treated as an income tax but need not be included in making estimated tax payments for the following tax year) is calculated based on whether the filer provided notice to dues-paying members of the non-deductibility of a portion of their dues.

Part III-B	Complete if the organization is exempt under section 501(c)(4), section 501(c)(5), or section 501(c)(6) and if either (a) BOTH Part III-A, lines 1 and 2, are answered "No," OR (b) Part III-A, line 3, is answered "Yes."		
1	Dues, assessments and similar amounts from members	1	
2	Section 162(e) nondeductible lobbying and political expenditures (**do not include amounts of political expenses for which the section 527(f) tax was paid).**		
a	Current year	2a	
b	Carryover from last year	2b	
c	Total	2c	
3	Aggregate amount reported in section 6033(e)(1)(A) notices of nondeductible section 162(e) dues . .	3	
4	If notices were sent and the amount on line 2c exceeds the amount on line 3, what portion of the excess does the organization agree to carryover to the reasonable estimate of nondeductible lobbying and political expenditure next year?	4	
5	Taxable amount of lobbying and political expenditures (see instructions)	5	

The instructions have helpful tables to summarize the rules by which notice (that members cannot take a trade or business expense deduction for the portion of their dues that are allocable to the organization's lobbying and political activities:

Dues, Lobbying, and Political Expenses

IF ...	THEN ...
The organization's lobbying and political expenses are more than its membership dues for the year,	The organization must: (a) Allocate all membership dues to its lobbying and political activities, and (b) Carry forward any excess lobbying and political expenses to the next tax year.
The organization: (a) Had only *de minimis* in-house expenses ($2,000 or less) and no other nondeductible lobbying or political expenses (including any amount it agreed to carryover); or (b) Paid a proxy tax, instead of notifying its members on the allocation of dues to lobbying and political expenses; or (c) Established that substantially all of its membership dues, etc., are not deductible by members.	The organization need not disclose to its membership the allocation of dues, etc., to its lobbying and political activities.

Proxy Tax

IF ...	THEN ...
The organization's actual lobbying and political expenses are more than it estimated in its dues notices,	The organization is liable for a proxy tax on the excess.
The organization: (a) Elects to pay the proxy tax, and (b) Chooses not to give its members a notice allocating dues to lobbying and political campaign activities,	All the members' dues remain eligible for a section 162 trade or business expense deduction.
The organization: (a) Makes a reasonable estimate of dues allocable to nondeductible lobbying and political activities, and (b) Agrees to adjust its estimate in the following year*.	The IRS may permit a waiver of the proxy tax.

*A facts and circumstances test determines whether or not a reasonable estimate was made in good faith.

The complete discussion of Part III rules is a course in itself. For our purposes, one pertinent Part III definition from the Part III instructions need be emphasized as three expenditures are exceptions:

Lobbying and political expenditures. For purposes of this section only, lobbying and political expenditures do not include:

1. Direct lobbying expenditures made to influence local legislation,
2. Any political campaign expenditures for which the tax under Section 527(f) was paid (see Part I-C).
3. Any expenditures with . . . covered executive branch official[s] in an attempt to influence the official actions or positions of that official.

Line 1. Enter here the amounts members paid in dues or assessments or both in the reporting year.

Line 2a. Total of the filer's lobbying and political expenditures, as defined within Section 162(e), (such expenses overall equating with *non*-deductible business expenses) goes here.

> **Reminder:** the 162(e) definitions differ from the 501(c)(3) definitions. Section 162(e) does *not* reach lobbying on a city or municipality level, but reaches communications with federal Cabinet officials even were such communications to fall outside of the 501(c)(3) definition of lobbying.

Line 2b. Last year, the filer failed to fully notice dues paying members (so the amount of all Section 162(e) lobbying and political expenditures failed to be covered by such notices), the amount from last year not covered was agreed to be carried-forward. Enter that amount here.

Line 2c. The total of 2a+ 2b.

Note: There are special rules for allocating costs to lobbying activities and in all cases a reasonable method must be used. The instructions give several examples of reasonable methods (the ratio method, the gross-up and alternative gross-up methods, the alternative gross-up method, and the Section 263A method.

Line 3. The total dues noticed to members as correlating to an organization's nondeductible 162(e) expenditures in the reporting year.

Line 4. If Line 3 is less than Line 2c, enter that shortfall the filer agrees to carry-over to next year.

Line 5. Enter here the portion of the reporting year shortfall to be subjected to proxy tax (that tax applies at highest corporate rates). Note the same is to be self-assessed upon Form 990-T.

KNOWLEDGE CHECK

4. A 501(c)(6) downtown chamber of commerce collects dues from its 100 members of $5,000 per year. In year 1, no notice was provided to members on any portion of their dues not being deductible in line with the 6033(e) reporting requirements. Year 1's actual political and lobbying expenditures were $200,000. The chamber of commerce anticipates that in its year 2 budget, $300,000 will be expended on 6033(e) political and lobbying efforts. Which scenario accurately describes the chamber's options for proxy tax payment in year 2 and notice requirements in year 2?

    1. Pay the proxy tax on year 1's shortfall ($200,000), and notice members that 60 percent of their year 2 dues will be non-deductible.
    2. Roll forward the year 1 shortfall ($200,000) and notice members that 100 percent of their year 2 dues will be non-deductible.
    3. Pay the proxy tax on combined year 1 shortfall plus anticipated year 2 political/ lobbying expenditures (total $500,000).
    4. Refund the members' year 1 dues, and double dues chargeable on year 2 to amount of $10,000; and notice members that 30 percent of year 2 dues will be non-deductible.

        a. 1 only.
        b. 2 only.
        c. 1 and 2.
        d. 1, 2 and 3.

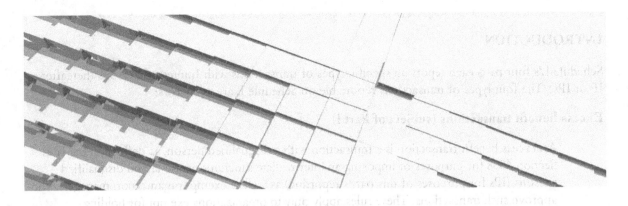

Chapter 6

THE INTERESTED PERSONS OF SCHEDULE L AND THE IMPACT OF THIS SCHEDULE ON FILING ORGANIZATIONS

LEARNING OBJECTIVES

After completing this chapter, you should be able to do the following:

- Identify the five categories of Interested Persons that apply uniformly across Parts II–IV of the Schedule, and the one additional category that applies as well to Part IV.
- Identify both Part IV's business transaction dollar thresholds that apply to disclosing compensation paid to an Interested Person's family member and to other types of business transactions undertaken with Interested Persons.
- Identify the criteria by which Part II requires disclosure of loans with Interested Persons.
- Identify the exceptions to reporting of grants and assistance provided to Interested Persons in Part III.
- Analyze the tenets by which an excess benefit transaction occurs and is then to be noticed via Part I disclosure.

INTRODUCTION

Schedule L's four parts each report on specific types of transactions with Interested Persons (hereafter, IP or IPs). The four types of transactions reportable on Schedule L are as follows:

Excess benefit transactions (subject of Part I)

An excess benefit transaction is a transaction with a disqualified person, as defined in the IRC Section 4958 for purposes of imposing an intermediate sanctions excise tax on disqualified persons (IPs for purposes of this part's reporting) as well as exempt organization managers who approve such transactions. These rules apply only to organizations exempt (or holding themselves out as exempt) under Sections 501(c)(3) [other than private foundations], 501(c)(4), or 501(c)(29).

[NOTE: Appendix G of the Form 990 instructions is dedicated to the intermediate sanctions scheme]

Loans (subject of Part II)

This part reports loans between the filing organization and any IP, if the loan is outstanding on the last day of the tax year).

Grants or other assistance (Part III)

This part reports grants or other assistance that were provided to an IP in the tax year

Business transactions (Part IV)

This part reports business transactions undertaken by the organization and an IP, subject to specific reporting thresholds.

WARNING: All preparers must understand the importance (and complexity) of Schedule L completion, both because the reporting demands sunshine and transparency on transactional intersections and what is reported impacts the independence of board members serving on the last day of the tax year (the count of such members the subject of Core Form, Part VI, Line 1b). Indeed, the IRS' FAQ (reprinted here) on the nature of the Schedule speaks to these points:

What types of transactions are reportable on Schedule L, Form 990?[1]

Transactions reportable on Schedule L include excess benefit transactions (see appendix G of Form 990 instructions), loans between the filing organization and interested persons, grants or other assistance to interested persons and business transactions between the organization and an interested person. Transactions between the organization and an interested person's family members or affiliated entities generally are included. Various thresholds and exceptions may determine whether a given transaction must be reported in one of these parts.

---

[1] Available at: www.irs.gov/ Charities-&-Non-Profits/ Exempt-Organizations-Annual-Reporting-Requirements-Form-990-Part-VI-and-Schedule-L-Transactions-Reportable [last checked February 21, 2017].

TIP: Form 990, Part VI, Line 1b asks for the number of independent voting members of the organization's governing body. One criterion for independence is whether a governing body member, or a family member of that person, was involved in a transaction that is reportable on the organization's Schedule L or on the Schedule L of a related organization. Thus, Form 990 filers should determine whether any of their governing board members were involved in a reportable Schedule L transaction before answering the independent board member question in Part VI, Line 1b.

The FAQ only hints at the complexity of this Schedule. Indeed, it is imperative that each part of the Schedule L be approached separately, and in order from Part I to Part IV. This is the case because:

1. The 2008–2013 Forms applied different definitions at each of the Schedule L's four parts for who was an Interested Person (hereafter, IP) in the part. The 2014 instructions standardized the categories of IPs applicable to Parts II through IV, applying at all times five categories. Parts III and IV as of the 2014 Form each employ their own additional categories of IPs [these are set out in table 1, in the next section of these materials].

2. Unfortunately, the 2014 instructions' "harmonization" furthered two points of additional confusion:
    *   One of the now-standardized five categories, creator or founder, is new as of 2014, but there is no supplied definition of either of the relevant terms; and
    *   Insufficient address was initially made as to how to deal with reasonable efforts related to the new, and sensitive, category for so-called "substantial contributors," which had not been prior-applied to either Parts II and IV.

3. As noted earlier, the Schedule L's importance relates not only to the sunlight[2] it shines on insider-type transactions (which presumably will lead filers to want to manage such transactions with more efficiency given that these are now the subject of public disclosure) but also due to the fact that the Schedule's reporting affects the reporting of independent board members (regardless of whether the transaction is ordinary and necessary or upon terms that may be extremely advantageous to the filer).

4. While the subjects and objects of Part I (that is, (c)(3)[3], (c)(4) and (c)(29) filers having suffered a Section 4958 disqualified person's participation in an excess benefit transaction) are set out in law and in Regulations, the topics and instructions related to reporting in Parts II–IV are not.
    a. Many of the IP categories originally applied in, as well as those now "standardized" throughout Parts II–IV are only employed in this Schedule and not necessarily elsewhere in the Form and are a creature of the Form 990 instructions, not tax law. (One example is that of the term *substantial contributor* as applied in Parts II–IV, which the instructions define as parties required to be disclosed on Schedule B; this definition is at odds with the same term's employ in Schedule A using the traditional statutory definition of the term that is applicable to private foundations under IRC section 4946.)
    b. Parts II–IV cannot be completed without accessing information from multiple sources outside of the organization, hence the need for the use of reasonable efforts in making inquiries.

5. Part II has no exceptions, Part III has several, and Part IV has dollar thresholds below which transactions are not required to be reported (see table 2, in the next section of these materials). A transaction reported on an earlier part is not reported on a latter part of the Schedule as all interested persons transactions are required to be reported on the earliest possible part of this Schedule.

---

[2] Sunlight references the famous quote by U.S. Supreme Court Justice Louis Brandeis ("Publicity is justly commended as a remedy for social and industrial diseases. Sunlight is said to be the best of disinfectants...") regarding the benefits of openness and transparency

[3] The lowercase letter c immediately followed by a number is used by the authors as a short-hand for 501(c).

Table 1: Definitions of Interested Persons for Schedule L's Parts II through IV

The following delineates the definitions in the 2014 and future years' Form 990 instructions, which attempted to harmonize the definitions by which parties hold IP status.

Party who is . . .	Part II	Part III	Part IV
1. A person who holds status on Form 990, Part VII, Section A as a current or former Trustee/Director, Officer, or Key Employee (hereafter, TDOKE)	Yes	Yes	Yes
2. A creator or founder of the filer[4]	Yes	Yes	Yes
3. A substantial contributor (a donor of $5,000 or more who is required to be reported by name on Schedule B)[5]	Yes	Yes	Yes
4. A *family member* of an individual with status as an IP via 1-3 preceding	Yes	Yes	Yes
5. A *35-percent controlled entity*[6] of one or more of the individuals or organizations captured as IPs via 1-4 preceding	Yes	Yes	Yes
6. A *management company* in which a former TDOKE was in the last 5 tax years (regardless of whether required to be reported on Form 990, Part VII, Section A as a former TDOKE) an officer, director, trustee or a direct or indirect 35 percent owner[7]	No	No	Yes
7. A member of the organization's grant selection committee	No	Yes	No
8. An employee (or child of an employee) of a substantial contributor or of a *35-percent controlled entity* of such person, but only if the employee (or child of employee) received the grant or assistance by the direction or advice of the substantial contributor or designee or of the *35-percent controlled entity*, or under a program funded by the substantial contributor that was intended primarily to benefit such employees (or their children)	No	Yes	No

---

[4] This category by definition also includes a VEBA's sponsoring organization(s).
[5] The Schedule's instructions state:
    For purposes of Schedule L, Parts II–IV, a substantial contributor is an individual or organization that made contributions during the tax year in the aggregate of at least $5,000 and is required to be reported by name in Schedule B . . . . A substantial contributor may include an employer that contributes to a VEBA.
[6] Italics in this table are employed to reflect glossary terms. This term's definition is reprinted on the next page.
[7] Ownership is measure by stock ownership (voting power or value, whichever is greater) of a corporation, profits or capital interest (which is greater) in a partnership or limited liability company, or beneficial interest in a trust.

Category #5's Glossary Definition[8]

35-percent Controlled Entity	An entity that is owned, directly or indirectly (for example, under constructive ownership rules of Section 267(c)), by a given person, such as the organization's current or former officers, directors, trustees, or key employees listed in Form 990, Part VII, Section [A], or the family members thereof (listed persons) as follows:
	• A corporation in which listed persons own more than 35 percent of the total combined voting power;
	• A partnership in which listed persons own more than 35 percent of the profits interest; or
	• A trust or estate in which listed persons own more than 35 percent of the beneficial interest.

Interested Party Exclusions

The previously noted IP categories do NOT reach entities who are:

- Exempt under 501(c)(3) or a foreign organization for which the filing organization has made a reasonable judgment (or has an opinion of counsel) that the foreign organization is described in Section 501(c)(3)
- Exempt under the same Section as the filing organization (for example, a 501(c)(4) with respect to another 501(c)(4) organization)
- A governmental unit or instrumentality

---

[8] Happily, this category has replaced the complex definition that had reached entities connected-to-other-IPs under the 2008–2013 Forms 990. In those years, Part IV required reporting of business transactions with the following two now-erased IP categories:
- "35 percent owned" entities of current or former TDOKEs and their family members [this category was only found in this Schedule/ Part and over time had some exclusions added in the case of 501(c) entities]
- Non-501(c) or non-governmental entities connected indirectly to the filer via one or more of filer's TDOKEs, or family members of those TDOKEs serving as a director/ trustee, officer, or in the case of a partnership or professional corporation, a partner member/ shareholder with greater than a 5 percent interest

KNOWLEDGE CHECK

1. Which individuals are Interested Persons for purposes of Schedule L's Parts II-IV?

    ___ 1. A taxable corporation denoted as the founder of the organization on the organization's website.

    ___ 2. An individual denoted as the founder of the organization on the organization's website.

    ___ 3. An individual who made three unconnected donations during the tax year of $2,000, $2,500, and $3,000.

    ___ 4. The same individual as in (2), but the payments were all to satisfy a $7,500 pledge made in the filing year.

    ___ 5. The executive director/ CEO of the filer, who is NOT an officer of the entity per the filer's organizational documents or resolutions of the board.

    a. 2/ 4/ 5.

    b. 1/ 2/ 4/ 5.

    c. 1/ 2/ 3/ 4/ 5.

    d. 1/ 2/ 5.

2. Which management company scenario would lead to exempt organization A's transactions with a management company disclosed on Schedule L, Part IV (assuming same were above the dollar thresholds that apply in that part)?

    a. The management company is owned by the ex-spouse of an individual who served on A's board five tax years ago.

    b. The management company is owned by an individual who should have been (but was not) reported as a key employee of A five tax years ago.

    c. The management company is owned by the domestic partner (but not spouse) of an individual who was an officer of A five tax years ago.

    d. The management company was owned until two years ago by an individual who was a TDOKE of the organization within the last five tax years.

Table 2: Dollar Thresholds and Relevant Time Periods Applied in Schedule L's Parts I through IV

	Part I	Part II	Part III	Part IV
$ Threshold(s)	None	none	none	• Amounts paid in the tax year total >$100k (in the aggregate) with any IP. • Amounts paid in the tax year on a single transaction exceed the greater of $10k or 1 percent of the filer's revenues. • Compensation paid to a family member of a current or former TDOKE reported on this tax year's Form 990 Part VII is >$10k. • Joint ventures (stand-alone rule).*

* The fact of engaging in joint venture (JV) with an IP is reportable when the filer has invested in the JV (at any time, irrespective of the tax year) greater than $10,000, and the profits or capital interest that both the filing organization and the IP held in the JV each exceeded 10 percent at *any time* during the tax year

	Part I	Part II	Part III	Part IV
Time period	Excess benefit transaction occurred either (a) during the tax year; or (b) in a prior year, but has not been reported on a prior-filed Form 990 or Form 990-EZ.	Loan to or from interested person was outstanding on the last day of the tax year.	Grant or assistance was provided to an interested person at any time during the tax year.	Payments for a business transaction with an interested person occurred at any time during the tax year (fact of a joint venture in place matters under a separate rule—see note at * in previous box).

PARTS II–IV REQUIRE REASONABLE EFFORTS

Unless possessing psychic powers, a filer's officials will not necessarily have knowledge of loans, grants or assistance provided to, or business transactions having occurred between, the filer and those who fall into characterization as IPs. Parts III and IV of Schedule L, from the inception of this Schedule in 2008 forward have required reasonable efforts be undertaken by the filer to gather information from all interested persons sufficient to allow completion of these two. Prior to the 2014 Form, the instructions provided separate address of what constitutes reasonable efforts for each of those parts.

All such text was removed from the 2014 Schedule L instructions as part of a change noted in the "What's New" section's explanation that the reasonable effort instructions have been harmonized. The Schedule's overarching "Specific Instructions" section now includes this note about what such efforts require. Furthermore, as of the 2015 Form and forward, the Schedule L instructions have the same address that through the 2013 Form had only been in place for Part III:

> **Reasonable effort.** The organization is not required to provide information about a transaction with an interested person if it is unable to secure sufficient information to conclude that the transaction is reportable after making a reasonable effort to obtain such information. An example of a reasonable effort is for the organization to distribute a questionnaire annually to each person that it believes may be an interested person, as described earlier, requesting information relevant to determine whether a transaction is reportable. The questionnaire may include the name and title of each person reporting information, blank lines for the person's signature and signature date, and the pertinent instructions and definitions for Schedule L interested persons and transactions.
>
> **Example.** A substantial contributor to the organization states that he would like Mr. X and Ms. Y to be beneficiaries of a grant. The organization inquires of the substantial contributor whether Mr. X or Ms. Y are interested persons with respect to the organization because of a family or business relationship they have with the substantial contributor (using the pertinent instructions and definitions), and the substantial contributor replies in writing that they are not. Whether they actually are interested persons or not, the organization has made a reasonable effort in this situation.

Given that substantial contributors were added to the overall list of interested persons for all parts of the Schedule L (not just Part III) as of the 2014 Form, the preceding example is especially important. It is recommended, as the example provides, to use a negative confirmation letter approach instead of a full questionnaire when conducting reasonable efforts with substantial contributors. Such a letter advises donors that as substantial contributors (due to their being listed on Form 990 Schedule B, albeit with names not open to public disclosure), they may have information that is subject to the organization's disclosure on Schedule L, Parts II–IV, such as the existence of other transactions the organization had with the donor (or others connected to the donor), and that for the purpose of completing Schedule L Part IV (or, as required, other Parts of that Schedule),[9] the organization is making additional inquiries of them related to that part's address of business transactions.

---

[9] As most organizations know both with whom they have debt or, if they make grant awards, who is a grantee, there is already a due diligence process that would allow them to know if they had loans outstanding with, or had made grants to, either the substantial contributor or that contributor's family member. Thus, there may be no need to make additional inquiries related to Schedule L's Parts II or III.

Such a negative confirmation letter would then provide the donor with the business transaction dollar thresholds, listing of other known IPs from the organization's board and staff, definition of family member and 35 percent controlled entity, and inform the recipient that if they have no knowledge to report they should disregard the inquiry. The letter would also state that if they do have something they think may need to report as being within the Schedule L, Part IV parameters, they should follow-up with the individual contact provided who will gather the required information and assist with getting the information necessary to proper Schedule L completion. Finally, the letter would thank them for their assistance in helping the filing organization be fully compliant with exempt organization reporting mandates.

This chapter now turns to discussion of each of the four parts of Schedule L, addressing them in the most common order of disclosure occurrence:

> **IV—Business Transactions**
>
> **II—Loans**
>
> **III—Grants or Assistance**
>
> **I—Excess Benefit Transactions**

Schedule L, Part IV—Business Transactions

Part IV reports a filer's payments in the course of transacting business with an IP (were the magnitude of the payments in the course of the tax year to be above the reporting thresholds). From the 2014 Form forward, an IP for this part is a: TDOKE, creator or founder, substantial contributor (SC), family member of any of the preceding, or a 35-percent Controlled Entity of any/ all IPs,[10] AND, IN ADDITION, a last category that is unique to this part: certain management companies.[11]

> Note: The three underlined categories appearing in the preceding paragraph were added to this part as of the 2014 Form.

WARNING. The trigger question at Core Form Part IV, Q.28a-c, shown in the following text box, was not updated by the IRS on the 2014–2016 Forms and thus does NOT reflect the current harmonization of the Schedule L's IP definitions.

This trigger question at 28c has always been misleading; since the 2014 IP-category harmonization, the entirety of Lines 28a, b, and c are imprecise and/or incorrect. Preparers need to understand that they misstate the relevant IP categories, as follows:

- Core Form Line 28a fails to include two categories—substantial contributors and creators/founders
- Core Form Line 28b, in the case of substantial contributors and creators/founders who are natural persons, omits the capture of their family members
- Core Form Line 28c fails to refer to the remaining categories of IPs: 35 percent-controlled entities and the unique-to-this-part category for certain management companies

Part IV, Line 28 reprint follows (but keep in mind the warning above!)

28	Was the organization a party to a business transaction with one of the following parties (see Schedule L, Part IV instructions for applicable filing thresholds, conditions, and exceptions):			
a	A current or former officer, director, trustee, or key employee? *If "Yes," complete Schedule L, Part IV* . .	28a		✓
b	A family member of a current or former officer, director, trustee, or key employee? *If "Yes," complete Schedule L, Part IV*	28b	✓	
c	An entity of which a current or former officer, director, trustee, or key employee (or a family member thereof) was an officer, director, trustee, or direct or indirect owner? *If "Yes," complete Schedule L, Part IV* . . .	28c		✓

---

[10] These are IP categories numbered 1-5 (the standardized categories) set out, with pertinent exclusions, in table 1 provided earlier in this chapter.

[11] This is IP category number 6 denoted in table 1.

The current instructions to Schedule L acknowledge the inadequacy of Part IV's Lines 28a-c. The first page of the Schedule L's instructions includes this note:

> The organization should answer "Yes" to Form 990, Part IV, Lines 28a, 28b, and 28c, only if the party to the transaction was an interested person as defined in these instructions.

UNDERSTANDING PART IV's REACH AND UNIQUE DEFINITIONS

As is the case for the Parts II and III of this Schedule, the point of the requisite disclosures here is transparency and sunlight, not judging the fact of a transaction. But this part of Schedule L is the most complicated of Parts II—IV, requiring not only an understanding of who must be reported (as noted in tables 1 and 2 provided at the beginning of this chapter), but also of what is a business transaction and then familiarity with the complicated *de minimis* dollar thresholds that set standard exceptions from reporting.

WHAT IS A BUSINESS TRANSACTION?

Business transactions for purposes of this part include both:

- **CONTRACTS** of every sort, regardless of when initiated (it is the fact of payment thereunder that is the reportable transaction, unless the transaction is one of the five types that are per se excluded, as detailed here). Accordingly, transactions include, but are not limited to:
  - Sales
  - Leases
  - Licenses
  - Insurance
  - Performance of services

- **JOINT VENTURES** (whether new or ongoing), in which the filer has invested $10,000 or more (whether or not said investment relates to the tax year being filed upon) and the profits or capital interest of the organization and an IP each exceeds 10 percent at some time during the tax year.

What Is <u>Not</u> A Business Transaction: Five Exclusions
(Aside from the de minimis amounts thresholds)

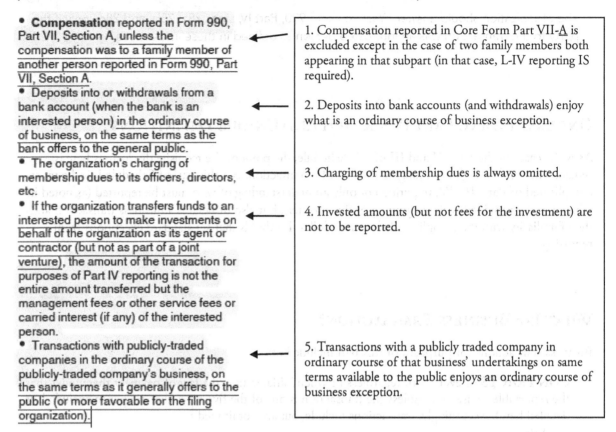

- **Compensation** reported in Form 990, Part VII, Section A, unless the compensation was to a family member of another person reported in Form 990, Part VII, Section A.
- Deposits into or withdrawals from a bank account (when the bank is an interested person) in the ordinary course of business, on the same terms as the bank offers to the general public.
- The organization's charging of membership dues to its officers, directors, etc.
- If the organization transfers funds to an interested person to make investments on behalf of the organization as its agent or contractor (but not as part of a joint venture), the amount of the transaction for purposes of Part IV reporting is not the entire amount transferred but the management fees or other service fees or carried interest (if any) of the interested person.
- Transactions with publicly-traded companies in the ordinary course of the publicly-traded company's business, on the same terms as it generally offers to the public (or more favorable for the filing organization).

1. Compensation reported in Core Form Part VII-<u>A</u> is excluded except in the case of two family members both appearing in that subpart (in that case, L-IV reporting IS required).

2. Deposits into bank accounts (and withdrawals) enjoy what is an ordinary course of business exception.

3. Charging of membership dues is always omitted.

4. Invested amounts (but not fees for the investment) are not to be reported.

5. Transactions with a publicly traded company in ordinary course of that business' undertakings on same terms available to the public enjoys an ordinary course of business exception.

Schedule L's Parts, and order of appearance, matter: If a transaction is reportable as an excess benefit transaction (for example, as having been conducted with a Section 4958 Disqualified Person without appropriate fair market value return to the filer), or as a loan, or as the provision of a grant or assistance, reporting on this part is voided to occur as same is superseded by entry in Schedule L's prior Parts, I–III. This is the case as filers need report a transaction or event on the first Schedule L part which applies to it.

THRESHOLDS FOR REPORTING

THE DOLLAR THRESHOLDS (APPLIED SOLELY TO PAYMENTS MADE DURING THE TAX YEAR) BY WHICH PART IV TRANSACTIONS ARE TO BE REPORTED ARE AS FOLLOWS:

- Compensation payments during the tax year to a *family member* of a TDOKE exceeded $10,000.[12]
- Payments during the tax year from a single transaction with an IP exceeded the greater of $10,000 or 1 percent of filer's total revenues for the tax year. (Note that this threshold is mooted where total

---

[12] Italicized terms are glossary terms.

payments for all transactions between the filer and one IP over the course of the reporting year aggregate to greater than $100,000, per the separate threshold that follows.)

- Aggregated payments during the tax year for business transactions with an IP exceeded $100,000.
- However, in the case of joint ventures, the preceding thresholds do not apply. Instead, investment in joint venture is to be disclosed as a reportable business transaction when the filer has at any time (whether or not during the tax year) invested $10,000 or more, and on the other side, an IP (or multiple IPs) of the filer at any point during the tax year AND the filer each had a profits or capital interest exceeding 10 percent.

Compensation payments to Family Members

The glossary definition of *compensation* states as follows [italicized terms are themselves also glossary terms:

Unless otherwise provided, all forms of cash and noncash payments or benefits provided in exchange for services, including salary and wages, bonuses, severance payments, deferred payments, retirement benefits, fringe benefits, and other financial arrangements or transactions such as personal vehicles, meals, housing, personal and family educational benefits, below-market loans, payment of personal or family travel, entertainment, and personal use of the organization's property. Compensation includes payments and other benefits provided to both *employees* and *independent contractors* in exchange for services. See also *deferred compensation, nonqualified deferred compensation, and reportable compensation.*

EXAMPLES—The instructions provide seven examples illustrating application of the Part IV dollar thresholds and their intersection with those who have IP status.

Example 1. T, a family member of an officer of the organization, serves as an employee of the organization and receives during the organization's tax year compensation of $15,000, which is not more than 1 percent of the organization's total revenue. The organization is required to report T's compensation as a business transaction in Schedule L, Part IV, because the organization's compensation to a family member of an officer exceeds $10,000, whether or not T's compensation is reported in Form 990, Part VII.

Example 2. X, the child of a current director listed in Form 990, Part VII, Section A, is a first-year associate at a law partnership that the organization pays $150,000 during the organization's tax year. The organization is not required to report this business transaction on account of X's employment relationship to the law firm.

Example 3. The facts are the same as in Example (2), except that X is a partner of the law firm and has an ownership interest in the law firm of 36 percent of the profits. The organization must report the business transaction because the law firm is a 35-percent controlled entity of X and the dollar amount is in excess of the $100,000 aggregate threshold.

Example 4. The facts are the same as in Example (3), except that the law firm entered into the transaction with the organization before X's parent became a director of the organization. X's parent became a director during the organization's tax year. The organization must report all payments made during its tax year to the law firm for the transaction.

Example 5. The facts are the same as in Example (3), except that X is the child of a former director listed in Form 990, Part VII, Section A. The organization is required to report the business transaction, as family members of former directors listed in Part VII are interested persons.

Example 6. The facts are the same as in Example (3), except that the organization pays $75,000 in total during the organization's tax year for 15 separate transactions to collect debts owed to the organization. None of the transactions involves payments to the law partnership in excess of $10,000. The organization is not required in this instance to report the business transactions, because the dollar amounts do not exceed either the $10,000 transaction threshold or the $100,000 aggregate threshold.

Example 7. The facts are the same as in Example (6), except that the organization pays $105,000 instead of $75,000. Because the aggregate payments for the business transactions exceed $100,000, the organization must report all the business transactions. The organization can report the transactions on an aggregate basis or list them separately.

FURTHER EXAMPLES (AND DISCUSSIONS OF FACTORS INFORMING RESULTS AS TO SCHEDULE L, PART IV DISCLOSURE REQUIREMENT):

1. Exempt organization B has a director, Beatrice, who is an architect and is experienced with construction project management. At the time that B comes onto the board in the midst of B's tax year, B has just had bonds issued in favor of a massive building project. Shortly thereafter, at the project's groundbreaking, the general contractor's principals are arrested under an indictment alleging that they had accepted bribes and kick-backs on unrelated government projects. The general contractor's assets are seized (including some materials procured by sub-contractors and paid for by B in advance of the groundbreaking).

In the course of the board's addressing the mess, Beatrice agrees to assist B through her sole proprietorship, SP, taking on a Project Manager/ Coordinator role to accomplish both a fast-tracked search for a general contractor replacement and in oversight of the new general contractor's progress from groundbreaking-do-over through the end of the next quarter. For SP's services (which are correctly posited as that of an independent contractor), she will be paid between $51,000 and $65,000 (the final amount tabbed to calendar dates upon which a signed agreement with the replacement contractor is procured and the do-over groundbreaking held). As part of the arrangement for services, SP is paid an initial $25,000 retainer on the last day of B's tax year.

2. Same facts as (1), although here the hired firm is not Beatrice's sole proprietorship, but a taxable company, TC, in which she holds 15 percent of the stock, her father has 10 percent, and her brother has 12 percent.

3. Same facts as (1), but here the service provider that Beatrice works for is a not-for-profit (NFP), a taxable not-for-profit corporation that has expertise and excess capacity it can devote to building construction management. NFP is neither a substantial contributor to B, nor a founder/ creator of B. Furthermore, NFP has not issued stock. 36 percent of the board members of NFP, during the course of B's tax year and thus throughout the time in which NFP and B have these arrangements occur, are comprised of Beatrice, her family members, and a family member of another one of B's board of directors.

4. Same facts as (3), but instead of NFP being a taxable not-for-profit corporation, it has tax-exemption under 501(c)(4).

RESULTS:

Both SP in (1) AND TC in (2) are 35-percent controlled entities (in the latter case, as TC's stock is held by Beatrice and her family members in a total proportion of 37 percent). As such, they are Interested Persons and assuming that the last-day-of-the-tax-year paid retainer in the amount of $25,000 exceeds the one-transaction threshold (greater of $10k or 1 percent of filer's gross receipts for the tax year), the transaction is reportable in Schedule L, Part IV.

A not-for-profit corporation is rarely reached by the definition of 35-percent controlled entity as the measure for inclusion in such category by a corporation is whether or not parties hold more than 35 percent of total combined voting power. Not-for-profit corporations, with rare exceptions, do not issue stock with voting rights. Thus, in scenario (3) unless NFP has issued voting stock, it cannot be a 35-percent controlled entity (board composition, as well as tax-exempt versus taxable status, are factors that are immaterial for these purposes). For scenario (4) it is likely, given the fact of 501(c)(4) tax-exemption, that NFP has not issued stock. However, were it to have issued stock with voting rights (an event which might be more likely with non-c4 categories, for example, with 501(c)(6) boards of trade or 501(c)(7) social clubs), it might be an Interested Person of B were B's Interested Persons to hold more than 35 percent of the voting stock.

3. Filer C has used the services of consulting firm F in the reporting year that in the prior year fit 35-percent controlled entity status because of ownership by family members of C's President. F's services were again availed of in the tax year now to be reported upon, but in this tax year the President's family had their stock voting and value interests reduced to a < 35 percent level. In which circumstance does that drop matter for purposes of the reporting tax year's Schedule L, Part IV reporting?

    a. If at the time of payment C makes to the firm, 35-percent controlled entity status no longer applied.

    b. If at the last day of C's tax year, 35-percent controlled entity status no longer applied.

    c. If on the first day of C's tax year, 35-percent controlled entity status no longer applied.

    d. If for more than half of C's tax year, 35-percent controlled entity status did not apply.

4. Organization B has annual gross receipts in the filing year of $11 million. Which transaction with Interested Person XYZ would NOT lead to Schedule L, Part IV disclosure?

    a. XYZ's services historically have been provided under ONE contract; the amount paid to B against same in the filing year totals under $110,000 but more than $100,000.

    b. Same as a, but B had XYZ remit payment to a third party on behalf of B.

    c. XYZ's services are and have been provided under FOUR separate contracts, and B remitted payments on each of those contracts in the amount of $26,000 apiece, paying a total of $104,000 in the tax year.

    d. Same as c, but payments on each of the 4 contracts were $24,000 apiece, so that the total paid in the tax year was $98,000.

5. Several of Organization D's current or former TDOKEs (reportable on Form 990 Core Form Part VII, Section A) have family members who are employed by D. For the relevant tax year, which is the calendar year, D's gross receipts were $2 million. One of the family members receives salary of $25,000 per year but no other remuneration or benefits and in order to NOT be reported on Schedule L Part IV for D's current tax comes forward early in the year and asks for a portion of their salary to be deferred to pay-out in a future tax year in order to avoid such disclosure. On these facts, which is a correct statement?

    a. Part IV disclosure only applies if the family member is paid in the tax year in excess of the greater of $10,000 or 1 percent of gross receipts, so a $5,000 deferral will avoid reporting.

    b. Part IV disclosure only applies if the family member is paid in the tax year in excess of $10,000, so a deferral of $15,000 will avoid reporting.

    c. Part IV disclosure only applies if the family member is paid in the tax year in excess of $10,000, but as compensation paid includes right to deferred payments, the reporting cannot be avoided.

    d. Part IV disclosure can be avoided by having the individual employee cut their pay by $5,000 for the year and take half ($10,000) as an employee and half ($10,000) as an independent contractor.

SCHEDULE L PART IV'S INTERSECTION WITH COMPENSATION REPORTING REQUIRED ON THE CORE FORM

Schedule L Tips and FAQs initially posted in November 2009 have been republished on the IRS website ever since. With respect to this question, the IRS states: [13]

Exempt Organizations Annual Reporting Requirements—Form 990, Part VI and Schedule L: Compensation

We compensate our chief financial officer $110,000 and the CFO's spouse (an employee) $20,000. Must we report one or both of these transactions in Schedule L, Part IV, Form 990?

The compensation to the CFO's spouse must be reported in Schedule L, Part IV, <u>assuming that it is not reported in Form 990, Part VII</u>** or Schedule L, Part I, because (1) the spouse is a family member of an officer, and therefore an *interested person* for purposes of Part IV; and (2) the compensation to the spouse exceeds $10,000. The organization does not need to report its compensation to the CFO in Schedule L, Part IV, though it does need to report that compensation in Part VII of the core Form 990.

*** WARNING. Underlining has been added to the text by the authors to denote that the cited phrase in this FAQ contradicts the current exclusion instruction. Same notes that compensation reported in Form 990, Part VII, Section A is excluded, <u>unless</u> the compensation was to a family member of another person reported in Form 990, Part VII, Section A.*

PREPARATION POINTS IN COMPLETING PART IV

Part IV	Business Transactions Involving Interested Persons.				
	Complete if the organization answered "Yes" on Form 990, Part IV, line 28a, 28b, or 28c.				
(a) Name of interested person	(b) Relationship between interested person and the organization	(c) Amount of transaction	(d) Description of transaction	(e) Sharing of organization's revenues?	
				Yes	No
(1) Ivan Somprivacy	Family member of	50,001	Employed as Development		✓
(2)	Flannie Flagg, CFO		Director		
(3)					

The required inputs for Part IV's columns are fairly simple:

- (Column a): Name of interested person.
- (Column b): Relationship between interested person and the filer (for example, spouse of director, [name] or entity owned > 35 percent by former director, [name] through her family). See example in box above.
- (Column c): Amount of transaction.

---

[13] Available at: www.irs.gov/Charities-&-Non-Profits/Exempt-Organizations-Annual-Reporting-Requirements-Form-990-Part-VI-and-Schedule-L-Compensation [last checked February 25, 2017].

- (Column d): Description of transaction. As noted in next passage, if more space is required, or desired, reference Schedule L's Part V blank lines.
- (Column e): Yes/No as to whether sharing of revenues occurred.

Use Part V for Additional Space

If lacking space and, particularly, if a filer wants to include more expansive, public relations information (for example, in line with the sample return snippet shown previously, to state that Mr. Somprivacy was the Development Director since 1999, well before the hire of Ms. Flagg), Column (d) can reference Part V's blank lines, where the longer statement can then be provided.

Aggregation Allowed for Multiple Transactions

> **Aggregate reporting.** The organization can aggregate multiple individual transactions between the same parties, or list them separately. If aggregation is chosen, report the aggregate amount in column (c) and describe the various types of transactions (for example, "consulting," "rental of real property") in column (d).

Schedule L—Part II, Loans To/From Interested Persons

Part II reports IPs who had a loan outstanding at year-end. From the 2014 Form forward, an IP for this part is a: TDOKE, <u>creator or founder</u>, <u>substantial contributor</u>, family member of any of the preceding, or a <u>35-percent Controlled Entity</u> of any/ all IPs.[14]

> Note: The three underlined categories appearing in the preceding paragraph were added to this part as of the 2014 Form.

> WARNING. The trigger question at Core Form Part IV, Q.26, shown in the following reprint, was not updated by the IRS on the 2014-2016 Forms and thus <u>does NOT reflect the current harmonization of the Schedule L's IP definitions.</u> The trigger question is wrong in these ways:
>
> - Core Form—Balance Sheet: Part X, Lines 5 and 22 reports loans undertaken with key employees, who are now omitted from characterization as Interested Persons on Schedule L, Part II, and thus the term "highest compensated employees" should not appear in Core Form Part IV, Q.26
> - Core Form—Balance Sheet: Part X, Lines 6 and 22 report loans undertaken with disqualified persons, who are now omitted from characterization as Interested Persons and thus the term "disqualified persons" should not appear in Core Form Part IV, Q.26
> - Core Form Part X, Lines 5, 6 and 22 do not reference creators/founders and substantial contributors and thus reference to these lines is imperfect, plus Core Form Part IV, Q.26 need not add such terms...

Core Form Part IV, Line 26 reprint follows (but note warning)

26	Did the organization report any amount on Part X, line 5, 6, or 22 for receivables from or payables to any current or former officers, directors, trustees, key employees, highest compensated employees, or disqualified persons? If so, complete Schedule L, Part II . . . .

SCHEDULE L, PART II'S HEADER MAKES THE SAME INACCURATE REFERENCES NOTED IN THE PRECEDING WARNING

Part II — **Loans to and/or From Interested Persons.**
Complete if the organization answered "Yes" on Form 990-EZ, Part V, line 38a or Form 990, Part IV, line 26; or if the organization reported an amount on Form 990, Part X, line 5, 6, or 22.

(a) Name of Interested person	(b) Relationship with organization	(c) Purpose of loan	(d) Loan to or from the organization?		(e) Original principal amount	(f) Balance due	(g) In default?		(h) Approved by board or committee?		(i) Written agreement?	
			To	From			Yes	No	Yes	No	Yes	No
(1)												
(2)												

---

[14] These are IP categories numbered 1-5 (the standardized categories) set out, with pertinent exclusions, in table 1 provided earlier in this chapter.

THE 990'S CORE FORM PART X CONTINUES THE MISREPRESENTATION OF WHEN SCHEDULE L, PART II IS TRIGGERED

- Core Form Part X's Lines 5, 6, and 22 (reprinted as followed) continue the Form's practice of referencing now-obsolete triggers. As noted in previous sections, as of the 2014 Form neither loans to/ from highest compensated employees (Lines 5 and 22) nor to disqualified persons (Lines 6 and 22) are reportable; furthermore, these lines of Core Form Part X do not necessarily capture creators/ founders and substantial contributors, both of which now constitute IPs on Schedule L, Part II. Accordingly, the highlighted phrases on the reprinted balance sheet lines are NOT triggers:

Part X	Balance Sheet		
	Check if Schedule O contains a response or note to any line in this Part X . . . . ☐	(A) Beginning of year	(B) End of year
5	Loans and other receivables from current and former officers, directors, trustees, key employees, and highest compensated employees. Complete Part II of Schedule L 5		
6	Loans and other receivables from other disqualified persons (as defined under section 4958(f)(1)), persons described in section 4958(c)(3)(B), and contributing employers and sponsoring organizations of section 501(c)(9) voluntary employees' beneficiary organizations (see instructions). Complete Part II of Schedule L 6		
22	Loans and other payables to current and former officers, directors, trustees, key employees, highest compensated employees, and disqualified persons. Complete Part II of Schedule L 22		

UNDERSTANDING PART II'S REACH AND UNIQUE DEFINITIONS

As is the case for the other parts of this Schedule (aside from Part I's reporting of excess benefit transactions), the point of the requisite disclosures here is transparency and sunlight, not judging the fact of a transaction. Preparers need understand both the details noted in tables 1 and 2 provided at the beginning of this chapter, the key timing detail (loan outstanding at year-end), and the bank deposits exception.

Note: Part II works in two directions, reporting both loans from filer-to-IP as well as loans from IP-to-filer.

- Trigger here is the fact of a year-end receivable or payable in any amount from or to any Interested Person.
- Salary advances outstanding on the last day of the tax year = loans for Part II purposes
- All OTHER receivables from employees (other than amounts reportable as excess benefit transactions in Schedule L, Part I) are reportable as loans for Part II purposes
- Salary advances and other advances and loans to or from non-employee IPs, as well as payments made pursuant to a split-dollar life insurance arrangement that are treated as loans under Treasury Regulation 1.7872-15, and other advances and receivables outstanding on the last day of the tax year (other than amounts reportable as excess benefit transactions in Schedule L, Part I) = loans for Part II purposes

There is no minimum threshold for reporting loans. Each loan must be separately listed on Schedule L, Part II. It does not matter if the original loan was originally between an IP and a third party; if on the last day of the year the loan is between the filing organization and an IP, except as subsequently noted, the loan should be reported on Part II of Schedule L.

Exceptions:

There are multiple common sense carve-outs limiting what is considered a loan (both for purposes of Core Form Part X (balance sheet) and corollary reporting here in Schedule L-II). Do not report the following as loans on Schedule L, Part II:

> * **Excess benefit transactions** reported in Schedule L, Part I.
> * Advances under an **accountable plan** as described in the instructions for Part II of Schedule J (Form 990), Compensation Information.
> * Pledges receivable that would qualify as charitable contributions when paid.
> * Accrued but unpaid **compensation** owed by the organization.
> * Loans from a credit union made to an interested person on the same terms as offered to other members of the credit union.
> * **Tax-exempt bonds** purchased from the filing organization and held by an interested person, so long as the interested person purchased the bonds on the same terms as offered to the general public.

> * Deposits into a bank account (when the bank is an interested person) in the ordinary course of business, on the same terms as the bank offers to the general public.
> * Receivables for a section 501(c)(9) voluntary employees' beneficiary organization from a sponsoring organization or contributing employer of the VEBA, if those receivables were created in the ordinary course of business and have been due for 90 days or fewer.
> * Receivables outstanding that were created in the ordinary course of the organization's business on the same terms as offered to the general public (such as receivables for medical services provided by a **hospital** to an officer of the hospital).

WHAT IS REQUIRED TO BE REPORTED IN PART II?

The following list shows the information that must be reported in Part II:

- Each loan is reported separately, regardless of amount, thus the details in Columns (c)–(i) will vary accordingly)
- Name (of interested person)—in Column (a)
- Relationship between the IP and the filer is inputted in Column (b)
- Purpose of transaction (can be cursory)—in Column (c); direction of transaction is reported in Column (d)
- Original principal as well as complete balance due at year end (instructions state to include not only accrued interest but any applicable penalties and collection costs) in Columns (e) and (f)
- Columns (g), (h), and (i) are there to promulgate (by reminder or otherwise) the need for good governance in handling insider loans

> PRACTICE TIP 1: It is never too late to have an outstanding loan approved by the board or committee of the board, thus allowing the filing on the tax year that must report the loan to earn a "Yes" answer in Column (h). Similarly, memorializing a loan's terms via a written agreement can be done to effect a later year "Yes" answer in Column (i).
>
> PRACTICE TIP 2: Expanded disclosures may be made in this Schedule's blank-lines part, Part V.

KNOWLEDGE CHECK

6. A bank is an IP of filer E. Which condition would void the exception by which the fact of a loan with the bank would be subject to reporting on Part II?

    a. E is offered a certificate of deposit that pays interest at four basis points higher than the bank makes available to any other customer.
    b. E deposits its cash reserve balance of $25,000 into a money market savings account at the bank.
    c. E uses the bank as a payroll depository and is not entitled to earnings on the float the bank retains.
    d. None of the above.

7. Which arrangement filer F makes with its board chair G IS reportable on Part II?

    a. G has pledged F a charitable contribution of $50,000 and same is outstanding at year-end.
    b. G takes travel advance of $2,000 at year-end attributable to business trip occurring first month of the next year which is subject to F's accountable plan reporting policy.
    c. G has taken a one-month salary advance at year-end.
    d. G enrolls in F's fee-for-service financial planning program and is billed $400 at year-end on the same basis as all others enrolling in the program.

Schedule L, Part III—Grants or Assistance Benefiting Interested Persons

Part III reports a filer's having provided an IP with grants or assistance (when same are outside the two exceptions). From the 2014 Form forward, an IP for this part is a TDOKE, creator or founder, substantial contributor (SC), family members of any of the preceding, or a 35-percent Controlled Entity of any/ all IPs, PLUS two more unique-to-this-part IP categories: [15] grant selection committee members (and their family members) and employees of a SC as well as employees of a 35-percent controlled entity of a SC, but only in certain circumstances[16]

Part III reporting is mandated via this trigger question at Core Form Part IV, Q.27 which has not been properly updated for the 2014 and forward instruction changes as it fails to include one IP category, that of <u>creator or founder</u>:

| 27 | Did the organization provide a grant or other assistance to an officer, director, trustee, key employee, substantial contributor or employee thereof, a grant selection committee member, or to a 35% controlled entity or family member of any of these persons? If "Yes," complete Schedule L, Part III . . . . | 27 | ✓ | |

Part III	Grants or Assistance Benefiting Interested Persons. Complete if the organization answered "Yes" on Form 990, Part IV, line 27.			
(a) Name of interested person	(b) Relationship between interested person and the organization	(c) Amount of assistance	(d) Type of assistance	(e) Purpose of assistance
(1)				

---

[15] See address of IP categories 1-5 (the standardized categories), as well as the two that are applicable only to this part, categories 7-8, and the pertinent exclusions from such characterization across all seven categories, in table 1 provided earlier in this chapter.

[16] This part's additional IP category (# 8 on page 5) for grants to an employee of (or child of an employee of) a substantial contributor (SC) OR to an employee of (or child of an employee of) a 35-percent controlled entity is only in place when

- *the employee or child of an employee received the grant/ assistance by the direction or advice of the SC or its 35-percent controlled entity; or*
- *the employee or child of an employee received the grant/ assistance under a program funded by the SC to primarily benefit such employees (or their children).*

Note: Both Part III exclusions (addressed on page 26) are relevant to this category of IP.

What to Report on Part III?
Definition of Grant or Other Assistance?

The Schedule L instructions for this part begin with this overarching instruction (note that the term grant or other assistance is not in bold type):

> Report each grant or other assistance (including provision of goods, services, or use of facilities), regardless of amount, provided by the organization to any interested person at any time during the organization's **tax year.** Examples of grants are scholarships, fellowships, discounts on goods or services, internships, prizes, and awards. A grant includes the gift portion of a part-sale, part-gift transaction.

The term "grant or other assistance" is defined in the glossary. The Schedule L instructions do not reference it in bold, apparently because the definition itself (reprinted as follows) does NOT refer to Schedule L.

> For purposes of Part IX, Lines 1-3; Schedule F (Form 990) and Schedule I (Form 990), includes awards, prizes, contributions, noncash assistance, cash allocations, stipends, scholarships, fellowships, research grants, and similar payments and distributions made by the organization during the tax year. It does not include salaries or other **compensation** to employees or payments to **independent contractors** if the primary purpose is to serve the direct and immediate needs of the organization (such as legal, accounting, or fundraising services); the payment of any benefit by a Section 501(c)(9) ...(VEBA) to employees of a sponsoring organization or contributing employer, if such payments is made under the terms of the VEBA and incompliance with Section 505...

Exceptions

Excepted from Part III reporting are transactions comprising excess benefit transactions or loans (these are instead reported in Parts I and II, respectively) as well as the following not intended to be caught here exceptions:

- Business transactions with IPs that do not contain any gift element and that are engaged to serve the direct and immediate needs of the organization. Examples include
  - compensation (including benefits) paid to an employee or contractor; and
  - compensation (including benefits) paid to an individual listed on Part VII of the Core Form.

These compensation transactions may be captured on Part IV of Schedule L if they exceed the reporting thresholds and are not excluded by one of Part IV's exceptions to reporting.

In addition, certain grants are excluded from reporting on Part III of Schedule L:

- Grants or assistance provided to an IP as a member of the charitable class or other class (such as a member of a 501(c)(5), 501(c)(6), or 501(c)(7) organization) that the organization intends to benefit in furtherance of its exempt purpose, if provided on similar terms as provided to other members of the class, such as short-term disaster relief, poverty relief, or trauma counseling. However, grants for travel, study (such as scholarships or fellowships), or other similar purposes (such as to achieve a specific objective, produce a report or other similar product, or improve or enhance a literary, artistic, musical, scientific, teaching, or other similar capacity, skill, or talent of the grantee) like those described in Section 4945(d)(3) are not excluded from reporting under this exception.
- Grants to employees (and their children) of a substantial contributor or 35-percent controlled entity of a substantial contributor, awarded on an objective and nondiscriminatory basis based on pre-established criteria and reviewed by a selection committee, as described in Regulations Section 53.4945-4(b).

Note that the first exception, for assistance and grants made to charitable class or other 501(c)-class intended beneficiaries provided in furtherance of exempt purpose on the same terms as provided to other members of the class, specifically does not reach (and thus does not exclude from reporting) grants for travel, study (including scholarships or fellowship) or similar purposes (including improvement of the individual, achievement of a specific objective, and so on).

8. The local chapter of a national disaster-relief organization, RO, and a wounded veterans support organization that works in the same geographic area, VO, pair together to provide training opportunities for VO's constituency to learn emergency medical physician's assistant services. In the course of the year, RO provides the following grants or assistance to VO's members. Which are NOT subject to reporting on Schedule L Part III by RO if delivered by RO to VO members who are also RO's IPs?

    a. Emergency medical physician assistant's field training in the course of an actual disaster-relief operation RO conducts.

    b. Tuition assistance in support of procuring college prerequisites necessary for medical physician assistant degree program.

    c. Temporary housing assistance to those who lost their homes in RO's local disaster-relief operation, qualifying for aid on the same basis as the public.

    d. Internship stipend to those who have lost their homes and agree to temporarily leave their jobs and assist in RO's local chapter disaster-relief operation.

What Schools and Colleges are to Report on Part III: NO Requirement to Identify Certain Individual Grantees

Schools and colleges have a special reporting convention: with respect to grants made to an interested person for travel, study, or similar purposes. In these cases, the identity of the individual who triggers the report is not required to be revealed. This convention provides an out whereby confidentiality of student-recipients will not be violated. Enunciation of this convention is in both the instructions and on the IRS website:

> *Schools.* Colleges, universities, and primary and secondary schools are not required to identify interested persons to whom they provided scholarships, fellowships, and similar financial assistance. Instead, these organizations must, in Part III, group each type of financial assistance (for example, need-based scholarships, merit scholarships, discounted tuition) provided to interested persons in separate lines. For each line, the school should report in Column (c) the aggregate dollar amount of each type of assistance, the type of assistance in Column (d), and the purpose of the assistance in Column (e), unless such reporting would be an unauthorized disclosure of student education records under the Family Educational Rights and Privacy Act (FERPA). Columns (a) and (b) should be left blank for these lines.

Grants to recipients in these circumstances are reported by group and type: one line is used for each type, and columns (a) and (b) are left blank:

Part III	Grants or Assistance Benefiting Interested Persons. Complete if the organization answered "Yes" on Form 990, Part IV, line 27.			
(a) Name of interested person	(b) Relationship between interested person and the organization	(c) Amount of assistance	(d) Type of assistance	(e) Purpose of assistance
(1)		1,000	Scholarship	Merit award
(2)		10,000	Fellowship	Laboratory research
(3)		6,920	Financial Aid	Needs-based award

It is also the case that no name (or other revealing information as to identity) is to be included in Part III reporting when a grantee is a Substantial Contributor (SC). But note that if an IP holds such status both as a SC and through another category, their non-SC status is to be reported as the rationale for inclusion in this part.

Column (b). Describe the relationship between the interested person that benefitted from the grant or assistance and the organization, such as spouse of Director John Smith. If substantial contributor was entered in Column (a), enter substantial contributor here as well. If related to substantial contributor was entered in Column (a), then describe the relationship without referring to specific names, for example: child of employee of *35-percent controlled entity* of substantial contributor.

If an interested person has interested person status other than by being a substantial contributor or related to a substantial contributor, then make no reference to the substantial contributor status. For example, if grantee Jane Smith is both a substantial contributor and the spouse of Director John Smith, then she must be listed by name in Column (a), and Column (b) must state spouse of Director John Smith or words to similar effect.

Anonymity provided under the previous two rules (for colleges or schools regarding scholarships, fellowships, and so on, and for those whose only status as IP derives from status as substantial contributor) does not change count of independent voting members of the governing body (a trustee or director) on the last day of the tax year. This is the case as the fact that an individual's name is not evidenced upon Schedule L, Part III does not change that they have failed one of the independence conditions per the (Core Form) Part VI, Line 1b definitions.

DISCUSSION EXAMPLES OF PARTIES/ FACTS LEADING TO SCHEDULE L, PART III DISCLOSURE

University D provided a fellowship to Diamond to support her graduate studies at the university early in the tax year. After that award/ payment, but prior to the end of that same tax year, Diamond's father joined D's governing body as a voting member and was still serving as a director of D at the close of the year. On these facts, the receipt by Diamond of the fellowship will be reportable on Schedule L, Part III and her father will fall outside of D's count of independent directors serving at yearend for purposes of the Core Form's Part VI, Q. 1b—a result in place even though neither he nor his family member will be required to have their name reported on Schedule L, Part III under the exception provided to schools and colleges or universities for naming recipients of scholarships, fellowships, and similar financial assistance.

Foundation D has a TDOKE, Dimitri who has a > 35 percent (by voting power) stock interest in a small business incubator, Demo-Donee. Demo-Donee received a demonstration project grant from D in the current tax year, after competing for the award in a national pool process that was judged by an objective and disinterested qualified panel of specialists. As these facts make Demo-Donee a 35-percent controlled entity, the grant will be reportable on Schedule L, Part III (and were Dimitri to still be a director of D at yearend, his status as a stake-holder in said entity will place him outside the count of D's independent directors on the current year's Form 990).

9. College H has a financial aid fund that is dedicated to assisting children of retired employees. One of the recipients is the child of the college's ex-president. The ex-president is reported on Core Form Part VII, Section A as a former Officer of H. On these facts, which statement is *incorrect*?

    a. Report of the financial aid award to H's child will be required on Part III.

    b. Report of the financial aid award to H's child will not be a subject of Part III disclosure because the fund is an element of employee benefit and thus not a grant or other assistance.

    c. The name of H's child who is the financial aid assistance need be disclosed.

    d. The dollar amount of the grant will be included on Core Form Part IX's grant lines.

Schedule L—Part I, Excess Benefit Transactions (501(c)(3), (c)(4) and (c)(29) organizations only)

Part I *reporting is mandated via this trigger question at* Core Form Part IV Q.25a/ b. This is an extremely rare reporting event to see on the Form 990. Although we spend time with definitions and how to determine who and whether an excess benefit transaction has occurred, it is a determination that is ordinarily made by the organization's board after learning of facts prior unknown to them relating to a board member or high ranking employee having transacted with the organization, or as the result of an IRS examination. Legal counsel experienced with this area of law should be consulted and with their input, information provided to the 990 preparer relating to required Form 990 disclosures and the potential need to file Form 4720.

25a	**Section 501(c)(3), 501(c)(4), and 501(c)(29) organizations.** Did the organization engage in an excess benefit transaction with a disqualified person during the year? *If "Yes," complete Schedule L, Part I*	**25a**		
b	Is the organization aware that it engaged in an excess benefit transaction with a disqualified person in a prior year, and that the transaction has not been reported on any of the organization's prior Forms 990 or 990-EZ? *If "Yes," complete Schedule L, Part I*	**25b**		

Part I is the mechanism by which 501(c)(3) public charities, 501(c)(4)s, and 501(c)(29)s report that they have had an excess benefit transaction undertaken with a disqualified person as such terms are defined in the *Intermediate Sanctions Excise Tax Scheme set out in Section 4958*. The potential liability for excise tax here vests not against the filer but against the disqualified person being reported upon (also, potentially, against organization managers who approved the transaction knowing it to convey excess benefit).

Part I	**Excess Benefit Transactions** (section 501(c)(3), section 501(c)(4), and 501(c)(29) organizations only). Complete if the organization answered "Yes" on Form 990, Part IV, line 25a or 25b, or Form 990-EZ, Part V, line 40b.				
1	**(a)** Name of disqualified person	**(b)** Relationship between disqualified person and organization	**(c)** Description of transaction	**(d)** Corrected?	
				Yes	No
(1)					
(2)					

2	Enter the amount of tax incurred by the organization managers or disqualified persons during the year under section 4958 . . . . ▶	$
3	Enter the amount of tax, if any, on line 2, above, reimbursed by the organization . . . . ▶	$

Three understandings are necessary to proper completion of this part:

1. **WHAT** is an excess benefit transaction (EBT)?
2. **WHO** qualifies as an interested person for this part–such as, as a disqualified person (DP)
3. **WHAT** is required to be reported were an excess benefit transaction to have occurred and thus be subject to reporting?

WHAT Are EBTs (and Why Does an Excise Tax Scheme Apply to Them)?

The notion of excess benefit transactions (a glossary term, see definition in following text box) was originally imposed by the 1996 enactment of Section 4958, setting out an excise tax scheme that 'punishes' certain insiders. The tax structure is modeled after the excise taxes in place to enforce the self-dealing prohibition for private foundations and their managers. Under Section 4958, the parties subject to sanctions are disqualified persons (DPs), and the taxes apply when they benefit from an uneven exchange with a 501(c)(3) public charity, 501(c)(4) or 501(c)(29) in the time period when they are in substantial influence or at any time in the five years after such status ceases.

An uneven exchange under the statute is one in which the DP provides less to the applicable tax exempt organization in any transaction than a like person would pay for like goods/services in like circumstances. In other words, an economic benefit is provided to the DP which exceeds the economic benefit garnered by the applicable exempt organization. [Pursuant to the Pension Protection Act of 2006, an additional set of EBTs are set out in the case of supporting organizations (to enforce prohibited transactions with such entities' substantial contributors) as well as with respect to donor-advised funds (to enforce prohibited transactions with donors or donor advisers – the latter a glossary term – of such funds).[17]]

The excise tax scheme in essence punishes a DP and compels them to return the affected organization to the position they would have been in had the EBT not been undertaken.[18]

> Excess benefit transaction. An excess benefit transaction generally is a transaction in which an applicable tax-exempt organization (see next paragraph) directly or indirectly provides to or for the use of a disqualified person an economic benefit the value of which exceeds the value of the consideration received by the organization for providing such benefit. For special Section 4958 rules governing transactions with donor advised funds and supporting organizations, see the special rules under Section 4958 Excess Benefit Transactions in appendix G in the Instructions for Form 990, or appendix E in the Instructions for Form 990-EZ.
>
> An applicable tax-exempt organization is an organizations which (without regard to any excess benefit) are 501(c)(3) public charities, 501(c)(4) or 501(c)(29) organizations, or organizations that had such status at any time during the 5-year period ending on the date of the excess benefit transaction.

---

[17] That extension is beyond the scope of this chapter. It imposes excess benefit transaction treatment upon impermissible intersections of those advising donor advised funds or connected in certain ways to 509(a)(3) supporting organizations.

[18] Under Section 4958, any disqualified person who benefits from an excess benefit transaction with an applicable tax-exempt organization is liable for a 25 percent tax on the excess benefit. The disqualified person is also liable for a 200 percent tax on the excess benefit if the excess benefit is not corrected by a certain date. Also, organization managers who participate in an excess benefit transaction knowingly, willfully, and without reasonable cause are liable for a 10 percent tax on the excess benefit, not to exceed $20,000 for all participating managers on each transaction.

Who Qualifies as an Interested Person (that is, What Makes a Party a Disqualified Person for Purposes of Section 4958)?

IP status here relates solely to characterization under Section 4958's definition of disqualified persons. Status as a disqualified person (DP) exists for parties who are listed in Section 4958(f)(1) as further amplified by the Regulations. As you will see, the list of characteristics that lead to Tier 1 DP status is complicated (Note: The term DP applied here is also employed in the Core Form's Parts IX (Statement of Functional Expenses) and X (Balance Sheet); the term disqualified person employed in Schedule A, Part III, Line 7b for public support purposes, is *not* the same term, as there it is used in the context of the private foundation rules, within the meaning of Section 4946.)

The Schedule L, Part I meaning of DP is as follows (ignoring the term's application to donor advised funds and sponsoring organizations of donor advised funds), bracketed notes and underlining applied for emphasis:

> **4958(f)(1) Disqualified person.** The term disqualified person means, with respect to any transaction—
>
> (A) [1st Degree DPs:] any person who was, at any time during the 5-year period ending on the date of such transaction, <u>in a position to exercise substantial influence over the affairs of the organization. This includes, for example:</u>
>   a. <u>Voting members of the governing body of the filing organization,</u>
>   b. <u>Persons holding the power of Presidents, CEO, COO, or</u>
>   c. <u>Treasurers and CFOs.</u>
>
> [2nd Degree DPs follow:]
>
> (B) a member of the family of an individual described in subparagraph (A),
> (C) a 35-percent controlled entity of anyone included in A or B, [per definition supplied in Section 4958(f)(3)[19]] or
> (D) any person who is described in subparagraph (A), (B), or (C) with respect to a supporting organization described in Section 509(a)(3) and organized and operated exclusively for the benefit of, to perform the functions of, or to carry out the purposes of the applicable tax-exempt organization is a disqualified person with respect to the supported organization.

---

[19] **4958(f)(3) 35-percent controlled entity.**
   (A) In general. The term 35-percent controlled entity means
      (i) a corporation in which persons described in subparagraph (A) or (B) of paragraph (1) own more than 35 percent of the total combined voting power,
      (ii) a partnership in which such persons own more than 35 percent of the profits interest, and
      (iii) a trust or estate in which such persons own more than 35 percent of the beneficial interest.
   (B) Constructive ownership rules. Rules similar to the rules of paragraphs (3) and (4) of Section 4946(a) shall apply for purposes of this paragraph.
This statutory definition is tracked in the Glossary's definition of the term.

SUMMARY

Per Section 4958(f)(1), a 1st Degree DP is one who is (or has been) in substantial influence (in the prior 60 months before a transaction). Voting board members, as well as an organization's President, CEO, COO, Treasurer, and CFO are automatically deemed to be in substantial influence.

Others are considered to have substantial influence on the basis of actual facts and circumstances.

Facts and Circumstances

The Form 990 instructions' appendix G summarizes the Regulations' provisions as to employees who do NOT need be tested for power to exercise substantial influence over the affairs of the organization, as follows:

- No testing is required of an employee who receives benefits and total compensation below the amount with which the IRS considers them highly compensated –
  - 2010 and 2011: $110,000
  - 2012-2015: $ 115,000
  - 2016: $120,000

> SO LONG AS the employee: (a) did NOT hold executive or voting powers by which those with such powers are automatically considered to have substantial influence; (b) is NOT a family member of a disqualified person; and (c) is NOT a substantial contributor (under the private foundation rules).

A tax-exempt organization described in Section 501(c)(3), or a Section 501(c)(4) organization engaging in transactions with other Section 501(c)(4) organizations, is automatically outside of substantial influence and thus cannot be a DP.

Statutory Exclusions from DP Status

- Tax-exempt organizations described in Section 501(c)(3)
- 501(c)(4) organizations engaging in transactions with other 501(c)(4) organizations.

Automatic 'substantial influence' and the factors by which factually or circumstantially being in substantial influence, are both addressed in appendix G of the 990 instructions, as follows (in the excerpts that follow, bold has been added for emphasis and reformatting or explanatory text applied via use of [brackets]):

A disqualified person [of the first degree—for example, not including family members and 35-percent controlled entities—such further degrees addressed later in these materials], regarding any transaction, is any person who was in a position to exert substantial influence over the affairs of the applicable tax-exempt organization at any time during a 5-year period ending on the date of the transaction.

Persons who hold certain powers, responsibilities, or interests are among those who are [or, for example, are automatically considered to be] in a position to exert substantial influence over the affairs of the organization

. . . and they are:

- voting members of the governing body . . .
- Presidents, chief executive officers, or chief operating officers...
- Treasurers and chief financial officers.

> **Facts and circumstances tending to show substantial influence.**
> - The person founded the organization.
> - The person is a substantial contributor to the organization under the section 507(d)(2)(A) definition, only taking into account contributions to the organization for the past 5 years.
> - The person's compensation is primarily based on revenues derived from the activities of the organization that the person controls.
> - The person has or shares authority to control or determine a substantial portion of the organization's capital expenditures, operating budget, or compensation for employees.
> - The person manages a discrete segment or activity of the organization that represents a substantial portion of the activities, assets, income, or expenses of the organization, as compared to the organization as a whole.
> - The person owns a controlling interest (measured by either vote or value) in a corporation, partnership, or trust that is a disqualified person.
> - The person is a nonstock organization controlled directly or indirectly by one or more disqualified persons.

> **Facts and circumstances tending to show no substantial influence.**
> - The person is an independent contractor whose sole relationship to the organization is providing professional advice (without having decision-making authority) for transactions from which the independent contractor will not economically benefit.
> - The person has taken a vow of poverty.
> - Any preferential treatment the person receives based on the size of the person's donation is also offered to others making comparable widely solicited donations.
> - The direct supervisor of the person is not a disqualified person.
> - The person does not participate in any management decisions affecting the organization as a whole or a discrete segment of the organization that represents a substantial portion of the activities, assets, income, or expenses of the organization, as compared to the organization as a whole.
>
> **What about persons who staff affiliated organizations?** In the case of multiple affiliated organizations, the determination of whether a person has substantial influence is made separately for each applicable tax-exempt organization. A person may be a disqualified person for more than one organization in the same transaction.

And finally, a look at the Core Form instructions' glossary definition of DP (in next paragraphs) both sets out a summary of 4958(f)(1)'s reach (altered for 990 purposes by one happy factor, that being that the glossary definition of family member employed in the 990 instructions applies, rather than the one 4958(f)(1) would otherwise apply.[20]) and notes that filers do not need apportion within any one year transactions with a DP solely to the months of the year in which they were still within 60 months of their last position of substantial influence:

---

[20] Under Section 4958(f)(4).

A. For purposes of section 4958; Form 990, Parts IX and X; and Schedule L (Form 990 or 990-EZ), Transactions With Interested Persons, Parts I and II, any person (including an individual, corporation, or other entity) who was in a position to exercise substantial influence over the affairs of the **applicable tax-exempt organization** at any time during a 5-year period ending on the date of the transaction. If the 5-year period ended within the organization's **tax year**, the organization may treat the person as a disqualified person for the entire tax year. Persons who hold certain powers, responsibilities, or interests are among those who are in a position to exercise substantial influence over the affairs of the organization.

A disqualified person includes:　　　　　　　／　Glossary definition reprint follows
- A disqualified person's **family member**,
- A **35% controlled entity** of a (1) disqualified person and/or (2) family members of the disqualified person,
- A donor or **donor advisor** to a **donor advised fund**, or
- An investment advisor of a **sponsoring organization**.

The **disqualified persons** of a **supported organization** include the disqualified persons of a section 509(a)(3) **supporting organization** that supports the supported organization.

See *Appendix G* for more information on **disqualified persons** and section 4958 **excess benefit transactions**.

Family member, family relationship	Unless specified otherwise, the family of an individual includes only his or her spouse (see Rev. Rul. 2013-17 regarding same-sex marriage), ancestors, brothers and sisters (whether whole or half blood), children (whether natural or adopted), grandchildren, great-grandchildren, and spouses of brothers, sisters, children, grandchildren, and great-grandchildren.

Note: The glossary definition fails to emphasize what these materials earlier covered – that certain individuals (board members with voting rights, presidents/ CEOs/ COOs, and treasurers/ CFOs) are deemed to automatically be considered as in a position to exercise substantial influence over the affairs of the ... organization (such as, to be a '1st degree' DP under Section 4958(f)(1)).

Once first degree DPs are determined, additional 4958(f)(1) DPs need be determined. These are:

- The family members of 1st degree DPs (a glossary term, see reprint prior page)
- 35-percent controlled entities (control by any/ all DPs and their family members; this is the same glossary definition printed in the footnote three pages earlier)
- Only for filers who are a supported organization of a 509(a)(3) supporting organization: the DPs of such 509(a)(3)s are also DPs of the filer

Information on the EBTs that uniquely apply in the case of:

- a 501(c)(3) entity classified as a supporting organization under Section 509(a)(3); or
- a sponsoring organization of one or more donor advised funds

With respect to supporting organizations:

EBT status is invoked to enforce the prohibition against grants, loan, compensation, or similar payments going to disqualified persons. For such purposes, first tier Disqualified Persons are substantial contributors (applying the definition of said term in place for private foundations – for example, any person who contributed or bequeathed an aggregate of more than $5,000 to the organization, if that amount is more than 2 percent of the total contributions and bequests received by the organization before the end of the tax year of the organization in which the contribution or bequest is received; however, not included are grantors of a trust). It is not only first tier DPs who cannot receive any such prohibited payments or loans—further tiers include first tier DPs' family members, and all 35-percent controlled entities of prior-enunciated DPs. Such status is set out in Section 4958(c)(3)(B):

> Person described. A person is described in this subparagraph if such person is—(i) a substantial contributor to such organization, (ii) a member of the family (determined under Section 4958(f)(4)) of an individual described in clause (i), or (iii) a 35-percent controlled entity (as defined in Section 4958(f)(3) by substituting persons described in clause (i) or (ii) of Section 4958(c)(3)(B) for persons described in subparagraph (A) or (B) of paragraph (1) in subparagraph (A)(i) thereof).

_____

With respect to sponsoring organizations of donor-advised funds:
EBT status is invoked to enforce the prohibition against grants, loan, compensation, or similar payments, going to disqualified persons. For such purposes, first tier Disqualified Persons are donors (to a donor advised fund) or donor advisers recognized by the sponsoring organization. Further tiers include first tier DPs' family members, and then all 35-percent controlled entities of prior-enunciated DPs.

Donor adviser is a glossary term:

> Any person appointed or designated by a donor to advise a **sponsoring organization** on the distribution or investment of amounts held in the donor's **donor advised fund**.

_____

PART I REPORTING

- Each excess benefit transaction is reported regardless of amount
- Line 1(a): Name (of interested person)—no need to disclose how or why they fall into DP status [aside from description of type of DP status at Line 1(b)]
- Line 1(a): Name (of organization manager(s)) who participated in the transaction (this includes 'approving' it) knowing that it was an excess benefit transaction.
- Line 1(b): Reports relationship of the DP to the filer, for example, officer (of the filer) or family member of director or 35-percent controlled entity
- Line 1(c): Description of the transaction—can be cursory; example in Instructions is compensation package
- Line 1(d): Check-the-box if correction has been made (and consult exempt organizations tax lawyer to know what comprises same and how to deal with Form 4720 reporting, if any, as well as income tax reporting with respect to the interested person having received an excess benefit)

Part I	Excess Benefit Transactions (section 501(c)(3), section 501(c)(4), and 501(c)(29) organizations only). Complete if the organization answered "Yes" on Form 990, Part IV, line 25a or 25b, or Form 990-EZ, Part V, line 40b.				
1 (a) Name of disqualified person	(b) Relationship between disqualified person and organization	(c) Description of transaction		(d) Corrected?	
				Yes	No
(1) Ima Inatrouble	Executive Director	Appropriated filer's vehicle for personal use of family members			✓
(2)					
(3)					
(4)					
(5)					
(6)					

Remember public relations opportunity is available via the Schedule L's blank-lines part: Part V. Taking advantage of same, a filer might now regarding the preceding reporting:

> Ima was the organization's top management official (as Executive Director) in 2008-2013. Since her departure, the organization has come to understand that the then-new Sprinter *FTC* purchased by the organization in late 2010 for Inatrouble to use when making presentations on behalf of the filer, was actually used full-time by one of her family members throughout all of 2011, 2012, and 2013. The value of that use was not intended (nor reported) as compensation to Ms. Inatrouble at the time in which it occurred and is thus comprises an 'excess benefit' reported in Part I.

In the presence of an excess benefit transaction, the DP (and in some cases, organization managers) would be required to file Form 4720 (same is the Form upon which DPs report and pay the tax on excess benefit transactions)—enforcement of such assessment lies with the IRS of course.

Having a filer reimburse a DP's assessed tax would create another excess benefit transaction. Such a possibility is inquired of in lines 2 and 3:

2	Enter the amount of tax incurred by the organization managers or disqualified persons during the year under section 4958 . . . . ▶	$ _____
3	Enter the amount of tax, if any, on line 2, above, reimbursed by the organization . . . . ▶	$ _____

The complex requirements implicated here, and the sophisticated minefield invigorated when an EBT has occurred, leads to the following:

> WARNING: In almost all cases of Section 4958 excess benefit, filers should obtain legal guidance from experienced exempt organizations tax counsel. This is essential as the organization's posture here is adverse to that of the disqualified person, and the Regulations under Section 4958 are both lengthy and nuanced. Careful in application of the law is key, as settlement terms between the filer and the disqualified person will likely create additional EBTs, and further, may lead to <u>organization managers</u> being exposed to excise tax as well.

10. Organization I is a 501(c)(3) public charity who learns in calendar 2016 that one of its board members, Z, who served from 2013 through 2015 had informed I's accounting department that he was to be paid under an independent contractor agreement the sum of $30,000 in both the 2013 and 2014 years (checks to I were in fact issued in such amount in each year). No such agreement was approved by the board and it thus would be voidable, as a matter of State law, even if such an arrangement had been authorized by others in the organization. (Voidable means not enforceable.) Which accurately describes I's Part I reporting obligation related to excess benefit transactions on the next filed Form 990 with respect to these facts?

    a. No reporting obligation if the organization voids the arrangement and obtains the funds back with interest from Z.

    b. No reporting obligation if I can determine that ordinary and necessary services were provided to I by Z and that the value of those services was no less than $60,000.

    c. Reporting of the $60,000 total remittance amount is required.

    d. Reporting of the $60,000 total remittance amount, less value of services received back that were ordinary and necessary, is required.

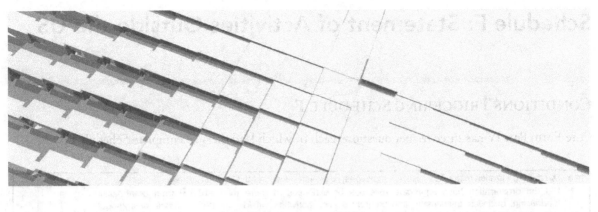

Chapter 7

FOREIGN ACTIVITIES (GRANT-MAKING AND BEYOND)

LEARNING OBJECTIVES

After completing this chapter, you should be able to do the following:

- Recognize what triggers the filing of Schedule F.
- Determine the level of detail required to be reported in each part of Schedule F.
- Identify when assistance to a foreign individual is reported at the entity versus individual level.

Schedule F: Statement of Activities Outside the US

CONDITIONS TRIGGERING SCHEDULE F

Core Form Part IV has three trigger questions each of which lead filers to complete Schedule F:

14 a Did the organization maintain an office, employees, or agents outside of the United States?	**14a**	
b Did the organization have aggregate revenues or expenses of more than $10,000 from grantmaking, fundraising, business, investment, and program service activities outside the United States, or aggregate foreign investments valued at $100,000 or more? *If "Yes," complete Schedule F, Parts I and IV.*	**14b**	
15 Did the organization report on Part IX, column (A), line 3, more than $5,000 of grants or other assistance to or for any foreign organization? *If "Yes," complete Schedule F, Parts II and IV*	**15**	
16 Did the organization report on Part IX, column (A), line 3, more than $5,000 of aggregate grants or other assistance to or for foreign individuals? *If "Yes," complete Schedule F, Parts III and IV.*	**16**	

Question 14a is actually not a trigger, but a survey question asking if the filer has maintained an office or employees outside of the US.

Question 14b is a trigger and a "Yes" to this question requires completion of Schedule F at both Parts I and IV. This question first asks the filer to add disparate amounts that are ordinarily netted (for financial statement purposes and potentially in part for Form 990 presentation). Specifically, the question asks if expenses PLUS revenues outside the United States during the year aggregate to greater than $10,000. The second question asked at 14b is whether foreign investments were valued, at any time during the tax year, at more than $100,000. A "Yes" to either trigger results in Schedule F, Part I filing.

PRACTICE TIP: When examining the possibility of foreign activities, a good internal check is to scan Schedule B to see if any contributors are listed with foreign addresses. Foreign fundraising is an often overlooked and underreported activity.

Note the instructions for Line 14b speak to the $100,000 investment threshold being tied to book value. The filing organization for Core Form Parts VIII, IX and X, may report income, expense and the investment in corporations and partnerships on the equity method. The IRS has agreed that filing organizations do not have to report the detailed K-1 activity on the Form 990. However, to determine if Schedule F is required, the instructions respect the difference in the tax law between a corporation and a partnership investment. The instructions note the difference in the tax rules for pass-thru of income and expenses of an investment in a corporation versus a partnership. Even though on a book basis the filer may record on the equity method, the filer must look at the revenue and expenses passed through from the partnership to determine if the partnership investment necessitates a Schedule F filing (this for Question 14b's first question, regarding revenue and expenses combined in excess of the $10,000 threshold). This may be problematic for organizations invested in alternative investments which do not receive schedules K-1 until after the May 15 filing deadline and want to file without extension.

PRACTICE TIP: For purposes of the $100,000 investment threshold (the second question of Question 14b, it is only DIRECT foreign investments that matter).

> **Lines 14a–14b.** Answer "Yes" to line 14a if the organization maintained an office, or had employees or agents, outside the **United States.** Answer "Yes," to line 14b if the organization had aggregate revenue or expenses of more than $10,000 from or attributable to grantmaking, **fundraising activities,** business, investment, and program service activities outside the **United States,** or if the book value of the organization's aggregate investments in foreign partnerships, foreign corporations, and other foreign entities was $100,000 or more at any time during the **tax year.**
>
> In the case of indirect investments made through investment entities, the extent to which revenue or expenses are taken into account in determining whether the $10,000 threshold is exceeded will depend upon whether the investment entity is treated as a partnership or corporation for U.S. tax purposes. For example, an organization with an interest in a foreign partnership would need to take into account its share of the partnership's revenue and expenses in determining whether the $10,000 threshold is exceeded. An organization with an investment in a foreign corporation would need to take into account dividends it receives from the corporation, but would not need to take into account or report any portion of the revenues, expenses, or expenditures of a foreign corporation in which it holds an investment, provided that the corporation is treated as a separate corporation for U.S. tax purposes.

Following Line 14, two more foreign activity questions follow. Lines 15 and 16 both relate to foreign grant-making activities. These questions specifically reach grants made to U.S. entities or individuals when such grants are restricted for foreign activity (that is, the funding's restrictions require the recipient to provide grants or other assistance to designated foreign organizations or foreign individuals—an example of the latter being earthquake victims in Haiti.) The Line 15 and 16 instructions, and the glossary definitions they apply follow:

> **Line 15.** Answer "Yes," if the organization reported on Part IX, Column (A), Line 3, more than $5,000 of **grants and other assistance** to <u>any</u> **foreign organization** or entity, (including a **foreign government**) or to a **domestic organization** or **domestic individual** for the purpose of providing grants or other assistance to a designated **foreign organization** or organizations.
>
> **Line 16.** Answer "Yes," if the organization reported on Part IX, Column (A), Line 3, more than $5,000 of <u>aggregate</u> **grants and other assistance** to **foreign individuals,** or to **domestic organizations** or **domestic individuals** for the purpose of providing grants or other assistance to a designed **foreign individual** or individuals.
>
> *Underlining added for emphasis in both lines' instructions.*

Foreign individual	A person, including a U.S. citizen or resident, who lives or resides outside the **United States.** For purposes of Form 990, Part IX, and Schedule F (Form 990), Statement of Activities Outside the United States, a person who lives or resides outside the United States at the time the grant is paid or distributed to the individual is a **foreign individual.**
Foreign organization	An organization that is not a **domestic organization.** A foreign organization includes an affiliate that is organized as a legal entity separate from the filing organization, but does not include any branch office, account, or **employee** of a domestic organization located outside the **United States.**

Part IV's Line 15 applies a > $5,000 threshold of grants or assistance having been paid to or incurred in favor of either any one foreign organization or entity OR (as emphasized above) to/ for any one domestic organization or individual for the purpose of providing grants or assistance to foreign organizations or individuals. Accordingly, the greater than $5,000 amount to trigger the Schedule need be evaluated on a by recipient basis by looking behind the entries at Core Form, Part IX, Line 3 (shown here) when the grant-making is effectively to or for the benefit of organizations or entities. [Line 16, the trigger with respect to reporting grantmaking to foreign individuals, or to domestic organizations or domestic individuals for the purpose of providing grants or other assistance to a designed foreign individual or individuals, uses $5,000 in the aggregate as the trigger.]

Part IX	Statement of Functional Expenses				
Section 501(c)(3) and 501(c)(4) organizations must complete all columns. All other organizations must complete column (A).					
Check if Schedule O contains a response or note to any line in this Part IX					
Do not include amounts reported on lines 6b, 7b, 8b, 9b, and 10b of Part VIII.		(A) Total expenses	(B) Program service expenses	(C) Management and general expenses	(D) Fundraising expenses
1	Grants and other assistance to domestic organizations and domestic governments. See Part IV, line 21	.			
2	Grants and other assistance to domestic individuals. See Part IV, line 22	1,596,299.	1,596,29		
3	Grants and other assistance to foreign organizations, foreign governments, and foreign individuals. See Part IV, lines 15 and 16	8,495,316.	8,495,31		

Activities Outside of the U.S.

Schedule F requires filers to provide more information on activities conducted outside the U.S. The glossary definition of that term and the Schedule R text both set out the activities to be reported, but each uses the word includes, so its list is not necessarily exhaustive; the term 'program related investments' (PRI) was added to the Schedule F instruction set in 2012. Note that the definition of PRI in the Form 990 instructions requires the primary purpose of the investment to be in furtherance of the reporting organization's exempt purpose, but does not extend the definition to include prohibition of engaging in lobbying which applies were this term being used in a private foundation context related to Section 4944 exception to the jeopardizing investment prohibition.

Form 990 glossary definitions:

> **With respect to what is *not* within (i.e., what is "outside") the US, the instructions provide this definition:**
>
> > **United States** is defined as the 50 states and the District of Columbia, the Commonwealth of Puerto Rico, the Commonwealth of the Northern Mariana Islands, Guam, American Samoa, and the United States Virgin Islands. A "foreign country" is any sovereignty that is not the **United States**.

> **Program-related Investment:**
>
> Investments made primarily to accomplish the organization's exempt purposes rather than to produce income. Examples of program-related investments include student loans and notes receivable from the other exempt organizations that obtained the funds to pursue the filing organization's exempt function.

KNOWLEDGE CHECK

1. Which fact scenario would not trigger a Schedule F filing?

    a. The filing organization contributed $50,000 to the United Way of San Diego restricted to its program to provide services in Tijuana, Mexico aiding families divided through U.S. deportation policies.

    b. The filing organization has a $1M investment in a domestic partnership that has a $200,000 investment in a foreign corporation.

    c. The filing organization is a calendar year taxpayer on the accrual method of accounting. They accrued and paid $8,000 on foreign travel to conferences and trainings in Japan, Korea and Canada in the year to be reported upon. In December of that year, they received an unconditional promise of a contribution from a Toronto, Ontario Canada donor in the amount of $4,500 USD. The gift was received in January of the following tax year.

    d. The filing organization invested $110,000 in a program-related investment for clean water filters. The company invested in is a U.S.-based company but the funds are to be used in Africa.

2. Which grantee, whose circumstances are described at the time they receive a grant, is a foreign individual?

    a. A U.S. citizen who has dual Canadian citizenship and is residing in the United States.

    b. A non-U.S. citizen who resides in the United States.

    c. A U.S. citizen who is temporarily living in Canada.

    d. A U.S. citizen who was born in Canada but is currently residing in the United States.

SCHEDULE F PREPARATION

A helpful first point of note: Filers do not have to list the specific countries in which their efforts are undertaken. The instructions group the world's countries into 10 regions, and those regions are reported when providing information on activities (in Schedule F, Part I) and when detailing grants and assistance provided to organizations/ entities and individuals (in Schedule F, Parts II and III). This methodology is employed due to security concerns to protect the identity of recipients or collaborators who might otherwise be identified if specific location was detailed. However, specific countries must be disclosed on other parts of the return (Part V, Line 4b FinCEN reporting) which removes some of the privacy provided by Schedule F.

The ten regions are:

- Antarctica
- Central America and the Caribbean
- East Asia and the Pacific
- Europe (Including Iceland and Greenland)
- Middle East and North Africa
- North America

- Russia and the newly independent states
- South America
- South Asia
- Sub-Saharan Africa

The instructions acknowledge that services provided over the Internet can make it difficult to determine if the users are domestic or foreign. Therefore, expenses for services provided in the United States that include recipients both inside and outside the United States should not be reported on Part I. The example used in the instructions is telemedicine and service provided via the Internet.

Part I—General Information on Activities Outside the United States

Part I starts with two questions that are only applicable to grant-making organizations, driving such filers to use Part V's blank lines to provide the required narrative answers. Note: Many grant makers will also be specifically required to complete the grant information required in Parts II and III. Organizations who are completing Schedule F solely because of non-grantmaking activities do not answer questions 1 and 2. However, if they make grants but not at a level triggering reporting on Part II or III, the organization should answer questions 1 and 2 and report those foreign grant-making activities on Part I as a separate line item.

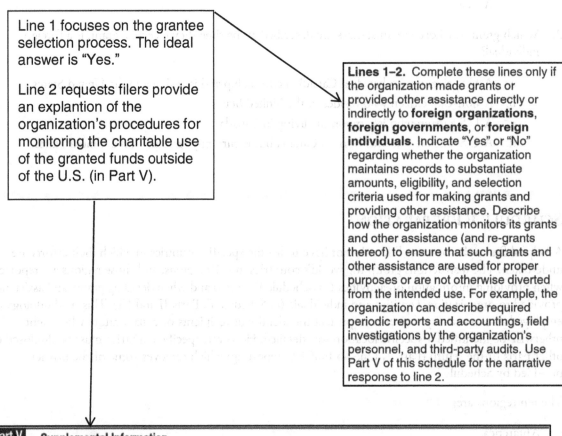

Line 1 focuses on the grantee selection process. The ideal answer is "Yes."

Line 2 requests filers provide an explantion of the organization's procedures for monitoring the charitable use of the granted funds outside of the U.S. (in Part V).

Lines 1–2. Complete these lines only if the organization made grants or provided other assistance directly or indirectly to **foreign organizations**, **foreign governments**, or **foreign individuals**. Indicate "Yes" or "No" regarding whether the organization maintains records to substantiate amounts, eligibility, and selection criteria used for making grants and providing other assistance. Describe how the organization monitors its grants and other assistance (and re-grants thereof) to ensure that such grants and other assistance are used for proper purposes or are not otherwise diverted from the intended use. For example, the organization can describe required periodic reports and accountings, field investigations by the organization's personnel, and third-party audits. Use Part V of this schedule for the narrative response to line 2.

Part V **Supplemental Information**

Provide the information required by Part I, line 2 (monitoring of funds); Part I, line 3, column (f) (accounting method; amounts of investments vs. expenditures per region); Part II, line 1 (accounting method); Part III (accounting method); and Part III, column (c) (estimated number of recipients), as applicable. Also complete this part to provide any additional information (see instructions).

Although provision of grants and assistance to individuals is also the subject of reporting on Parts II and III, these activities are also addressed in Part I. Though grantmaking reporting in Parts II and III will only provide information on grants to parties receiving > $5,000, Part I completion is still required even had no one recipient been provided grants or assistance valued at more than $5,000. If other activities trigger a Schedule F, Part I filing and there are grantmaking activities below the $5,000 per grantee threshold, there will still be grant-making activity disclosed in Part I AND answers will be required for questions 1 and 2 of this part.

Thereafter, Line 3 (reprint follows after the Line 3 instruction) is to be completed for all organizations with any type of activity outside the US hitting the thresholds denoted in the Core Form Part IV's question 14b.

Line 3. Enter the details for each type of activity conducted at any time during the **tax year** for each region on a separate line of Part I. If multiple activities are conducted per region, list each type of activity on a separate line and repeat regions in column (a) as necessary. Use the regions listed earlier.

Report each activity conducted in each region. Do not report more than one activity per region on a single line.

(a) Region	(b) Number of offices in the region	(c) Number of employees, agents, and independent contractors in region	(d) Activities conducted in region (by type) (e.g., fundraising, program services, investments, grants to recipients located in the region)	(e) If activity listed in (d) is a program service, describe specific type of service(s) in region	(f) Total expenditures for and investments in region
Central America/Caribbean	5	166	Program services	See Part V	3,314,373.
East Asia & the Pacific	11	208	Program services	See Part V	3,578,393.
Europe	0	0	Program services	See Part V	3,156.
Middle East & North Africa	0	0	Program services	Veterinary services	12,820.
North America	0	0	Program services	Veterinary services	15,984.
Central America	0	0	Grantmaking	N/A	211,788
East Asia Pacific	0	0	Grantmaking	N/A	411,985
Sub-Saharan Africa	15	198	Program services	See Part V	16,236,445.
3 a Sub-total	76	935			23,784,944.
b Total from continuation sheets to Part I	0	0			9,700.
c **Totals** (add lines 3a and 3b)	76	935			23,794,644.

Key points of the instructions to Part I are:

- Start reporting at the region level
- Report one activity per line
- Activities are reported if they are conducted at any time during the filing year
- Number of offices being reported in Column (b) should not be duplicated (reference to the regional office on the line above if necessary)
- Do not duplicate the number of employees, agents, and independent contractors reported in Column (c) (reference to the regional office on the line above if necessary)
- Number of volunteers is not sought for reporting on Schedule F
- Investments are to be reported separately (on a region-by-region basis) from other activities.
- Investments in a region may be aggregated for reporting and only Columns (a), (d), and (f) must be completed. Leave Columns (b), (c) and (e) blank for investments.
- Foreign investments are direct foreign investments. Schedule F does not include indirect foreign investments held through domestic pass-through investments. Similarly, if the foreign investment is traded on a U.S. exchange, it will not be treated as a foreign investment for Schedule F reporting purposes.

Three reporting conventions of note:

1. Types of activities in Column (d) should reflect specifics (for example, conducting board meetings or sending representatives to speak at conferences); when program services are an apt description in Column (d), the same are to be described in Column (e) or Part V if additional space is required.
2. Total amount of expenditures AND book value of investments (including program-related investments) for Column (f) reporting may be rounded to nearest $1,000
3. Indirect expenditure allocations for foreign activities do not need be reported in Column (f) if the filer does not separately track them

Parts II and III

Each of these parts report specifically on fact of grants or assistance having been provided. In both cases, it is only grants of > $5,000 to a specific grantee that are to be disclosed.

Part II

Although identifying information on grantees is not reported, the information for each grant of > $5,000 is entered on a separate line on Part II. Use duplicate Parts II if additional lines are needed. Report cash and non-cash grants. If grants are accrued but unpaid because the filing organization uses the accrual method of accounting, explain this on Part V of Schedule F as well of an explanation of when the organization expects the accrual to be fulfilled.

Schedule F reports grants made by the filing organization (whether restricted or unrestricted) and also reports sub-recipient awards where the filing organization did not select the grantee but the grantee was selected by the funder or some other organization. Filing organizations often want to report sub-recipients as subcontractors or something other than grantees. The proper reporting treats these as grants of the filer in the Core Form's Part IX (at either Line 1 or Line 3) with corollary reporting on either Schedule I or F depending upon whether the sub- recipient qualifies as having received a domestic or foreign grant.

Part II Grants and Other Assistance to Organizations or Entities Outside the United States. Complete if the organization answered "Yes" on Form 990, Part IV, line 15, for any recipient who received more than $5,000. Part II can be duplicated if additional space is needed.

1 (a) Name of organization	(b) IRS code section and EIN (if applicable)	(c) Region	(d) Purpose of grant	(e) Amount of cash grant	(f) Manner of cash disbursement	(g) Amount of non-cash assistance	(h) Description of non-cash assistance	(i) Method of valuation (book, FMV, appraisal, other)
		Central America	Health	0.		204,480.	De-worming	Red Book Value
		Central America	Veterinary service	0.		7,308.	Vet medicine/Supply	Red Book Value
		East Asia/Pacific	Earthquake relief	5,000.	Cash	0.		
		East Asia/Pacific	Vocational training	25,807.	cash	0.		
		East Asia/Pacific	Child protection	36,340.	Wire Transfer	0.		
		East Asia/Pacific	Child protection	44,719.	Wire Transfer	0.		
		East Asia/Pacific	Earthquake relief	42,780.	Wire Transfer	0.		
		East Asia/Pacific	Veterinary service	287,339.	Wire Transfer	0.		

2   Enter total number of recipient organizations listed above that are recognized as charities by the foreign country, recognized as tax-exempt by the IRS, or for which the grantee or counsel has provided a section 501(c)(3) equivalency letter .... ▶ 21

3   Enter total number of other organizations or entities .... ▶ 0

Part III Grants and Other Assistance to Individuals Outside the United States. Complete if the organization answered "Yes" on Form 990, Part IV, line 16. Part III can be duplicated if additional space is needed.

(a) Type of grant or assistance	(b) Region	(c) Number of recipients	(d) Amount of cash grant	(e) Manner of cash disbursement	(f) Amount of non-cash assistance	(g) Description of non-cash assistance	(h) Method of valuation (book, FMV, appraisal, other)
(1)							
(2)							

> Neither part seeks names of recipients (Column (a) is *grayed out* in Part II; Part III makes no request at all).

The treatment of Part II's Columns (d)–(i) and of Part III's Columns (c)–(h) are analogous to Schedule I's Parts I and II, with columns that are titled similarly.

If the recipient organization has no foreign office, report the foreign region where the grant funds will be used in Column (c).

Column (d), as with other parts of the form, should not state a general exempt purpose, such as educational or religious, but should be specific, such as de-worming or veterinary services.

In a nod to the accounting rules, the Form instructions state that the grant reported in Column (e) for accrual based tax payers should be the net present value reported on the audited financial statements.

However, this is not how most organizations record grants. (Filers typically record the entire grant for book purposes and then record one adjustment to the entire grants payable account for the net present value adjustment based upon the payables inside the account and make an overall annual adjustment each year.) In that situation, the filer is not adjusting each grant and thus the organization should report the amount it has on its books and records for each grant, as stated in the instructions. If a filer does record an allowance against specific grants, this information should be reported in Schedule F.

Column (i) should indicate the method used to determine the fair market value of any non-cash grants or assistance. This may include appraisal, a known authoritative literature, or estimated value.

Part III

Part III is similar to Part II, but here the subject is reporting direct grants or assistance the filer has paid to or incurred for foreign individuals. Use a separate line for each type of assistance to grant to a group of individuals in a particular region. Use duplicate Parts III for more space.

Grants to individuals are only reported as grants to individuals if the filing organization is making the grants directly to the individuals, or the amounts are specifically earmarked for specifically for identified individuals. If the grant is to a hospital for the medical care of individuals, that is a grant to a foreign organization reported on Part II. Similarly, if the grant is to a foreign school for scholarships, it is reported on Part II. However, if the organization selects 7 specific students to receive scholarships that would be assistance reported on Part III.

Use the principles of reporting previously described for Part II for Part III's columns.

For each type of assistance, explain the number of individuals who received the assistance. If the filing organization has no way to obtain an exact count, it may estimate the number receiving benefits. If an estimate is used the filing organization must explain Part V of how the estimate was determined.

KNOWLEDGE CHECK

3. Which type of assistance is reported on Part III of Schedule F?

    a. Seeds and educational materials provided to individual farmers in Southeast Asia farming collectives.
    b. Scholarship funds granted to a foreign university where the filing organization has a seat on the board that is advisory to the scholarship selection committee.
    c. Funds granted to a foreign orphanage for the care of 100 specific children under 18 years of age.
    d. Funds granted to a foreign health clinic to cover the cost of vaccinations of all children in the village under the age of 6.

Part IV

This Part serves the purpose of reminding filers of additional filing requirements that may reach their connection to foreign transactions or assets. Preparers should note that a "Yes" answer to any of this part's inquiries does not mean that the cited form automatically applies.

The instructions for each of these forms need be consulted to determine if the filing organization is subject to the relevant form's filing requirements.

Part IV	Foreign Forms	

1   Was the organization a U.S. transferor of property to a foreign corporation during the tax year? *If "Yes," the organization may be required to file Form 926, Return by a U.S. Transferor of Property to a Foreign Corporation (see Instructions for Form 926)* . . . . ☐ Yes   ☐ No

2   Did the organization have an interest in a foreign trust during the tax year? *If "Yes," the organization may be required to file Form 3520, Annual Return To Report Transactions With Foreign Trusts and Receipt of Certain Foreign Gifts, and/or Form 3520-A, Annual Information Return of Foreign Trust With a U.S. Owner (see Instructions for Forms 3520 and 3520-A; do not file with Form 990)* . . . . . . ☐ Yes   ☐ No

3   Did the organization have an ownership interest in a foreign corporation during the tax year? *If "Yes," the organization may be required to file Form 5471, Information Return of U.S. Persons With Respect to Certain Foreign Corporations (see Instructions for Form 5471)* . . . . ☐ Yes   ☐ No

4   Was the organization a direct or indirect shareholder of a passive foreign investment company or a qualified electing fund during the tax year? *If "Yes," the organization may be required to file Form 8621, Information Return by a Shareholder of a Passive Foreign Investment Company or Qualified Electing Fund (see Instructions for Form 8621)*. . . . . ☐ Yes   ☐ No

5   Did the organization have an ownership interest in a foreign partnership during the tax year? *If "Yes," the organization may be required to file Form 8865, Return of U.S. Persons With Respect to Certain Foreign Partnerships (see Instructions for Form 8865)* . . . . ☐ Yes   ☐ No

6   Did the organization have any operations in or related to any boycotting countries during the tax year? *If "Yes," the organization may be required to file Form 5713, International Boycott Report (see Instructions for Form 5713; do not file with Form 990)* . . . . ☐ Yes   ☐ No

KNOWLEDGE CHECK

4. With respect to completing Schedule F, which statements is correct?

    a. Organizations need report all grants to foreign organizations on Part II regardless of the amounts paid or incurred to each grantee.

    b. All organizations report both direct and indirect foreign expenses (of activities the form reaches) regardless of whether indirect expenses are tracked.

    c. Organizations may round amounts reported on Part I to the nearest $1,000.

    d. Organizations should only report amounts of revenue and expenses from the direct conduct of charitable activities and need not report expenses incurred in other activities outside of the United States (such as investment or fundraising).

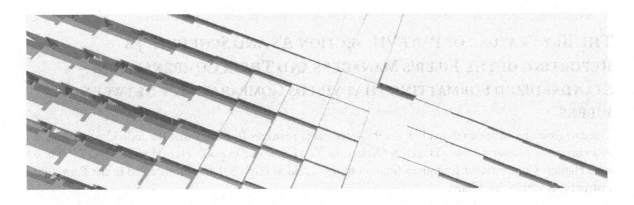

Chapter 8

FULLY DISCLOSING COMPENSATION ON SCHEDULE J—THE REST OF THE CORE FORM PART VII STORY

LEARNING OBJECTIVES

After completing this chapter, you should be able to do the following:

- Identify the triggers which lead to the filing organization being required to complete Schedule J-II[1] and appreciate that with such completion comes the requirement to prepare Schedule J-I, which addresses compensation practices and policy implementation overall.
- Recognize the details of what compensation is not required to be reported on Part VII of the Core Form but IS required to be reported on Schedule J-II.

---

[1] Parts of the Schedule J are each referenced by Schedule letter and part number. For example, Part II is J-II.

THE KEY FEATURE OF PART VII-SECTION A'S AND SCHEDULE J'S REPORTING OF THE FILER'S MANAGERS AND THEIR COMPENSATION— STANDARDIZED FORMATTING THAT YIELDS COMPARABILITY BETWEEN FILERS

The categories by which an individual is a 990-reportable manager (meaning that the individual qualifies as a current or former Trustee/ Director, Officer, or Key Employee (a pool referred to as TDOKEs) or a Five Highest Compensated Employee (known to the world as High 5's) are summari2ed in the Form 990 instructions within this Chart:

Position	Current or former	Enter on Form 990, Part VII, Section A . . .	Enter on Schedule J (Form 990), Part II . . .
Directors and Trustees	Current	All	If reportable and other compensation is greater than $150,000 in the aggregate from organization and related organizations (do not report institutional trustees)
	Former	If reportable compensation in capacity as former director or trustee is greater than $10,000 in the aggregate from organization and related organizations	If listed on Form 990, Part VII, Section A (do not report institutional trustees)
Officers	Current	All	If reportable and other compensation is greater than $150,000 in the aggregate from organization and related organizations
	Former	If reportable compensation is greater than $100,000 in the aggregate from organization and related organizations	If listed on Form 990, Part VII, Section A
Key employees	Current	All	All
	Former	If reportable compensation is greater than $100,000 in the aggregate from organization and related organizations	If listed on Form 990, Part VII, Section A
Other Five Highest Compensated Employees	Current	If reportable compensation is greater than $100,000 in the aggregate from organization and related organizations	If reportable and other compensation is greater than $150,000 in the aggregate from organization and related organizations
	Former	If reportable compensation is greater than $100,000 in the aggregate from organization and related organizations	If listed on Form 990, Part VII, Section A

Note: The IRS table makes several misstatements by omission:

1. The table fails to note that current Key Employees are limited in current number to 20; and
2. The table notes the rule for status as a Former Trustee/ Director, but fails to note that if such individual served as a Trustee/ Director as well as an Officer (or Key Employee), they will also need be evaluated for status as Former under such category.

Schedule J's compensation reporting expands upon that reported by the filing organization on the Core Form's Part VII, Section A. Accordingly, we first begin this chapter's work with a review of the Form 990's overall definitions of compensation (and their application to measurements of dollars to be reported).

The basis of standardization is the use of two categories of compensation disclosure: reportable compensation and other compensation. The former is the glossary term, and it is the underlying definition applied in both the Core Form's Part VII-A at Columns D and E and in Schedule J-II's Column B:

Reportable Compensation

In general, the aggregate *compensation* that is reported (or required to be reported, if greater) on Form W-2, Box 1 or 5 (whichever amount is greater), or Form 1099-MISC, Box 7, for the calendar year ending with or within the organization's *tax year*. If the amount reported on Form W-2, Box 5 is zero, or less than the amount in Form W-2, Box 1, such as for certain clergy and religious workers not subject to social security and Medicare taxes as employees, reportable compensation includes the Box 1 amount rather than the Box 5 amount. For foreign persons who receive U.S. source income, reportable compensation includes the amount reportable on Form 1042-S, Box 2. For persons for whom compensation reporting on Form W-2, 1099-MISC, or 1042-S is not required (certain foreign persons, institutional trustees, and persons whose compensation was below the $600 reporting threshold for Form 1099-MISC), reportable compensation includes the total value of the compensation paid in the form of cash or property during the calendar year ending with or within the organization's tax year.

As evidenced by the definition's utilization of data from Form W-2, 1099-MISC, and 1042-S, reportable compensation always relates to the calendar year ending with or within the tax year that the filer is reporting upon. This same rule is followed for reporting a manager's other compensation disclosed in Core Form's Part VII-A at Column F and in Schedule J-II's Columns C and D.

In accord with this convention, all 2015 990s will show compensation provided to each listed manager in and throughout calendar 2015, all 2016 990s will show compensation provided to each listed manager in and throughout calendar 2016, and all 2017 990s will show compensation provided to each listed manager in calendar 2017. Because filers use the tax form numbered for the year in which the tax year began, those with a December 31 year-end will find their tax year and Form year reporting of compensation tie to the same twelve months period. Fiscal year filers do not have such synchronicity.

For organizations filing a short year return, there may be no reporting of compensation if no calendar year ends with or within the short year. The instructions specify that only in the case of a final return would compensation be reported for such a short year return:

For a short year return in which there is no calendar year that ends with or within the short year, leave Columns (D) and (E) blank, unless the return is a final return. If the return is a final return, report the compensation that is reportable compensation on Forms W-2 and 1099 for the short year, from both the filing organization and related organizations, whether or not Forms W-2 or 1099 have been filed yet to report such compensation.

REPORTING CONVENTIONS: CORE FORM VERSUS SCHEDULE J

Form 990 (CORE FORM): PART VII, SECTION A

(A) Name and Title	(B) Average hours per week (list any hours for related organizations below dotted line)	(C) Position (do not check more than one box, unless person is both an officer and a director/trustee)						(D) Reportable compensation from the organization (W-2/1099-MISC)	(E) Reportable compensation from related organizations (W-2/1099-MISC)	(F) Estimated amount of other compensation from the organization and related organizations
		Individual trustee or director	Institutional trustee	Officer	Key employee	Highest compensated employee	Former			
(1)										

Form 990 (CORE FORM): PART VII, SECTION A

Schedule J (Form 990) 2015   Page **2**

Part II   **Officers, Directors, Trustees, Key Employees, and Highest Compensated Employees.** Use duplicate copies if additional space is needed.

For each individual whose compensation must be reported on Schedule J, report compensation from the organization on row (i) and from related organizations, described in the instructions, on row (ii). Do not list any individuals that are not listed on Form 990, Part VII.

Note: The sum of columns (B)(i)–(iii) for each listed individual must equal the total amount of Form 990, Part VII, Section A, line 1a, applicable column (D) and (E) amounts for that individual.

(A) Name and Title		(B) Breakdown of W-2 and/or 1099-MISC compensation			(C) Retirement and other deferred compensation	(D) Nontaxable benefits	(E) Total of columns (B)(i)–(D)	(F) Compensation in column (B) reported as deferred on prior Form 990
		(i) Base compensation	(ii) Bonus & incentive compensation	(iii) Other reportable compensation				
1	(i)							
	(ii)							

DOLLAR AMOUNTS CONSTITUTING REPORTABLE COMPENSATION: THE CORE FORM'S PART VII-A EMPLOYS TWO COLUMNS FOR REPORTING OF REPORTABLE COMPENSATION.

- Column D for that paid by the filer and unrelated organizations (Schedule J-II reporting uses column B, top row)
- Column E for that paid by the filer's Related Organizations (Schedule J-II reporting uses Column B, bottom row)

Here, reportable compensation paid by related organizations—subject of Column E reporting—is disclosed subject to three rules, the first of which does not apply at Schedule J-II:

1. The reporting organization has no responsibility to report amounts of reportable compensation provided by a related organization if they total less than $10,000 (again, reporting amounts provided in the calendar year ending with or within the filer's tax year). This exception is referred to as the $10,000-per-related-organization exception. This rule does not apply when reporting in Schedule J.

Note: Were an individual a former trustee or director; the $10,000-per-related-organization exception does not apply with respect to compensation paid for that individual's services to the filer in the person's capacity as a trustee or director.

[The subject of Schedule J's lack of this and one other $10,000 exception is taken up again in this chapter's discussion of Part VII-A Column F reporting.]

2. The reporting organization is not required to include income paid by a related organization during times (of the calendar year) in which the related organization was outside of the conditions by which related organization status vests (those dollars can be reported, they just don't have to be.) The relevant instruction on this point follows:

> Reportable compensation paid to the person by a **related organization** at any time during the entire calendar year ending with or within the filing organization's tax year should be reported in column (E). If the related organization was related to the filing organization for only a portion of the tax year, then the filing organization may choose to report only compensation paid or accrued by the related organization during the time it was actually related. If the filing organization reports compensation on this basis, it must explain in Schedule O (Form 990 or 990-EZ) and state the period during which the related organization was related.

3. The reporting organization need not report in Core Form Part VII Section A's Column E (nor in Column F when reporting amounts of other compensation) amounts paid to the filer's board members or officers by a taxable related organization who is not controlled by the filer and is also not being paid to provide management services when the board member or officer is volunteering their services to the filer. The relevant instruction for this Volunteer Exception follows:

> ***Volunteer exception.*** The organization need not report in column (E) or (F) compensation from a related organization paid to a **volunteer officer, director,** or **trustee** of the filing organization if the related organization is a for-profit organization, is not owned or controlled directly or indirectly by the organization or one or more related tax-exempt organizations, and does not provide management services for a fee to the organization.

The Core Form's Part VII-A also sets out (in Lines 3-5) trigger questions by which Schedule J applies. The last of those implicates the need for further Part VII-A reporting of compensation (in Column D), and, of course companion Schedule J inclusion, when the filer knows that an unrelated organization or an individual is providing to one of the organization's Part VII-A disclosable managers compensation for services the manager provides to the organization.

5	Did any person listed on line 1a receive or accrue compensation from any unrelated organization or individual for services rendered to the organization? If "Yes," complete Schedule J for such person . . . .

When a "Yes" results, the reporting requirements applicable to Core Form Part VII-A, Column D, as well as F, are as follows (per the Core Form instructions):

Compensation from unrelated organizations or individuals. If a current or former **officer, director, trustee, key employee, or highest compensated employee** received or accrued compensation or payments from an **unrelated organization** (other than from **management companies** or leasing companies, as discussed above) or an individual for services rendered to the filing organization in that person's capacity as an officer, director, trustee, or employee of the filing organization, then the filing organization must report (subject to the *taxable organization employee exception*, next) such amounts as **compensation** from the filing organization <u>if it has knowledge of the arrangement</u>, whether or not the unrelated organization or the individual treats the amounts as compensation, grants, contributions, or otherwise. Report such compensation from unrelated organizations in Section A, Columns (D) and (F), as appropriate. If the organization cannot distinguish between reportable compensation and other compensation from the unrelated organization, report all such compensation in Column (D).

Taxable organization employee exception.

Do not report as compensation any payments from an unrelated taxable organization that employs the individual and continues to pay the individual's regular compensation while the individual provides services without charge to the filing organization, but only if the unrelated organization does not treat the payments as a charitable contribution to the filing organization.

Highlighting and underlining added for emphasis by the authors

In addition to the taxable organization employee exception, there are three other conditions in which compensation from an unrelated organization is not subject to reporting, as follow:

1. The unrelated organization is a management company or a leasing company.
2. Common paymaster's remittances are not included as remittances by an unrelated organization (the instructions mandate that the receiver of the individual's services report the paymaster's compensation as that they directly provided).
3. Deferred compensation plans'/trusts' remittances are not included.

The Part VII-A Line 5 instructions further delineate the intent of the compensation-capture here, and also provide examples.

Line 5. Complete Schedule J (Form 990) for any individual listed on Form 990, Part VII, Section A if the person receives or accrues compensation from an unrelated organization (other than certain management companies and leasing companies, as discussed earlier) for services rendered to the filing organization in the person's capacity as an officer, director, trustee, or employee of the filing organization. Also, specify on Schedule J (Form 990), Part III, the name of the unrelated organization, the type and amount of compensation it paid or accrued, and the person receiving or accruing such compensation.

Example 1: A is the CEO (and the top management official) of the organization. In addition to compensation paid by the organization to A, A receives payments from B, an unrelated corporation (using the definition of relatedness on Schedule R (Form 990)), for services provided by A to the organization. B also makes rent payments for A's personal residence. The organization is aware of the compensation arrangement between A and B, and does not treat the payments as paid by the organization for Form W-2 reporting purposes. A, as the top management official of the organization, must be listed as an officer of the organization in Part VII, Section A. However, the amounts paid by B to A require that the organization answer "Yes" on Line 5 and complete Schedule J (Form 990) about A.

Example 2: C is an attorney employed by a law firm that is not a related organization to the organization. The organization and the law firm enter into an arrangement where C serves the organization, a 501(c)(3) legal aid society pro bono, on a full-time basis as its vice-president and as a board member while continuing to receive her regular compensation from the law firm. The organization does not provide any compensation to C for the services provided by C to the organization, and does not report C's compensation on Form W-2 or Form 1099-MISC. The law firm does not treat any part of C's compensation as a charitable contribution to the legal aid society. Under these circumstances, the amounts paid by the law firm to C do not require that the organization answer "Yes" on Line 5, about C. Also, nothing in these facts would prevent C from qualifying as an independent member of the organization's governing body for purposes of Form 990, Part VI, Line 1b.

Example 3: D, a volunteer director of the organization, is also the sole owner and CEO of M management company (an unrelated organization), which provides management services to the organization. The organization pays M an annual fee of $150,000 for management services. Under the circumstances, the amounts paid by M to D (in the capacity as owner and CEO of M) do not require that the organization answer "Yes" on Line 5, regarding D. However, the organization must report the transaction with M, including the relationship between D and M, on Schedule L (Form 990 or 990-EZ), Part IV. Also, D does not qualify as an independent member of the organization's governing body because D receives indirect financial benefits from the organization through M that are reportable on Schedule L (Form 990 or 990-EZ), Part IV.

KNOWLEDGE CHECK

1. Which is NOT an element of reportable compensation?

   a. Nontaxable health and medical benefits provided to a current-to-the-tax-year manager who is providing services to the filer as an employee.

   b. Remunerative payment of $1,000 provided to a current-to-the-tax-year manager for services provided in the ordinary course of the manager's business in which services are provided as an independent contractor.

   c. Settlement payments provided to a former manager (reported on the current tax year 990) with respect to release of claims stemming from their prior employment.

   d. Compensation payments provided to a former manager for current service to the filer that is completely unrelated to the basis by which they have status as a prior year manager.

2. Filer Z learns of a sibling organization, WW, after its tax year closes, and realizes that one of its managers was paid by WW in the calendar year that Part VII-A will report upon. If WW's status as a related organization only vests for October-December of the calendar year, which statement *most accurately and fully* reflects the amounts of the affected manager's compensation that Z may report?

   a. One-quarter of the manager's entire calendar year remuneration from WW.

   b. 100 percent of the manager's entire calendar year remuneration from WW.

   c. October-December remuneration provided to the manager from WW.

   d. Either b or c.

3. For an individual whose compensation is to be disclosed on the Form 990, which statement is accurate to reporting on Part VII, Section A's Columns D and E and Schedule J Column B when that individual received reportable compensation (in the relevant calendar year) of $9,999 from the filer and reportable compensation of $9,000 from one of the filer's related organizations and $3,000 from another of the filer's related organizations?

   a. Columns D and E will both report -0-. Schedule J will report $9,999 and $12,000, respectively, in column B's two rows.

   b. Column D will report $9,999 and Column E will report -0-. Schedule J will report $9,999 and $-0-, respectively, in Column B's two rows.

   c. Column D will report $9,999 and Column E will report -0-. Schedule J will report $9,999 and $2,000, respectively, in Column B's two rows.

   d. Column D will report $9,999 and Column E will report -0-. Schedule J will report $9,999 and $12,000, respectively, in Column B's two rows.

4. X is an unrelated organization of ABC charity. It is not providing ABC with management company services. ABC unexpectedly loses its CFO and seeks an interim CFO for a six-month period. Andreas, the CFO of X, is in the midst of negotiating a 16 months sabbatical from X, and interviews for the position saying he will volunteer his time. Andreas serves as ABC's CFO for six months, without compensation from ABC but while drawing salary from X. Which most accurately states the reporting requirement ABC is subject to given this arrangement?

   a. ABC must disclose the amount of compensation the CFO is paid by X attributable to the portion of the calendar year that closed in the tax year in which Andreas served as its CFO.

   b. ABC must disclose the amounts the CFO is paid by X attributable to the portion of the calendar year that closed in the tax year in which Andreas served as its CFO f it has knowledge of the arrangement by which Andreas is being paid by X while serving ABC.

   c. ABC need not disclose the amounts the CFO is paid by X (attributable to the portion of the calendar year that closed in the tax year in which the CFO provided services to X) if it has knowledge of the arrangement by which Andreas is being paid by X while serving ABC and knows that X is not treating the payment of X's salary as a charitable contribution.

   d. ABC need not disclose the amounts the CFO is paid by X (attributable to the portion of the calendar year that closed in the tax year in which the CFO provided services to X) if a condition of Andreas' hire was that XYZ would keep these compensation arrangements confidential.

Non-taxable Benefits Comprising Other Compensation

The Core Form's Part VII-A employs Column F for reporting remunerative amounts that fall outside of the definition of reportable compensation, combining in this column both amounts paid by the filer as well as by all of the filer's related organizations

Column F discloses amounts paid in the form of other compensation (a category reaching amounts other than reportable compensation) provided to the listed managers by the filer or its related organizations. The term other compensation relates to all compensation other than reportable compensation, and includes deferred compensation as well as certain nontaxable benefits. The instruction for the column begins as follows:

> **Column (F). Other compensation** generally includes compensation not currently reportable on Form W-2, box 1 or 5 or Form 1099-MISC, box 7, including nontaxable benefits other than disregarded benefits, as discussed in **Disregarded benefits** and in the instructions for Schedule J, (Form 990), Part II. Treat amounts paid or accrued under a **deferred compensation** plan, or held by a deferred compensation trust, that is established, sponsored, or maintained by the organization (or a **related organization**) as paid, accrued, or held directly by the organization (or the related organization). |

The instructions' continuation mandates the reporting of the three most common employee benefits or non-taxable compensation arrangements (the authors refer to these as the Big 3 as noted in the following text) in any amount, but then provide that other benefits are only disclosed in Part VII-A when, by type of benefit, their value is greater than $10,000.

The Big 3 benefits whose value in any dollar amount are always to be disclosed are derived from the following instruction which enumerate in five numbered points a total of three types of non-taxed remunerative benefits, as follow:

- Points 1 and 2 = Big 3's #1: qualified pension plans
- Point 3 = Big 3's #2: health and medical benefits
- Points 4 and 5 = Big 3's #3: non-qualified pension plans' provision of tax-deferred compensation

The following items of compensation provided by the filing organization and related organizations must be reported as "other compensation" in column (F) in all cases regardless of the amount, to the extent they are not included in column (D).

1. Tax-deferred contributions by the employer to a qualified defined contribution retirement plan.

2. The annual increase or decrease in actuarial value of a qualified defined benefit plan, whether or not funded or vested.

3. The value of health benefits provided by the employer, or paid by the employee with pre-tax dollars, that are not included in reportable compensation. For this purpose, health benefits include: (1) payments of health benefit plan premiums; (2) medical reimbursement and flexible spending programs, and (3) the value of health coverage (rather than actual benefits paid) provided by an employer's self-insured or self-funded arrangement. Health benefits include dental, optical, drug, and medical equipment benefits. They do not include disability or long-term care insurance premiums or allocated benefits for this purpose.

4. Tax-deferred contributions by the employer and employee to a funded nonqualified defined contribution plan, and deferrals under an unfunded nonqualified defined contribution plan, whether or not such plans are vested or subject to a substantial risk of forfeiture. See examples in Schedule J (Form 990), Part II instructions.

5. The annual increase or decrease in actuarial value of a nonqualified defined benefit plan, whether or not funded, vested, or subject to a substantial risk of forfeiture.

Again, it is the combination of the instructions five numbered into the three realms they relate to that yield the Big 3:

1. Retirement benefits (that is, tax-deferred contributions to a qualified defined contribution retirement plan and annual increase in actuarial value of a qualified defined benefit plan)
2. Health benefits (that is, the value of non-taxable health benefits provided by the employer - per Point 3 relating to health and medical benefits)
3. Deferred compensation (tax-deferred contributions to a nonqualified defined contribution plan and annual increase in actuarial value of a nonqualified defined benefit plan)

Reminder: Other compensation for Part VII-A purposes ignores benefits outside of the Big 3 if (by type) their value is less than $10,000. Under this Column F rule, these other types of nontaxable benefits are not captured in Column F reporting unless the amount the employer provided for any one of those is $10,000 or more (in which case 100 percent of the cost of the particular item(s) hitting that threshold is entered).

Note: Both Part VII-A and Schedule J-II do not include the value of benefits excluded under IRC Section 132 as disregarded benefits – these materials cover that topic shortly.

TIP: The two Part VII-A $10,000 exceptions (Column E – $10,000-per-related-organization exception; and Column F – <$10,000-per-non-Big-3-benefit) apply only to Core Form Part VII, NOT to reporting for the same individuals upon Schedule J, Part II.

The Schedule J instructions note the impact of this disparity as follows:

Amounts excluded under the two separate exceptions . . . are to be excluded from compensation in determining whether an individual's total reportable compensation and other compensation exceeds the thresholds set forth on Form 990, Part VII, Section A, Line 4 [this is the total reported Part VII-A remuneration exceeds $150,000 trigger to Schedule J-II]. **[However] If the individual's total compensation exceeds the relevant threshold, then the amounts excluded under the $10,000 exceptions are *included* in the individual's compensation reported on Schedule J-II (Form 990).** Thus, the total amount of compensation reported on [Sch. J] can be higher than the amount reported on Form 990, Part VII, Section A.

Italics, bold and bracketed notes added by authors

A helpful example illustrating the two exceptions and their application (or lack thereof) on Part VII, Section A versus Schedule J follows:

Example (from the 990 instructions): Organization X provides the following compensation to its current officer:

$110,000 Reportable compensation(includes pre-tax employee contributions: $5,000 to a qualified defined contrib. retirement plan & $2,500 to qualified health benefit plan)

5,000   Tax-deferred employer contribution to qualified defined contrib. retirement plan

5,000   Nontaxable employer contributions to health benefit plan

4,000   Nontaxable dependent care assistance

500   Nontaxable group life insurance premium

8,000   Moving expense (nontaxable as qualified under Section 132)

Organization Y, a related organization, also provides compensation to the officer as follows:

$21,000   Reportable compensation (including $1,000 pre-tax employee contribution to qualified defined contribution retirement plan)

1,000   Tax-deferred employer contribution to qualified defined contribution retirement plan

5,000   Nontaxable tuition assistance

The officer receives no compensation in the capacity as a former director or trustee of X, and no unrelated organization pays the officer for services provided to X.

The organization can disregard as other compensation the

(a) $4,500 in dependent care and group life insurance payments from the organization (under the $10,000-per-item exception);

(b) the $8,000 moving expense from the organization (excluded under Section 132) on both Form 990, Part VII and Schedule J (Form 990), Part II; and

(c) the $5,000 in tuition assistance from the related organization (under the $10,000-per-item exception) in determining whether the officer's total reportable and other compensation from the organization and related organizations exceeds $150,000.

In this case, total reportable compensation is $131,000, and total other compensation (excluding the excludible items below $10,000) is $11,000. Under these circumstances, the officer's dependent care, group life, moving expenses, and tuition assistance items need not be reported as other compensation on Form 990, Part VII, Section A, Column (F), and the officer's total reportable and other compensation ($142,000) is not reportable on Schedule J (Form 990).

If instead, the officer's reportable compensation from Y were $30,000 rather than $21,000, then the officer's total reportable and other compensation ($151,000) would be reportable on Schedule J (Form 990), including the dependent care, group life, and tuition assistance items, even though these items would not have to be reported as other compensation in Form 990, Part VII.

KNOWLEDGE CHECK

5. Which IS NOT reportable as other compensation for purposes of Core Form Part VII-A's Column F but IS reportable upon Schedule J-II?

    a. $8,000 of payments for long-term care insurance for a current-to-the-tax-year manager who is providing services to the filer as an employee.

    b. Reimbursements under an accountable plan totaling $9,000.

    c. A working condition fringe benefit (properly qualified as a section disregarded benefit).

    d. Health benefits valued at less than $10,000.

NON-TAXABLE BENEFITS AND DISREGARDED BENEFITS

As to the exclusion of disregarded benefits, the Core Form instructions (for Part VII) state as follows:

> Disregarded benefits under Regs. Sec. 53.4959-4(a)(4) need not be reported in Column (F). Disregarded benefits generally include fringe benefits excluded from gross income under Section 132. These benefits include the following:
>
> > No-additional cost service
> > Qualified employee discount
> > Working condition fringe
> > De minimis fringe
> > Qualified transportation fringe
> > Qualified moving expense reimbursement
> > Qualified retirement planning services
> > Qualified military base realignment and closure fringe
>
> For descriptions of each of these disregarded benefits, see instructions for Schedule J, *Compensation Information*.

Further, regarding non-taxability of benefits overall (which effects them not being within reportable compensation), the Schedule J instructions remind filers that:

> The taxability of a benefit can depend upon the form in which it is provided. For example, a cash housing allowance is ordinarily reportable in Form W-2, Box 5. Under Section 119, housing provided for the convenience of the employer can be excludable, and the fair rental value of in-kind housing provided to certain school employees can be part taxable and part excludable, depending on facts and circumstances. Taxable benefits must be reported on Form W-2.
>
> *Highlighting reflects specific topic covered next page*

The following benefits provided for a listed person must be reported in Column D to the extent not reported as taxable compensation in Form W-2, Box 1 or 5, or Form 1099-MISC, Box 7:

- Value of housing provided by the employer, except to the extent such value is a working condition fringe.
- Educational assistance.
- Health insurance.
- Medical reimbursement programs.
- Life insurance.
- Disability benefits.
- Long-term care insurance.
- Dependent care assistance.
- Adoption assistance.
- Payment or reimbursement by the organization of (or payment of liability insurance premiums for) any penalty, tax, or expense of correction owed under chapter 42 of the IRC, any expense not reasonably incurred by the person in connection with a civil judicial or civil administrative proceeding arising out of the person's performance of services on behalf of the organization, or any expense resulting from an act or failure to act with respect to which the person has acted willfully and without reasonable cause.

The list above is not all-inclusive.

NOTE REGARDING EMPLOYER-PROVIDED HOUSING:

Whether the value of such housing is not taxable as a working condition fringe benefit (for example, qualifies as one of the enumerated disregarded benefits under Section 132) and thus not reported for Form 990 purposes as a disregarded benefit in accord with Regulations Section 53.4958-4(a)(4)) depends on whether the taxpayer's specific facts and circumstances meet Section 132's requirements.

Just because a benefit sounds like it could be a working condition fringe, does not make it so. Witness the disjunction between nontaxable housing offered by educational institutions, typically to college Presidents, which frequently would not qualify as an Section 132 working condition fringe (requiring it to not only be for the convenience of the employer, but also on the employer's business premises; and, furthermore, yielding taxable income to the extent of the employee's personal use of the residence). IF 132 working condition exception does not apply, the housing's value is not excepted from reporting upon Schedule J, or Part VII-A of the Core Form if >$10,000 in value.

Educational institutions should look to avoid taxation of such benefit (to the employee) under Section 119(d)[2]), but in such case the value of same would then be reported as other compensation upon both Form 990 Part VII-A and Schedule J.

The Schedule J-II instructions further address disregarded benefits, specifically detailing:

- de minimis fringe benefits
- working condition fringe benefits, and
- explaining that accountable plan amounts are also disregarded

---

[2] Section 119(d), following, was enacted by Congress in response to court case rulings in the early 1980s disallowing convenience of the employer working condition fringe benefit exception to colleges who had the president's house outside of the college's campus (or business premises):

(d) Lodging furnished by certain educational institutions to employees.

(1) In general. In the case of an employee of an educational institution, gross income shall not include the value of qualified campus lodging furnished to such employee during the taxable year.

(2) Exception in cases of inadequate rent. Paragraph (1) shall not apply to the extent of the excess of—

(A) the lesser of—

(i) 5 percent of the appraised value of the qualified campus lodging, or

(ii) the average of the rentals paid by individuals (other than employees or students of the educational institution) during such calendar year for lodging provided by the educational institution which is comparable to the qualified campus lodging provided to the employee, over

(B) the rent paid by the employee for the qualified campus lodging during such calendar year.

The appraised value under subparagraph (A)(i) shall be determined as of the close of the calendar year in which the taxable year begins, or, in the case of a rental period not greater than 1 year, at any time during the calendar year in which such period begins.

(3) Qualified campus lodging. For purposes of this subsection, the term qualified campus lodging means lodging to which subsection (a) does not apply and which is—

(A) located on, or in the proximity of, a campus of the educational institution, and

(B) furnished to the employee, his spouse, and any of his dependents by or on behalf of such institution for use as a residence.

(4) Educational institution, etc. For purposes of this subsection—

(A) In general. The term educational institution means—

(i) an institution described in Section 170(b)(1)(A)(ii) (or an entity organized under state law and composed of public institutions so described), or

(ii) an academic health center.

(B) Academic health center. ....Omitted....

<table>
<tr>
<td>

Accountable plan amounts. An accountable plan is a reimbursement or other expense allowance arrangement that meets each of the following rules:

1. The expenses covered under the plan must be reasonable employee business expenses that are deductible under section 162 or other provisions of the Code.

2. The **employee** must adequately account to the employer for the expenses within a reasonable period of time.

3. The employee must return any excess allowance or reimbursement within a reasonable period of time. See Regulations section 1.62-2 and Pub. 535, Business Expenses, for explanations of accountable plans.

</td>
<td>

De minimis fringe. A "de minimis fringe" is a property or service the value of which, after taking into account the frequency with which similar fringes are provided by the employer to the **employees**, is so small as to make accounting for it unreasonable or administratively impractical.

Working condition fringe. A working condition fringe is any property or service provided to an **employee** to the extent that, if the employee paid for the property or service, the payment would be deductible by the employee under section 162 (ordinary and necessary business expense) or section 167 (depreciation). In some cases, property provided to employees may be used partly for business and partly for personal purposes, such as automobiles. In that case the value of the personal use of such property is taxable **compensation**, and the value of the use for business purposes properly accounted for is a working condition fringe benefit.

</td>
</tr>
</table>

PART VII, COLUMN F'S DEFINITION OF HEALTH OR MEDICAL BENEFITS

With respect to health benefits, the Core Form instructions state that health benefits provided include

1. payments of health benefit plan premiums; and
2. value of health coverage (rather than actual benefits paid) provided by an employer's self-insured or self-funded arrangement.

Health benefits include dental, optical, drug, and medical equipment benefits. They do not include disability or long-term care insurance premiums or allocated benefits for these purposes.

Thus, self-insured medical plans may be valued based on the estimated cost of providing coverage for the year if the employer paid a third-party insurer for similar benefits, as determined on an actuarial basis, rather than basing same on actual benefits paid.

Example. Organization S provides health benefits to B (its CEO) under a self-insured medical reimbursement plan. The value of the plan benefits for the tax year is $10,000, which represents the estimated cost of providing coverage for the year if the employer paid a third-party insurer for similar benefits, as determined on an actuarial basis. The actual benefits paid for B and B's family for the year are $30,000. If the benefits are not reportable compensation to B, then Organization S must report the $10,000 value of plan benefits as other compensation to B in Form 990, Part VII, Section A, Column (F).

KNOWLEDGE CHECK

6. The value of nontaxable health benefits required to be disclosed on Part VH's Column F does not include which?

    a. Value of health coverage (rather than actual benefits paid) provided by an employer self-insured or self-funded arrangement.

    b. Payments the filer or related organizations provide under a nontaxable plan provided to the employee dental services, drug purchases, or medical equipment benefits.

    c. Health insurance premiums, including premiums for long-term care insurance.

    d. Fair market value of health care coverage protection available to an employee through the filer's self-insured or self-funded arrangement.

COLUMN F'S DEFINITION OF DEFERRED COMPENSATION

The third item of Big 3 benefits that are the subject of other compensation disclosure are tax-deferred nonqualified defined benefit and contribution plans (also known as deferred compensation plans). Appropriate disclosure of remunerative amounts attributable to such benefit plans requires understanding the extent to which unvested benefits attributable to an employee's services are reached by this category and are to be reported. Remember that other compensation includes these items of compensation – which are to be reported as other compensation in Column (F) in all cases regardless of the amount, to the extent they are not included in Column (D):

> Tax-deferred contributions by the employer and employee to a funded nonqualified defined contribution plan, and deferrals under an unfunded nonqualified defined contribution plan, whether or not such plans are vested or subject to a substantial risk of forfeiture.
>
> The annual increase or decrease in actuarial value of a nonqualified defined benefit plan, whether or not funded, vested, or subject to a substantial risk of forfeiture.

The Core Form instructions refer to the examples in Schedule J, Part II for when to count contributions to nonqualified defined contribution plans. The four examples there follow:

Example 1. An executive participates in Organization A's nonqualified deferred compensation plan. Under the terms of the plan beginning on January 1 of calendar year 1, she earns for each year of service an amount equal to 2 percent of her base salary of $100,000 for that year. These additional amounts are deferred and are not vested until the executive has completed 3 years of service with Organization A. In year 4 the deferred amounts for years 1–3 are paid to the executive. For each of the years 1–3, Organization A enters $2,000 of deferred compensation for the executive in Column (C). For year 4, Organization A enters $6,000 in Column (B)(iii) and $6,000 in Column (F).

Example 2. Under the terms of his employment contract with Organization B beginning July 1 of calendar year 1, an executive is entitled to receive $50,000 of additional compensation after he has completed 5 years of service with the organization. The compensation is contingent only on the longevity of service. The $50,000 is treated as accrued or earned ratably over the course of 5 years of service, even though it is not funded or vested until the executive has completed the 5 years. Organization B makes payment of $50,000 to the executive in calendar year 6. Organization B enters $5,000 of deferred compensation in Column (C) for calendar year 1 and $10,000 for each of calendar years 2–5. For calendar year 6, Organization B enters $50,000 in Column (B)(iii) and $45,000 in Column (F).

Example 3. An executive participates in Organization C's incentive compensation plan. The plan covers calendar years 1–5. Under the terms of the plan, the executive is entitled to earn 1 percent of Organization C's total productivity savings for each year during which Organization C's total productivity savings exceeds $100,000. Earnings under the incentive compensation plan will be payable in year 6, to the extent funds are available in a certain incentive compensation pool. For years 1 and 2, Organization C's total productivity savings are $95,000. For each of years 3, 4, and 5, Organization C's total productivity savings are $120,000. Accordingly, the executive earns $1,200 of incentive compensation in each of years 3, 4, and 5. She does not earn anything under the incentive compensation plan in years 1 and 2 because the relevant performance criteria were not met in those years. Although the amounts earned under the plan for years 3, 4, and 5, are dependent upon there being a sufficient incentive compensation pool from which to make the payment, Organization C enters $1,200 of deferred compensation in Column (C) in years 3, 4 and 5. In year 6, Organization C pays $3,600 attributable to years 3, 4, and 5, and enters $3,600 in Column (B)(ii) and $3,600 in Column (F).

Example 4. A new executive participates in Organization D's nonqualified defined benefit plan, under which she will receive a fixed dollar amount per year for a fixed number of years beginning with the first anniversary of her retirement. The benefits do not vest until she serves for 15 years with Organization B. Because the benefits should be treated as accruing ratably over the 15 years, for year 1 the actuarial value of 1/15th of the benefits is reported as deferred compensation in Column (C). For year 2, the actuarial value of 2/15ths of the benefits minus last year's value of 1/15th is reported as deferred compensation in Column (C). For year 3, the actuarial value of 3/15ths of the benefits minus last year's value of 2/15ths is reported, and so on.

And finally, the instructions note that deferred compensation does *not* include amounts deferred at year end but paid within 2½ months after the tax year's end:

> Deferred compensation to be reported in Column (F) includes compensation that is earned or accrued in one year and deferred to a future year, whether or not funded, vested, qualified or nonqualified, or subject to a substantial risk of forfeiture. But do not report in Column (F) a deferral of compensation that causes an amount to be deferred from the tax year to a date that is not more than 2 1/2 months after the end of the tax year.
>
> Enter an amount in Column (F) for each person listed in Part VII, Section A. (Enter -0- if applicable.) Report a reasonable estimate if actual numbers are not readily available.

There are two further points to be made concerning provision of compensation by related organizations:

(1) Relative to other compensation provided to volunteer board members or officers that is provided by related organizations, an exception (as earlier noted on page 5) may cover amounts of reportable compensation and other compensation.

A filer need not report in Column F amounts of other compensation from related organizations paid to the filer's board members or officers by a taxable related organization who is not controlled by the filer and is also not being paid to provide management services when the board member or officer is volunteering their services to the filer per the instructions:

> ***Volunteer exception.*** The organization need not report in column (E) or (F) compensation from a related organization paid to a **volunteer officer, director,** or **trustee** of the filing organization if the related organization is a for-profit organization, is not owned or controlled directly or indirectly by the organization or one or more related tax-exempt organizations, and does not provide management services for a fee to the organization.

(2) Requiring the filer's obligation to make reasonable efforts to report amounts of remuneration its managers (subject to Part VII-A reporting) have received from related organizations, and in certain instances as noted earlier in this chapter, from unrelated organizations, the instructions state:

> *Reasonable effort.* The organization is not required to report compensation from a related organization to a person listed on Form 990, Part VII, Section A, if the organization is unable to secure the information on compensation paid by the related organization after making a reasonable effort to obtain it, and if it is unable to make a reasonable estimate of such compensation. If the organization makes reasonable efforts but is unable to obtain the information or provide a reasonable estimate of compensation from a related organization in Column (E) or (F), then it must report the efforts undertaken on Schedule O (Form 990 or 990-EZ). An example of a reasonable effort is for the organization to distribute a questionnaire annually to each of its current and former officers, directors, trustees, key employees, and highest compensated employees that includes the name and title of each person reporting information, blank lines for those persons' signatures and signature dates, and the pertinent instructions and definitions for Form 990, Part VII, Section A, Columns (E) and (F).
>
> *Highlighting and bold added by the authors for emphasis*

Note the requirement to report one's efforts to obtain the information if unable to get information from one or more of the relevant managers. There is no requirement to name the non-reporting manager or any other details.

Overall help to check which columns to use in Schedule J's Part II and the Core Form's VII, Section A, Columns D-F are available in the instructions' chart which compares reportable compensation (Part VII's Columns D and E) with other compensation (Part VII, Column F).

Type of Compensation	Where to Report				
	Form 990, Part VII, Section A, column (D) or (E)			Form 990, Part VII, Section A, column (F)	
	Schedule J (Form 990), Part II, column B(i)	Schedule J (Form 990), Part II, column B(ii)	Schedule J (Form 990), Part II, column B(iii)	Schedule J (Form 990), Part II, column C	Schedule J (Form 990), Part II, column D
Base salary/wages/fees paid	x				
Base salary/wages/fees deferred (taxable)	x				
Base salary/wages/fees deferred (nontaxable)				x	
Bonus paid (including signing bonus)		x			
Bonus deferred (taxable in current year)		x			
Bonus deferred (not taxable in current year)				x	
Incentive compensation deferred (taxable in current year)		x			
Incentive compensation deferred (not taxable in current year)				x	
Severance or change of control payments made			x		
Sick pay paid by employer	x				
Third party sick pay			x		
Other compensation amounts deferred (taxable in current year)		x			
Other compensation amounts deferred (not taxable in current year)				x	
Tax gross-ups paid			x		
Vacation/sick leave cashed out			x		
Stock options at time of grant				x	
Stock options at time of exercise			x		
Stock awards paid by taxable organizations substantially vested			x		
Stock awards paid by taxable organizations not substantially vested				x	
Stock equivalents paid by taxable organizations substantially vested			x		
Stock equivalents paid by taxable organizations not substantially vested				x	
Loans—forgone interest or debt forgiveness			x		
Contributions (employer) to qualified retirement plan				x	
Contributions (employee deferrals) to section 401(k) plan	x				
Contributions (employee deferrals) to section 403(b) plan	x				
Qualified or nonqualified retirement plan defined benefit accruals (reasonable estimate of increase or decrease in actuarial value)				x	
Qualified retirement (defined contribution) plan investment earnings or losses (not reportable or other compensation)					
Taxable distributions from qualified retirement plan (reported on Form 1099-R but not reportable or other compensation on Form 990)					

Type of Compensation	Where to Report				
	Form 990, Part VII, Section A, column (D) or (E)			Form 990, Part VII, Section A, column (F)	
	Schedule J (Form 990), Part II, column B(i)	Schedule J (Form 990), Part II, column B(ii)	Schedule J (Form 990), Part II, column B(iii)	Schedule J (Form 990), Part II, column C	Schedule J (Form 990), Part II, column D
Distributions from nongovernmental section 457(b) plan (not reportable or other compensation on Form 990)					
Amounts includible in income under section 457(f)			x		
Amounts deferred by employer or employee (plus earnings) under section 457(b) plan (substantially vested)			x		
Amounts deferred by employer or employee under section 457(b) or 457(f) plan (not substantially vested)				x	
Amounts deferred under nonqualified defined contribution plans (substantially vested)			x		
Earnings or losses of nonqualified defined contribution plan (substantially vested)			x		
Earnings or losses of nonqualified defined contribution plan (not substantially vested)					
Scholarships and fellowship grants (taxable)			x		
Health benefit plan premiums paid by employer (taxable)	x				
Health benefit plan premiums paid by the employee (taxable)	x				
Health benefit plan premiums (nontaxable)					x
Medical reimbursement and flexible spending programs (taxable)			x		
Medical reimbursement and flexible spending programs (nontaxable)					x
Other health benefits (taxable)			x		
Other health benefits (nontaxable)					x
Life, disability, or long-term-care insurance (taxable)			x		
Life, disability, or long-term-care insurance (nontaxable)					*
Split-dollar life insurance (see Notice 2002-8, 2002-1 C.B. 398)			x		
Housing provided by employer or ministerial housing allowance (taxable)			x		
Housing provided by employer or ministerial housing allowance (nontaxable) (but see Schedule J instructions regarding working condition fringes)					*
Personal legal services (taxable)			x		
Personal legal services (nontaxable)					*
Personal financial services (taxable)			x		
Personal financial services (nontaxable)					*
Dependent care assistance (taxable)			x		
Dependent care assistance (nontaxable)					*
Adoption assistance (taxable)			x		
Adoption assistance (nontaxable)					*

Type of Compensation	Where to Report				
	Form 990, Part VII, Section A, column (D) or (E)			Form 990, Part VII, Section A, column (F)	
	Schedule J (Form 990), Part II, column B(I)	Schedule J (Form 990), Part II, column B(ii)	Schedule J (Form 990), Part II, column B(iii)	Schedule J (Form 990), Part II, column C	Schedule J (Form 990), Part II, column D
Split-dollar life insurance (see Notice 2002-8, 2002-1 C.B. 398)			x		
Housing provided by employer or ministerial housing allowance (taxable)			x		
Housing provided by employer or ministerial housing allowance (nontaxable) (but see Schedule J instructions regarding working condition fringes)					*
Personal legal services (taxable)			x		
Personal legal services (nontaxable)					*
Personal financial services (taxable)			x		
Personal financial services (nontaxable)					
Dependent care assistance (taxable)			x		
Dependent care assistance (nontaxable)					*
Adoption assistance (taxable)			x		
Adoption assistance (nontaxable)					*
Tuition assistance for family (taxable)			x		
Tuition assistance for family (nontaxable)					*
Cafeteria plans (nontaxable health benefit)					x
Cafeteria plans (nontaxable benefit other than health)					*
Liability insurance (taxable)			x		
Employer-provided automobile (taxable)			x		
Employer-subsidized parking (taxable)			x		
Travel (taxable)			x		
Moving (taxable)			x		
Meals and entertainment (taxable)			x		
Social club dues (taxable)			x		
Spending account (taxable)			x		
Gift cards			x		
Disregarded benefits under Regulations section 53.4958-4(a)(4) (see Schedule J, Part II instructions)					

Note. Items marked with asterisk "*" instead of an "x" are excludible from Form 990, Part VII, Section A, column (F), if below $10,000.

SCHEDULE J, PART II (AND CORE FORM PART VII-A) COMPLEXITY: REPORTING MANAGERS' COMPENSATION PAID BY THIRD PARTIES

Confusion commonly occurs when considering how to report amounts paid by third parties to a filer's current or former TDOKEs and High 5's.

It is helpful to employ a framework that looks to a hierarchy of third-party payers, as Core Form Part VII-A and Schedule J instructions treat different third parties differently, but in this relative order:

1. A disregarded entity of the filer
2. In a common paymaster relationship with the filer
3. Neither of the preceding, but a related organization
4. None of the above (thus, an unrelated organization who is not a common paymaster)—

Note: Categories 3 and 4 may be trumped if the third party is providing leasing company or management company services to the filer.

The Core Form instructions are complicated, to say the least, as to when a third party's payments actually should be reflected as that OF the filer (such as, in Column D of Part VII-A for reportable compensation). Here, in order, is what the instructions require in each of the four preceding scenarios:

Disregarded Entity

Revenues and expenses of a disregarded entity (per glossary: an entity wholly owned that is not a separate entity for federal tax purposes) are reported as those of the filer. Thus, amounts paid by a disregarded entity are included with those paid by the filer in Part VII-A's Columns D and F.

Common Paymaster

The Instructions for Part VII-A's Columns D and E required filers to report the paymaster's amounts for services to the filer (or to a related organization) as paid directly by the filer (or by the related organization).

> Compensation from common paymasters [and] payroll/reporting agents . . . (except for compensation from management companies or leasing companies) must be treated as reportable compensation in determining whether the dollar thresholds are met for reporting . . . . If the Form 990, Part VII thresholds for reporting are met, then the compensation from the common paymaster [or] payroll/reporting agent . . . . must be reported as compensation from the filing organization in Part VII [and] Form 990, Schedule J, Part II.

Leased Employees (a trump category that supersedes related or unrelated organization characterization)

Assuming that one's leased employees are not being paid by a common paymaster or disregarded entity there are two choices as to whom the lessor is – either a related organization of the filer or one that is unrelated.

Here are the rules for reporting of remuneration provided to a manager who is acquired through a leasing company or management company (but not in a common paymaster or payroll/ reporting agent context):

> **Employee leasing companies and professional employer organizations.** In some cases, instead of hiring a management company, an exempt organization "leases" one or more employees from another company, which may be in the business of leasing employees. Alternatively, the organization
>
> may enter into an agreement with a professional employer organization to perform some or all of the federal employment tax withholding, reporting, and payment functions related to workers performing services for the organization. The organization should treat employees of an employee leasing company, a professional employer organization (whether or not certified under the new *Certified Professional Employer Organization* or a management company as the organization's own employees if such persons are common law employees of the filing organization under state law. Otherwise, the compensation paid to leasing companies and professional employer organizations should be treated like compensation to a management company for purposes of Form 990 compensation reporting.

> NOTE: the concluding paragraph in the above instruction applies to **both** leased employees and those from management companies.

Management Companies (a trump category that supersedes related or unrelated organization characterization)

A filer's procuring the services of an individual from a management company (rather than from the individual themselves) changes Part VII/ Schedule J-II reporting. In this case the filer does NOT have an employee to be reported at all in Part VII, Section A (and Schedule J-II). Instead, the filer will denote at Part VII, Section B that it has procured the services of the company as an independent contractor if the contractor's compensation for the calendar year ending with or within the tax year exceeds the $100,000 threshold and falls into one of the top five contractors' compensation.

However, if an officer of the filer comes from a management company, they do need be listed (such as, in their individual capacity as an officer) at Part VII, Section A, but the compensation provided to them (by filer and related organizations) will be -0- on Part VII and Schedule J-II (assuming management company is not related and that the individual is NOT a common law employee of the filing organization under state law).

The entire instruction with respect to reporting on management company's services (and individuals procured therefrom) follows [highlighting reflects changes to text in 2013 instructions from that of prior year, which actually are not a change, but rather emphasizing/ clarifying a long-misunderstood point]:

> **Management companies. Management companies**, as **independent contractors**, are reported on Form 990, Part VII (if at all) only in Section B. *Independent Contractors*, and are not reported on Schedule J (Form 990), Part II. If a current or former **officer, director, trustee, or key employee** has a relationship with a management company that provides services to the organization, then the relationship may be reportable on Schedule L (Form 990 or 990-EZ), Part IV. A key employee of a management company must be reported as a current officer of the filing organization if he or she is the filing organization's **top management official** or **top financial official** or is designated as an officer of the filing organization. However, that person does not qualify as a key employee of the filing organization solely on the basis of being a key employee of the management company. If a current or former officer, director, trustee, key employee, or **highest compensated employee** received **compensation** from a management company that provided services to the organization and was a **related organization** during the **tax year**, then the individual's compensation from the management company must be reported on Form 990, Part VII, Section A, columns (E) and (F). If the management company was not a related organization during the tax year, the individual's compensation from the management company is not reportable in Part VII, Section A. Questions pertaining to management companies also appear on Form 990, Part VI, line 3 and Schedule H (Form 990), Part IV.

Related Organization

(But not a disregarded entity of the filer nor acting as a common paymaster or payroll/ reporting agent, nor captured by the preceding leasing company or management company scenarios)
Reporting of pay by related organizations has multiple aspects. Part VII-A's Column E (dedicated to related organizations' pay of reportable compensation) and F (other compensation) report remuneration provided to the filer's listed managers by related organizations; indeed, Column E-reportable compensation factors into determining whether the dollar thresholds are met for reporting such persons in the first place (that is, as a Key Employee, as one of the five highest compensated employees or as a former TDOKE or High 5).

Unrelated Organization

(But not a disregarded entity of the filer nor acting as a common paymaster or payroll/ reporting agent, nor captured by the preceding leasing company or management company scenarios)
In these instances, the filer is aware that an unrelated organization is providing compensation to a manager for services that person is rendering to the filer and the Part VII-A Q. 5 trigger to Schedule J is invoked.

The instructions with respect to reporting in such instances in Part VII-Section A's Columns D-F state that IF the filer knows what the unrelated org is paying these individuals, such amounts must be reported as though paid by the filer (Note: This topic was addressed earlier in the chapter.):

Compensation from unrelated organizations or individuals. If a current or former **officer, director, trustee, key employee, or highest compensated employee** received or accrued compensation or payments from an **unrelated organization** (other than from **management companies** or leasing companies, as discussed above) or an individual for services rendered to the filing organization in that person's capacity as an officer, director, trustee, or employee of the filing organization, then the filing organization must report (subject to the *taxable organization employee exception* on this page) such amounts as **compensation** from the filing organization if it has knowledge of the arrangement, whether or not the unrelated organization or the individual treats the amounts as compensation, grants, contributions, or otherwise. Report such compensation from unrelated organizations in Section A, columns (D) and (F), as appropriate. If the organization cannot distinguish between reportable compensation and other compensation from the unrelated organization, report all such compensation in column (D).

Taxable organization employee exception. Do not report as compensation any payments from an unrelated taxable organization that employs the individual and continues to pay the individual's regular compensation while the individual provides services without charge to the filing organization, but only if the unrelated organization does not treat the payments as a charitable contribution to the filing organization.

In addition to that reporting, and note discussed in this chapter's earlier address, the ScheduleJ, Part II instructions note that a "Yes" answer to Core Form Part VII-A, Q. 5 requires specific disclosures to be made in J's Part III:

> • Each of the organization's current and former officers, directors, trustees, key employees, and five highest compensated employees who received or accrued compensation from any unrelated organization or individual for services rendered to the filing organization, as reported on line 5 of Form 990, Part VII, Section A. List in Part III the name of each unrelated organization that provided compensation to such persons, the type and amount of compensation it paid or accrued, and the person receiving or accruing such compensation, as explained in the instructions for Form 990, Part VII, Section A, line 5.

KNOWLEDGE CHECK

7. With regard to compensation from an unrelated organization being a subject of additional reporting or not, what information is NOT a factor?
    a. If the employer is a for-profit or tax exempt organization.
    b. How long the individual is committed to volunteering for the filing organization.
    c. If the employer is taking a deduction for the employee's salary under Section 170.
    d. If the employer is continuing to pay the employee's salary while they volunteer for the filing organization.

8. When an individual listed on Part VII holds an officer position but serves as such by virtue of being placed with the reporting organization by a management company, which disclosure is NOT required in respect of this arrangement?

    a. Part VI, Line 3 will be checked "Yes."

    b. Compensation paid to the individual by the management company for services to the filing organization is required to be disclosed on Part VII, Section A.

    c. Details of the management company arrangement, including compensation paid to the individual who is listed on Part VII, Section A, is to be provided on Schedule O.

    d. Compensation paid to the management company is only reported on Part VII, Section B if total compensation exceeds $100,000 and the company's compensation total makes it one of the top 5 highest compensated independent contractors.

SCHEDULE J TRIGGERS: HERE, FORM 990, PART VII-A'S LINES 3 AND 4

		Yes	No
3	Did the organization list any **former** officer, director, or trustee, key employee, or highest compensated employee on line 1a? *If "Yes," complete Schedule J for such individual* **3**		✓
4	For any individual listed on line 1a, is the sum of reportable compensation and other compensation from the organization and related organizations greater than $150,000? *If "Yes," complete Schedule J for such individual* **4**	✓	
5	Did any person listed on line 1a receive or accrue compensation from any unrelated organization or individual for services rendered to the organization? *If "Yes," complete Schedule J for such person* **5**		✓

TRIGGER QUESTIONS OVERALL

The point of each of the three trigger questions is to have the filer reveal more on two fronts:

First, providing more detail on compensation provided to individuals listed in Part VII-A who have status as the following:

- A former officer, key employee, director, or trustee
- Either a 'Key Employee' (in which case their total reportable compensation was greater than $150k) OR as a listed manager who otherwise had total reportable compensation (Column D and E) plus other compensation (Column F) totaling more than $150k [in other words, are handsomely remunerated]
- One whose compensation for services to the filer has been paid by an unrelated organization—this, the subject of Question 5, was already addressed in these materials.

Second, answering more management or governance inquiries related to the filer's practices in setting managers' compensation, overseeing provision of employment perks, and, for (c)(3) or (c)(4)'s, venturing into arenas subject to so-called intermediate sanctions excise tax.

TRIGGER QUESTIONS 3 AND 4—THE MOST COMMON LINK TO SCHEDULE J

Required disclosures for these triggers are self-evident:

Question 3: A filer must answer "Yes" were they to have entered any individual as a Former

Question 4: A filer must answer "Yes" to 4 if they have either a key employee or any other individual other than a Former (for example, a current Trustee, Director, Officer High 5) whose remuneration across the part's three columns is greater than $150k

> *Issue* for Question 4 is whether Columns D + E + F add up to $150,000.01 [or more]

Note again, as addressed earlier, the two so-called $10,000 exceptions that are employed in Part VII, Section A are a permitted part of the methodology to determine whether Schedule J does or does not apply via Question 4. This is the case regardless of the fact that such exceptions will not be applied in completing Schedule J-II for that individual were that Schedule to be invoked for the individual.

Question 4 does have one nuance—the amount that may be in Column (F) of Part VII-A is to be ignored for purposes of this math text. Specifically disregarded are any decreases in the actuarial value of defined benefit plans (to the extent otherwise properly included in Column (F) of Part VII-A)

[That command is noted both in the Core Form's instructions (which require inclusion of such negative number in Column (F), and then notes that same is to be ignored for Schedule J trigger purposes) and the Schedule J Instructions, which are highlighted to show their address of this in the following excerpt:]

Enter information for certain individuals listed on Form 990, Part VII, Section A, as described below. Report **compensation** for the calendar year ending with or within the organization's **tax year** paid to or earned by the following individuals:
• Each of the organization's former **officers**, former **directors**, former **trustees**, former **key employees**, and former five **highest compensated employees** listed on Form 990, Part VII, Section A.
• Each of the organization's current officers, directors, trustees, key employees, and five highest compensated employees for whom the sum of Form 990, Part VII, Section A, Columns (D), (E), and (F) (disregarding any decreases in the actuarial value of defined benefit plans) is greater than $150,000.

• Each of the organization's current and former officers, directors, trustees, key employees, and five highest compensated employees who received or accrued compensation from any unrelated organization or individual for services rendered to the filing organization, as reported on line 5 of Form 990, Part VII, Section A.

Do not list any individuals in Schedule J, Part II that are not listed on Form 990, Part VII, Section A. Do not list in Part II **management companies** or other organizations providing services to the organization. Do not list highest compensated **independent contractors** reported on Form 990, Part VII, Section B.

For each individual listed, enter compensation from the organization on row (i), and compensation from all **related organizations** on row (ii).

9. Under which fact scenario will filer L, whose tax year is the calendar year, NOT be required to complete Schedule J-II?

   a. L paid a voting member of the board of directors $15,000 in director fees in respect of 25 years of faithful service to the organization (he had never accepted compensation in prior years for service as a member of board).

   b. L reports at least one Key Employee in Core Form Part VII-A.

   c. L has a volunteer board member who receives compensation from an unrelated for-profit company for providing marketing services to the organization.

   d. L's treasurer resigned at the end of the prior tax year and was in the following year, the reporting year, hired as the director of major gifts with a base salary of $120,000 plus the ability to earn an additional 10 percent of base salary as a bonus if certain milestones are achieved by the development committee this year. That benchmark was achieved and the resulting bonus paid in the reporting year.

Working with Form 990 Compensation Reporting Mandates—Specifically, Schedule J's Part II

SCHEDULE J, PART II

Schedule J, Part II is completed to provide specific detail on the individuals whose circumstances (evidenced upon the Core Form's Part VII, Section A) led to the triggering of Schedule J. Only managers who generated a "Yes" response to Section A's questions 3, 4, or 5 are reported here.

Part II	Officers, Directors, Trustees, Key Employees, and Highest Compensated Employees. Use duplicate copies if additional space is needed.						

For each individual whose compensation must be reported in Schedule J, report compensation from the organization on row (i) and from related organizations, described in the instructions, on row (ii). Do not list any individuals that are not listed on Form 990, Part VII.

Note. The sum of columns (B)(i)–(iii) for each listed individual must equal the total amount of Form 990, Part VII, Section A, line 1a, applicable column (D) and (E) amounts for that individual.

(A) Name and Title	(B) Breakdown of W-2 and/or 1099-MISC compensation			(C) Retirement and other deferred compensation	(D) Nontaxable benefits	(E) Total of columns (B)(i)–(D)	(F) Compensation in column (B) reported as deferred in prior Form 990
	(i) Base compensation	(ii) Bonus & incentive compensation	(iii) Other reportable compensation				
1 (i)							
(ii)							

For each individual listed there are (as on the Core Form Part VII Section A) two sub-rows in play: Row (i) provides information on compensation that was remitted by the filer and unrelated organizations; row (ii) provides information on compensation that was remitted by the filer's related organizations.

There are four cautions to be aware of in completing Part II:

1. Do not include any individuals in this part if they are not already listed on Part VII, Section A of the Core Form *and* the cause of one or more "Yes" answers to the trigger questions found in Part VII, Section A's Lines 3–5.

2. As emphasized earlier in this chapter, the sum of columns (B)(i)–(iii) in this Part will not necessarily equal the total reported on Part VII Section A's Columns D and E for each individual if the $10,000 (or less) reportable compensation from related organization exception was availed of in completing Column E in the Core Form (note, though, that filers who want to have Core Form Part VII, Section A and Schedule J Part II compensation amounts tie can achieve that result by perfecting the Core Form's reporting by adding back in amounts that otherwise would be omitted by application of that exception).

3. Also as emphasized earlier in this chapter, the other $10,000 exception available on the Core Form, the non-Big 3 fringe benefits valued at less than $10,000 exception available in the Core Form at Column F is not applicable in this part of Schedule J.

4. Same as in Core Form Part VII, Section A, amounts of compensation paid by a related organization in periods of time in which it did not meet the conditions for being a related organization, may be omitted.

Here are the pertinent Schedule J instructions behind cautions 3 and 4, preceding:

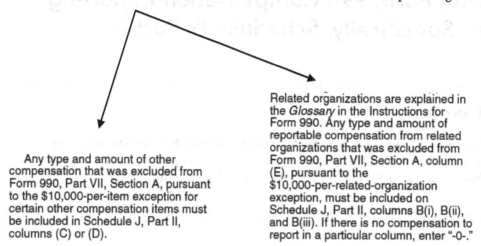

Any type and amount of other compensation that was excluded from Form 990, Part VII, Section A, pursuant to the $10,000-per-item exception for certain other compensation items must be included in Schedule J, Part II, columns (C) or (D).

Related organizations are explained in the *Glossary* in the Instructions for Form 990. Any type and amount of reportable compensation from related organizations that was excluded from Form 990, Part VII, Section A, column (E), pursuant to the $10,000-per-related-organization exception, must be included on Schedule J, Part II, columns B(i), B(ii), and B(iii). If there is no compensation to report in a particular column, enter "-0-."

SCHEDULE J PART II PREPARATION

Column B's Entries:

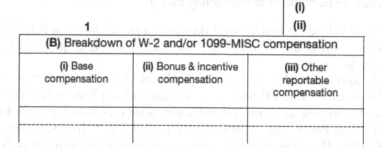

Part II	Officers, Directors, Trustees, Key Employees, and Highest Compensated Employees. Use duplicate copies if additional space is needed.

For each individual whose compensation must be reported in Schedule J, report compensation from the organization on row (i) and from related organizations, described in the instructions, on row (ii). Do not list any individuals that are not listed on Form 990, Part VII.

Note. The sum of columns (B)(i)–(iii) for each listed individual must equal the total amount of Form 990, Part VII, Section A, line 1a, applicable column (D) and (E) amounts for that individual.

		(i)
1		(ii)

(B) Breakdown of W-2 and/or 1099-MISC compensation		
(i) Base compensation	(ii) Bonus & incentive compensation	(iii) Other reportable compensation

The framework of Column B is to take what had been total amounts in Columns D and E in Core Form Part VII-A and break them out into three sub-columns by which reportable compensation provided by both the filer [row (i)] and all related organizations [row (ii)] are parsed out:

      (B)(i) = Base compensation

      (B)(ii) = Bonus & incentive compensation

      (B)(iii) = Other reportable compensation

- (B)(i)—Base compensation

> **Column (B)(i).** Enter the listed person's base compensation that was included in box 1 or box 5 of Form W-2 (whichever is greater) or box 7 of Form 1099-MISC, issued to the person. Base compensation means nondiscretionary payments to a person agreed upon in advance, contingent only on the payee's performance of agreed-upon services (such as salary or fees).

- (B)(ii)—Bonus compensation

> **Column (B)(ii).** Enter the listed person's bonus and incentive compensation that is included in box 1 or box 5 of Form W-2 (whichever is greater) or box 7 of Form 1099-MISC, issued to the person. Examples include payments based on satisfaction of a performance target (other than mere longevity of service), and payments at the beginning of a contract before services are rendered (for example, signing bonus).

- (B)(iii)—All other compensation

> **Column (B)(iii).** Enter all other payments to the listed person included in box 1 or box 5 of Form W-2 (whichever is greater) or box 7 of Form 1099-MISC issued to the person but not reflected in columns (B)(i) or (B)(ii). Examples include, but are not limited to, current-year payments of amounts earned in a prior year, payments under a severance plan, payments under an arrangement providing for payments upon the change in ownership or control of the organization or similar transaction, deferred amounts and earnings or losses in a nonqualified defined contribution plan subject to section 457(f) when they become substantially vested, and awards based on longevity of service.

- (C)—Retirement or deferred compensation

> **Column (C).** Enter all current-year deferrals of compensation for the listed person under any retirement or other deferred compensation plan, whether qualified or nonqualified, that is established, sponsored, or maintained by or for the organization or a related organization. Report as deferred compensation the annual increase or decrease in actuarial value, if any, of a defined benefit plan, but do not report earnings or losses accrued on deferred amounts in a defined contribution plan. Do not enter in column (C) any payments to a listed person of compensation that are included in box 1 or box 5 of Form W-2 (whichever is greater), or box 7 of Form 1099-MISC, issued to the person for the calendar year ending with or within the organization's **tax year**. Enter a reasonable estimate if actual numbers are not readily available.

- (D)—Non-taxable benefits

> Instructions provide useful additional explanations

> **Column (D).** "Nontaxable benefits" are benefits specifically excluded from taxation under the Internal Revenue Code. Report the value of all nontaxable benefits provided to or for the benefit of the listed person, other than benefits disregarded for purposes of section 4958 under Regulations section 53.4958-4(a)(4). Common nontaxable and section 4958 disregarded benefits, referred to as "fringe benefits," below are discussed in detail beginning on this page.

- (E)—Total (self-explanatory, no address in the instructions for this column)
- (F)—Compensation previously reported

> **Column (F).** Enter in column (F) any payment reported in this year's column (B) to the extent such payment was already reported as deferred compensation to the listed person in a prior Form 990, 990-EZ, or 990-PF. For this purpose, the amount must have been reported as compensation specifically for the listed person on the prior form.

10. Which remunerative amount is NOT the source of a possible discrepancy in compensation disclosure between Core Form Part VII Section A and Schedule J-II?

    a. Compensation of $8,000 paid by a related organization.

    b. Deferred compensation plan contribution made by the filing organization to the employer's deferred compensation account.

    c. $5,000 in adoption benefits.

    d. $6,000 of tuition assistance and $5,000 of dependent care benefits.

Working with Schedule J's Reporting on Compensation Practices—Schedule J, Part I

SCHEDULE J, PART I

Tip: To prepare Schedule J properly, the filer's related organizations need not only be identified, but their intersection(s) with managers scrutinized in order to gather the data necessary to complete Schedule J's Part I. This is the case as Part I's Lines 4-6 address circumstances of both the filer and its related organizations.

Part I asks questions regarding certain **compensation** practices of the organization. Part I generally pertains to all **officers**, **directors**, **trustees** and **employees** of the organization listed on Form 990, Part VII, Section A, regardless of whether the organization answered "Yes" to line 23 of Part IV for all such individuals. However, only the organizations that are described in *Who Must File* must complete Part I. Part I, lines 1, 2, 3, 7, 8, and 9 require reporting on the compensation practices of the filing organization, but not of **related organizations**. Lines 4 through 6 require information regarding both the filing organization and its related organizations. Part I, lines 5 through 9, must be completed only by section 501(c)(3), section 501(c)(4), and section 501(c)(29) organizations.

Name of the organization	Employer Identification number

NOTE THIS PART ASKS ABOUT PRACTICES WITH RESPECT TO SOME OR ALL PART VII-A LISTED-INDIVIDUALS, NOT ONLY THOSE WHO HIT A SCHEDULE J-TRIGGER!

Part I   Questions Regarding Compensation

		Yes	No
1a	Check the appropriate box(es) if the organization provided any of the following to or for a person listed in Form 990, Part VII, Section A, line 1a. Complete Part III to provide any relevant information regarding these items.		

☐ First-class or charter travel   ☐ Housing allowance or residence for personal use
☐ Travel for companions   ☐ Payments for business use of personal residence
☐ Tax indemnification and gross-up payments ☐ Health or social club dues or initiation fees
☐ Discretionary spending account   ☐ Personal services (e.g., maid, chauffeur, chef)

If 1 or more yes on 1a

b	If any of the boxes on line 1a are checked, did the organization follow a written policy regarding payment or reimbursement or provision of all of the expenses described above? If "No," complete Part III to explain	**1b**		

2	Did the organization require substantiation prior to reimbursing or allowing expenses incurred by all directors, trustees, and officers, including the CEO/Executive Director, regarding the items checked in line 1a?	**2**		

3 Indicate which, if any, of the following the filing organization used to establish the compensation of the organization's CEO/Executive Director. Check all that apply. Do not check any boxes for methods used by a related organization to establish compensation of the CEO/Executive Director, but explain in Part III.

3 Indicate which, if any, of the following the filing organization used to establish the compensation of the organization's CEO/Executive Director. Check all that apply. Do not check any boxes for methods used by a related organization to establish compensation of the CEO/Executive Director, but explain in Part III.

☐ Compensation committee   ☐ Written employment contract
☐ Independent compensation consultant ☐ Compensation survey or study
☐ Form 990 of other organizations   ☐ Approval by the board or compensation committee

b	Participate in, or receive payment from, a supplemental nonqualified retirement plan?	**4b**		
c	Participate in, or receive payment from, an equity-based compensation arrangement?	**4c**		
	If "Yes" to any of lines 4a–c, list the persons and provide the applicable amounts for each item in Part III.			

Line 1a

Which, if any, of the expenses or benefits shown were provided by the filer to any of the managers listed in Part VII, Section A?

Pertinent Line 1 Instructions: [the three types shown reach non-intuitive scenarios**]

Line 1a. Check the appropriate box(es) if the organization provided any of the listed benefits to any of the persons listed on Form 990, Part VII, Section A, regardless of whether such benefits are reported as **compensation** on Form W-2, Wage and Tax Statement, boxes 1 or 5, or Form 1099-MISC, Miscellaneous Income, box 7. For each of the listed benefits provided to or for a listed person, provide in Part III the following information:

* The type of benefit.
* The listed person who received the benefit, or a description of the types (for example, all directors) and number of listed persons that received the benefit.
* Whether the benefit, or any part of it, was treated as taxable compensation to the listed person.

First-class travel refers to any travel on a passenger airplane, train, or boat with first-class seats or accommodations by a listed person or his or her companion if any portion of the cost above the lower-class fare is paid by the organization. First-class travel does not include intermediate classes between first class and coach, such as business class on commercial airlines. Bump-ups to first class free of charge or as a result of using frequent flyer benefits, or similar arrangements that are at no additional cost to the organization, can be disregarded.

Charter travel refers to travel on an airplane, train, or boat under a charter or rental arrangement. Charter travel also includes any travel on an airplane or boat that is owned or leased by the organization.

Travel for companions refers to any travel of a listed person's guest not traveling primarily for bona fide business purposes of the organization. It also refers to any travel of a listed person's **family members**, whether or not for bona fide business purposes.

** <u>First-class charges</u> include at the gate low-cost option provided to premium flyers.

Charter travel includes travel on organization's own planes or boats.

Travel for companions picks up travel of a listed person's family members, even if the listed person IS traveling for bona fide business purposes.

Line 1b

If any were provided, did the filer follow a written policy for reimbursing or payment of all of those expenses?

Line 2

Did the filer, in providing any of the Line 1a listed expenses or benefits to its trustees or directors, officers, and top management official (for example, CEO or executive director) [but not Core Form Part VII, Section A Key Employees and High 5s], handle payment of such expenses under Accountable Plan methods?

2 Did the organization require substantiation prior to reimbursing or allowing expenses incurred by all directors, trustees, and officers, including the CEO/Executive Director, regarding the items checked in line 1a? **2**		

> **Line 2 instructions state:** An organization can answer "Yes" if it checked the "Discretionary spending account" box on line 1 and required substantiation of expenses under the rules for accountable plans for all listed benefits on line 1 other than for discretionary spending accounts.

Line 3

Check the methods by which the filer established its top management official's compensation:

3 Indicate which, if any, of the following the filing organization used to establish the compensation of the organization's CEO/Executive Director. Check all that apply. Do not check any boxes for methods used by a related organization to establish compensation of the CEO/Executive Director, but explain in Part III.
☐ Compensation committee ☐ Written employment contract
☐ Independent compensation consultant ☐ Compensation survey or study
☐ Form 990 of other organizations ☐ Approval by the board or compensation committee

Question 3 is tricky as a box cannot be checked if the filing organization relies on its related organization to set compensation. If that is the case, an explanation can be included in Schedule J's Part III as to why no boxes are checked. The 2013 instructions add a sentence concerning filer's being able to check the boxes for methods utilized by a compensation consultant hired to help determine compensation.

> **Line 3.** Check the appropriate box(es) to indicate which methods, if any, the organization used to establish the **compensation** of the organization's **top management official**. If the organization relied on a compensation consultant that used a method described in line 3 to help determine compensation for the top management official, the organization may check the box for that method in line 3. Do not check any box(es) for methods used by a related organization to establish the filing organization's compensation of the filing organization's top management official. Explain in Part III if the organization relied on a **related organization** that used one or more of the methods described below to establish the top management official's compensation.

Line 3 surveys what inputs or methods were used or accessed in setting compensation. The instructions discuss each method (in an attempt to be educational):

Compensation committee refers to a committee of the organization's **governing body** responsible for determining the top management official's compensation package, whether or not the committee has been delegated the authority to make an employment agreement with the top management official on behalf of the organization. The compensation committee can also have other duties.

Independent compensation consultant refers to a person outside the organization who advises the organization regarding the top management official's compensation package, holds himself or herself out to the public as a compensation consultant, performs valuations of nonprofit executive compensation on a regular basis, and is qualified to make valuations of the type of services provided. The consultant is independent if he or she does not have a **family**

relationship or **business relationship** with the top management official, and if a majority of his or her appraisals are performed for persons other than the organization, even if the consultant's firm also provides tax, audit, and other professional services to the organization.

Form 990 of other organizations refers to compensation information reported on Form 990, 990-EZ, Short Form Return of Organization Exempt From Income Tax; or 990-PF, Return of Private Foundation, of similarly situated organizations.

Written employment contract refers to one or more recent or current written employment agreements to which the top management official and another organization are or were parties, written employment agreements involving similarly situated top management officials with similarly situated organizations, or written employment

offers to the top management official from other organizations dealing at arm's length.

Compensation survey or study refers to a study of top management official compensation or functionally comparable positions in similarly situated organizations.

Approval by board or compensation committee refers to the ultimate decision by the governing body or compensation committee on behalf of the organization regarding whether to enter into an employment agreement with the top management official, and the terms of such agreement.

Line 4a

Did any of the managers listed in Part VII, Section A receive from the filer or any of its related organizations?

- A severance payment *or* change-of-control payment (including settlement payments related to wrongful termination) (4a)
- Participate in supplemental nonqualified retirement plans (for example, a plan not open to all employees and favoring the highest paid) (See Section 457(f)(4)(b))
- Participate in equity-based compensation arrangements (4c) (See instruction for detail required when "Yes" results)

4	During the year, did any person listed in Form 990, Part VII, Section A, line 1a, with respect to the filing organization or a related organization:			
a	Receive a severance payment or change-of-control payment?	4a		
b	Participate in, or receive payment from, a supplemental nonqualified retirement plan?	4b		
c	Participate in, or receive payment from, an equity-based compensation arrangement?	4c		
	If "Yes" to any of lines 4a–c, list the persons and provide the applicable amounts for each item in Part III.			

> **Line 4.** List in Part III the names of listed persons paid amounts during the year by the filing organization or a **related organization** under any arrangement described in lines 4a through 4c, and report the amounts paid during the year to each such listed person. Also describe in Part III the terms and conditions of any arrangement described in lines 4a through 4c in which one or more listed persons participated during the year, regardless of whether any payments to the listed person were made during the year.

Instructions also provide examples, which are not included in these materials.

> **Line 4a.** Answer "Yes" if a listed person received a severance or change-of-control payment from the organization or a **related organization**. A severance payment is a payment made if the right to the payment is contingent upon the person's severance from service in specified circumstances,

> such as upon an involuntary separation from service or under a separation or termination agreement voluntarily entered into by the parties. Payments under a change-of-control arrangement are made in connection with a termination or change in the terms of employment resulting from a change in control of the organization. Treat as a severance payment any payment to a listed person by the organization or a related organization in satisfaction or settlement of a claim for wrongful termination or demotion.

> **Line 4b.** Answer "Yes" if a listed person participated in or received payment from any supplemental nonqualified retirement plan established, sponsored, or maintained by or for the organization or a **related organization**. A supplemental nonqualified retirement plan is a nonqualified retirement plan that is not generally available to all employees but is available only to a certain class or classes of management or highly compensated **employees**. For this purpose, include as a supplemental nonqualified retirement plan a plan described in section 457(f) (but do not include a plan described in section 457(b)) and a split-dollar life insurance plan.

> **Line 4c.** Answer "Yes" if a listed person participated in or received payment from the organization or a **related organization** of any equity-based compensation (such as stock, stock options, stock appreciation rights, restricted stock, or phantom or shadow stock), or participated in or received payment from any equity compensation plan or arrangement sponsored by the organization or a **related organization**, whether the compensation is determined by reference to equity in a partnership, limited liability company, or corporation. Equity-based compensation does not include compensation contingent on the revenues or net earnings of the organization, which are addressed by lines 5 and 6 later.

Lines 5-9 are for 501(c)(3), 501(c)(4), and 501(c)(29) filers only:

5	For persons listed in Form 990, Part VII, Section A, line 1a, did the organization pay or accrue any compensation contingent on the revenues of:			
a	The organization?	5a		
b	Any related organization?	5b		
	If "Yes" to line 5a or 5b, describe in Part III.			
6	For persons listed in Form 990, Part VII, Section A, line 1a, did the organization pay or accrue any compensation contingent on the net earnings of:			
a	The organization?	6a		
b	Any related organization?	6b		
	If "Yes" to line 6a or 6b, describe in Part III.			
7	For persons listed in Form 990, Part VII, Section A, line 1a, did the organization provide any non-fixed payments not described in lines 5 and 6? If "Yes," describe in Part III	7		

Line 5

Was compensation of any of the managers listed in Part VII, Section A based on revenues (gross or net) of the filer or any of its related organizations? For these purposes, net revenue is gross revenues less certain expenses, but not net income or net earnings.

Line 6

Was compensation of any of the managers listed in Part VII, Section A based on net earnings of the filer or any of its related organizations?

Line 7

Were any of the managers listed in Part VII, Section A compensated by the filer by non-fixed payments? Payments that are not fixed payments are defined in Treas. Reg. Sec. 53.4958-4(a)(3)(ii).

The reach of Lines 5–7 are further explicated in the instructions, which should be consulted for further explanation and examples:

Line 5. Answer "Yes" if the organization paid or accrued with respect to a listed person any **compensation** contingent upon and determined in whole or in part by the revenues (gross or net) of one or more activities of the organization or a **related organization**, or by the revenues (gross or net) of the organization or a related organization as a whole. For this purpose, net revenues means gross revenues less certain expenses, but does not mean net income or net earnings. Describe such arrangements in Part III.

Example. A, a listed person, is a physician employed by organization B. As part of A's compensation package, A is to be paid a bonus equal to x percent of B's net revenues from a particular department operated by B for a specified period of time. This arrangement is a payment contingent on revenues of the organization, and must be reported on Line 5, regardless of whether the payment is contingent on achieving a certain revenue target.

However, if instead the bonus payment is a specific dollar amount (for instance, $5,000) to be paid only if a gross revenue or net revenue target of the department is achieved, the payment is not contingent on revenues of the organization for this purpose.

Line 6. Answer "Yes" if the organization paid or accrued with respect to a listed person any **compensation** contingent upon and determined in whole or in part by the net earnings of one or more activities of the organization or a **related organization**, or by the net earnings of the organization or a related organization as a whole. Describe such arrangements in Part III.

Example. A, a listed person, is an **employee** of organization B. As part of A's compensation package, A is to be paid a bonus equal to x percent of B's net earnings for a specified period of time. This arrangement is a payment contingent on net earnings of the organization for Line 6 purposes, regardless of whether the payment is contingent on achieving a certain net earnings target. However, if instead the bonus payment is a specific dollar amount to be paid only if a net earnings target is achieved, the payment is not contingent on the net earnings of the organization for this purpose.

Line 7. Answer "Yes" if the organization provided any non-fixed payments, not described on Lines 5 and 6, for a listed person. Describe such arrangements in Part III. A fixed payment is an amount of cash or other property specified in the contract, or determined by a fixed formula specified in the contract, which is to be paid or transferred in exchange for the provision of specified services or property. A fixed formula can incorporate an amount that depends upon future specified events or contingencies, provided that no person exercises discretion when calculating the amount of a payment or deciding whether to make a payment, such as a bonus. Amounts paid or accrued to any listed person that are not fixed amounts as defined above are non-fixed payments. For example, any amount paid to a person under a reimbursement arrangement where discretion is exercised by any person as to the amount of expenses incurred or reimbursed is a non-fixed payment. See Regs. Sec. 53.4958-4(a)(3).

Exception. Amounts payable under a qualified pension, profit-sharing, or stock bonus plan under Section 401(a) or under an employee benefit program that is subject to and satisfies coverage and nondiscrimination rules under the Internal Revenue Code (for example, Sections 127 and 137), other than nondiscrimination rules under Section 9802, are treated as fixed payments for purposes of Line 7, regardless of the organization's discretion with respect to the plan or program. The fact that a person contracting with the organization is expressly granted the choice to accept or reject any economic benefit is disregarded in determining whether the benefit constitutes a fixed payment for purposes of Line 7.

8	Were any amounts reported in Form 990, Part VII, paid or accrued pursuant to a contract that was subject to the initial contract exception described in Regulations section 53.4958-4(a)(3)? If "Yes," describe in Part III	8		
9	If "Yes" to line 8, did the organization also follow the rebuttable presumption procedure described in Regulations section 53.4958-6(c)?	9		

Line 8

Have there been payments made to any of the managers listed in Part VII, Section A or to independent contractors listed in Part VII, Section B that the filer would situate under the initial contract exception which makes same outside of the reach of Section 4958 (also known as intermediate sanctions)?

> The reach of this exception ends when the initial contract terminates (as set out in Regs. Sec. 53.4958-4(a)(3)(v). The authors urge filers to use extreme caution in making this claim, as even the smallest change to a contract will kick it out of the initial contract exception.

Line 9

If Line 8 has been answered "Yes," was the so-called rebuttable presumption procedure followed in establishing the terms of the contract by which payments were made?

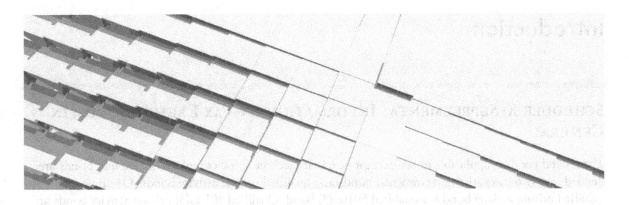

Chapter 9

TAX EXEMPT BONDS AND SCHEDULE K

LEARNING OBJECTIVES

After completing this chapter, you should be able to do the following:

- Recognize triggers that necessitate filing Schedule K
- Distinguish compliance issues indicating when an organization may have a problem regarding its tax-exempt bonds
- Recognize when to engage external experts for additional assistance with tax-exempt bond compliance

Introduction

SCHEDULE K: SUPPLEMENTAL INFORMATION ON TAX EXEMPT BONDS, IN GENERAL

The federal tax rules applicable to tax-exempt bonds are technical and complex. Tax-exempt bonds are divided into two categories: governmental bonds and qualified private activity bonds. One type of qualified private activity bond is a qualified 501(c)(3) bond. Qualified 501(c)(3) private activity bonds are issued by state and local governmental entities on behalf of other organizations (such as a 501(c)(3) organization). Those other organizations are called conduit borrowers. The 501(c)(3) organization is responsible not only for the payment of principal and interest, but also for adhering to the on-going compliance requirements regarding its tax-exempt bonds. Schedule K is employed demonstrate to the IRS (and the general public) that the organization is complying with the rules for the entire life of the bonds. Schedule K requires the bond holder to report on the proceeds, the qualified and nonqualified use of the bond financed property, and the yield on investments acquired with bond proceeds. Failure to comply with federal tax requirements may jeopardize the tax-exempt status of the bonds.

CONDITIONS TRIGGERING SCHEDULE K

Schedule K is only required of full Form 990 filers and is not required for Form 990-EZ.

Core Form's Part IV, Line 24a sets out the trigger to Schedule K; Lines 24b through 24d augment the initial trigger question with additional compliance questions.

24a	Did the organization have a tax-exempt bond issue with an outstanding principal amount of more than $100,000 as of the last day of the year, that was issued after December 31, 2002? *If "Yes," answer lines 24b through 24d and complete Schedule K. If "No," go to line 25a*	**24a**	
b	Did the organization invest any proceeds of tax-exempt bonds beyond a temporary period exception? . .	**24b**	
c	Did the organization maintain an escrow account other than a refunding escrow at any time during the year to defease any tax-exempt bonds?	**24c**	
d	Did the organization act as an "on behalf of" issuer for bonds outstanding at any time during the year? . .	**24d**	

Once it is determined (and disclosed on Part IV, Line 24a) that the filing organization had more than $100,000 of outstanding tax exempt bonds on the last day of the tax year, or the last day of the 12-month reporting period selected, and the relevant bonds were issued after December 31, 2002, Schedule K completion is required.

Note that the criteria is whether there was outstanding principal at the end of the year. Meaning, if the bond issue was not a liability of the organization on the last day of the year (due to refinancing, defeasance, and so on), then no Schedule K is required.

Also, as to whether Schedule K is required, if bonds were legally defeased, and as a result are no longer treated as a liability of the organization, they are not considered outstanding.

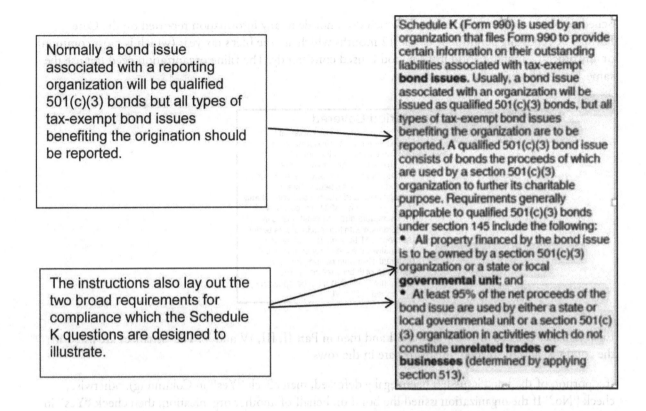

Normally a bond issue associated with a reporting organization will be qualified 501(c)(3) bonds but all types of tax-exempt bond issues benefiting the origination should be reported.

Schedule K (Form 990) is used by an organization that files Form 990 to provide certain information on their outstanding liabilities associated with tax-exempt **bond issues**. Usually, a bond issue associated with an organization will be issued as qualified 501(c)(3) bonds, but all types of tax-exempt bond issues benefiting the organization are to be reported. A qualified 501(c)(3) bond issue consists of bonds the proceeds of which are used by a section 501(c)(3) organization to further its charitable purpose. Requirements generally applicable to qualified 501(c)(3) bonds under section 145 include the following:
• All property financed by the bond issue is to be owned by a section 501(c)(3) organization or a state or local **governmental unit**; and
• At least 95% of the net proceeds of the bond issue are used by either a state or local governmental unit or a section 501(c) (3) organization in activities which do not constitute **unrelated trades or businesses** (determined by applying section 513).

The instructions also lay out the two broad requirements for compliance which the Schedule K questions are designed to illustrate.

SCHEDULE K, PART I—BOND ISSUES

The filing organization begins by completing Part I for each outstanding bond issue over $100,000 outstanding on the last day of the tax year. If there are over four issuances outstanding at year end, the filer should use multiple Schedule K pages and disclose such use on the first-employed Schedule K's Part VI.

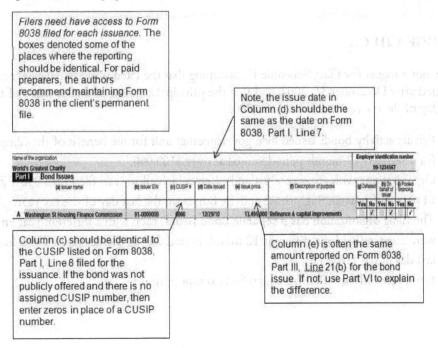

Filers need have access to Form 8038 filed for each issuance. The boxes denoted some of the places where the reporting should be identical. For paid preparers, the authors recommend maintaining Form 8038 in the client's permanent file.

Note, the issue date in Column (d) should be the same as the date on Form 8038, Part I, Line 7.

Column (c) should be identical to the CUSIP listed on Form 8038, Part I, Line 8 filed for the issuance. If the bond was not publicly offered and there is no assigned CUSIP number, then enter zeros in place of a CUSIP number.

Column (e) is often the same amount reported on Form 8038, Part III, Line 21(b) for the bond issue. If not, use Part VI to explain the difference.

Schedule K is a supplemental schedule which does not tie to any information reported on the Core Form. The reporting period may be the 12 months which are the filer's tax year (which is most common) or any other 12-month period if the period is used consistently. The filing organization need not use the same 12-month period for each issuance.

> **Period Covered**
>
> The organization can complete this schedule for any tax-exempt liability using the same period as the Form 990 with which it is filed. Alternatively, the organization can use any other 12-month period or periods selected by the organization and which, used consistently for a tax-exempt liability for purposes of this schedule and computations, is in accordance with the requirements under sections 141 through 150. Under this alternative, the organization can use different 12-month periods for each tax-exempt liability reported. The alternative period(s) must be specifically described in Part VI.

Each issuance is listed in a row on Parts I and then in Part II, III, IV and V. The issuances are listed in the columns, and the related disclosures are in the rows.

If a portion of the bond issue has been legally defeased, then check "Yes" in Column (g); otherwise, check "No." If the organization issued the bond on behalf of another organization, then check "Yes" in Column (h); otherwise, check "No."

Sometimes, the governmental entity issues a bond on behalf of a group of organizations where each organization is allocated, and responsible for, a portion of the bond proceeds. Here, the bond is a Pooled financing, and each organization should check the box "Yes" in Column (i) on their respective returns; otherwise, check "No."

KNOWLEDGE CHECK

1. Which is not a trigger for filing Schedule K, assuming that the cited bond issuance(s) are tax-exempt, were issued after December 31, 2002, and that the principal amount of one or more of the bonds on the last day of the tax year exceeded $100,000?

    a. Private activity bonds issued by a governmental unit for the benefit of the filing organization for a selected 12-month period valued at over $100,000.

    b. Organizations with gross receipts and assets which allow it to file Form 990-EZ but have $110,000 of outstanding private activity bonds on the last day of the tax year.

    c. The filing organization has 3 separate bond issues, each with a different year end. All three were outstanding for a different 12 month period during the tax year all of which include the last day of the tax year.

    d. Bond proceeds are used for a qualified exempt purpose.

Schedule K, Part II—Proceeds

Part II requests detailed information on how the bond proceeds were spent. Some questions ask for amounts spent through the end of the reporting period; other questions ask for the disposition of unspent amounts. After the bond-financed project is complete, answers to some questions will remain the same every year, and answers to other questions may change each year. The organization should carefully read the instructions for each line and answer accordingly.

Unless the organization is only paying interest on the debt, Part II, Line 1, the bonds retired, should increase each year to reflect the total principal paid through the end of the reporting period (not simply the principal paid during the 12-month reporting period).

Part II, Line 2 may change if the organization has legally defeased any portion of the bonds since the bonds were issued.

Part II, Line 4, gross proceeds in reserve funds, may also change each year. The remaining lines will stay the same.

Part II, Line 3, total proceeds of issue, may differ from the amount reported on Form 8038 (Part III, Line 21(b)) due to investment earnings. If there is a difference, then Part VI can explain.

The amount reported on Part II, Line 7, issuance costs, should match the amount reported on Form 8038 (Part IV, Line 24).

Note that the instructions for Line 10, capital expenditures from proceeds, indicates that the organization should only report capital expenditures from the bond proceeds. Amounts spent refunding prior bond issues spent on capital projects should be reported on Line 11.

Line 16 asks whether a final allocation of the bond proceeds have been made, and Line 17 asks whether the organization has adequate books and records to support the final allocation. Written documentation should include substantiation of the final allocation of bond proceeds, evidence of expenditures, and evidence of placed in serve dates. The person within the organization responsible for the post-issuance compliance should be able to locate this documentation required to be kept for the life of the bond plus three years.

		A
1	Amount of bonds retired	1,038,455
2	Amount of bonds legally defeased	
3	Total proceeds of issue	13,495,000
4	Gross proceeds in reserve funds	
5	Capitalized interest from proceeds	
6	Proceeds in refunding escrows	
7	Issuance costs from proceeds	200,000
8	Credit enhancement from proceeds	
9	Working capital expenditures from proceeds	
10	Capital expenditures from proceeds	5,000,000
11	Other spent proceeds	8,295,000
12	Other unspent proceeds	
13	Year of substantial completion	2012

		Yes	No
14	Were the bonds issued as part of a current refunding issue?	✓	
15	Were the bonds issued as part of an advance refunding issue?		✓
16	Has the final allocation of proceeds been made?	✓	
17	Does the organization maintain adequate books and records to support the final allocation of proceeds?	✓	

Part III   Private Business Use

		A	
		Yes	No
1	Was the organization a partner in a partnership, or a member of an LLC, which owned property financed by tax-exempt bonds?		✓
2	Are there any lease arrangements that may result in private business use of bond-financed property?		✓

Note that Lines 3 and 5–12 concern the net proceeds of the bond issue, but Line 4 concerns gross proceeds of the bond issue. Because of this, the aggregate of the amounts entered on Lines 4–12 may not equal the amount entered on Line 3.

SCHEDULE K, PART III—PRIVATE BUSINESS USE

Bonds issued prior to January 1, 2003 (and those refunding bonds issued prior to this date) do not have to complete Part III.

Practice Tip: Although such bonds escape Schedule K reporting, the bonds are still candidates for IRS audit. Therefore, this same information should be maintained and accessible for the older bonds.

Part III's questions relate to the prohibition by which no more than 5 percent of the net proceeds of the bonds may be used for a private business use, including issuance costs (as only 2 percent of bond proceeds can be used for issuance costs, additional private business use cannot exceed 3 percent over the life of the bond).

Private business use is measured over the life of the bond. Schedule K reporting provides the private use percentage for the reporting year, which is not the measure of compliance (or lack thereof). The private business use in any one year may be high but still the bond issue remains compliant. Consequently, the organization may choose to use Part VI to explain high private business use in any year.

Part III	Private Business Use		A	
			Yes	No
1	Was the organization a partner in a partnership, or a member of an LLC, which owned property financed by tax-exempt bonds?			✓
2	Are there any lease arrangements that may result in private business use of bond-financed property?			✓

Part III	Private Business Use *(Continued)*		A	
			Yes	No
3a	Are there any management or service contracts that may result in private business use of bond-financed property?			✓
b	If "Yes" to line 3a, does the organization routinely engage bond counsel or other outside counsel to review any management or service contracts relating to the financed property?			
c	Are there any research agreements that may result in private business use of bond-financed property?			✓
d	If "Yes" to line 3c, does the organization routinely engage bond counsel or other outside counsel to review any research agreements relating to the financed property?			
4	Enter the percentage of financed property used in a private business use by entities other than a section 501(c)(3) organization or a state or local government . . . . ▶			0.0 %
5	Enter the percentage of financed property used in a private business use as a result of unrelated trade or business activity carried on by your organization, another section 501(c)(3) organization, or a state or local government . . . ▶			0.0 %
6	Total of lines 4 and 5			0.0 %
7	Does the bond issue meet the private security or payment test?			✓
8a	Has there been a sale or disposition of any of the bond-financed property to a nongovernmental person other than a 501(c)(3) organization since the bonds were issued?			✓
b	If "Yes" to line 8a, enter the percentage of bond-financed property sold or disposed of			%
c	If "Yes" to line 8a, was any remedial action taken pursuant to Regulations sections 1.141-12 and 1.145-2?			
9	Has the organization established written procedures to ensure that all nonqualified bonds of the issue are remediated in accordance with the requirements under Regulations sections 1.141-12 and 1.145-2?		✓	

All bond-financed property must be owned by a governmental entity or 501(c)(3) organization (Part III, question 1). In questions 2-4, the schedule asks if there are any arrangements or contracts that may cause private business use. The organization should still answer these questions "Yes," even if it meets certain safe harbor tests. If a safe harbor applies, then do not include the use in the percentages reported on Lines 4 and 5.

Note that question 5 applies the term "unrelated trade or business" but same is captures conducted activity even when it is not subject to the unrelated business income tax due to exception (for example, lawful conduct of bingo under IRC Section 513(f)) or not being regularly carried on and thus modified out of unrelated business taxable income per Section 512's general rule. A lack of taxable income per the unrelated business income tax scheme does not mean the taxpayer is free of private business use.

Question 7 asks whether the bond meets the private security or private payment test. The structure of this question implies that a "Yes" answer would be correct if there is no private business use. However, a qualified 501(c)(3) bond issue meets the private security or payment test if over 5 percent of the payment of principal or interest is either made or secured by payments or property used for private business use.

Therefore, if an organization has no private business use of bond-financed property, then the answer to this question should be "No."

Question 9 asks whether the organization has established written procedures to ensure proper remediation of any violation under Regulations Section 1.141-12 and 1.145-2. If the organization has not established written procedures, then answer the question "No," but explain in Part VI when such written procedures will be adopted.

SCHEDULE K, PART IV—ARBITRAGE

Part IV questions relate to how the bond proceeds were invested prior being expended. The person within the organization who is responsible for post-issuance compliance should know the timing and status of any required rebate calculations and analysis, and should also be able to locate the most recent calculations.

Part IV	Arbitrage	A	
		Yes	No
1	Has the issuer filed Form 8038-T, Arbitrage Rebate, Yield Reduction and Penalty in Lieu of Arbitrage Rebate?		✓
2	If "No" to line 1, did the following apply?		
a	Rebate not due yet?	✓	
b	Exception to rebate?		✓
c	No rebate due?		✓
	If "Yes" to line 2c, provide in Part VI the date the rebate computation was performed		
3	Is the bond issue a variable rate issue?		✓
4a	Has the organization or the governmental issuer entered into a qualified hedge with respect to the bond issue?		✓
b	Name of provider		
c	Term of hedge		
d	Was the hedge superintegrated?		
e	Was the hedge terminated?		

Part IV	Arbitrage (Continued)	A	
		Yes	No
5a	Were gross proceeds invested in a guaranteed investment contract (GIC)?		✓
b	Name of provider		
c	Term of GIC		
d	Was the regulatory safe harbor for establishing the fair market value of the GIC satisfied?		
6	Were any gross proceeds invested beyond an available temporary period?		✓
7	Has the organization established written procedures to monitor the requirements of section 148?	✓	

Arbitrage is the ability to borrow at tax-exempt rates and invest the proceeds at a higher rate incurring no additional risk. If there is any net positive arbitrage, the amount cannot be kept by the organization and must be remitted to the federal government as a rebate. The reporting cycle for the arbitrage rebate is every fifth bond year and at the final maturity date of the bonds unless the bond meets the criteria for ending reporting sooner.

Because Form 8038-T may be due only once every five years, the organization should check Line 1 either "Yes" or "No" to indicate whether it has filed the form for the most recent due date (not whether the form was filed in the current tax year). If an organization answers "No" to question 1, then it must answer "Yes" for questions 2a, 2b or 2c. If the bond is in its first five years, then the organization would likely answer Line 1 "No" and Line 2a "Yes." If there was no rebate due at the last computation date, then answer line 2c "Yes" and use Part VI to provide the date of the rebate calculation demonstrating that no rebate was due.

Question 7 asks whether the organization has established written procedures to monitor compliance with Section 148 (the section regarding arbitrage and rebates). If the organization has not established written procedures, then answer the question No, but explain in Part VI when such written procedures will be adopted.

SCHEDULE K, PART V—PROCEDURES TO UNDERTAKE CORRECTIVE ACTION

Similar to other questions on Schedule K about written procedures, if the organization has not established written procedures, then answer the question "No," but explain in Part VI when such written procedures will be adopted. A filing organization may only check "Yes" if the procedures are both written and were in place within the 12-month period used to report on the bond issues on Part I.

Part V	Procedures To Undertake Corrective Action		
		A	
		Yes	No
	Has the organization established written procedures to ensure that violations of federal tax requirements are timely identified and corrected through the voluntary closing agreement program if self-remediation is not available under applicable regulations?	✓	

SCHEDULE K, PART VI—SUPPLEMENTAL INFORMATION

Part VI is where organizations provide supplemental information related to Schedule K, such as the following:

- Is more than one schedule used to report all of the bond issuances?
- Part I, Columns (e) and (f)
- Explanation of why total proceeds in Part I do not equal total proceeds in Part II
- Explaining information on issuances by related organizations
- Explanation of high private use percentages
- Notice of when written procedures are to be put in place.
- Describing any assumptions used to prepare Schedule K

Filers must identify what each Part VI disclosure relates to (via Schedule K Part and line number) and should report disclosures in the order in which they relate to the schedule.

ENGAGING OUTSIDE COUNSEL

The rules regarding tax exempt bonds are a specialized area of the law with significant consequences for compliance errors. Often, an organization works with bond counsel during initial issuance of the bonds, but fails to engage outside experts throughout the life of the bond. An outside service provider can assist with many aspects of post-issuance compliance, such as the following:

- Make recommendations regarding policies, procedures and systems.
- Draft written policies that comply with IRS requirements
- Analyze facility use contracts or changes in using the property
- Prepare or review Schedule K
- Perform rebate calculations

The consequences of noncompliance with federal tax law requirements could cause the loss of the tax-exempt status of the bonds. Most organizations do not have an internal expert knowledgeable in post-issuance compliance matters, and therefore many organizations contact external experts for assistance.

KNOWLEDGE CHECK

2. When is an organization required to include Schedule K with its Form 990 filing?

    a. The organization has any tax-exempt bond issues outstanding.
    b. The organization has at least one tax-exempt bond issue with outstanding principal of more than $100,000 on the last day of the year that was issued after December 31, 2002.
    c. The organization is preparing to issue debt, but the debt is not issued after year-end.
    d. The organization has at least one tax-exempt bond issue with outstanding principal of more than $100,000 on the last day of the year.

3. What facts might prompt an organization to contact external experts in tax-exempt bonds for assistance?

    a. Analysis of a contract for space financed with tax-exempt bonds
    b. Preparation of Schedule K
    c. Disposal of property purchased with tax-exempt bond proceeds.
    d. All of the above.

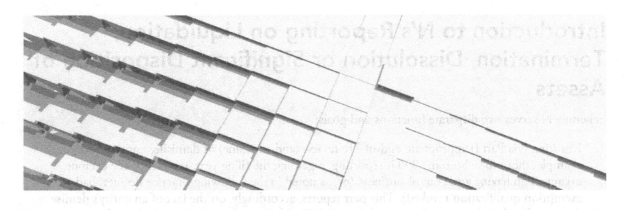

Chapter 10

THE FINAL CHAPTER: SCHEDULE N—EXEMPT ENTITY IS NO MORE, IS IN WIND-UP, OR HAS EXPERIENCED ASSET CONTRACTION/ EXPANSION

LEARNING OBJECTIVES

After completing this chapter, you should be able to do the following:

- Recognize the underlying rationales behind this Schedule's two parts and their required disclosures
- Recognize the in-depth disclosures required when asset transfers have been accomplished in the course of liquidation, dissolution, or merger

Introduction to N's Reporting on Liquidation, Termination, Dissolution or Significant Disposition of Assets

Schedule N serves two disparate functions and goals:

1. Ensuring (via Part I) appropriate end-of-life review (and sunshine) of demising entities—for example, those for whom the 990 is reporting, regarding the filing year, the fact of the exempt organization having gone out of business (or, as noted in the following Practice Pointer, had exemption qualification revoked). This part reports, accordingly, on the fact of an entity's demise through dissolution, merger (into another entity), liquidation or termination, the latter being a condition that apparently reaches loss of 501(c) tax-exempt status, regardless of whether the organization plans to continue operations as taxable thereafter or not. The Form's disclosures in all of these situations are there to confirm what has happened to and with the organization's assets, which presumably through the time of dissolution, merger, liquidation or exemption termination had been dedicated to both not-for-profit and/ or exempt purposes. The obvious purpose of the required disclosures are to ensure that the assets have been handled properly with those dedications honored and maintained. [In addition, as noted via the Caution note that appears in the Schedule's instructions, 990 reporting is the means mandated by which notice to the IRS of such conditions is provided.]

2. Effecting (via Part II) disclosure, in situations other than those reported in Part I, on asset transfers of any type (other than ordinary course of business exempt function asset sales, stock market investing, or exempt-purpose granting) when the transfer(s) comprises a significant disposition of the organization's net assets. As with Part I, the disclosures required in such situation are there to allow scrutiny of whether such significant dispositions have honored and maintained the dedication of the organization's assets in accord with exemption mandates.

 An organization must support any claim to have liquidated, terminated, dissolved, or merged by attaching a certified copy of its articles of dissolution or merger, resolutions, or plans of liquidation or merger. An organization filing Schedule N should not report its liquidation, termination, or dissolution in a letter to IRS Exempt Organizations, Determinations ("EO Determinations"). EO Determinations no longer issues letters confirming that the organization's tax-exempt status was terminated upon its liquidation, termination, or dissolution.

Separate trigger questions in Core Form Part IV invoke each of Schedule N's two parts:

Schedule N is *required of all* 990 filers who had a yes answer to Part IV Q.31 or 32:

31   Did the organization liquidate, terminate, or dissolve and cease operations? *If "Yes," complete Schedule N, Part I* . . . .

32   Did the organization sell, exchange, dispose of, or transfer more than 25% of its net assets? *If "Yes," complete Schedule N, Part II* . . . .

The Schedule N instructions (for Part I) specifically require a "Yes" answer to trigger question 31 when an organization has ceased operations and has no plans to continue any activities or operations in the future. This includes an organization that has dissolved, liquidated, terminated, or merged into a successor organization.

> **Practice Pointer:** For organizations who have lost their exempt status via revocation, the trigger question's reference to cessation of operations appears to not apply. Both the Core Form instruction to Question 31 (reprinted in following paragraphs) and the Schedule N instructions use the two sentences that appeared previously. But the N's instructions provide no definition of termination, nor do they explain if termination by revocation of exemption trumps the requirement that the entity has ceased operations and have no plans to continue any activities or operations in the future. The authors presume it does, pointing to the instructions for the header box of the Core Form, regarding the Block B box for final return, which state:
>
> ***Final return/terminated.*** Check this box if the organization has terminated its existence or ceased to be a Section 501(a) or Section 527 organization and is filing its final return as an exempt organization or Section 4947(a)(1) trust. For example, an organization should check this box when it has ceased operations and dissolved, merged into another organization, <u>or has had its exemption revoked by the IRS</u>. <u>An organization that checks this box because it has liquidated, terminated, or dissolved during the tax year must also attach Schedule N (Form 990 or 990-EZ).</u>
>
> *Highlighting and underlining added by the authors for emphasis*

The Schedule N instructions (for Part II) specifically require a "Yes" answer to trigger question 32 when an organization has not met the conditions to complete Part I, but has experienced transactions that equate to a significant disposition of the organization's net assets (the latter is a glossary term reprinted in this text's Part II address).

The entire Core Form Part IV instruction for this part's trigger questions says only this:

Lines 31–32. The organization must answer "Yes," if it liquidated, terminated, dissolved, ceased operations, or engaged in a **significant disposition of net assets** during the year. See the Instructions for Schedule N (Form 990 or 990-EZ) for definitions and explanations of these terms and transactions or events, and a description of articles of dissolution and other information that must be filed with Form 990.

Note that a significant disposition of net assets may result from either an expansion or contraction of operations.

Organizations that answer "Yes" on either of these questions must also check the box in Part I, Line 2, and complete Schedule N (Form 990 or 990-EZ), Part I or Part II.

NOTE: Filers required to file either Schedule N's Part I or Part II will also find disclosure of that Schedule's application front and center on Page 1 of the Core Form (Line 2):

| 2 | Check this box ▶ ☐ if the organization discontinued its operations or disposed of more than 25% of its net assets. |

COMPLETION OF PART I

Disclosures required in this part relate to the issues when an organization has ended its existence through dissolution or merger into a successor, or has otherwise had its life cycle 'terminated' (through non-dissolution/ non-merger liquidation or other means and apparently, as discussed on the first substantive page, revocation of exemption) and ceased operations (aside from revoked organizations).

Part I requires first noting both all assets distributed and expenses paid upon Line 1, with enumeration in specific columns as follows:

Column (a) discloses

- all transferred assets, aggregated into categories (categories are to be sufficiently described); and
- all transaction expenses (that is, those paid for services to assist in the transaction or in the winding down of the organization's activities); requirement is to separately list related transaction expenses of at least $10,000.

The remaining Line 1 columns require disclosure of

- date of distribution of assets;
- date of payment of transaction expenses;
- fair market value assigned to each category of assets (with stock transfers, brokers' fees are not to be subtracted);
- fair market value assigned to each category of transaction expense;
- method by which fair market value was ascribed to assets (appraisals, comparables, book value, actual cost – with or without depreciation, and offers);
- method by which fair market value was employed for transactional expenses reported (hourly rate or fixed fee); and
- disclosure of the EIN, name and address or each recipient of assets or transaction expenses paid, and if such parties are themselves tax-exempt, disclosing the Section by which same vests, or if the recipient is not tax-exempt, disclosing their type (for example, government agency, limited liability company or corporation).

Part I   **Liquidation, Termination, or Dissolution.** Complete this part if the organization answered "Yes" to Form 990, Part IV, line 31, or Form 990-EZ, line 36.
Part I can be duplicated if additional space is needed.

1	(a) Description of asset(s) distributed or transaction expenses paid	(b) Date of distribution	(c) Fair market value of asset(s) distributed or amount of transaction expenses	(d) Method of determining FMV for asset(s) distributed or transaction expenses	(e) EIN of recipient	(f) Name and address of recipient	(g) IRC section of recipient(s) (if tax-exempt) or type of entity

		Yes	No
2	Did or will any officer, director, trustee, or key employee of the organization:		
a	Become a director or trustee of a successor or transferee organization? **2a**		
b	Become an employee of, or independent contractor for, a successor or transferee organization? **2b**		
c	Become a direct or indirect owner of a successor or transferee organization? **2c**		
d	Receive, or become entitled to, compensation or other similar payments as a result of the organization's liquidation, termination, or dissolution? **2d**		
e	If the organization answered "Yes" to any of the questions on lines 2a through 2d, provide the name of the person involved and explain in Part III. ▶		

Part I   **Liquidation, Termination, or Dissolution** (continued)

Note. If the organization distributed all of its assets during the tax year, then Form 990, Part X, column (B), line 16 (Total assets), and line 26 (Total liabilities), should equal -0-.

			Yes	No
3	Did the organization distribute its assets in accordance with its governing instrument(s)? If "No," describe in Part III	**3**		
4a	Is the organization required to notify the attorney general or other appropriate state official of its intent to dissolve, liquidate, or terminate?	**4a**		
b	If "Yes," did the organization provide such notice?	**4b**		
5	Did the organization discharge or pay all of its liabilities in accordance with state laws?	**5**		
6a	Did the organization have any tax-exempt bonds outstanding during the year?	**6a**		
b	If "Yes" to line 6a, did the organization discharge or defease all of its tax-exempt bond liabilities during the tax year in accordance with the Internal Revenue Code and state laws?	**6b**		
c	If "Yes" to line 6b, describe in Part III how the organization defeased or otherwise settled these liabilities. If "No" to line 6b, explain in Part III.			

Part II, Line 2 instructions are fully reprinted in the following passage. Highlighting is applied to denote text that is not evidenced on face of the Form:

Line 2. Report whether any **officer, director, trustee,** or **key employee** listed in Form 990, Part VII, Section A, is (or is expected to become) involved in a successor or transferee organization by governing, controlling, or having a financial interest in that organization. "Having a financial interest" includes receiving payments from a successor or transferee organization as an **employee, independent contractor,** or in any other capacity.

Line 2a. Check "Yes" if any officer, director, trustee, or key employee listed in Form 990, Part VII, Section A, is (or is expected to become) a director or trustee of a successor or transferee organization.

Line 2b. Check "Yes" if any officer, director, trustee, or key employee listed in Form 990, Part VII, Section A, is (or is expected to become) an employee of, or independent contractor for, a successor or transferee organization.

Line 2c. Check "Yes" if any officer, director, trustee, or key employee listed on Form 990, Part VII, Section A, is (or is expected to become) an owner, whether direct or indirect, in a successor or transferee organization.

Line 2d. Check "Yes" if any officer, director, trustee, or key employee listed on Form 990, Part VII, Section A, has received or is expected to receive "**compensation** or other similar payment" as a result of the liquidation, termination, or dissolution of the organization, whether paid by the organization or a successor or transferee organization. For this purpose, "compensation or other similar payment" includes a severance payment, a "change in control" payment, or any other payment that would not have been made to the individual if the dissolution, liquidation, or termination of the organization had not occurred.

Line 2e. If the organization checked "Yes" to any of the other questions on lines 2a through 2d, provide the name of the person involved, and explain in Part III the nature of the listed person's relationship with the successor or transferee organization and the type of benefit received or to be received by the person.

Note that Line 2 requires disclosure of whether officers, trustees/directors, or key employees have a connection to either transferee organizations or a successor organization. Although the latter term is not defined, a surviving corporation in a merger constitutes a successor.

COMPLETION OF PART II

Part II's disclosures relate to asset transfers (unless excepted) by filers that comprise a significant disposition of the organization's net assets. That glossary-term's definition is reprinted fully below; note that the Core Form instructions specifically state that that a significant disposition of net assets may result from either an expansion or contraction of operations:

Significant disposition of net assets

A disposition of net assets, consisting of a sale, exchange, disposition or other transfer of more than 25% of the FMV of the organization's net assets during the year, whether or not the organization received full or adequate consideration. A significant disposition of net assets involves:

*1. One or more dispositions during the organization's **tax year**, amounting to more than 25% of the FMV of the organization's net assets as of the beginning of its tax year; or*

2. One of a series of related dispositions or events begun in a prior year that, when combined, comprise more than 25% of the FMV of the organization's net assets as of the beginning of the tax year when the first disposition in the series was made. Whether a significant disposition of net assets occurred through a series of related dispositions depends on the facts and circumstances in each case.

Examples of the types of transactions that are "a significant disposition of net assets" required to be reported on Schedule N (Form 990 or 990-EZ), Liquidation, Termination, Dissolution or Significant Disposition of Assets, Part II include:

- *Taxable or tax-free sales or exchanges of exempt assets for cash or other consideration (a social club described in section 501(c)(7) selling land or an exempt organization selling assets it had used to further its exempt purposes);*
- *Sales, **contributions** or other transfers of assets to establish or maintain a partnership, **joint venture**, or a corporation (for-profit or nonprofit) whether or not the sales or transfers are governed by section 721 or section 351, whether or not the transferor received an ownership interest in exchange for the transfer;*
- *Sales of assets by a partnership or joint venture in which the exempt partner has an ownership interest; and*
- *Transfers of assets pursuant to a reorganization in which the organization is a surviving entity.*

The following types of situations aren't considered significant dispositions of net assets for purposes of Schedule N, Part II:

- *The change in composition of **publicly traded securities** held in an exempt organization's passive investment portfolio;*
- *Asset sales made in the ordinary course of the organization's exempt activities to accomplish the organization's exempt purposes, for instance, gross sales of inventory;*
- *Grants or other assistance made in the ordinary course of the organization's exempt activities to accomplish the organization's exempt purposes, for instance, the regular charitable distributions of a United Way or other federated fundraising organization;*
- *A decrease in the value of net assets due to market fluctuation in the value of assets held by the organization; and*
- *Transfers to a **disregarded entity** of which the organization is the sole member.*

The Part II instructions provide no more information than that in the reprint (point 2 of the definition prior to examples of what are considered/not-considered "significant dispositions" for this Part's purposes) as to how to do the 25 percent calculation. All that the instructions do is define "net assets":

net assets means **total assets** less total liabilities. The determination of a significant disposition of net assets is made by reference to the FMV of the organization's net assets at the beginning of the tax year (in the case of a series of related dispositions that commenced in a prior year at the beginning of the tax year during which the first disposition was made).

| Part II | Sale, Exchange, Disposition, or Other Transfer of More Than 25% of the Organization's Assets. Complete this part if the organization answered "Yes" to Form 990, Part IV, line 32, or Form 990-EZ, line 36. Part II can be duplicated if additional space is needed. |

1	(a) Description of asset(s) distributed or transaction expenses paid	(b) Date of distribution	(c) Fair market value of asset(s) distributed or amount of transaction expenses	(d) Method of determining FMV for asset(s) distributed or transaction expenses	(e) EIN of recipient	(f) Name and address of recipient	(g) IRC section of recipient(s) (if tax-exempt) or type of entity

		Yes	No
2	Did or will any officer, director, trustee, or key employee of the organization:		
a	Become a director or trustee of a successor or transferee organization? 2a		
b	Become an employee of, or independent contractor for, a successor or transferee organization? 2b		
c	Become a direct or indirect owner of a successor or transferee organization? 2c		
d	Receive, or become entitled to, compensation or other similar payments as a result of the organization's significant disposition of assets? 2d		
e	If the organization answered "Yes" to any of the questions on lines 2a through 2d, provide the name of the person involved and explain in Part III . ▶		

> **Practice Pointer:** If Part I is completed, Part II is inapplicable and should not be completed. The instructions note that for filers who are in wind up toward dissolution throughout the year being reported upon, it is ONLY Part II that is required:
>
> > An organization that completely liquidated, terminated, or dissolved and ceased operations during the **tax year** must complete Part I. An organization that was still in the process of winding up its affairs at the end of the tax year, but had not completely liquidated, terminated, or dissolved and ceased operations, should not complete Part I, but may need to complete Part II. An organization that has made a **significant disposition of net assets** must complete Part II.

Part II's inquiries mirror exactly those of Part I's Lines 1 and 2. There are no separate instructions for these lines in Part II as citation is made back to the Part I instructions.

WARNING: Because Part II does not reprise Part I's Lines 3-6, there is no query in part about notice having been provided to state regulators (the subject of Line 4 in Part I). However, some states do require such notice be undertaken prior to a substantial contraction or substantial transfer of assets when organizations hold assets for state-law defined charitable purposes.

KNOWLEDGE CHECK

1. A 501(c)(6) professional association YY contemplated moving specific programming to an affinity organization, AO, three years ago, at which time it had $10 million in net assets at beginning of that year (year A); in each of the ensuing years (B and C), YY had $7.2 million and $5 million in net assets at the beginning of the year, respectively. YY made the following distributions to AO of specific program assets:

   year A – $ 800,000
   year B –   1,800,000
   year C –   800,000

   On these facts, which answer BEST describes YY's Schedule N reporting requirements in these three years, assuming that the noted transfers fit the definition of "related dispositions" ?

   a. All three years.
   b. Year B only.
   c. Year C only.
   d. Years B and C.

2. A filing organization undergoes a merger with another exempt organization and is NOT the surviving corporation (the merger ends its corporation existence). On such facts, the Schedule N for the organization's last tax year must note which of these details in Part I?

   1. The name of the surviving corporation and its EIN and address, with its tax-exempt status.
   2. The name of the surviving corporation and its EIN and address, with its tax-exempt status IF the filer reports that it transferred assets to it.
   3. Whether any of the filer's board members became board members of the surviving corporation.
   4. Whether any of the filer's officers, board members, or key employees became employees of the surviving corporation.

   a. None of the above.
   b. 1, 3 and 4
   c. 2, 3 and 4
   d. 2 only

3. A charitable organization G had $8 million in net assets; at the beginning of the tax year G made multiple transfers of assets during the year. Which transfer will NOT be the subject of Part II reporting?

    a. A sale or exchange of the organization's headquarters that comprised $4.5 million of the organization's beginning of the year net assets.

    b. A contribution of $3 million in cash and assets to a new not-for-profit corporation that is under the control of G through majority control of the not-for-profit corporation's board of directors.

    c. Assets sales made throughout the year by which more than $2 million of the organization's beginning of the year net assets (in the form of inventory sold in the accomplishment of the organization's exempt) were converted to cash.

    d. Liquidation of G's investment partnership interest (the value of G's interest in that partnership comprised more than $2 million of the organization's beginning of the year net assets).

GLOSSARY

NOTES:

- Words in bold within a definition are defined elsewhere within the Glossary.
- All section references are to the Internal Revenue Code (Title 26 of U.S. Code) or regulations under Title 26, unless otherwise specified.
- Definitions are for purposes of filing Form 990 (and Schedules) only.
- Appendix references within this Glossary refer to the appendices to the IRS instructions, which may be obtained online.

35% Controlled Entity – An entity that is owned, directly or indirectly (for example, under constructive ownership rules of section 267(c)), by a given person, such as the organization's current or former **officers, directors, trustees,** or **key employees** listed on Form 990, Part VII, Section 1, or the **family members** thereof (listed persons) as follows:

1. A corporation in which listed persons own more than 35% of the total combined voting power;
2. A partnership in which listed persons own more than 35% of the profits interest; or
3. A trust or estate in which listed persons own more than 35% of the beneficial interest.

Accountable Plan – A reimbursement or other expense allowance arrangement that satisfies the requirements of section 62(c) by meeting the requirements of business connection, substantiation, and returning amounts in excess of substantiated expenses. See Regulations section 1.62-2(c)(2).

Activities Conducted Outside the United States – For purposes of Schedule F (Form 990), Statement of Activities Outside the United States, include grantmaking, **fundraising, unrelated trade or business,** program services, **program-related investments,** other investments, or **maintaining offices, employees, or agents** in particular regions outside the **United States.**

Applicable Tax-Exempt Organization – A section 501(c)(3), 501(c)(4), or 501(c)(29) organization that is tax-exempt under section 501(a), or that was such an organization at any time during the 5-year period ending on the day of the **excess benefit transaction.**

Art – See **Works of Art.**

ASC 740 – See **FIN 48 (ASC 740).**

Audit – A formal examination of an organization's financial records and practices by an independent, certified public accountant with the objective of issuing a report on the organization's financial statements as to whether those statements are fairly stated according to generally accepted accounting principles (or other recognized comprehensive basis of accounting).

Audited Financial Statements – Financial statements accompanied by a formal opinion or report prepared by an independent, certified public accountant with the objective of assessing the accuracy and reliability of the organization's **financial statements.**

Audit Committee – A committee, generally established by the **governing body** of an organization, with the responsibilities to oversee the organization's financial reporting process, monitor choice of accounting policies and principles, monitor internal control processes, or oversee hiring and performance of any external auditors.

Bingo – A game of chance played with cards that are generally printed with five rows of five squares each. Participants place markers over randomly called numbers on the cards in an attempt to form a pre-selected pattern such as a horizontal, vertical, or diagonal line, or all four corners. The first participant to form the pre-selected pattern wins the game. To be a bingo game, the game must be of the type described in which wagers are placed, winners are determined, and prizes or other property are distributed in the presence of all persons placing wagers in that game. Satellite, Internet, and progressive or event bingo are not bingo, because they are conducted in many different places simultaneously, and the winners are not all present when the wagers are placed, the winners are determined, and the prizes are distributed. Thus, all revenue and expenses associated with satellite, Internet, and progressive or event bingo generally should be included under **pull tabs.** Certain bingo games within a hybrid gaming event (such as progressive or event bingo) can also qualify as bingo if the individual game meets the preceding definition of bingo.

Board-Designated Endowment – See **Quasi-Endowment.**

Bond Issue – An issue of two or more bonds that are:

1. Sold at substantially the same time;
2. Sold under the same plan of financing; and
3. Payable from the same source of funds.

See Regulations section 1.150-1(c).

Business Relationship – For purposes of Part VI, line 2, business relationships between two persons include the following.

1. One person is employed by the other in a sole proprietorship or by an organization with which the other is associated as a **trustee, director, officer,** or greater-than-35% owner.
2. One person is transacting business with the other (other than in the ordinary course of either party's business on the same terms as are generally offered to the public), directly or indirectly, in one or more contracts of sale, lease, license, loan, performance of services, or other transaction involving transfers of cash or property valued in excess of $10,000 in the aggregate during the organization's tax year. Indirect transactions are transactions with an organization with which the one person is associated as a trustee, director, officer, or greater-than-35% owner. Such transactions do not include charitable contributions to tax-exempt organizations.
3. The two persons are each a director, trustee, officer, or greater-than-10% owner in the same business or investment entity (but not in the same tax-exempt organization).

Ownership is measured by stock ownership (either voting power or value) of a corporation, profits or capital interest in a partnership or limited liability company, membership interest in a nonprofit organization, or beneficial interest in a trust. Ownership includes indirect ownership (for example, ownership in an entity that has ownership in the entity in question); there can be ownership through multiple tiers of entities.

Cash Contributions – **Contributions** received in the form of cash, checks, money orders, credit card charges, wire transfers, and other transfers and deposits to a cash account of the organization.

Central Organization – The organization, sometimes referred to as the parent organization, that holds a **group exemption** letter for one or more **subordinate organizations** under its general supervision and control.

CEO, Executive Director, or Top Management Official – See **Top Management Official.** "CEO" stands for chief executive officer.

Certified Historic Structure – Any building or structure listed in the National Register of Historic Places as well as any building certified as being of historic significance to a registered historic district. See section 170(h)(4)(B) for special rules that apply to **contributions** made after August 17, 2006.

Church – Certain characteristics are generally attributed to churches. These attributes of a church have been developed by the IRS and by court decisions. They include: distinct legal existence; recognized creed and form of worship; definite and distinct ecclesiastical government; formal code of doctrine and discipline; distinct religious history; membership not associated with any other church or denomination; organization of ordained ministers; ordained ministers selected after completing prescribed courses of study; literature of its own; established places of worship; regular congregations; regular religious services; Sunday schools for the religious instruction of the young; schools for the preparation of its ministers. The IRS generally uses a combination of these characteristics, together with other facts and circumstances, to determine whether an organization is considered a church for federal tax purposes. A convention or association of churches is generally treated like a church for federal tax purposes. See Pub. 1828, Tax Guide for Churches and Religious Organizations.

Closely Held Stock – Generally, shares of stock in a closely held company that is not available for sale to the general public or which is not widely traded (see further explanation in the instructions for Part X, line 12 and Schedule M (Form 990), Noncash Contributions, line 10).

Collectibles – Include autographs, sports memorabilia, dolls, stamps, coins, books (other than books and publications reported on line 4 of Schedule M), gems, and jewelry (other than costume jewelry reportable on line 5 of Schedule M).

Collections of Works of Art, Historical Treasures, and Other Similar Assets – Include collections, as described in **SFAS 116** (ASC 958-360-20), of **works of art, historical treasures,** and other similar assets held for public exhibition, education, or research in furtherance of public service.

Compensation – Unless otherwise provided, all forms of cash and noncash payments or benefits provided in exchange for services, including salary and wages, bonuses, severance payments, deferred payments, retirement benefits, fringe benefits, and other financial arrangements or transactions such as personal vehicles, meals, housing, personal and family educational benefits, below-market loans, payment of personal or family travel, entertainment, and personal use of the organization's property. Compensation includes payments and other benefits provided to both **employees** and **independent contractors** in exchange for services. See also **Deferred Compensation, Nonqualified Deferred Compensation,** and **Reportable Compensation.**

Compilation (Compiled Financial Statements) – A compilation is a presentation of **financial statements** and other information that is the representation of the management or ownership of an organization and which has not been reviewed or audited by an independent accountant.

Conflict of Interest Policy – A policy that defines conflict of interest, identifies the classes of individuals within the organization covered by the policy, facilitates disclosure of information that can help identify conflicts of interest, and specifies procedures to be followed in managing conflicts of interest. A conflict of interest arises when a person in a position of authority over an organization, such as an **officer,**

director, or manager, can benefit financially from a decision he or she could make in such capacity, including indirect benefits such as to **family members** or businesses with which the person is closely associated. For this purpose, a conflict of interest does not include questions involving a person's competing or respective duties to the organization and to another organization, such as by serving on the boards of both organizations, that do not involve a material financial interest of, or benefit to, such person. For a description of "conflict of interest" for purposes of determining whether **governing body** members who are reviewing a potential **excess benefit transaction** have a conflict of interest, pursuant to Regulations section 53.4958-6(c)(1)(iii), see instructions for Part VI, line 15.

Conservation Easement – A restriction (granted in perpetuity) on the use that may be made of real property granted exclusively for conservation purposes. Conservation purposes include preserving land areas for outdoor recreation by, or for the education of, the general public; protecting a relatively natural habitat of fish, wildlife, or plants, or a similar ecosystem; preserving open space, including farmland and forest land, where such preservation will yield a significant public benefit and is either for the scenic enjoyment of the general public or pursuant to a clearly defined federal, state, or local governmental conservation policy; and preserving a historically important land area or a certified historic structure. For more information see section 170(h) and Notice 2004-41, 2004-2 C.B. 31.

Contributions – Unless otherwise provided, includes donations, gifts, bequests, grants, and other transfers of money or property to the extent that adequate consideration is not provided in exchange and that the contributor intends to make a gift, whether or not made for charitable purposes. A transaction can be partly a sale and partly a contribution, but discounts provided on sales of goods in the ordinary course of business should not be reported as contributions. Neither donations of services (such as the value of donated advertising space, broadcast air time, or discounts on services) nor donations of use of materials, equipment, or facilities should be reported as contributions. For purposes of Form 990, a distribution to a section 501(c)(3) organization from a split interest trust (for example, charitable remainder trust, charitable lead trust) is reportable as a contribution. See also **Cash Contributions** and **Noncash Contributions.**

Control – For purposes of determining **related organizations:**

Control of a nonprofit organization (or other organization without owners or persons having beneficial interests, whether the organization is taxable or tax-exempt)

One or more persons (whether individuals or organizations) control a nonprofit organization if they have the power to remove and replace (or to appoint, elect, or approve or veto the appointment or election of, if such power includes a continuing power to appoint, elect, or approve or veto the appointment or election of, periodically or in the event of vacancies) a majority of the nonprofit organization's directors or trustees, or a majority of members who elect a majority of the nonprofit organization's directors or trustees. Such power can be exercised directly by a (parent) organization through one or more of the (parent) organization's officers, directors, trustees, or agents, acting in their capacity as officers, directors, trustees, or agents of the (parent) organization. Also, a (parent) organization controls a (subsidiary) nonprofit organization if a majority of the subsidiary's directors or trustees are trustees, directors, officers, employees, or agents of the parent.

Control of a stock corporation

One or more persons (whether individuals or organizations) control a stock corporation if they own more than 50% of the stock (by voting power or value) of the corporation.

Control of a partnership or limited liability company

One or more persons control a partnership if they own more than 50% of the profits or capital interests in the partnership (including a limited liability company treated as a partnership or disregarded entity for federal tax purposes, regardless of the designation under state law of the ownership interests as stock, membership interests, or otherwise). A person also controls a partnership if the person is a managing partner or managing member of a partnership or limited liability company which has three or fewer managing partners or managing members (regardless of which partner or member has the most actual control), or if the person is a general partner in a limited partnership which has three or fewer general partners (regardless of which partner has the most actual control). For this purpose, a "managing partner" is a partner designated as such under the partnership agreement, or regularly engaged in the management of the partnership even though not so designated.

Control of a trust with beneficial interests

One or more persons control a trust if they own more than 50% of the beneficial interests in the trust. A person's beneficial interest in a trust shall be determined in proportion to that person's actuarial interest in the trust as of the end of the tax year. See Regulations sections 301.7701-2, 3, and 4 for more information on classification of corporations, partnerships, disregarded entities, and trusts. Control can be indirect. See the Schedule R (Form 990) instructions for a description of indirect control.

Controlled Entity – An organization controlled by a **controlling organization under section 512(b)(13).** A controlled entity may be a nonprofit organization. For the definition of control in this context, see section 512(b)(13)(D) and Regulations section 1.512(b)-1(l)(4) (substituting "more than 50%" for "at least 80%" in the regulation, for purposes of this definition). Controlled entities are a subset of **related organizations.** For purposes of Form 990, controlled entities do not include **disregarded entities** of the filing organization.

Controlling Organization Under Section 512(b)(13) – An exempt organization that controls a **controlled entity.** Section 512(b)(13) treats payments of interest, annuity, royalties, and rent from a controlled entity to a controlling organization as unrelated business taxable income under certain circumstances. Control in this context means (i) in the case of a corporation, ownership (by vote or value) of more than 50 percent of the stock in such corporation, (ii) in the case of a partnership, ownership of more than 50 percent of the profits interests or capital interests in such partnership, or (iii) in any other case, ownership of more than 50 percent of the beneficial interests in the entity. Section 318 (relating to constructive ownership of stock) shall apply for purposes of determining ownership of stock in a corporation. Similar principles shall apply for purposes of determining ownership of interests in any other entity.

Core Form – The Form 990, *Return of Organization Exempt From Income Tax Under section 501(c), 527, or 4947(a)(1) of the Internal Revenue Code (except for private foundations).* It does not include any schedules that may be attached to Form 990.

Credit Counseling Services – Include the providing of information to the general public on budgeting, personal finance, and saving and spending practices, or assisting individuals and families with financial problems by providing them with counseling. See section 501(q)(4)(A).

Current Year – The **tax year** for which the Form 990 is being filed; see also **Fiscal Year.**

Debt Management Plan Services – Services related to the repayment, consolidation, or restructuring of a consumer's debt, including the negotiation with creditors of lower interest rates, the waiver or reduction of fees, and the marketing and processing of debt management plans. See section 501(q)(4)(B).

Defeasance Escrow – An irrevocable escrow established to redeem the bonds on their earliest call date in an amount that, together with investment earnings, is sufficient to pay all the principal of, and interest and call premiums on, bonds from the date the escrow is established to the earliest call date. See Regulations section 1.141-12(d)(5).

Deferred Compensation – **Compensation** that is earned or accrued in, or is attributable to, one year and deferred to a future year for any reason, whether or not funded, vested, qualified or nonqualified, or subject to a substantial risk of forfeiture. However, a deferral of compensation that causes an amount to be deferred from the calendar year ending with or within the tax year to a date that is not more than 2 V2 months after the end of the calendar year ending with or within the tax year is not treated as deferred compensation for purposes of Form 990, if such compensation is currently reported as reportable compensation. Deferred compensation may or may not be included in **reportable compensation** for the **current year.**

Director – See **Director or Trustee.**

Director or Trustee – Unless otherwise provided, a member of the organization's **governing body** at any time during the tax year, but only if the member has any voting rights. A member of an advisory board that does not exercise any governance authority over the organization is not considered a director or trustee.

Disqualified Person – A. For purposes of section 4958; Form 990, Parts IX and X; and Schedule L (Form 990 or 990-EZ), Transactions With Interested Persons, Parts I and II, any person (including an individual, corporation, or other entity) who was in a position to exercise substantial influence over the affairs of the **applicable tax-exempt organization** at any time during a 5-year period ending on the date of the transaction. If the 5-year period ended within the organization's **tax year,** the organization may treat the person as a disqualified person for the entire tax year. Persons who hold certain powers, responsibilities, or interests are among those who are in a position to exercise substantial influence over the affairs of the organization.

A disqualified person includes:

- A disqualified person's **family member,**
- A **35% controlled entity** of a (1) disqualified person and/ or (2) family members of the disqualified person,
- A donor or **donor advisor** to a **donor advised fund,** or
- An investment advisor of a **sponsoring organization.**

The **disqualified persons** of a **supported organization** include the disqualified persons of a section 509(a)(3) **supporting organization** that supports the supported organization.

See *Appendix G* for more information on **disqualified persons** and section 4958 **excess benefit transactions.**

B. Under section 4946, a disqualified person includes:

1. A substantial contributor, which is any person who gave an aggregate amount of more than $5,000, if that amount is more than 2% of the total **contributions** the foundation or organization received from its inception through the end of the year in which that person's contributions were received. If the organization is a trust, a substantial contributor includes the creator of the trust (without regard to the amount of contributions the trust received from the creator and related persons). Any person who is a substantial contributor at any time generally remains a substantial contributor for all future

periods even if later contributions by others push that person's contributions below the 2% figure discussed above. Gifts from the contributor's spouse are treated as gifts from the contributor. Gifts are generally valued at FMV as of the date the organization received them.

2. A foundation manager, defined as an **officer, director,** or **trustee** of the organization or any individual having powers or responsibilities similar to those of officers, directors, or trustees.

3. An owner of more than 20% of the voting power of a corporation, profits interest of a partnership, or beneficial interest of a trust or an unincorporated enterprise that is a substantial contributor to the organization.

4. A family member of an individual in the first three categories. For this purpose, "family member" includes only the individual's spouse, ancestors, children, grandchildren, great-grandchildren, and the spouses of children, grandchildren, and great-grandchildren.

5. A corporation, partnership, trust, or estate in which persons described in (1) through (4) above own more than 35% of the voting power, profits interest, or beneficial interest.

For purposes of section 509(a)(2), as referenced in Schedule A (Form 990 or 990-EZ), Public Charity Status and Public Support, a disqualified person is defined in section 4946, except that it does not include an organization described in section 509(a)(1).

For purposes of section 509(a)(3), as referenced in Schedule A (Form 990 or 990-EZ), a disqualified person is defined in section 4946, except that it does not include a foundation manager or an organization described in section 509(a)(1) or 509(a)(2).

Disregarded Entity or Entities – An entity wholly owned by the organization that is generally not treated as a separate entity for federal tax purposes (for example, single-member limited liability company of which the organization is the sole member). See Regulations sections 301.7701-2 and 3. A disregarded entity generally must use the **EIN** of its sole member. An exception applies to employment taxes: for wages paid to **employees** of a disregarded entity, the disregarded entity must file separate employment tax returns and use its own EIN on such returns. See Regulations sections 301.6109-1(h) and 301.7701-2(c)(2)(iv).

Domestic Government – See **Governmental Unit.**

Domestic Individual – An individual who lives or resides in the **United States** and is not a **foreign individual.**

Domestic Organization – A corporation or partnership is domestic if created or organized in the United States or under the law of the United States or of any state or possession. A trust is domestic if a court within the United States or a **U.S. possession** is able to exercise primary supervision over the administration of the trust, and one or more U.S. persons (or persons in possessions of the United States) have the authority to control all substantial decisions of the trust.

Donor Advised Fund – A fund or account:

1. That is separately identified by reference to **contributions** of a donor or donors;
2. That is owned and controlled by a **sponsoring organization;** and
3. For which the donor or **donor advisor** has or reasonably expects to have advisory privileges in the distribution or investment of amounts held in the donor advised funds or accounts because of the donor's status as a donor.

A donor advised fund does not include any fund or account:

1. That makes distributions only to a single identified organization or governmental entity, or
2. In which a donor or donor advisor gives advice about which individuals receive grants for travel, study, or other similar purposes, if:
    a. The donor or donor advisor's advisory privileges are performed exclusively by such person in his or her capacity as a committee member in which all of the committee members are appointed by the sponsoring organization;
    b. No combination of donors or donor advisors (and related persons as defined below) directly or indirectly control the committee; and
    c. All grants from the fund or account are awarded on an objective and nondiscriminatory basis following a procedure approved in advance by the board of directors of the sponsoring organization. The procedure must be designed to ensure that all grants meet the requirements of section 4945(g)(1), (2), or (3); or
3. That the IRS exempts from being treated as a donor advised fund because either such fund or account is advised by a committee not directly or indirectly controlled by the donor or donor advisor or such fund benefits a single identified charitable purpose. For example, see Section 5.01 of Notice 2006-109, 2006-51 I.R.B. 1121, and any future related guidance.

Donor Advisor – Any person appointed or designated by a donor to advise a **sponsoring organization** on the distribution or investment of amounts held in the donor's **donor advised fund.**

EIN – Employer identification number, a nine-digit number. Use Form SS-4 to apply for an EIN.

Employee – Any individual who, under the usual common law rules applicable in determining the employer-employee relationship, has the status of an employee, and any other individual who is treated as an employee for federal employment tax purposes under section 3121(d). See Pub. 1779 for more information.

Endowment – See **Temporarily Restricted Endowment, Permanent Endowment,** and **Quasi-Endowment.** See also **SFAS 117** (ASC 958-205-45).

Escrow or Custodial Account – Refers to an account (whether a segregated account at a financial institution or a set-aside on the organization's books and records) over which the organization has signature authority, in which the funds are held for the benefit of other organizations or individuals, whether or not the funds are reported on Part X, line 21, and whether or not the account is labeled as "escrow account," "custodial account," "trust account," or some similar term. An escrow or custodial account does not include a split-interest trust (or the beneficial interest in such trust) described in section 4947(a)(2) for which the filing organization is a trustee, other than a trust in the trade or business of lending money, repairing credit, or providing debt management plan services, payment processing, or similar services.

Excess Benefit Transaction – In the case of an **applicable tax-exempt organization,** any transaction in which an excess benefit is provided by the organization, directly or indirectly to, or for the use of, any **disqualified person,** as defined in section 4958. Excess benefit generally means the excess of the economic benefit received from the applicable organization over the consideration given (including services) by a disqualified person, but see the special rules below regarding donor advised funds and supporting organizations. See *Appendix G* for more information.

Donor advised fund. For a **donor advised fund,** an excess benefit transaction also includes a grant, loan, **compensation,** or similar payment from the fund to a:

- Donor or **donor advisor;**
- **Family member** of a donor or donor advisor;
- **35% controlled entity** of a donor or donor advisor; or
- 35% controlled entity of a family member of a donor or donor advisor.

The excess benefit in this transaction is the amount of the grant, loan, **compensation,** or similar payments.

For additional information see the Instructions for Form 4720.

Supporting organization. For any **supporting organization,** defined in section 509(a)(3), an excess benefit transaction also includes grants, loans, **compensation,** or similar payments provided by the supporting organization to a:

- Substantial contributor,
- Family member of a substantial contributor,
- 35% controlled entity of a substantial contributor, or
- 35% controlled entity of a family member of a substantial contributor.

For this purpose, the excess benefit is defined as the amount of the grant, loan, **compensation,** or similar payments. Additionally, an excess benefit transaction includes any loans provided by the supporting organization to a disqualified person (other than an organization described in section 509(a)(1), (2), or (4)).

Exempt Bond – See **Tax-Exempt Bond.**

Fair Market Value (FMV) – The price at which property, or the right to use property, would change hands between a willing buyer and a willing seller, neither being under any compulsion to buy, sell, or transfer property or the right to use property, and both having reasonable knowledge of relevant facts.

Family Member, Family Relationship – Unless specified otherwise, the family of an individual includes only his or her spouse (see Rev. Rul. 2013-17 regarding same-sex marriage), ancestors, brothers and sisters (whether whole or half blood), children (whether natural or adopted), grandchildren, great-grandchildren, and spouses of brothers, sisters, children, grandchildren, and great-grandchildren.

FIN 48 (ASC 740) – Financial Accounting Standards Board (FASB) Interpretation No. 48, *A accounting for Uncertainty in Income Taxes -an interpretation of FASB Statement No. 109,* now codified in FASB Accounting Standards Codification 740, Income Taxes (ASC 740). The organization can be required to provide in Schedule D (Form 990), Supplemental Financial Statements, the text of the footnote to its **financial statements** regarding the organization's liability for uncertain tax positions under FIN 48 (ASC 740).

Financial Statements – An organization's statements of revenue and expenses and balance sheet, or similar statements prepared regarding the financial operations of the organization.

Fiscal Year – An annual accounting period ending on the last day of a month other than December. See also **Tax Year** and **Current Year.**

Foreign Government – A governmental agency or entity, or a political subdivision thereof, that is not classified as a **United States** agency or **governmental unit,** regardless of where it is located or operated.

Foreign Individual – A person, including a U.S. citizen or resident, who lives or resides outside the **United States.** For purposes of Form 990, Part IX, and Schedule F (Form 990), Statement of Activities Outside the United States, a person who lives or resides outside the United States at the time the grant is paid or distributed to the individual is a **foreign individual.**

Foreign Organization – An organization that is not a **domestic organization.** A foreign organization includes an affiliate that is organized as a legal entity separate from the filing organization, but does not include any branch office, account, or **employee** of a domestic organization located outside the **United States.**

Fundraising – See **Fundraising Activities.**

Fundraising Activities – Activities undertaken to induce potential donors to contribute money, securities, services, materials, facilities, other assets, or time. They include publicizing and conducting **fundraising** campaigns; maintaining donor mailing lists; conducting **fundraising events,** preparing and distributing fundraising manuals, instructions, and other materials; **professional fundraising services;** and conducting other activities involved with soliciting **contributions** from individuals, foundations, governments, and others. Fundraising activities do not include **gaming,** the conduct of any trade or business that is regularly carried on, or activities substantially related to the accomplishment of the organization's exempt purpose (other than by raising funds).

Fundraising Events – Include dinners and dances, door-to-door sales of merchandise, concerts, carnivals, sports events, auctions, casino nights (in which participants can play casino-style games but the only prizes or auction items provided to participants are noncash items that were donated to the organization), and similar events not regularly carried on that are conducted for the primary purpose of raising funds. Fundraising events do not include the following:

1. The conduct of a trade or business that is regularly carried on;
2. Activities substantially related to the accomplishment of the organization's exempt purposes (other than by raising funds);
3. Solicitation campaigns that generate only **contributions,** which may involve gifts of goods or services from the organization of only nominal value, or sweepstakes, lotteries, or raffles in which the names of contributors or other respondents are entered in a drawing for prizes of only nominal value; and
4. Gaming.

GAAP – See **Generally Accepted Accounting Principles.**

Gaming – Includes (but is not limited to): **bingo, pull tabs/ instant bingo** (including satellite and progressive or event bingo), Texas Hold-Em Poker, 21, and other card games involving betting, raffles, scratch-offs, charitable gaming tickets, break-opens, hard cards, banded tickets, jar tickets, pickle cards, Lucky Seven cards, Nevada Club tickets, casino nights/ Las Vegas nights (other than events not regularly carried on in which participants can play casino-style games but the only prizes or auction items provided to participants are noncash items that were donated to the organization, which events are **fundraising events),** and coin-operated gambling devices. Coin-operated gambling devices include slot machines, electronic video slot or line games, video poker, video blackjack, video keno, video bingo, video pull tab games, etc. See Pub. 3079, Tax-Exempt Organizations and Gaming.

Generally Accepted Accounting Principles/ GAAP – The accounting principles set forth by the Financial Accounting Standards Board (FASB) and the American Institute of Certified Public Accountants (AICPA) that guide the work of accountants in reporting financial information and preparing **audited financial statements** for organizations.

Governing Body – The group of 1 or more persons authorized under state law to make governance decisions on behalf of the organization and its shareholders or members, if applicable. The governing body is, generally speaking, the board of **directors** (sometimes referred to as board of **trustees)** of a corporation or association, or the trustee or trustees of a trust (sometimes referred to as the board of trustees).

Government Official – A federal, state, or local official described within section 4946(c).

Governmental Issuer – A state or local governmental unit that issues a **tax-exempt bond.**

Governmental Unit – A state, a **possession of the United States,** or a **political subdivision** of a state or U.S. possession, the United States, or the District of Columbia. See section 170(c)(1).

Grants and Other Assistance – For purposes of Part IX, lines 1-3; Schedule F (Form 990); and Schedule I (Form 990), includes awards, prizes, contributions, noncash assistance, cash allocations, stipends, scholarships, fellowships, research grants, and similar payments and distributions made by the organization during the tax year. It does not include salaries or other **compensation** to **employees** or payments to **independent contractors** if the primary purpose is to serve the direct and immediate needs of the organization (such as legal, accounting, or fundraising services); the payment of any benefit by a section 501(c)(9) voluntary employees' beneficiary association (VEBA) to employees of a sponsoring organization or contributing employer, if such payment is made under the terms of the VEBA and in compliance with section 505; or payments or other assistance to affiliates or branch offices that are not organized as legal entities separate from the filing organization.

Gross Proceeds – For purposes of Schedule K (Form 990), Supplemental Information on Tax-Exempt Bonds, generally any sale **proceeds,** investment proceeds, transferred proceeds, and replacement proceeds of an issue. See Regulations sections 1.148-1(b) and 1(c).

Gross Receipts – The total amounts the organization received from all sources during its tax year, without subtracting any costs or expenses. See *Appendix B. How to Determine Whether an Organization's Gross Receipts Are Normally $50,000 (or $5,000) or Less* and *Appendix C. Special Gross Receipts Tests for Determining Exempt Status of section 501(c)(7) and 501(c)(15) Organizations.*

Group Exemption – Tax exemption of a group of organizations all exempt under the same Code section, applied for and obtained by a **central organization** on behalf of **subordinate organizations** under the central organization's general supervision or control. See Rev. Proc. 80-27, 1980-1 C.B. 677, Rev. Proc. 96-40, 1996-2 C.B. 301, and *Appendix E. Group Returns—Reporting Information on Behalf of the Group,* for more information.

Group Return – A Form 990 filed by the **central organization** of a **group exemption** for two or more of the **subordinate organizations.** See *General Instructions, Section I. Group Return, earlier,* and *Appendix E. Group Returns—Reporting Information on Behalf of the Group,* for more information.

Highest Compensated Employee – One of the five highest compensated **employees** of the organization (including employees of a **disregarded entity** of the organization), other than current **officers, directors, trustees,** or **key employees,** whose aggregate **reportable compensation** from the organization and **related organizations** is greater than $100,000 for the calendar year ending with or within the organization's **tax year.** These employees should be reported in Part VII, Section A of Form 990.

Historical Treasure – A building, structure, area, or property (real or personal) with recognized cultural, aesthetic, or historical value that is significant in the history, architecture, archeology, or culture of a country, state, or city.

Hospital/ Hospital Facility – For purposes of Schedule H (Form 990), Hospitals, a hospital, or hospital facility, is a facility that is, or is required to be, licensed, registered, or similarly recognized by a state as a hospital. This includes a hospital facility that is operated through a **disregarded entity** or a **joint venture** treated as a partnership for federal income tax purposes. It does not include hospital facilities that are located outside the **United States.** It also does not include hospital facilities that are operated by entities organized as separate legal entities from the organization that are taxable as a corporation for federal tax purposes (except for members of a **group exemption** included in a **group return** filed by an organization).

Hospital Organization – An organization which operates one or more **hospital facilities.**

Hospital (or Cooperative Hospital Service Organization) – For purposes of Schedule A (Form 990 or 990-EZ), Public Charity Status and Public Support, a hospital (or cooperative hospital service organization) is an organization whose main purpose is to provide hospital or medical care. For purposes of Schedule A, a rehabilitation institution or an outpatient clinic can qualify as a hospital if its principal purposes or functions are the providing of hospital or medical care, but the term does not include medical schools, medical research organizations, convalescent homes, homes for children or the aged, animal hospitals, or vocational training institutions for handicapped individuals.

Household Goods – Include furniture, furnishings, electronics, appliances, linens, and other similar items. They do not include food, paintings, antiques and other objects of art, jewelry and gems (other than costume jewelry), and collections.

Independent Contractor – An individual or organization that receives compensation for providing services to the organization but who is not treated as an **employee.** See Pub. 1779 for more information.

Independent Voting Member of Governing Body – A **voting member of the governing body,** if all four of the following circumstances applied at all times during the organization's tax year:

1. The member was not compensated as an **officer** or other **employee** of the organization or of a **related organization** (see the instructions for Schedule R (Form 990), Related Organizations and Unrelated Partnerships), except as provided in the religious exception discussed in the instructions for Form 990, Part VI.
2. The member did not receive total **compensation** or other payments exceeding $10,000 during the organization's tax year from the organization or from related organizations as an **independent contractor,** other than **reasonable compensation** for services provided in the capacity as a **member of the governing body.** For example, a person who receives reasonable expense reimbursements and reasonable compensation as a **director** of the organization does not cease to be independent merely because he or she also received payments of $7,500 from the organization for other arrangements.
3. Neither the member, nor any **family member** of the member, was involved in a transaction with the organization (whether directly or indirectly through affiliation with another organization) required to be reported on Schedule L (Form 990 or 990-EZ), Transactions With Interested Persons, for the organization's tax year.
4. Neither the member, nor any family member of the member, was involved in a transaction with a taxable or tax-exempt related organization of a type and amount that would be reportable on Schedule L (Form 990 or 990-EZ) if required to be filed by the related organization.

A member of the governing body is not considered to lack independence merely because of any of the following circumstances.

1. The member is a donor to the organization, regardless of the amount of the contribution.
2. The member has taken a *bona fide* vow of poverty and either:
   a. Receives **compensation** as an agent of a **religious order** or a section 501(d) religious or apostolic organization, but only under circumstances in which the member does not receive taxable income (for example, Rev. Rul. 77-290, 1977-2 C.B. 26; Rev. Rul. 80-332, 1980-2 C.B. 34); or
   b. Belongs to a religious order that receives sponsorship or payments from the organization that do not constitute taxable income to the member.
3. The member receives financial benefits from the organization solely in the capacity of being a member of the charitable or other class served by the organization in the exercise of its exempt function, such as being a member of a section 501(c)(6) organization, so long as the financial benefits comply with the organization's terms of membership.

Initial Contract – A binding written contract between an **applicable tax-exempt organization** and a person who was not a **disqualified person** immediately before entering into the contract.

Instant Bingo – See **Pull Tabs.**

Institutional Trustee – A **trustee** that is not an individual or natural person but an organization. For instance, a bank or trust company serving as the trustee of a trust is an institutional trustee.

Joint Venture – Unless otherwise provided, a partnership, limited liability company, or other entity treated as a partnership for federal tax purposes, as described in Regulations sections 301.7701-1 through 301.7701-3.

Key Employee – For purposes of Form 990, an **employee** of an organization (other than an **officer, director,** or **trustee**) who meets all three of the following tests applied in the following order:

1. $150,000 Test. Receives **reportable compensation** from the organization and all **related organizations** in excess of $150,000 for the **calendar year** ending with or within the organization's **tax year.**
2. Responsibility Test. The employee:
   a. has responsibilities, powers or influence over the organization as a whole similar to those of officers, directors, or trustees;
   b. manages a discrete segment or activity of the organization that represents 10% or more of the activities, assets, income, or expenses of the organization, as compared to the organization as a whole; or
   c. has or shares authority to control or determine 10% or more of the organization's capital expenditures, operating budget, or compensation for employees.
3. Top 20 Test. Is one of the 20 employees (that satisfy the $150,000 Test and Responsibility Test) with the highest reportable compensation from the organization and related organizations for the calendar year ending with or within the organization's tax year.

See instructions for Part VII for examples of **Key Employees.**

Legislation – Includes action by Congress, any state legislature, any local council, or similar governing body about acts, bills, resolutions, or similar items, or action by the public in referenda, ballot initiatives, constitutional amendments or similar procedures. It does not include actions by executive, judicial, or administrative bodies.

Lobbying – See **Lobbying Activities.**

Lobbying Activities – All activities intended to influence foreign, national, state, or local **legislation.** Such activities include direct lobbying (attempting to influence the legislators) and grassroots lobbying (attempting to influence legislation by influencing the general public).

Maintaining Offices, Employees, Or Agents – For purposes of Schedule F (Form 990), Statement of Activities Outside the United States, includes principal, regional, district, or branch offices, such offices maintained by agents, and persons situated at those offices paid wages for services performed. "Agent" is defined under traditional agency principles (but does not include **volunteers).**

Management Company – An organization that performs management duties for another organization customarily performed by or under the direct supervision of the other organization's **officers, directors, trustees,** or **key employees.** These management duties include, but are not limited to, hiring, firing, and supervising personnel; planning or executing budgets or financial operations; and supervising exempt operations or **unrelated trades or businesses.**

Medical Research – For purposes of a medical research organization operated in conjunction with a hospital (see Schedule A (Form 990 or 990-EZ), Public Charity Status and Public Support), medical research means investigations, studies and experiments performed to discover, develop, or verify knowledge relating to physical or mental diseases and impairments and their causes, diagnosis, prevention, treatment, or control.

Member of the Governing Body – A person who serves on an organization's **governing body,** including a **director** or **trustee,** but not if the person lacks voting power.

Noncash Contributions – **Contributions** of property, tangible or intangible, other than money. Noncash contributions include, but are not limited to, stocks, bonds, and other **securities;** real estate; **works of art;** stamps, coins, and other **collectibles;** clothing and **household goods;** vehicles, boats, and airplanes; inventories of food, medical equipment or supplies, books, or seeds; intellectual property, including patents, trademarks, copyrights, and trade secrets; donated items that are sold immediately after donation, such as publicly traded stock or used cars; and items donated for sale at a charity auction. Noncash contributions do not include **volunteer** services performed for the reporting organization or donated use of materials, facilities, or equipment.

Nonexempt Charitable Trust – A trust that meets the following conditions:

- Is not exempt from tax under section 501(a),
- All of its unexpired interests are devoted to charitable purposes, and
- A charitable deduction was allowed for **contributions** to the trust under section 170, section 545(b)(2), section 642(c), section 2055, section 2106(a) (2), or section 2522, or for amounts paid by or permanently set aside by the trust under section 642(c).

Nonqualified Deferred Compensation – **Deferred compensation** that is earned pursuant to a nonqualified plan or nongovernmental section 457 plan. Different rules can apply for purposes of identifying arrangements subject to sections 83, 409A, 457(f), and 3121(v). Earned but unpaid incentive compensation can be deferred pursuant to a nonqualified deferred compensation plan.

Officer – Unless otherwise provided (for example, Signature Block, principal officer in *Heading),* a person elected or appointed to manage the organization's daily operations at any time during the **tax year,** such as a president, vice-president, secretary, treasurer, and, in some cases, Board Chair. The officers of an organization are determined by reference to its organizing document, bylaws, or resolutions of its governing body, or as otherwise designated consistent with state law, but at a minimum include those officers required by applicable state law. For purposes of Form 990, treat the organization's **top management official** and **top financial official** as officers.

"On Behalf Of" Issuer – A corporation organized under the general nonprofit corporation law of a state whose obligations are considered obligations of a state or local **governmental unit.** See Rev. Proc. 82-26, 1982-1 C.B. 476, for a description of the circumstances under which the Service will ordinarily issue an advance ruling that the obligations of a nonprofit corporation were issued on behalf of a state or local governmental unit. See also Rev. Rul. 63-20, 1963-1 C.B. 24; Rev. Rul. 59-41, 1959-1 C.B. 13; and Rev. Rul. 54-296, 1954-2 C.B. 59. An "on behalf of" issuer also includes any corporation organized by a state or local governmental unit specifically to issue **tax-exempt bonds** to further public purposes. See Rev. Rul. 57-187, 1957-1 C.B. 65.

Organization Manager – For purposes of section 4958, any **officer, director,** or **trustee** of an **applicable tax-exempt organization,** or any individual having powers or responsibilities similar to officers, directors, or trustees of the organization, regardless of title.

Permanent (True) Endowment – An **endowment** fund established by donor-restricted gifts that is maintained to provide a permanent source of income, with the stipulation that principal must be invested and kept intact in perpetuity, while only the income generated can be used by the organization. See **SFAS 117** (ASC 958-205-45).

Political Campaign Activities – All activities that support or oppose candidates for elective federal, state, or local public office. It does not matter whether the candidate is elected. A candidate is one who offers himself or is proposed by others for public office. Political campaign activity does not include any activity to encourage participation in the electoral process, such as voter registration or voter education, provided that the activity does not directly or indirectly support or oppose any candidate.

Political Subdivision – A division of any state or local **governmental unit** which is a municipal corporation or which has been delegated the right to exercise part of the sovereign power of the unit. Sovereign power includes the power to make and enforce laws.

Possession of the United States – Includes the Commonwealth of Puerto Rico, the Commonwealth of the Northern Mariana Islands, Guam, American Samoa, and the U.S. Virgin Islands.

Principal Officer – For purposes of the *Heading* on page 1 of Form 990 (but not for the purposes of the Signature Block or other parts of the Form 990), an officer of the organization who, regardless of title, has ultimate responsibility for implementing the decisions of the organization's **governing body,** or for supervising the management, administration, or operation of the organization.

Private Business Use – For purposes of Schedule K (Form 990), Supplemental Information on Tax-Exempt Bonds, use by the organization or another 501(c)(3) organization in an **unrelated trade or business.** Private business use also generally includes any use by a nongovernmental person other than a section 501(c)(3) organization unless otherwise permitted through an exception or safe harbor provided under the regulations or a revenue procedure.

Private Foundation – An organization described in section 501(c)(3) that is not a **public charity.** Some private foundations are classified as operating foundations (also known as private operating foundations) under section 4942(j)(3) or exempt operating foundations under section 4940(d)(2). A private foundation retains its private foundation status until such status is terminated under section 507. Thus, a tax-exempt private foundation becomes a taxable private foundation if its section 501(c)(3) status is revoked.

Proceeds – For purposes of Schedule K (Form 990), Supplemental Information on Tax-Exempt Bonds, generally the sale proceeds of an issue (other than those sale proceeds used to retire bonds of the issue that are not deposited in a reasonably required reserve or replacement fund). Proceeds also include any investment proceeds from investments that accrue during the project period (net of rebate amounts attributable to the project period). See Regulations section 1.141-1(b).

Professional Fundraising Services – Services performed for the organization requiring the exercise of professional judgment or discretion consisting of planning, management, preparation of materials (such as direct mail solicitation packages and applications for grants or other assistance), provision of advice and consulting regarding solicitation of **contributions,** and direct solicitation of **contributions,** such as soliciting restricted or unrestricted grants to provide services to the general public. However, professional fundraising does not include services provided by the organization's **employees** in their capacity as employees (except as provided in the instructions for Part I, line 16a), nor does professional fundraising include purely ministerial tasks, such as printing, mailing services, or receiving and depositing contributions to a charity, such as services provided by a bank or caging service.

Program-Related Investment – Investments made primarily to accomplish the organization's exempt purposes rather than to produce income. Examples of program-related investments include student loans and notes receivable from other exempt organizations that obtained the funds to pursue the filing organization's exempt function.

Public Charity – An organization described in section 501(c)(3) and that is excepted from private foundation status because it is described in section 509(a)(1) (which cross-references sections 170(b)(1)(A)(i) through (vi)), 509(a)(2), 509(a)(3), or 509(a)(4).

Publicly Traded Securities – Generally, include common and preferred stocks, bonds (including governmental obligations such as bonds and Treasury bills), mutual fund shares, and other investments listed and regularly traded in an over-the-counter market or an established exchange and for which market quotations are published or are otherwise readily available. (See further explanation in the instructions for Part X, line 11, and Schedule M (Form 990), Noncash Contributions, line 9).

Pull Tabs – Includes games in which an individual places a wager by purchasing preprinted cards that are covered with pull tabs. Winners are revealed when the individual pulls back the sealed tabs on the front of the card and compares the patterns under the tabs with the winning patterns preprinted on the back of the card. Included in the definition of pull tabs are "instant bingo," "mini bingo," and other similar scratch-off cards. Satellite, Internet, and progressive or event bingo are games conducted in many different places simultaneously and the winners are not all present when the wagers are placed, the winners are determined, and the prizes are distributed. Revenue and expenses associated with satellite, Internet, and progressive bingo should be included under this category. However, certain bingo games within a hybrid gaming event (such as progressive or event bingo) can also qualify as bingo if the individual game meets the preceding definition of **bingo.**

Qualified 501(c)(3) Bond – A **tax-exempt bond,** the proceeds of which are used by a section 501(c)(3) organization to advance its charitable purpose. Requirements generally applicable to a qualified section 501(c)(3) bond under section 145 include the following.

1. All property financed by the bond issue is to be owned by a section 501(c)(3) organization or a **governmental unit.**
2. At least 95% of net proceeds of the **bond issue** are used either by a **governmental unit** or a section 501(c)(3) organization in activities that are not **unrelated trades or businesses** (determined by applying section 513).

Qualified Conservation Contribution – Any **contribution** of a qualified real property interest to a qualified organization exclusively for conservation purposes. A "qualified real property interest" means any of the following interests in real property:

1. The entire interest of the donor,
2. A remainder interest, or
3. A restriction (such as an easement), granted in perpetuity, on the use which may be made of the real property.

A "qualified organization" means an organization which is:

    a. a **governmental unit** described in section 170(c)(1);

    b. a publicly supported charitable organization described in sections 501(c)(3) and 170(b)(1)(A)(vi) or section 509(a)(2) (see the instructions for Parts II and III of Schedule A (Form 990 or 990-EZ)); or

    c. a **supporting organization** described in sections 501(c)(3) and 509(a)(3) that is controlled by a governmental unit or a publicly supported charitable organization.

In addition, a qualified organization must have a commitment to protect the conservation purposes of a qualified conservation contribution, and have the resources to enforce the restrictions.

A "conservation purpose" means:

1. The preservation of land areas for outdoor recreation by, or the education of, the general public;
2. The protection of a relatively natural habitat of fish, wildlife, plants, or similar ecosystems;
3. The preservation of open space (including farm and forest land) where such preservation will yield a significant public benefit and is for the scenic enjoyment of the general public or is pursuant to a clearly delineated federal, state, or local governmental conservation policy; or
4. The preservation of an historically important land area or a certified historic structure.

See section 170(h) for additional information, including special rules about the conservation purpose requirement for buildings in registered historic districts. See also **Conservation Easement.**

Qualified state or local political organization A type of political organization that meets the following requirements:

- It limits its exempt function to the selection process relating solely to any state or local public office or office in a state or local political organization;
- It is required under a state law to report to a state agency (and does report) information that otherwise would be required to be reported on Form 8872, Political Organization Report of Contributions and Expenditures, or it is required to report under state law (and does report) at least the following information:
  1. The name and address of every person who contributes a total of $500 or more during the calendar year and the amount of each contribution;
  2. The name and address of every person to whom the organization makes expenditures aggregating $800 or more during the calendar year, and the amount of each expenditure; and
  3. Any additional information specified in section 527(j)(3), if state law requires the reporting of that information to the state agency.
- The state agency makes the reports filed by the organization publicly available;
- The organization makes the reports filed with the state agency publicly available in the manner described in section 6104(d); and
- No federal candidate or office holder controls or materially participates in the direction of the organization, solicits **contributions** to the organization, or directs any of the organization's disbursements.

Quasi-Endowment – An **endowment** fund established by the organization itself, either from unrestricted donor or organizational funds, over which the organization itself imposes restrictions on their use, and which restrictions can be temporary or permanent in nature. These funds are sometimes referred to as board-designated endowments. See **SFAS 117** (ASC 958-205-45).

Reasonable Compensation – The value that would ordinarily be paid for like services by like enterprises under like circumstances.

Reasonable Effort – A reasonable amount of effort in information gathering that the organization is expected to undertake in order to provide information requested on the Form 990. See the specific instructions for Part VI, lines 1b and 2; Part VII, Section A (compensation from related organizations); and Schedule L (Form 990 or 990-EZ), Parts III and IV, for examples of reasonable efforts.

Refunding Escrow – One or more funds established as part of a single transaction or a series of related transactions, containing **proceeds** of a **refunding issue** and any other amounts to provide for payment of principal or interest on one or more prior issues. See Regulations section 1.148-1(b).

Refunding Issue – An issue of obligations, the **proceeds** of which are used to pay principal, interest, or redemption price on another issue (a prior issue), including the issuance costs, accrued interest, capitalized interest on the refunding issue, a reserve or replacement fund, or similar costs, if any, properly allocable to that refunding issue. A current refunding issue is a refunding issue that is issued not more than 90 days before the last expenditure of any proceeds of the refunding issue for the payment of principal or interest on the prior issue. An advance refunding issue is a refunding issue that is not a current refunding issue. See Regulations sections 1.150-1(d)(1), 1.150-1(d)(3), and 1.150-1(d)(4).

Related Organization – An organization, including a nonprofit organization, a stock corporation, a partnership or limited liability company, a trust, and a **governmental unit** or other government entity, that stands in one or more of the following relationships to the filing organization at any time during the **tax year.**

- Parent: an organization that **controls** the filing organization.
- Subsidiary: an organization **controlled** by the filing organization.
- Brother/ Sister: an organization **controlled** by the same person or persons that control the filing organization. However, if the filing organization is a trust that has a bank or financial institution trustee that is also the trustee of another trust, the other trust is not a Brother/ Sister related organization of the filing organization on the ground of common control by the bank or financial institution trustee.
- Supporting/ Supported: an organization that claims to be at any time during the **tax year,** or that is classified by the IRS at any time during the tax year, as (i) a **supporting organization** of the filing organization within the meaning of section 509(a)(3), if the filing organization is a **supported organization** within the meaning of section 509(f)(3); (ii) or a supported organization, if the filing organization is a supporting organization.
- Sponsoring Organization of a VEBA: an organization that establishes or maintains a section 501(c)(9) voluntary employees' beneficiary association (VEBA) during the tax year. A sponsoring organization of a VEBA also includes an employee organization, association, committee, joint board of trustees, or other similar group of representatives of the parties which establish or maintain a VEBA. Although a VEBA must report a sponsoring organization as a related organization, a sponsoring organization should not report a VEBA as a related organization, unless the VEBA is related to the sponsoring organization in some other capacity described in this definition.
- Contributing Employer of a VEBA: an employer that makes a contribution or contributions to the VEBA during the tax year. Although a VEBA must report a contributing employer as a related organization, a contributing employer should not report a VEBA as a related organization, unless the VEBA is related to the contributing employer in some other capacity described in this definition.

The organization must determine its related organizations for purposes of completing Form 990, Parts VI (Governance), VII (Compensation), VIII (Statement of Revenue) and X (Balance Sheet), Schedule D (Form 990), Schedule J (Form 990), and Schedule R (Form 990). See instructions for those parts and schedules for related organization reporting requirements.

Religious Order – An organization described in Rev. Proc. 91-20, 1991-1 C.B. 524.

Reportable Compensation – In general, the aggregate **compensation** that is reported (or required to be reported, if greater) on Form W-2, box 1 or 5 (whichever amount is greater); and/ or Form 1099-MISC, box 7, for the calendar year ending with or within the organization's **tax year.** For foreign persons who receive U.S. source income, reportable compensation includes the amount reportable on Form 1042-S, box 2. For persons for whom compensation reporting on Form W-2, 1099-MISC, or 1042-S is not required (certain foreign persons, institutional trustees, and persons whose compensation was below the $600 reporting threshold for Form 1099-MISC), reportable compensation includes the total value of the compensation paid in the form of cash or property during the calendar year ending with or within the organization's tax year.

Review of Financial Statement – An examination of an organization's financial records and practices by an independent accountant with the objective of assessing whether the **financial statements** are plausible, without the extensive testing and external validation procedures of an audit.

School – An organization, the primary function of which is the presentation of formal instruction, and which has a regular faculty, curriculum, an enrolled body of students, and a place where educational activities are regularly conducted.

Security/ Securities – Any bond, debenture, note, or certificate or other evidence of indebtedness issued by a corporation, government or **political subdivision,** share of stock, voting trust certificate, or any certificate of interest or participation in, certificate of deposit or receipt for, temporary or interim certificate for, or warrant or right to subscribe to or purchase, any of the foregoing.

SFAS 116 – Statement of Financial Accounting Standards No. 116, Accounting for Contributions Received and Contributions Made, now codified in FASB Accounting Standards Codification 958, Not-for-Profit Entities (ASC 958).

SFAS 117 – Statement of Financial Accounting Standards No. 117, Financial Statements of Not-for-Profit Organizations, now codified in FASB Accounting Standards Codification 958, Not-for-Profit Entities (ASC 958).

Short Accounting Period – An accounting period of less than 12 months, which exists when an organization changes its annual accounting period, and which can exist in its initial or final year of existence (see **Tax Year).**

Short Period – See **Short Accounting Period.**

Significant Disposition of Net Assets – A disposition of net assets, consisting of a sale, exchange, disposition or other transfer of more than 25% of the FMV of the organization's net assets during the year, whether or not the organization received full or adequate consideration. A significant disposition of net assets involves:

1. One or more dispositions during the organization's **tax year,** amounting to more than 25% of the FMV of the organization's net assets as of the beginning of its tax year; or
2. One of a series of related dispositions or events begun in a prior year that, when combined, comprise more than 25% of the FMV of the organization's net assets as of the beginning of the tax year when

the first disposition in the series was made. Whether a significant disposition of net assets occurred through a series of related dispositions depends on the facts and circumstances in each case.

Examples of the types of transactions that are "a significant disposition of net assets" required to be reported on Schedule N (Form 990 or 990-EZ), Liquidation, Termination, Dissolution or Significant Disposition of Assets, Part II include:

- Taxable or tax-free sales or exchanges of exempt assets for cash or other consideration (a social club described in section 501(c)(7) selling land or an exempt organization selling assets it had used to further its exempt purposes);
- Sales, **contributions** or other transfers of assets to establish or maintain a partnership, **joint venture,** or a corporation (for-profit or nonprofit) whether or not the sales or transfers are governed by section 721 or section 351, whether or not the transferor received an ownership interest in exchange for the transfer;
- Sales of assets by a partnership or joint venture in which the exempt partner has an ownership interest; and
- Transfers of assets pursuant to a reorganization in which the organization is a surviving entity.

The following types of situations are not considered significant dispositions of net assets for purposes of Schedule N, Part II:

- The change in composition of **publicly traded securities** held in an exempt organization's passive investment portfolio;
- Asset sales made in the ordinary course of the organization's exempt activities to accomplish the organization's exempt purposes, for instance, gross sales of inventory;
- Grants or other assistance made in the ordinary course of the organization's exempt activities to accomplish the organization's exempt purposes, for instance, the regular charitable distributions of a United Way or other federated fundraising organization;
- A decrease in the value of net assets due to market fluctuation in the value of assets held by the organization; and
- Transfers to a **disregarded entity** of which the organization is the sole member.

Sponsoring Organization – Any organization which is all of the following:

- Described in section 170(c), other than governmental units described in section 170(c)(1) and without regard to section 170(c)(2)(A);
- Not a **private foundation** as defined in section 509(a); and
- Maintains one or more **donor advised funds.**

State of Legal Domicile – For a corporation, the state of incorporation (country of incorporation for a foreign corporation formed outside the United States). For a trust or other entity, the state whose law governs the organization's internal affairs (the foreign country whose law governs for a foreign organization other than a corporation).

Subordinate Organization – One of the organizations, typically local in nature, that is recognized as exempt in a **group exemption** letter and subject to the general supervision and control of a **central organization.**

Supported Organization – A **public charity** described in section 509(a)(1) or 509(a)(2) supported by a **supporting organization** described in section 509(a)(3).

Supporting Organization – A public charity claiming status on Form 990 or otherwise under section 509(a)(3). A supporting organization is organized and operated exclusively to support one or more **supported organizations.** A supporting organization that is operated, supervised, or controlled by one or more supported organizations is a Type I supporting organization. The relationship of a Type I supporting organization with its supported organization(s) is comparable to that of a parent-subsidiary relationship. A supporting organization supervised or controlled in connection with one or more supported organizations is a Type II supporting organization. A Type II supporting organization is controlled or managed by the same persons that control or manage its supported organization(s). A supporting organization that is operated in connection with one or more supported organizations is a Type III supporting organization. A Type III supporting organization is further considered either functionally integrated with its supported organization(s) or not functionally integrated with its supported organization(s) (Type III other). Finally, a supporting organization cannot be controlled directly or indirectly by one or more **disqualified persons** (as defined in section 4946), other than foundation managers and other than one or more public charities described in section 509(a)(1) or (2).

Tax-Exempt Bond – An obligation issued by or on behalf of a **governmental issuer** on which the interest paid is excluded from the holder's gross income under section 103. For this purpose, a bond can be any form of indebtedness under federal tax law, including a bond, note, loan, or lease-purchase agreement.

Tax Year – The annual accounting period for which the Form 990 is being filed, whether the calendar year ending December 31st or a fiscal year ending on the last day of any other month. The organization may have a short tax year in its first year of existence, in any year when it changes its annual accounting period (for example, from a December 31 year-end to a June 30 year-end), and in its last year of existence (for example, when it merges into another organization or dissolves). See also **Current Year, Fiscal Year,** and **Short Period.**

Temporarily Restricted Endowment – Includes **endowment** funds established by donor-restricted gifts that are maintained to provide a source of income for either a specified period of time or until a specific event occurs (see **SFAS 117** (ASC 958-205-45)), as well as all other temporarily restricted net assets held in a donor-restricted endowment, including unappropriated income from **permanent endowments** that is not subject to a permanent restriction.

Top Financial Official – The person who has ultimate responsibility for managing the organization's finances, for example, the treasurer or chief financial officer.

Top Management Official – A person who has ultimate responsibility for implementing the decisions of the organization's **governing body** or for supervising the management, administration, or operation of the organization (for example, the organization's president, CEO, or executive director).

Total Assets – The amount reported on Form 990, Part X, line 16, column (B).

Trustee – See **Director or Trustee.**

United States – Unless otherwise provided, includes the 50 states, the District of Columbia, the Commonwealth of Puerto Rico, the Commonwealth of the Northern Mariana Islands, Guam, American Samoa, and the United States Virgin Islands.

Unrelated Business – See **Unrelated Trade or Business.**

Unrelated Business income – Income from an **unrelated trade or business** as defined in section 513.

Unrelated Business Gross Income – Gross income from an **unrelated trade or business** as defined in section 513.

Unrelated Organization – An organization that is not a **related organization** to the filing organization.

Unrelated Trade or Business – Any trade or business, the conduct of which is not substantially related to the exercise or performance by the organization of its charitable, educational, or other purpose or function constituting the basis for its exemption. See Pub. 598 and the instructions for Form 990-T for a discussion of what is an unrelated trade or business.

U.S. Possession – See **Possession of the United States.**

Volunteer – A person who serves the organization without compensation, for instance, a member of the organization's governing body who serves the organization without compensation. "Compensation" for this purpose includes tips and noncash benefits, except for:

- Reimbursement of expenses under a reimbursement or other expense allowance arrangement in which there is adequate accounting to the organization,
- Working condition fringe benefits described in section 132,
- Liability insurance coverage for acts performed on behalf of the exempt organization, and
- *De minimis* fringe benefits.

Voting Member of the Governing Body – A member of the organization's **governing body** with power to vote on all matters that may come before the governing body (other than a conflict of interest that disqualifies the member from voting).

Works of Art – Include paintings, sculptures, prints, drawings, ceramics, antiques, decorative arts, textiles, carpets, silver, photography, film, video, installation and multimedia arts, rare books and manuscripts, historical memorabilia, and other similar objects. Art does not include **collectibles.**

Year of Formation – The year in which the organization was created or formed under applicable state law (if a corporation, the year of incorporation).

TAX GLOSSARY

401(k) Plan – A qualified retirement plan to which contributions from salary are made from pre-tax dollars.

Accelerated Depreciation – Computation of depreciation to provide greater deductions in earlier years of equipment and other business or investment property.

Accounting Method – Rules applied in determining when and how to report income and expenses on tax returns.

Accrual Method – Method of accounting that reports income when it is earned, disregarding when it may be received, and expense when incurred, disregarding when it is actually paid.

Acquisition Debt – Mortgage taken to buy, hold, or substantially improve main or second home that serves as security.

Active Participation – Rental real estate activity involving property management at a level that permits deduction of losses.

Adjusted Basis – Basis in property increased by some expenses (for example, by capital improvements) or decreased by some tax benefit (for example, by depreciation).

Adjusted Gross Income (AGI) – Gross income minus above-the-line deductions (such as deductions other than itemized deductions, the standard deduction, and personal and dependency exemptions).

Alimony – Payments for the support or maintenance of one's spouse pursuant to a judicial decree or written agreement related to divorce or separation.

Alternative Minimum Tax (AMT) – System comparing the tax results with and without the benefit of tax preference items for the purpose of preventing tax avoidance.

Amortization – Write-off of an intangible asset's cost over a number of years.

Applicable Federal Rate (AFR) – An interest rate determined by reference to the average market yield on U.S. government obligations. Used in Sec. 7872 to determine the treatment of loans with below-market interest rates.

At-Risk Rules – Limits on tax losses to business activities in which an individual taxpayer has an economic stake.

Backup Withholding – Withholding for federal taxes on certain types of income (such as interest or dividend payments) by a payor that has not received required taxpayer identification number (TIN) information.

Bad Debt – Uncollectible debt deductible as an ordinary loss if associated with a business and otherwise deductible as short-term capital loss.

Basis – Amount determined by a taxpayer's investment in property for purposes of determining gain or loss on the sale of property or in computing depreciation.

Cafeteria Plan – Written plan allowing employees to choose among two or more benefits (consisting of cash and qualified benefits) and to pay for the benefits with pretax dollars. Must conform to Sec. 125 requirements.

Capital Asset – Investments (such as stocks, bonds, and mutual funds) and personal property (such as home).

Capital Gain/ Loss – Profit (net of losses) on the sale or exchange of a capital asset or Sec. 1231 property, subject to favorable tax rates, and loss on such sales or exchanges (net of gains) deductible against $3,000 of ordinary income.

Capitalization – Addition of cost or expense to the basis of property.

Carryovers (Carryforwards) and Carrybacks – Tax deductions and credits not fully used in one year are chargeable against prior or future tax years to reduce taxable income or taxes payable.

Conservation Reserve Program (CRP) – A voluntary program for soil, water, and wildlife conservation, wetland establishment and restoration and reforestation, administered by the U.S. Department of Agriculture.

Credit – Amount subtracted from income tax liability.

Deduction – Expense subtracted in computing adjusted gross income.

Defined Benefit Plan – Qualified retirement plan basing annual contributions on targeted benefit amounts.

Defined Contribution Plan – Qualified retirement plan with annual contributions based on a percentage of compensation.

Depletion – Deduction for the extent a natural resource is used.

Depreciation – Proportionate deduction based on the cost of business or investment property with a useful life (or recovery period) greater than one year.

Earned Income – Wages, bonuses, vacation pay, and other remuneration, including self-employment income, for services rendered.

Earned Income Credit – Refundable credit available to low-income individuals.

Employee Stock Ownership Plan (ESOP) – Defined contribution plan that is a stock bonus plan or a combined stock bonus and money purchase plan designed to invest primarily in qualifying employer securities.

Estimated Tax – Quarterly payments of income tax liability by individuals, corporations, trusts, and estates.

Exemption – A deduction against net income based on taxpayer status (such as single, head of household, married filing jointly or separately, trusts, and estates).

Fair Market Value – The price that would be agreed upon by a willing seller and willing buyer, established by markets for publicly-traded stocks, or determined by appraisal.

Fiscal Year – A 12-month taxable period ending on any date other than December 31.

Foreign Tax – Income tax paid to a foreign country and deductible or creditable, at the taxpayer's election, against U.S. income tax.

Gift – Transfer of money or property without expectation of anything in return, and excludable from income by the recipient. A gift may still be affected by the unified estate and gift transfer tax applicable to the gift's maker.

Goodwill – A business asset, intangible in nature, adding a value beyond the business's tangible assets.

Gross Income – Income from any and all sources, after any exclusions and before any deductions are taken into consideration.

Half-Year Convention – A depreciation rule assuming property other than real estate is placed in service in the middle of the tax year.

Head-of-Household – An unmarried individual who provides and maintains a household for a qualifying dependent and therefore is subject to distinct tax rates.

Health Savings Account (HSA) – A trust operated exclusively for purposes of paying qualified medical expenses of the account beneficiary and thus providing for deductible contributions, tax-deferred earnings, and exclusion of tax on any monies withdrawn for medical purposes.

Holding Period – The period of time a taxpayer holds onto property, therefore affecting tax treatment on its disposition.

Imputed Interest – Income deemed attributable to deferred-payment transfers, such as below-market loans, for which no interest or unrealistically low interest is charged.

Incentive Stock Option (ISO) – An option to purchase stock in connection with an individual's employment, which defers tax liability until all of the stock acquired by means of the option is sold or exchanged.

Income in Respect of a Decedent (IRD) – Income earned by a person, but not paid until after his or her death.

Independent Contractor – A self-employed individual whose work method or time is not controlled by an employer.

Indexing – Adjustments in deductions, credits, exemptions and exclusions, plan contributions, AGI limits, and so on, to reflect annual inflation figures.

Individual Retirement Account (IRA) – Tax-exempt trust created or organized in the U.S. for the exclusive benefit of an individual or the individual's beneficiaries.

Information Returns– Statements of income and other items recognizable for tax purposes provided to the IRS and the taxpayer. Form W-2 and forms in the 1099 series, as well as Schedules K-1, are the prominent examples.

Installment Method– Tax accounting method for reporting gain on a sale over the period of tax years during which payments are made, such as, over the payment period specified in an installment sale agreement.

Intangible Property– Items such as patents, copyrights, and goodwill.

Inventory – Goods held for sale to customers, including materials used in the production of those goods.

Involuntary Conversion – A forced disposition (for example, casualty, theft, condemnation) for which deferral of gain may be available.

Jeopardy – For tax purposes, a determination that payment of a tax deficiency may be assessed immediately as the most viable means of ensuring its payment.

Keogh Plan – A qualified retirement plan available to self-employed persons.

Key Employee – Officers, employees, and officers defined by the Internal Revenue Code for purposes of determining whether a plan is "top heavy."

Kiddie Tax – Application of parents' maximum tax rate to unearned income of their child under age 19. Full-time students under 24 are also subject to the kiddie tax.

Lien – A charge upon property after a tax assessment has been made and until tax liability is satisfied.

Like-Kind Exchange – Tax-free exchange of business or investment property for property that is similar or related in service or use.

Listed Property – Items subject to special restrictions on depreciation (for example, cars, computers, cell phones).

Lump-Sum Distribution – Distribution of an individual's entire interest in a qualified retirement plan within one tax year.

Marginal Tax Rate – The highest tax bracket applicable to an individual's income.

Material Participation – The measurement of an individual's involvement in business operations for purposes of the passive activity loss rules.

Mid-month Convention – Assumption, for purposes of computing depreciation, that all real property is placed in service in the middle of the month.

Mid-quarter Convention – Assumption, for purposes of computing depreciation, that all property other than real property is placed in service in the middle of the quarter, when the basis of property placed in service in the final quarter exceeds a statutory percentage of the basis of all property placed in service during the year.

Minimum Distribution – A retirement plan distribution, based on life expectancies, that an individual must take after age 70 ½ in order to avoid tax penalties.

Minimum Funding Requirements – Associated with defined benefit plans and certain other plans, such as money purchase plans, assuring the plan has enough assets to satisfy its current and anticipated liabilities.

Miscellaneous Itemized Deduction – Deductions for certain expenses (for example, unreimbursed employee expenses) limited to only the amount by which they exceed 2% of adjusted gross income.

Money Purchase Plan – Defined contribution plan in which the contributions by the employer are mandatory and established other than by reference to the employer's profits.

Net Operating Loss (NOL) – A business or casualty loss for which amounts exceeding the allowable deduction in the current tax year may be carried back two years to reduce previous tax liability and forward 20 years to cover any remaining unused loss deduction.

Nonresident Alien – An individual who is neither a citizen nor a resident of the United States. Nonresidents are taxed on U.S. source income.

Original Issue Discount (OID) – The excess of face value over issue price set by a purchase agreement.

Passive Activity Loss (PAL) – Losses allowable only to the extent of income derived each year (such as by means of carryover) from rental property or business activities in which the taxpayer does not materially participate.

Passive Foreign Investment Company (PFIC) – A foreign based corporation subject to strict tax rules which covers the treatment of investments in Sections 1291 through 1297.

Pass-Through Entities – Partnerships, LLCs, LLPs, S corporations, and trusts and estates whose income or loss is reported by the partner, member, shareholder, or beneficiary.

Personal Holding Company (PHC) – A corporation, usually closely-held, that exists to hold investments such as stocks, bonds, or personal service contracts and to time distributions of income in a manner that limits the owner(s) tax liability.

Qualified Subchapter S Trust (QSST) – A trust that qualifies specific requirements for eligibility as an S corporation shareholder.

Real Estate Investment Trust (REIT) – A form of investment in which a trust holds real estate or mortgages and distributes income, in whole or in part, to the beneficiaries (such as investors).

Real Estate Mortgage Investment Conduit (REMIC) – Treated as a partnership, investors purchase interests in this entity which holds a fixed pool of mortgages.

Realized Gain or Loss – The difference between property's basis and the amount received upon its sale or exchange.

Recapture – The amount of a prior deduction or credit recognized as income or affecting its characterization (capital gain vs. ordinary income) when the property giving rise to the deduction or credit is disposed of.

Recognized Gain or Loss – The amount of realized gain or loss that must be included in taxable income.

Regulated Investment Company (RIC) – A corporation serving as a mutual fund that acts as investment agents for shareholders and customarily dealing in government and corporate securities.

Reorganization – Restructuring of corporations under specific Internal Revenue Code rules so as to result in nonrecognition of gain.

Resident Alien – An individual who is a permanent resident, has substantial presence, or, under specific election rules is taxed as a U.S. citizen.

Roth IRA – Form of individual retirement account that produces, subject to holding period requirements, nontaxable earnings.

S Corporation – A corporation that, upon satisfying requirements concerning its ownership, may elect to act as a pass-through entity.

Saver's Credit – Term commonly used to describe Sec. 25B credit for qualified contributions to a retirement plan or via elective deferrals.

Sec. 1231 Property – Depreciable business property eligible for capital gains treatment.

Sec. 1244 Stock – Closely held stock whose sale may produce an ordinary, rather than capital, loss (subject to caps).

Split-Dollar Life Insurance – Arrangement between an employer and employee under which the life insurance policy benefits are contractually split, and the costs (premiums) are also split.

Statutory Employee – An insurance agent or other specified worker who is subject to social security taxes on wages but eligible to claim deductions available to the self-employed.

Stock Bonus Plan – A plan established and maintained to provide benefits similar to those of a profit-sharing plan, except the benefits must be distributable in stock of the employer company.

Tax Preference Items – Tax benefits deemed includable for purposes of the alternative minimum tax.

Tax Shelter – A tax-favored investment, typically in the form of a partnership or joint venture, that is subject to scrutiny as tax-avoidance device.

Tentative Tax – Income tax liability before taking into account certain credits, and AMT liability over the regular tax liability.

Transportation Expense – The cost of transportation from one point to another.

Travel Expense – Transportation, meals, and lodging costs incurred away from home and for trade or business purposes.

Unearned Income – Income from investments (such as interest, dividends, and capital gains).

Uniform Capitalization Rules (UNICAP) – Rules requiring capitalization of property used in a business or income-producing activity (such as items used in producing inventory) and to certain property acquired for resale.

Unrelated Business Income (UBIT) – Exempt organization income produced by activities beyond the organization's exempt purposes and therefore taxable.

Wash Sale – Sale of securities preceded or followed within 30 days by a purchase of substantially identical securities. Recognition of any loss on the sale is disallowed.

INDEX

FORM 990: EXPLORING THE FORM'S COMPLEX SCHEDULES

BY EVE ROSE BORENSTEIN, J.D. AND
JANE M. SEARING, CPA, M.S. TAXATION,
TAX SHAREHOLDER - CLARK NUBER P.S.

Solutions

The AICPA offers a free, daily, e-mailed newsletter covering the day's top business and financial articles as well as video content, research and analysis concerning CPAs and those who work with the accounting profession. Visit the CPA Letter Daily news box on the www.aicpa.org home page to sign up. You can opt out at any time, and only the AICPA can use your e-mail address or personal information.

Have a technical accounting or auditing question? So did 23,000 other professionals who contacted the AICPA's accounting and auditing Technical Hotline last year. The objectives of the hotline are to enhance members' knowledge and application of professional judgment by providing free, prompt, high-quality technical assistance by phone concerning issues related to: accounting principles and financial reporting; auditing, attestation, compilation and review standards. The team extends this technical assistance to representatives of governmental units. The hotline can be reached at 1-877-242-7212.

SOLUTIONS

CHAPTER 1

Solutions to Knowledge Check Questions

1.
  a. Incorrect. Schedules C and O are required: All filers need to include Schedule O to provide required Core Form Part VI disclosures; the 501(h) lobbying election is a trigger to Schedule C.
  b. Correct. Schedules A, B, C, E, G and O are all required filings due to the dollar amounts listed.
  c. Incorrect. Schedules B and G are required: Schedule B is required to report donors of more than $5,000; Schedule G, Part II is triggered when a fundraising event's *gross receipts* exceed $15,000 and the facts provided show same was exceeded.
  d. Incorrect. Schedule C is used by both 990 and 990-EZ filers to report lobbying activities or the presence of the 501(h) election.

2.
  a. Incorrect. Understanding the applicable definitions is key to Form 990 completion.
  b. Incorrect. Applying the stated outcomes to reporting furthers proper completion of Form 990.
  c. Correct. The IRS helpline is not a source for Form 990 completion guidance.
  d. Incorrect. A key to Form 990 completion is understanding the applicable definitions.

3.
  a. Incorrect. Schedule A reports the basis by which the filer is qualified as a public charity.
  b. Incorrect. Schedule L reports transactions with interested persons.
  c. Correct. Although Core Form Part III reports program accomplishments and changes to programs, there is no Schedule requiring such information.
  d. Incorrect. Schedule B reports contributions from donors.

CHAPTER 2

Solutions to Knowledge Check Questions

1.

    a. Incorrect. Control over not-for-profit corporations is deemed to exist in the presence of majority representation on the board of directors, which occurs when a party directs who is elected or appointed to a majority of board seats.

    b. Incorrect. Control over not-for-profit corporations is deemed to exist in the presence of majority representation on the board of directors, which occurs when a party has its officers, board members, employees, or agents in a majority of board seats.

    c. Correct. That board members of another entity are related to board members of a filer is immaterial to control.

    d. Incorrect. Common control over not-for-profit corporations is present when the same person or persons have majority representation on each entity's board of directors, which occurs when such persons directs who is elected or appointed to a majority of each board's seats.

2.

    a. Correct. Who created the filer is immaterial to the factors by which control of the board is evaluated and the condition of having a founder/ creator does not alone denote a related organization.

    b. Incorrect. The condition of being in a supported/ supporting organization relationship as set out in 509(a)(3) is a stand-alone basis by which a related organization is deemed to exist.

    c. Incorrect. That two of three board members of the filer were board members or officers of another organization establishes majority board representation which equates to control.

    d. Incorrect. That two of three board members are appointed by another organization's officer establishes majority board representation which equates to control.

3.

    a. Incorrect. The condition of being in a supported/ supporting organization relationship as set out in 509(a)(3) is a stand-alone basis by which a related organization is deemed to exist.

    b. Correct. A filer having a partnership interest of greater than 50 percent is a condition by which a related organization is deemed to exist.

    c. Incorrect. The condition of being in a supported/ supporting organization relationship as set out in 509(a)(3) is a stand-alone basis by which a related organization is deemed to exist.

    d. Incorrect. A filer having a greater than 50 percent stock position is a condition by which a related organization is deemed to exist.

4.

    a. Incorrect. Whether or not a disregarded entity would have taxable income as a stand-alone taxpayer is immaterial to its operations and financial statements being included with those of the filer.

    b. Incorrect. The disregarded entity's ability to operate within tax-exempt parameters is immaterial to its operations and financial statements being included with those of the filer.

    c. Incorrect. A disregarded entity is not eligible to file its own income tax return.

    d. Correct. A filer that has a disregarded entity reports that fact on Schedule R, Part I and then has its operations and financial statements included with those of the filer.

5.

    a.   Incorrect. The identity of the related organization is required to be reported.

    b.   Incorrect. Part III requires reporting of the predominant category of income (exempt function, unrelated, or excluded from tax ...)

    c.   Correct. The amount of non-exempt function income is not disclosed.

    d.   Incorrect. The share the filer has of the partnership's total income is required to be reported.

6.

    a.   Incorrect. The identity of split interest trusts (such as charitable remainder trusts) is not required to be reported.

    b.   Incorrect. With name and EIN identifying information omitted, there is also no requirement to report address.

    c.   Incorrect. The identity of split interest trusts (such as charitable remainder trusts) is not required to be reported

    d.   Correct. Part IV requires reporting of all trusts' (including charitable remainder trusts') legal domicile and share of end-of-year assets.

7.

    a.   Incorrect. The name of a related organization that is a corporation is reported.

    b.   Incorrect. The legal domicile of Part IV related organizations is always reported.

    c.   Correct. Although the filer's share of year-end assets is to be reported, the dollar value of that share, or of the corporation's total assets, is not.

    d.   Incorrect. The fact that a related organization is a 512(b)(13) controlled entity is reported.

CHAPTER 3

Solutions to Knowledge Check Questions

1.

    a.   Incorrect. Classification as a public charity exists until such time as the organization is either audited by the IRS resulting in reclassification or the organization or is required to self-report as a private foundation due to no longer qualifying under IRC Section 509(a)(1)-(4).

    b.   Correct. Schedule A is required of all entities classified as public charities who retain qualification (as denoted upon this Schedule) under Section 509(a)(1)-(4).

    c.   Incorrect. Schedule A reporting is fluid to each year and reclassification ruling requests are not required.

    d.   Incorrect. Original (or later year update) IRS classification letter is indeterminate of current year reporting and is not to be attached.

2.

    a. Incorrect. A charity advocating to meet the needs of a charitable constituency (1) without other facts does not meet an identity basis; and an organization advancing knowledge of various religions is conducting education (as in 4), but without other facts, lacks an identity basis.

    b. Incorrect. An organization advancing knowledge of various religions is conducting education (4), but without other facts, lacks an identity basis.

    c. Incorrect. A shelter that is an agency of the county (2), is a governmental unit and thus has an identity basis.

    d. Correct. A shelter that is an agency of the county (2), is a governmental unit and thus has an identity basis; a hospital (3) has an identity basis; and an association of churches (5) has an identity basis.

3.

    a. Incorrect. Filer checks only one box in Schedule A, Part I, correlating to its primary basis of qualification in the reporting year.

    b. Incorrect. Basis of initial qualification is not determinative of the filer's primary basis of qualification in the reporting year.

    c. Correct. Filers self-declare their primary basis of qualification on each reporting year and any other explanation is optional.

    d. Incorrect. Filers self-declare their primary basis of qualification on each reporting year and there is no requirement to explain that same differs from what IRS rostering has.

4.

    a. Incorrect. In-kinds from government payers count toward public support under both the first and second tests.

    b. Incorrect. Program service revenue is not taken into consideration for either public support or total support in the first test.

    c. Correct. The first test applies a 2 percent limit across the test period to the amount contributions provided by certain large donors.

    d. Incorrect. The contributions of large contributors (substantial contributors) do not count toward public support in the second test, regardless of whether the contributors remitted program service revenue to the filer.

5.

    a. Incorrect. This event is the reason a grant would be sought to be classified as unusual.

    b. Correct. This would ONLY be a factor if the donor meets the definition of substantial contributor, but if not the length of relationship is not a factor.

    c. Incorrect. This is a factor weighing in favor of a grant being considered unusual.

    d. Incorrect. A donor's provision of general operating support is a factor if it lacks an express limitation to one year's operating expenses.

6.

    a.   Incorrect. A current member of the governing board is a foundation manager and is thus a disqualified person whose remittances are reported on Line 7a.

    b.   Incorrect. A spouse of a governing board member is, like the governing board member, a disqualified person whose remittances are reported on Line 7a.

    c.   Incorrect. An executive director has powers akin to that of an officer and is considered a foundation manager and thus a disqualified person whose remittances are reported on Line 7a.

    d.   Correct. An entity owned more than 35 percent by disqualified persons is a disqualified person; but here the > 35 percent threshold is held solely by siblings of disqualified persons and siblings are not within the definition of family of disqualified persons so they have no such status.

7.

    a.   Incorrect. The cited forms of passive income are considered part of total support in both tests.

    b.   Incorrect. These forms of in-kind contributed revenue from a governmental unit count towards both public support and total support in both tests.

    c.   Incorrect. The cited form of income is considered part of total support in both tests.

    d.   Correct. Capital gains, on their own, factor into neither test.

8.

    a.   Incorrect. That a contributor has or has not engaged in insider transactions is not a factor as to whether its contributions are excluded from public support.

    b.   Correct. Contributions remitted by disqualified persons will be reported on Line 7a as excluded from the public support calculation.

    c.   Incorrect. That program service revenue has come from persons who have engaged in insider transactions does not affect that program service revenue is included in total support and potentially excluded from public support if the payer's remittances are above specific per-year amounts.

    d.   Incorrect. That program service revenue is or is not paid by donors who may or may not be substantial contributors or meet other donation thresholds. Program service revenue is included in total support and potentially excluded from public support if the payer's remittances are above specific per-year amounts.

9.

    a.   Correct. The test is only available when the calculated public percentage is greater than 10 percent.

    b.   Incorrect. Fundraising events are not mentioned as a factor in the facts and circumstances test.

    c.   Incorrect. A broadly representative community board is a factor, but the number of directors is not a factor in the facts and circumstances test.

    d.   Incorrect. Although connection to the community is a factor, the presence in any one community is not a factor in the facts and circumstances test.

10.

a. Correct. The results here indicate that the filer has automatically met the 509(a)(1)/ 170(b)(1)(A)(vi) test.

b. Incorrect. As the results here indicate, the filer has automatically met the 509(a)(1)/ 170(b)(1)(A)(vi) test, there is no reason why the filer would need to disclose that they had met the facts and circumstances test.

c. Incorrect. The results here indicate that the filer has failed to establish 509(a)(1)/ 170(b)(1)(A)(vi) qualification because the percentage of public support is < 10 percent.

d. Incorrect. The results cited would require the filer to narrate that they met the facts and circumstances test, not that they have been including unusual grants in the calculation.

11.

a. Incorrect. A new exemption application cannot be filed by a currently qualified 501(c)(3) organization to seek other 501(c) exemption or change its public charity classification.

b. Incorrect. The facts here do not specify that the filer has failed to qualify under the first test for two consecutive years; at issue on the cited facts is whether the filer would qualify on years 1–5 even though completing the calculation on years 1–5 support was not required on the prior year's return.

c. Incorrect. A failure to retain public charity classification does not subject an exempt organization to income taxation as a corporation or trust.

d. Correct. At issue (assuming Part III testing is not appropriate) is the filer's qualification as a public charity based on years 1–5 on Part II; success on those years is inputted on the year 6 return and covers year 6.

12.

a. Incorrect. The statement is true, as passing either the Part II or Part III tests on one year covers the next year.

b. Incorrect. The statement is true, as passing either of the Part II or Part III tests on one year covers the next year.

c. Correct. Taxpayers are required to complete the public support test based on the method they kept their books; a retroactive change to a back year's method to pick up pledged amounts is a tax distortion.

d. Incorrect. The statement is true, as two consecutive years' failure of the public support tests yields private foundation classification on the second year.

CHAPTER 4

Solutions to Knowledge Check Questions

1.

   a. Incorrect. The facts provided relate to whether or not the fair market value of the wearing apparel item reduces the amount of the attendee's charitable contribution and whether the charity need not include that fair market value in making a Section 6115 quid pro quo disclosure, but results in those realms do not affect the charity's Line 8a reporting requirement for the wearing apparel exchange.

   b. Incorrect. The amount to be included upon Line 8a is the gift certificate's fair market value, not a lower amount reflecting the effective usage rate of all certificates provided.

   c. Correct. The values shown properly reflect the fair market value measure of the goods the charity provided at the fundraising event to those who paid the event's entry fee.

   d. Incorrect. The amount to be included upon Line 8a is not altered by the fact that fewer meals and pieces of wearing apparel than number sold were actually disbursed to attendees.

2.

   a. Incorrect. These costs are reported by the filer on Form 990 and when, as here, are direct expenses of a fundraising event, are reportable on Line 8b.

   b. Correct. These costs, the expenditure of donated services, are not reported by the filer for Form 990 Part IX purposes (nor is their contribution reported on Part VIII).

   c. Incorrect. These costs are reported by the filer on Form 990 and when, as here, are direct expenses of a fundraising event, are reportable on Line 8b.

   d. Incorrect. These costs are reported by the filer on Form 990 when, as here, are direct expenses of a fundraising event, are reportable on Line 8b.

3.

   a. Incorrect. The donated item's fair market value at time of contribution is, for Form 990 purposes, to be reported as income, regardless of the donor's basis in the item. The same item's disbursement at the fundraising event yields that same amount (fair market value at time of donation) as a direct expense of the fundraising sale.

   b. Correct.

   c. Incorrect. Because it is the donated item's fair market value at time of contribution that is reported, for Form 990 purposes, as income, it is that same amount that is then disbursed when the filer sells the item at a fundraising sale.

   d. Incorrect. Although this approach is taken under GAAP, Form 990 reporting demands that fair market value of a noncash contribution is reported as income. That item's disbursement at a fundraising sale then washes out the income item.

4.

   a.   Incorrect. The first item is a pledge of donated services that *will be used by the filer* and the second is the provision of a discount on services; neither of these items are within the definition of noncash contributions reportable on Form 990.

   b.   Incorrect. The first item is the provision of a discount on services and the second is both donated services and discount on use of the contributor's property; neither of these items are within the definition of noncash contributions reportable on Form 990.

   c.   Correct. A transferable certificate for services that the filer will sell should be treated as an intangible property right because it represents the right to access services and is thus equivalent to a prepaid gift certificate.

   d.   Incorrect. This is the provision of a discount on services that is not in the definition of noncash contributions.

5.

   a.   Incorrect. A gift of stock or securities is a noncash contribution regardless of whether the filer immediately undertakes sale of the donated property to convert the contributed property to cash.

   b.   Incorrect. Filers choose how to report number and may use either number of donations or number of items.

   c.   Correct. Amount of revenue attributed by the filer to noncash contributions should tie to the values of all noncash contributions detailed in Schedule M.

   d.   Incorrect. There is no requirement that taxpayers who do not capitalize collections of such items keep records of fair market value of the donations that are not capitalized and thus booked at $-0-.

6.

   a.   Incorrect. A *quid pro quo* donor acknowledgment letter would be required if someone were to buy three entry fees (as $90 is greater than the reporting threshold, which is someone making gifts and procuring goods or services via a payment of greater than $75).

   b.   Incorrect. The *quid pro quo* solicitation is for attendance at an event in which dinner is being returned; it is immaterial that a buyer may have made other payments in the year in *quid pro quo* contexts.

   c.   Correct. A quid pro quo donor acknowledgment is required for any payer who buys three or more tickets unless the right to the dinner meals are renounced. This is because a payment of greater than $75 has been made.

   d.   Incorrect. If the buyer renounces the right to the proffered *quid pro quo* goods or services, there is no exchange portion of their payment to report.

CHAPTER 5

Solutions to Knowledge Check Questions

1.

a.   Incorrect. A filer who has made the 501(h) election must complete Part II-A, *even if no lobbying expenditures have been made in the year.*

b.   Incorrect. A filer who has made the 501(h) election must complete Part II-A, regardless of whether any lobbying expenditures were made in the year.

c.   Correct. A filer who has made the 501(h) election must complete Part II-A, regardless of whether any lobbying expenditures were made in the year.

d.   Incorrect. The presented fact that the filer has made the 501(h) election is determinative as a filer who has made the 501(h) election must complete Part II-A, regardless of whether any lobbying expenditures were made in the year.

2.

a.   Correct. Part II-B requires reporting by type of activities (the lines specify different types and any entry on the other line requires narration of what activities were undertaken) and each line is required to show expenditures made.

b.   Incorrect. There is no requirement to detail that board members volunteered efforts in favor of lobbying.

c.   Incorrect. The source of funding for lobbying is immaterial to the reporting obligation in Part II-B.

d.   Incorrect. A filer who has made the 501(h) election must complete Part II-A, regardless of whether any lobbying expenditures were made in the year and regardless of the source of funding for lobbying.

3.

a.   Correct. Reporting ties to what occurred in the filing year, regardless of whether campaign laws were violated.

b.   Incorrect. Consistency of reporting is required.

c.   Incorrect. Reporting must reflect what occurred in the filing year, regardless of whether campaign laws were violated.

d.   Incorrect. Reporting must reflect what occurred in the filing year, regardless of whether campaign laws were violated.

4.

    a.   Incorrect. This scenario is correct, but scenario 2 is also accurate in that rolling forward the year 1 shortfall ($200,000) and noticing the members that 100 percent of their year 2 dues will be non-deductible would apply.

    b.   Incorrect. This statement is correct, but scenario 1 is also correct in that paying the proxy tax on year 1's shortfall ($200,000), and noticing members that 60 percent of their year 2 dues will be non-deductible would apply.

    c.   Correct. 1 is accurate, as the year 1 shortfall of $200,000 does not survive to the succeeding year's notice requirement when the proxy tax is assessed and thus the second year notice would project that $300,000 of the $500,000 anticipated dues, 60 percent, are non-deductible. 2 is accurate in that if the filer does not self-assess the proxy tax on the year 1 shortfall of $200,000, that amount needs to be carried over to the next year's notice and thus that amount plus the projected $300,000 for year 2, a total of $500,000, has to be noticed (100 percent of anticipated dues collection).

    d.   Incorrect. Option 3 is in error, as the proxy tax is only assessed paid on shortfalls on the filing year.

CHAPTER 6

Solutions to Knowledge Check Questions

1.

    a.   Incorrect. Founders, whether taxable corporations or individuals, are interested persons and the answer omits the founder in 1. Without more information, it is not clear whether individual donor in 4 is subject to classification as a substantial contributor, because his or her appearance on Schedule B cannot be ascertained.

    b.   Incorrect. Without more information, it is not clear whether individual donor in 4 is subject to classification as a substantial contributor, because his or her appearance on Schedule B cannot be ascertained.

    c.   Incorrect. Founders, whether taxable corporations or individuals, are interested persons and the answer omits the founder in 1. Without more information, it is not clear whether the individual donor in either 3 or 4 is subject to classification as a substantial contributor, because his or her appearance on Schedule B cannot be ascertained.

    d.   Correct. Founders are interested persons and the top management official of the organization is automatically an officer for Core Form Part VII-A reporting purposes and thus is an interested person.

2.

    a. Incorrect. That the management company is owned more than 35 percent by an ex-spouse of a former board member (former meaning served in any of the prior five tax years) does not make that company indirectly owned by that individual as ex-spouses are not captured in the Form 990 definition of family member.

    b. Correct. The facts state that the management company is owned more than 35 percent by a former key employee (former meaning served in any of the prior five tax years); that the individual was not properly reported on the prior tax year return is immaterial.

    c. Incorrect. That the management company is owned more than 35 percent by a domestic partner of a former officer (former meaning served in any of the prior five tax years) does not make that company indirectly owned by that individual, as domestic partners who are not legal spouses are not captured in the Form 990 definition of family member.

    d. Incorrect. The management company is no longer owned by a TDOKE who served within the last five years, and thus is not captured by the management company interested person definition.

3.

    a. Incorrect. Status as a 35-percent controlled entity exists if specified parties' aggregate ownership interests are greater than 35 percent *at any time in the filer's tax year*.

    b. Incorrect. If at any time during the filer's tax year the specified parties' aggregate ownership interests exceed 35 percent, then a status as a 35-percent controller entity exists.

    c. Correct. In this tax year the family's interest was below the threshold as of the first day of the year and the facts state that the reduced from prior years' level was in place in this tax year.

    d. Incorrect. Status as a 35-percent controlled entity exists if specified parties' aggregate ownership interests are greater than 35 percent *at any time in the filer's tax year*.

4.

    a. Incorrect. One threshold for reporting is determined by whether any one transaction exceeded the greater of 1 percent of the year's gross receipts OR $10,000, but that threshold is here trumped by the other threshold that reaches transactions which in the aggregate are greater than $100,000.

    b. Incorrect. Payment to an interested person being made on their behalf to a third party does not change the fact of the interested person having been paid.

    c. Incorrect. The facts here exceed the reporting threshold that reaches transactions in the aggregate greater than $100,000.

    d. Correct. The facts here do not meet reporting threshold that reaches transactions in the aggregate greater than $100,000.

5.

    a. Incorrect. Part VII-A disclosure of family member's compensation is invoked by a greater than $10,000 threshold.

    b. Incorrect. Part VII-A disclosure reaches compensation as same is reportable in Part VII-A's Columns D-F, and thus includes all deferred compensation.

    c. Correct. Part VII-A disclosure reaches compensation as same is reportable in Part VII-A's Columns D-F, and thus includes all deferred compensation.

    d. Incorrect. Part VII-A disclosure reaches compensation as same is reportable in Part VII-A's Columns D-F, and requires in Column D payment whether remitted to an employee (using W-2 reporting measures) or an independent contractor (using 1099-MISC reporting measure ignoring the $600 threshold), thus both amounts will be captured.

6.

    a.   Correct. Accessing a certificate of deposit falls neither into the deposit into a bank account . . . in the ordinary course of business, on the same terms as the bank offers to the general public exception nor the loan from a credit union . . . on the same terms as offered to other members of the credit union exception.

    b.   Incorrect. Depositing its cash reserve balance of $25,000 into a money market savings account at the bank would fit the deposit into a bank account . . . in the ordinary course of business, on the same terms as the bank offers to the general public exception.

    c.   Incorrect. Using the bank as a payroll depository fits the deposit into a bank account . . . in the ordinary course of business, on the same terms as the bank offers to the general public exception.

    d.   Incorrect. E's investment via a certificate of deposit is not a deposit into a bank account.

7.

    a.   Incorrect. G has made a pledge that will qualify as a charitable contribution when paid and thus the receivable on F's book falls within a reporting exception.

    b.   Incorrect. G has received an advance under an accountable plan and thus the outstanding amount fits a reporting exception.

    c.   Correct. The fact that G has received a salary advance equates to F having made a loan that has no reporting exception.

    d.   Incorrect. The facts here show a receivable outstanding on F's books that was created in the ordinary course of the organization's business on the same terms as offered to the general public, which fits a reporting exception.

8.

    a.   Incorrect. The training provided by RO is provided to improve the skills of the recipients, and though laudable in its charitable outcome, falls outside of grants or assistance to a charitable class that the organization intends to benefit, which in RO's case would be those in need of disaster relief.

    b.   Incorrect. Tuition assistance provides aid to improve capacity and skill of the recipient, and though laudable in its charitable outcome, falls outside of grants or assistance to a charitable class that the organization intends to benefit, which in RO's case would be those in need of disaster relief.

    c.   Correct. RO's provision of temporary housing assistance to victims of disaster circumstances fits the exception for grants or assistance to a charitable class that the organization intends to benefit.

    d.   Incorrect. The stipend provided by RO goes beyond immediate assistance to recipients who have lost their homes as same is provided on the condition that they temporarily leave their jobs and assist in RO's local chapter disaster-relief operation; that condition moves the aid outside of grants or assistance to a charitable class that the organization intends to benefit.

9.

    a.   Incorrect. The statement is correct, as the grant of the award will be reported.

    b.   Correct. The characterization of the fund as an employee benefit does not alter that a grant is being provided to the recipient student, and thus reporting on Part III will be required.

    c.   Incorrect. The statement is correct, as schools, including colleges and universities, are not required to report the names of grantees receiving financial assistance when reporting grants in Part III.

    d.   Incorrect. The statement is correct, as the amount provided is reported on Part IX as a grant expenditure.

10.

    a.   Incorrect. The payment of the amounts in the 2013 and 2014 years equates to an excess benefit transaction regardless of whether correction has been effected.

    b.   Incorrect. An unenforceable obligation cannot be converted to an effective obligation by latter-determined facts (that same is unenforceable as a matter of state law is a result to the organization's benefit, and rights retained by the beneficiary of the transaction equate to an impermissible gift!)

    c.   Correct. Reporting of the $60,000 total remittance amount would be required.

    d.   Incorrect. An unenforceable obligation cannot in part be converted to an effective obligation on equitable grounds. The explanation at b notes that unenforceability as a matter of state law benefits the organization and cannot retroactively assert rights retained by the beneficiary of the transaction yields an impermissible gift.

CHAPTER 7

Solutions to Knowledge Check Questions

1.

    a.   Incorrect. The facts trigger Schedule F reporting because the domestic beneficiary is obligated to apply the funds outside of the United States in an amount greater than $10,000.

    b.   Incorrect. Because the investment vehicle is a partnership, $200,000 of the book value of the $1 million investment is attributable to the filer, and that $200,000 exceeds the $100,000 or greater trigger for investments in foreign entities.

    c.   Incorrect. The filer's revenues and expenses for the year will reflect both the pledge (at present value of close to or at $4,500) and the expenditure of $8,000; accordingly, the filer's aggregate expenses are in excess of the greater than $10,000 trigger for reporting.

    d.   Correct. No Schedule F trigger is reached: the filer has invested in a corporation, not a partnership, and it is *a U.S. company.* That the investment is program related, and the intended use of the funds by the investee, is immaterial.

2.

    a.   Incorrect. Where the individual is residing or living at the time they receive the grant is determinative; here with the individual residing in the U.S., the grant is <u>not</u> to a foreign individual.

    b.   Incorrect. Where the individual is residing or living at the time they receive the grant is determinative; with the individual residing in the U.S., the grant is <u>not</u> to a foreign individual.

    c.   Correct. Where the individual is residing or living at the time they receive the grant is determinative; here the individual is living in Canada and thus is a foreign individual.

    d.   Incorrect. Even though the U.S. citizen was born in Canada, he is still a U.S. citizen. Also, where the individual is residing or living at the time they receive the grant is determinative; here, with the individual residing in the U.S., the grant is <u>not</u> to a foreign individual.

3.

    a.   Correct. The facts here show that individual farmers are being directly assisted via the provision of seeds and educational materials.

    b.   Incorrect. The funds are being provided to a university, and the advisory posture of the funder is immaterial.

    c.   Incorrect. The grantee is the orphanage. That a specified group of children amongst the fundee's constituents will be served does not make the grant one that is imputed to each of the constituents.

    d.   Incorrect. The grantee is the health clinic. That a specified group of individuals will be served does not make the grant one that is imputed to each of the goes to those individuals.

4.

    a.   Incorrect. Only grants to foreign organizations who received more than $5,000 are to be reported.

    b.   Incorrect. Indirect expenses are to be reported only if they are tracked by the filer.

    c.   Correct. The instructions specifically allow reporting to the nearest $1,000.

    d.   Incorrect. All expenses are to be reported for activities that occur outside the United States.

CHAPTER 8

Solutions to Knowledge Check Questions

1.

    a.   Correct. With the cited benefits outside of taxable income (and not subject to Medicare taxation) they are reported as other compensation.

    b.   Incorrect. An individual's provision of independent contractor services is included in reportable compensation.

    c.   Incorrect. A settlement related to claims stemming from prior employment is taxable income to the individual and is thus within the definition of reportable compensation.

    d.   Incorrect. Remuneration of any sort is considered reportable compensation.

2.

   a.   Incorrect. Filer can report either the entire year's remuneration provided by WW or only that specific to the period of the year in which WW was a related organization, October–December.
   b.   Incorrect. Filer can report either the entire year's remuneration provided by WW **or** only that specific to the period of the year in which WW was a related organization, October–December.
   c.   Incorrect. Although filer may report solely the October-December remuneration paid by WW, it may report the entire year's remuneration.
   d.   Correct. Filer can report either the entire year's remuneration provided by WW or only that specific to the period of the year in which WW was a related organization, October–December.

3.

   a.   Incorrect. The filer's payment of reportable remuneration of $9,999 must be reported in Column D. The rest of the statements are correct: E can be rounded down to $-0- and ScheduleJ's two rows will report $9,999 from filer and $12,000 from related organizations.
   b.   Incorrect. ScheduleJ's 2nd row must report $12,000 from related organizations. The rest of the statements are correct: D will report $9,999, E can be rounded down to $-0- and ScheduleJ's 1st row will report $9,999 from filer.
   c.   Incorrect. ScheduleJ's 2nd row must report $12,000 from related organizations (there is no $10,000 offset). The rest of the statements are correct.
   d.   Correct. The entirety of statements is correct in that Column D will report $9,999 and Column E will report -0-.

4.

   a.   Incorrect. The taxable organization employee exception may apply to void the need for disclosure (it would apply IF ABC was aware of Andreas' arrangement with X and X does not treat the payments to Andreas as a charitable contribution to ABC).
   b.   Incorrect. If X does not treat the payments it makes to Andreas as a charitable contribution to ABC, the taxable organization employee exception applies.
   c.   Correct. The facts recited fit squarely within the taxable organization employee exception.
   d.   Incorrect. Form 990 reporting disclosures cannot be avoided by the excuse that contractual obligations prevent disclosure; the only out from disclosure available is through the taxable organization employee exception.

5.

   a.   Correct. Long-term care insurance of $10,000 or less is not required to be reported in Part VII-A's Column F but the actual amount is reportable upon Schedule J-II.
   b.   Incorrect. Accountable plan reimbursements are not compensatory and are not reportable in either Part VII-A or Schedule J-II.
   c.   Incorrect. Working condition fringe benefits are excepted from compensation reporting in both Part VII-A and Schedule J-II.
   d.   Incorrect. Health benefits of any amount are reportable in Part VII-A (as well as in Schedule J-II).

6.

a. Incorrect. Health benefits, in this case the fair market value of an employer's self-insured or self-funded arrangements to the benefit of the employee, are reportable in Part VII-A's Column F.

b. Incorrect. The cited benefits (reimbursement in whole or part of dental services, drug purchases and medical equipment costs) are considered health benefits and are reportable in Part VII-A's Column F.

c. Correct. Although health insurance premiums are disclosable in Part VII-A's Column F, long-term care insurance is not considered health benefits and is susceptible to the $10,000 exception from reporting.

d. Incorrect. The cited benefits and the valuation methodology for same comprise reportable health benefits reportable in Part VII-A's Column F.

7.

a. Incorrect. The taxable organization employee exception is in part predicated on the status of the unrelated organization being taxable and not tax-exempt.

b. Correct. The period of time in which the filer is accepting services that it does not have to pay for is immaterial to whether or not compensation provided to the individual from an unrelated organization will need be disclosed.

c. Incorrect. The taxable organization employee exception is in part predicated on whether the employer who pays the individual's remuneration while they are providing services to the filer is taking a charitable contribution deduction.

d. Incorrect. Whether or not compensation from an unrelated organization is the subject of reporting by a filer is not dependent on how the unrelated organization comes to make such payment.

8.

a. Incorrect. The Governance Part of the Core Form, Part VI, asks at Line 3 if the filer is procuring services of a management company.

b. Incorrect. A filer accessing services of an officer through a management company does NOT disclose remuneration paid to the officer by the management company unless the company is a related organization of the filer.

c. Incorrect. There is no such requirement (however, Part VI, Line 3 does call for such disclosure).

d. Correct. If the management company is a High 5 independent contractor, this information disclosure will be required.

9.

a. Correct. The facts recite here do no more than state that the voting member of the board will have $15,000 of reportable compensation disclosed on Core Form Part VII-A. That disclosure is not a trigger to Schedule J reporting.

b. Incorrect. Having a Key Employee reported in Core Form Part VII-A means that the conditions asked of in Part VII-A's Question 4 (which is a trigger to Schedule J reporting) will be answered yes.

c. Incorrect. The facts recited here do not trip the taxable organization employee exception and thus L would answer yes at Part VII-A's Question 5 (which is a trigger to Schedule J).

d. Incorrect. The facts recited here confirm that L has a former officer reportable in Core Form Part VII-A as the now-former treasurer is receiving, in one of the next five tax years, more than $100,000 in reportable compensation. Having a former is a condition asked of in Part VII-A's Question 3, and the "Yes" required here is a trigger to Schedule J reporting.

10.

    a.   Incorrect. The $10,000-per-related organization exception from reporting is available on Core Form Part VII-A's Column E but NOT available on Schedule J-II.

    b.   Correct. The facts recited here do no more than state that the voting member of the board will have $15,000 of reportable compensation disclosed on Core Form Part VII-A. That disclosure is not a trigger to Schedule J reporting.

    c.   Incorrect. Adoption benefits are outside of the Big 3 employee benefit types always reported regardless of amount, and are thus not reported under the $10,000-per-other-benefits exception from reporting available on Core Form Part VII-A's Column F but NOT available on Schedule J-II.

    d.   Incorrect. These are outside of the Big 3 types reported regardless of amount.

CHAPTER 9

Solutions to Knowledge Check Questions

1.

    a.   Incorrect. The trigger question to Schedule K is not dependent on whether or not a 12-month period (other than filer's tax year) is selected for reporting.

    b.   Correct. A Form 990-EZ filer does NOT complete Schedule K.

    c.   Incorrect. Number of bond issuances and reporting periods on each are immaterial to the triggering of Schedule K.

    d.   Incorrect. Use of the bond proceeds is immaterial to the triggering of Schedule K.

2.

    a.   Incorrect. The amount at year-end of one or more of the bond issuances must be greater than $100,000.

    b.   Correct. The statement sets out the complete trigger question.

    c.   Incorrect. The amount of the bond obligation on the filer's book at year-end must be greater than $100,000.

    d.   Incorrect. The issuance must have occurred after December 31, 2002.

3.

    a.   Incorrect. Analysis of a contract for space financed with tax-exempt bonds could be one of the factors that leads to assistance, but is not the only correct option.

    b.   Incorrect. Preparation of Schedule K could lead to assistance, but is not the only correct option.

    c.   Incorrect. Disposal of property purchased with tax-exempt bond proceeds that is purchased with tax-exempt bond proceeds could prompt an organization to contact external experts, but is not the only correct option.

    d.   Correct. The rules regarding tax-exempt bonds are a specialized area of the law and there are significant adverse consequences for compliance errors. Preparation of Schedule K highlights multiple compliance needs, which both implicate need for policies and require understanding of the 95 percent private activity use limits along with limits as to the use of bond proceeds.

CHAPTER 10

Solutions to Knowledge Check Questions

1.

    a. Incorrect. For year A, only $500,000 had been distributed against beginning of year assets of $10 million, so the 25 percent threshold was not met to trigger the Schedule.

    b. Incorrect. For year B there will be a Schedule N filing requirement (the cumulative A+ B year distribution, $2.6 million, is tested against year A's beginning of year assets of $10 million, and exceeds the 25 percent threshold to trigger the Schedule). However, year C will also have a Schedule N filing requirement, as noted in solution C, following.

    c. Incorrect. For year C there will be a Schedule N filing requirement (the cumulative A+ B+ C year distribution, $3.4 million, is tested against year A's beginning of year assets of $10 million, and exceeds the 25 percent threshold to trigger the Schedule). However, year B also had a Schedule N filing requirement, as noted in solution B, preceding.

    d. Correct. As noted in solutions B and C, both years have a Schedule year filing requirement.

2.

    a. Incorrect. The name, EIN, address, and tax-exempt status of the surviving corporation (successor) will be noted because, in a merger, assets transfer to the surviving corporation. In addition, whether any board members became board members of the successor, or if board members, officers, or key employees of the filer became employees of the successor also is required to be disclosed. Thus, 1, 3, and 4 are accurate.

    b. Correct. The cited three statements include required disclosures.

    c. Incorrect. Regardless of whether assets are listed as having been transferred, the successor should be identified because it will have taken on intangible assets from the demised filer.

    d. Incorrect. Questions regarding the overlap of board members, officers, key employees on the board, or becoming employees, of the survivor/ successor need to be answered.

3.

    a. Incorrect. The amount here exceeds 25 percent of the $8 million in net assets, and the type of transfer is not one of the five exceptions to what is considered a significant disposition of net assets, but more to the point is within the examples of what is a significant disposition of net assets (specifically, a taxable or tax-free sale or exchange of exempt assets for cash or other consideration).

    b. Incorrect. The amount here exceeds 25 percent of the $8 million in net assets, and the type of transfer is not one of the five exceptions to what is considered a significant disposition of net assets (specifically, it is not a transfer to a sole-member limited liability company, which thus would qualify as a disregarded entity).

    c. Correct. Asset sales made in the ordinary course of the organization's exempt activities to accomplish the organization's exempt purpose are one of the five exceptions to what is considered a significant disposition of net assets.

    d. Incorrect. The amount here exceeds 25 percent of the $8 million in net assets, and the type of transfer is not one of the five exceptions to what is considered a significant disposition of net assets, but more to the point is within the examples of what is a significant disposition of net assets (specifically, sales of assets by a partnership or joint venture in which the exempt partner has an ownership interest).

Learn More

AICPA CPE

Thank you for selecting AICPA as your continuing professional education provider. We have a diverse offering of CPE courses to help you expand your skillset and develop your competencies. Choose from hundreds of different titles spanning the major subject matter areas relevant to CPAs and CGMAs, including:

- Governmental & Not-for-Profit accounting, auditing, and updates
- Internal control and fraud
- Audits of Employee Benefit Plans and 401(k) plans
- Individual and corporate tax updates
- A vast array of courses in other areas of accounting & auditing, controllership, management, consulting, taxation, and more!

Get your CPE when and where you want

- Self-study training options that includes on-demand, webcasts, and text formats with superior quality and a broad portfolio of topics, including bundled products like –
  - ➤ CPExpress for immediate access to hundreds of one and two-credit hour online courses for just-in-time learning at a price that is right
  - ➤ Annual Webcast Pass offering live Q&A with experts and unlimited access to the scheduled lineup, all at an incredible discount.
- Staff training programs for audit, tax and preparation, compilation and review
- Certificate programs offering comprehensive curriculums developed by practicing experts to build fundamental core competencies in specialized topics
- National conferences presented by recognized experts
- Affordable AICPA courses on-site at your organization – visit **aicpalearning.org/on-site** for more information.
- Seminars sponsored by your state society and led by top instructors. For a complete list, visit **aicpalearning.org/publicseminar**.

Take control of your career development

The AICPA I CIMA Competency and Learning website at **https://competency.aicpa.org** brings together a variety of learning resources and a self-assessment tool, enabling tracking and reporting of progress toward learning goals.

Visit the AICPA store at cpa2biz.com/CPE to browse our CPE selections.

Why AICPA?

Think of All the Great Reasons to Join the AICPA.

CAREER ADVOCACY SUPPORT

On behalf of the profession and public interest on the federal, state and local level.

PROFESSIONAL & PERSONAL DISCOUNTS

Save on travel, technology, office supplies, shipping and more.

ELEVATE YOUR CAREER

Five specialized credentials and designations (ABV®, CFF®, CITP®, PFS™ and CGMA®) enhance your value to clients and employers.

HELPING THE BEST AND THE BRIGHTEST

AICPA scholarships provide more than $350,000[1] to top accounting students.

GROW YOUR KNOWLEDGE

Discounted CPE on webcasts, self-study or on-demand courses & more than 60 specialized conferences & workshops.

PROFESSIONAL GUIDANCE YOU CAN COUNT ON

Technical hotlines & practice resources, including Ethics Hotline, Business & Industry Resource Center and the Financial Reporting Resource Center.

KEEPING YOU UP TO DATE

With news and publications from respected sources such as the *Journal of Accountancy*.

MAKING MEMBERS HAPPY

We maintain a 94%+ membership renewal rate.

FOUNDED ON INTEGRITY

Representing the profession for more than 125 years.

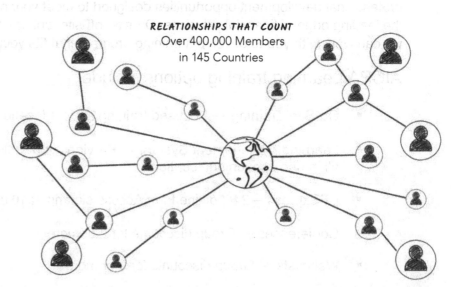

RELATIONSHIPS THAT COUNT
Over 400,000 Members in 145 Countries

®

TO JOIN, VISIT:
aicpa.org/join or call 888.777.7077.